Islam's Reformation Of Christianity

To Mohibul Roh with

Love

Islam's Reformation Of Christianity

Zulfiqar Ali Shah

CLARITAS
BOOKS

1 2 3 4 5 6 7 8 9 10

CLARITAS BOOKS

Bernard Street, Swansea, United Kingdom
Milpitas, California, United States

CLARITAS
BOOKS

First Published in May 2022

Typeset in Minion Pro 14/11

Islam's Reformation of Christianity
By Zulfiqar Ali Shah

Series Editor: Sharif H. Banna

A CIP catalogue record for this book is available from the British Library

ISBN: 978-1-80011-993-2

Dedicated to Ammarah, Zubair and
Zoya with love

ZULFIQAR ALI SHAH received his B.A. and M.A. (Hons) in Comparative Religions from the International Islamic University in Islamabad,
Pakistan and his Ph.D. in Theology and Religious Studies from the University of Wales, UK. He has taught at the International Islamic University in Islamabad, the University of Wales in the UK, the University
of North Florida and Cardinal Stritch University in the US. He is the
former President of the Islamic Circle of North America and the Sha-
riah Scholars Association of North America. Dr. Zulfiqar Shah is currently the Executive Director and Secretary General of the Fiqh Council of North America and Religious Director of the Islamic Society of
Milwaukee, USA. He has authored many articles and books including
*Anthropomorphic Depictions of God: The Concept of God in the Juda-
ic, Christian and Islamic Traditions*. His forthcoming ground-breaking
books include *St Thomas Aquinas and Muslim Thought, Islam and the
English Enlightenment: The Untold Story, Islam and the French Enlightenment* and *Islam and the Founding Fathers of America*.

Contents

CHAPTER 1 **Christianity: An Introduction**   11

  The Greco-Roman Context   11

  Christ and the Christian Theology   13

  The New Testament   14

  Multiple Christologies   18

  Christian Apologists and Early Church Fathers   24

  The Monarchians   30

  Dynamic Monarchianism   34

  Arianism   36

  The Council of Nicaea   40

  The Person of Jesus Christ   47

  The Council of Chalcedon   53

  Trinitarian and Christological Models   60

  What is Salvation?   64

  Human Depravity   66

  Original Sin or Original Forgiveness?   69

  Trinity or Tri-theism?   71

CHAPTER 2 **Some Manifestations of Roman Christianity**   75

  Antinomianism   75

  St. Paul's Christocentrism   76

  Paul, the Lying Spouter   78

  Jame's Work-based Salvation Scheme   80

  Spiritual Arrogance   82

  Christian Libertinism   87

Anti-Rationalism   95

Celsus, Porphyry and Christian Mysteries   98

Multiple Christianities   102

Christianity and State   111

Unqualified Submission to Authorities   115

The Hierarchical Universe   119

Paul's Legacy of Pacifism   123

Eusebius and Constantine   129

Augustine and Theology of Governance   134

Christianity and Persecutions   140

Constantine and Christian Unity   142

Theodosius and Edict of Salonica   145

Augustine and Rationalization of Coercion   148

The Saint and Politics   153

Augustine's Legacy   156

John Chrysostom and Violence   159

Justinian and Religious Persecution   160

Some Conclusions   166

CHAPTER 3 **Islam: The Southern Reformation of Christianity**   179

Islam and Christian Background   180

Islamic Reformation of Christianity   186

The Quran and Trinitarian Christology   190

The Quran and Divine Sonship   192

The Quran and Mariolatry   196

The Quran, Modalism, Dynamic Monarchians,
Social Trinitarians and Monophysites   198

The Quran and Augustinian and Cappadocian Models   202

The Quran and Social Trinity   203

Christian Apologists and Quranic Christology   208

Quranic Christology vs John's Christology   214

Tawhid: The Islamic Monotheism   221

Transcendence of God and the Quran   223

The Islamic Creed   224

Categories of Tawhid   231

Tawhid, Islamic Art and God Talk   238

Tawhid: The Ethical Monotheism   239
Salvation   244
The Quran and Human Reason   247
What is Reason?   248
Quranic Rationality   252
Reason and Revelation   255
The Quran and Qualitative Rationality   257
Islamic Monotheism and Religious Diversity   263
The Adam Connection   265
The Abrahamic Connection   266
The Word of God or Jesus Connection   274
Islamic Nomianism   275
Islam and Divine Right Monarchy   280
Islam and Religious Freedom   287
The Constitution of Medina   288
Conclusion   296

ENDNOTES   297
BIBLIOGRAPHY   337
INDEX   353

Christianity: An Introduction

The Christian faith is very unique. It revolves around a historical person, Jesus, who is simultaneously considered full God and full man. Its incarnational and Trinitarian metaphysics and faith-based salvation schemes are also very distinctive. Its theology is totally paradoxical, and its mysteries are real mysteries- very difficult to untangle. Its concept of human nature, society and human destiny is amazingly arbitrary, puzzling and complex. It is a faith which is neither fully Semitic nor fully Hellenistic; it is a synthesis of both Jewish and Roman traditions. Its central doctrines and dogmas are so unintelligible that centuries of hard work have not been able to untangle their perplexing knots. In this chapter I will try to unravel some of the dogmatic perplexities and their side effects.

Jesus lived among the Jews and inherited the Semitic monotheistic consciousness. The occupying Roman Empire was ruled by pagan emperors. Jesus and the early Christians were at a loss to fight the overpowering Roman authorities, and early Christianity was severely persecuted by Roman officials.

The Greco-Roman Context

The Greco-Roman world was filled with religions and cults which preached mystical cleansing of sins through the sacrificial death of a saviour. The tragedy and sacrificial ritual narratives were central to Greco-Roman culture, drama and religion. The early Christian Church had difficulties in winning over Roman pagans to Semitic monotheism. Its long conflict with the mystery religions left an indelible impact upon Church theology.[1] It is impossible to deny such a long-lasting influence. Consequently, the Church developed a number of dogmas using the biblical vocabulary, but incorporating Greco-Roman concepts. The result was a Roman Christianity at odds with the original Semitic monotheistic consciousness of Jesus and his surroundings.

The central Christian concepts, such as the cosmic threat to man due to inherent human depravity, the need for a cosmic saviour and substitutionary sacrifice, incarnation, belief in the saving acts of the saviour, initiation in the cult, and salvation through the atoning death were reflections of the dominant Greco-Roman culture and tradition. Once incorporated, they rendered human participation in the Christian scheme of salvation insignificant while emphasising the divine incentive and grace. Faith in the mystery of incarnation and atoning death was required over and beyond knowledge, reason and human actions. True faith was reflected through the tradition of the Church, therefore the Church was central to human salvation as the dispenser of divine knowledge and grace; there was no salvation out of Church. The Church discouraged Greco-Roman philosophical and religious traditions, as they were the results of Roman paganism; they were evil and must be discarded in favor of the divinely inspired Church tradition. Consequently, the Greco-Roman philosophical traditions were used to serve the Church teachings and not as intellectual guides or rational luminaries.

The fourth century AD saw a merger of the Church and State when Emperor Constantine declared Christianity as the state religion. The Church and its teachings were supplied with state tools to enhance its authority, rendering it virtually irresistible. In return the Church elevated the state's authority to transcendental realms by equating obedience to the Emperor with submission to God. This was the birth of absolute monarchy and absolute Church, the model mostly followed by Latin Christendom to premodern times. Roman Christianity, with its emphasis upon faith, human depravity, mysteries of incarnation and crucifixion and salvation through the redeeming acts of Christ dispensed through the Church, led Christendom to intellectual stagnation, obliterating the philosophical tradition of Greco-Roman world. A culture of anti-law, anti-philosophy, anti-reasoning and anti-intellectualism was created to subject the masses to an absolute Church authority, resulting in what is now considered the Dark Ages. Church dogmas, especially Trinitarian theology, contributed to this mystery-filled anti-intellectual culture. W. C. Dampier states that "in order to appreciate the causes which produced the great failure of Europe to increase the stores of natural knowledge in the Middle Ages, it is necessary to trace the development of the mediaeval mind. We must first realize the general outlines of the theology of Christian faith and ethics framed by the early Fathers."[2] The Trinitarian theology, with its corollaries such as the dogmas of original sin, human depravity and redemption through the atoning death of Christ, were mainly responsible for the intellectual stagnation of Medieval Latin Christendom. The fact that the eighteenth-century Enlightenment figures attacked these Christian mysteries to usher an age of reason and freedom substantiates the claim.

Therefore we now turn to the Trinitarian theology, its development and long lasting cultural impact on Christendom.

Christ and the Christian Theology

The orthodox Christian tradition is a Trinitarian faith where monotheism is reflected through the prism of a triune God; God the Holy Father, Son and Holy Spirit make up the Godhead. They are considered equal in Godhead, from the same divine substance, having three different persons, identities and consciousness. However, in Christian liturgy and daily life Lord Jesus Christ, the Son of God, plays a lot more visible role than God the Father and God the Holy Spirit. The Christian tradition in reality is obsessed with Jesus Christ; there is a tremendous concentration on one man, Jesus of Nazareth, who is considered simultaneously a full man and a full God. He is described in different terms, concepts and ways; he is addressed as the Son of man, Son of God, the Word, the Prophet, the Messiah, the Kyrios or Lord and even as God. S. C. Guthrie Jr. observes that "all the doctrines of the Christian faith are related to Christ as spokes to the hub of a wheel. We could not talk about who God is, how we know Him, what He is like and what He wants with us, without talking about the revelation of himself, His will and work in Christ [...] Everything else Christians believe stands or falls with what they believe about Jesus."[3] The distinctively Christian understanding of God is based on the claim that God is most fully revealed through what Christians claim is his self-revelation in the life, teaching, death, and resurrection of Jesus Christ. "The final revelation of Christianity," observes William Blake, "is, therefore, not that Jesus is God, but that God is Jesus."[4] I. R. Netton confirms it by observing that "the *traditional* Christian theological paradigm, of course, despite much debate, was that Jesus's 'self-consciousness was always consciously of Himself as God.'"[5]

The God of Christianity is fully known through the writings of the New Testament, the Christian Scripture. The New Testament is not centered on God Almighty; it is Christocentric. Richard Burridge has shown, by manual analysis of the four Gospels, that God the Almighty/ Father occupies a sum total of just 2.5% of the Gospels, while the rest of the Gospels are concerned with Jesus in various capacities i.e., his person, teachings, his disciples, his recipients, his dialogue with Jewish leaders etc. (Mark gives only a 0.2% place to the verbs whose subject is God/Father in his Gospel, with Matthew 0.6%, Luke 1.1% and John 0.6%).[6] Charles Gore pinpointed this fact a long time ago by observing that "Christianity is faith in a certain person Jesus Christ, and by faith in Him is meant such unreserved self-committal as is only possible, because faith in Jesus is understood to be faith in God, and union with Jesus union with God."[7]

The New Testament

Even though the central pivot of all New Testament writings is Jesus Christ and crucial information about his life, teachings, death, and resurrection, are contained in the books, none of them in fact were written by him or under his supervision. Philip Schaff observes: "The Lord chose none of his apostles, with the single exception of Paul, from the ranks of the learned; he did not train them to literary authorship, nor gave them, throughout his earthly life, a single express command to labor in that way."[8] There is a consensus among biblical scholars re-garding this issue: "Whereas we possess documents originally written by Paul," observes J. Jeremias, "not a single line has come down to us from Jesus's own hand."[9] These books were the product of later genera-tions, and are commonly accepted as the earliest classical responses to the many-faceted aspects of Christ's life and existence. R.M. Grant ob-serves that the New Testament "is the basic collection of the books of the Christian Church. Its contents, unlike those of the Old Testament, were produced within the span of a single century, under the auspices of disciples of Jesus or their immediate successors. The collection is unlike the Koran in that it contains not a word written by the founder of the community, though his spoken words are recorded by evangelists and apostles and reflected in almost all the documents."[10]

The New Testament, in its present shape, number, and order was not available to the early Christians for centuries after the departure of Jesus and his disciples. Clarke observes that the New Testament writings were "written for the special needs of particular groups of people, and the idea of combining them into one authoritative volume was late and not in the mind of the authors. Christians, therefore, and the Christian Church might conceivably have gone on indefinitely without Christian scriptures."[11] One of the leading factors may have been the existence of an already compiled Hebrew Bible. "Throughout the whole patristic age," observes Kelly, "as indeed in all subsequent Christian centuries, the Old Testament was accepted as the word of God, the unimpeachable sourcebook of saving doctrine."[12] The compilation, collection, and identification of this particular group of writings (the canonisation process) as a distinct and authoritative entity resulted from a complex development within the Christian Church. It took the Church 367 years to produce a list of writings and a canon that would contain all the present day (New Testament) canonical writings. The oldest indisputable witness to the New Testament canon is Athanasius, a fourth-century bishop of Alexandria. Throughout these long centuries the Hebrew Bible, with its strict monotheistic bent, was accepted as the scripture of the Christian community. The New Testament's universal acceptance and authority was gradual.

Moreover, Jesus historically existed among the Jews, respected their Scripture, thought himself as a fulfillment of their law, struggled with the Jewish religious hierarchy and claimed to be sent to the lost sheep of the house of Israel. There may have been features distinctive to Jesus's understanding of God and His transcendence, but the concept as a whole would probably be not at odds with Jewish understanding of the Deity. The earliest Christians would, perforce, have obviously inherited the themes of divine transcendence and monotheism from the developed Judaism around them, meaning that the unity, uniqueness and sublimity of the Creator God must have been the indisputable premise of the original Church's faith tradition. One can deduce from available historical data that the Church has used the same Unitarian, transcendental and monotheistic premise against polytheists, Gnostic emanationists and Marcionite dualists to refute their monotheistic violations. Loving God and loving thy neighbour was the essence of this original Unitarian Christianity. The original Christian monotheistic morality was in line with the Jewish ethical monotheism. Unitarian Christianity, with its strict ethical monotheism, on the other hand, was at odds with the Roman pagan imperial designs. Consequently the Christians were persecuted for centuries by the Roman imperial machine.

Finally tired of Christian persecution and internal Roman strife, the Emperor Constantine co-opted Christianity in the 4th century by issuing the edict of toleration in 313. The pagan population was forced to join the new religion, and they brought along with them their old beliefs, practices and ideas. The Christian Church was overwhelmed by accommodating the new converts and their religious ideals. The metamorphosis of pagan and original Christian belief systems produced a new synthesis; the Roman Church Christianity of the fourth century. It was neither Roman paganism nor strict Jewish monotheism, but a unique Trinitarian version of monotheism. The imperial hands played an important role in giving Christianity this strange anti-Semite twist, because the Church was unable to reconcile the contradictions inherent in its new theology. The task was impossible because the new hodgepodge was arbitrary, artificial and mostly political. It was not theology per se, but an amalgamation of politics and theology. Jewish monotheism and pagan polytheism were worlds apart, and the Church was at a loss to create a viable synthesis. Self-contradictions, unintelligibility and circular reasoning became the hallmarks of the new enterprise. The source of these contradictions was the multiple authors of the New Testament books and their divergent outlooks.

The four Gospels, the most significant of the New Testament books, were not the biographies of Jesus in the strict sense of the term;[13] they were a mythical account of a few weeks of his presumed activity. They did not present a systematic, objective, progressive or developmental account of Jesus's life but were highly selective, following a loose chronological framework bent on theological significance and moralizing anthology of Jesus's sayings and actions. The gospel writers were faith-driven preachers who had axes to grind; the gospel of John made this fact abundantly clear. (20:30-31) The Gospels were good news, exactly as the word "gospel" meant. Moreover, there were other Christian gospels and writings, probably written before some of the so-called canonical gospels, which were later rejected by the Church during the long canonisation process. Luke's confessed frustrations in the prologue of his gospel attested to this very fact. Even the carefully handpicked gospels did not present a systematic view of Jesus. John D. Crossan rightly observes that if one reads "those four texts vertically, as it were, from start to finish and one after another, you get generally persuasive impression of unity, harmony, and agreement. But if you read them horizontally, focusing on this or that unit and comparing it across two, three, or four versions, it is disagreement rather than agreement that strikes one most forcibly. By even the middle of the second century, pagan opponents, like Celsus, and Christian apologists, like Justin, Tatian and Marcion were well aware of those discrepancies, even if only between, say, Matthew and Luke."[14]

The Church has, over the centuries, been selective when it comes to scripture, using only those documents validating its own theological position and credentials. In other words, the documents chosen were mainly those which allowed the Church to prove what it wanted to have proven. Yet ironically, even these carefully selected documents contain no one single uniform picture of the person around whom the entire material is supposed to revolve. Following the New Testament, Christianity has always grappled with the question of Jesus's identity, forever trying to understand who he really is and what he represented. D. Cupitt rightly observes that "more than any other religion Christianity has revolved obsessively around one particular man: it has loved him, worshipped him, mediated upon him, portrayed him, and sought to imitate him – but he slips away."[15] There is no single preached Christ:

> An immense variety of ideals of character have been based upon the example of Jesus: an historical man who lived only one life has been made the exemplar of a great range of different forms of life. Jesus has been declared to be a model for hermits, peasants, gentlemen, revolutionaries, pacifists, feudal lords, soldiers and others. If we restrict attention to the religious life of men in the Latin West alone, the diversity is great among the ideals of Benedict, Francis, Bruno, and Ignatius Loyola.[16]

Even contemporary scholarship is polarised over which picture or image of Jesus is to be accepted as authentic. In a presidential address to the Catholic Biblical Association at Georgetown University on 6 August 1986, Daniel J. Harrington categorised this variety into seven different images of Jesus currently prevailing in contemporary scholarship. We have Jesus the political revolutionary (S. G. F. Brandon), the magician (Morton Smith), Galilean charismatic (Geza Vermes), Galilean rabbi (Bruce Chilton), Hillelite or proto-Pharisee or an essene (Harvey Falk), and eschatological prophet (E. P. Sanders). To Crossan, this "stunning diversity is an academic embarrassment."[17]

This "embarrassing" diversity of pictures, ideals, concepts and interpretations of Jesus Christ has led some to conclude that "everyone who writes a life of Jesus sees his own face at the bottom of a deep well."[18] To compound matters, there exists only a very limited number of reliable narrations concerning Jesus, which even if combined fail to give us access to the man himself. One is left with no choice but to conclude with R. H. Lightfoot that "the form of the earthly no less than of the heavenly Christ is for the most part hidden from us."[19]

Multiple Christologies

The multiplicity of Gospels resulted in diversity of Christologies. The central question "What think ye of Christ?" was answered in a number of different ways. He was a Prophet (Mk 6:14-15; Matt. 20:10-11; Lk. 7.16; Jn. 4.19; 6.14; 7.40, 52; 9.17), an angelic prince (Mk. 8:38; Matt. 13:41; Lk. 22:43), the Messiah (the *Jewish mashiach)* (Mk. 8:29-30; Lk. 22:67-69), the Son of Man (Matt. 12:8, 26:64; Mk. 8:38, 13:26, 14:62; Lk. 22:69), the Son of God (Mk. 1:1, 14:61-62; Matt. 26:63-64; Lk. 22:70; Jn. 5:25, 11:4), *Kyrios* meaning 'Lord' (Romans 1:3, 7, 5:1-11, 10:9, 16:24; 1 Corinthians 1:2, 3, 7, 8, 9, 10) and even *Logos* or *Theos*. (Jn. 1:1, 20:26-28) The *Theos* Christology was found only in the Gospel of John. The beginning and end chapter of John contained references to Jesus which were traditionally translated as "God". Nothing of that sort existed in the first three Gospels. Jesus never called himself God, nor did the first three evangelists, authors of the Synoptic Gospels. It was the Gospel of John and Epistles to Hebrews that seemingly attributed of *Oeos (divinity)* to Jesus; this was an odd fact.

It was against all human logic that the one who lived a human life, prayed to God (Mk. 14:32; Lk. 6:12; Matt. 26:39; Heb. 5:7), confessed being God's servant (Matt. 12:18; Acts 3:13, 4:27), was sent by God (Jn. 12:49-50), was confessedly dependent upon God (Jn. 14:28), died a human death, at his crucifixion cried out loud "O My God, why have you forsaken me?" was in actuality God the Almighty. "How then can man be justified with God? Or how can he be clean that is born of a woman?" (Job 25:4) The mutually antithetical and logically impossible claims could not be proved by logical probabilities. Being the man and the God Almighty at the same time, being mercilessly crucified and being the Omnipotent God, not knowing the hour and being the Omniscient God all at the same time, were mutually improbable and exclusive logical categories. Additionally, some Christians argued that the *Theos* Christology was interpolated; they contended that the highly poetic style of John 1:1 was missing in the rest of the Gospel, and Jesus was never called the "Word" elsewhere in the Gospel.

There were also problems related to the translation of John 1.1. The popular translation "and the Word was God" was disputed by many translators. There were multiple other possible translations such as "the Word was a god" and "godlike sort was the Logos" and "so the Word was divine." The source of the problem lay in the original Greek manuscripts of the Gospels, which were all in capital letters. The original word in the manuscript was *theos,* and could not have the definite article in accordance with grammatical rules. John 10:35 used it for human rulers as "gods." Origen of Alexandria, the third-century Church Father and a specialist in Greek grammar, highlighted the difference by stating that John used "the article, when the name of God refers to the uncreated cause of all things, and omits it when the Logos is named God [...] The true God, then, is The God"[20] The term used was "*ho theos*" and not just "*theos*". This observation alluded to the fact that when the anarthrous noun "*theos*" was applied to the Word it was not a definite but an indefinite one. These grammatical intricacies were quite often used to manipulate meanings and to substantiate specific theological positions, the Orthodoxy preferring the popular rendition as it vindicated its "Jesus God" theology and the opposing groups favouring the other translations to prove Jesus's subordination to God the Father.

Likewise, the Greek word *Logos* carried multiple meanings such as thought, speech, reason, principle, logic, meaning, account, in addition to the popular translation "Word." It also had varying connotations in different time periods. Middle Platonism was the prevalent philosophical worldview of the pre- and post-Jesus era. The emanation theory of Platonism was used by transcendental Jews, like Philo of Alexandria, to protect transcendent God's absolute purity beyond this material existence, an existence marked by evils and immoralities. Philo contended that the pure God brought this defective cosmos into being, not because of a direct act of creation, but through a pure act of intellectual will. The result of this pure intellectual will was *Logos, the Word*. The material cosmos was brought forth through the intermediary agency of Logos and other Intellects, the Logos here comparable to Plato's World Soul. God, the One and the Infinite source of existence was not equal to the derivative and secondary existences such as the *Logos*. The Church Fathers, such as Origen and Justin Martin, effectively used this derivative ideology in treating Jesus as the Word of God. This benign Logos theology was later translated into the lofty hard divinity of Jesus by the Church. The Orthodoxy amalgamated the possibly interpolated "theos" and manipulated "Logos" Christologies to create the later synthetic Incarnation Christology where the demarcation line between God and Logos was completely blurred; this was nothing short of violence to the Gospel text.

The New Testament books, which the Church carefully selected to defend its peculiar theology, were at a loss to do so. The embarrassing hodgepodge of Christologies presented by the New Testament writers was contradictory and mutually exclusive. The son of man, Prophet, Messiah and even angels were not ontologically God Almighty; they were the creatures of God and hence mutually exclusive (Numbers 23:19). It was easy to claim- but hard to prove - that the man who spent nine months in Mary's womb, had a natural human delivery, ate, drank and had all other low human needs, grew in power, energy, knowledge, and was killed by the Roman soldiers was also Almighty God, proclaimed by Moses and worshipped by Abraham. It violated all logic, monotheistic history and scriptural axioms. At the same time the Roman Church, under the influence of Greco-Roman tragedy and sacred violence traditions, wanted to kill god at the altar of their sins. They created an irrational synthesis of incarnation, as discussed in the previous pages, impossible to reconcile with human reasoning. It seems that once the Church had decided that Jesus was God, especially in light of the Easter experience, the *theos* of John, which might have been used by John just as a communicative tool, was loaded with absolute tones of *ho theos* against the original backdrop. The later Church gambits were thus theologically motivated.

Like the Prologue, there were numerous issues with John 20:28. The Church had used this climactic confession of Thomas as the supreme Christological pronouncement of faith in Jesus as Lord and God. The dissenters contended that this designation was applied to Jesus in a broader sense, current in contemporary Judaism. John, who did not equate God with Logos in the Prologue, could not have obliterated all distinctions between God and Logos at the end of his Gospel. Moreover, the scriptures also designated Moses as God and king, and Adam as God over the earth. John actually alluded to this broader use of the designation "God" in 10:33-35. Many insinuated that the absolute article *ho* (the) did not exist in the fifth century codex Bezae and other earlier church manuscripts. This meant that Thomas did not address Jesus with an absolute divine tone, but called him "My divine lord". Theodore of Mopsuestia (c.350-428), the Bishop of Mopsuestia, understood this verse as directed to God the Father and not to Jesus arguing that Thomas' words were nothing but exclamations of surprise: "My God!" or "My Lord!" Additionally, the God designation for Jesus never occurred in any of the Synoptic Gospels. Thomas the doubter was not a recognised disciple. Even in the Gospel of John this designation was used for the risen lord, the heavenly Christ and not for the earthly Jesus. Therefore, there was no definite proof of Jesus's divinity in the Johannian corpus.

Outside the Johannine corpus it was only Hebrews 1:6-8 that applied the title 'God' to Jesus in one of its possible translations. Just like the earlier discussed passages, it had been translated in more than one way. There was no definite proof of the *theos* Christology in the Hebrews either.

In brief, the material, which was neither authored nor authorised by the Jesus of history, was implied to substantiate his hard divinity without much rational support. The process was gradual, much like the canonisation process itself. The otherwise mutually-exclusive Christologies of Jesus as a prophet, angel, Messiah and Lord were metamorphosed to describe a human being with divine attributes and qualities and ultimately godhead. Hence humanity and divinity became somehow merged in the historical man, Jesus of Nazareth. The Pauline and Johannine corpus' fluid style proved to be handy providing the context, terminology and conceptual framework for the later Christians to take the hazardous leap against the Semitic monotheistic consciousness. This contentious and dubious approach was thoroughly problematic, especially in light of the other strictly monotheistic passages. There were several passages, particularly in the Synoptic Gospels, that emphasised Almighty God's absolute unity and uniqueness (Mk. 12:29-32), Jesus's subordination to God the Father and his adoption at baptism (Lk. 6:12, 10:22; Matt. 19:17, 11:27; Jn. 7:29-33, for adoption see Matt. 3:16-17; Lk. 3:22).

The passages of adoption, distinction, derivation and subordination poked serious holes in the hard divinity of Jesus; derivative, finite or subordination divinity is no divinity in absolute sense. Additionally, whilst the derivative passages could have been interpreted as giving a divine status to Jesus, they nevertheless left a number of important issues unresolved regarding Jesus's relationship with God and with human beings. The Church used shady and shaky scriptural arguments to describe the divinity to Jesus, assigning him full-scale divinity, including the designation of absolute divine titles, actions, attributes and functions. This ascription of divinity did not cause many problems as long as the faith remained confined to Christians interested solely in the salvation. It was God and God alone, and nobody less than Him, who could have brought salvation to the humanity engulfed in sin. This is the implication we get from the oldest surviving sermon of the Christian Church after the New Testament writings: "Brethren, we ought so to think of Jesus Christ as of God, as of the judge of living and dead. And we ought not to belittle our salvation; for when we belittle him, we expect also to receive little."[21]

The problem surfaced when the Church had to face the external world, and to prove to them the significance and wisdom of Christian teachings. For the one whom Christians had called God was also the one who was born, lived an ordinary natural life for thirty or so years, ate, drank, suffered and was relentlessly crucified. These were the realities which the Church itself witnessed. The Alexandrian pagan philosopher Celsus's observations pinpointed the problem accurately: "Everyone saw his suffering, but only a disciple and a half crazed woman saw him risen. His followers then made a God of him, like Antinous [...] The idea of the coming down of God is senseless. Why did God come down for justification of all things? Does not this make God changeable?"[22]

The pagan Celsus vehemently attacked the Christian concept of the Deity and dubbed it as thoroughly corporeal and anthropomorphic. He concluded that "Christianity is not merely a religious revolution with profound social and political consequences; it is essentially hostile to all positive human values. The Christians say [...] 'Do not ask questions, only believe.' They say, 'Wisdom is foolishness with God' [...] they will flee to the last refuge of the intellectually destitute, 'Anything is possible to God.'[23]

In the words of Grillmeier:

The hour had come for the birth of speculative theology, of theological reflection, of *theoligie savante*. The confession of Jesus Christ as the Son of God, the *novum* of Christian faith... demanded of Christian theology a twofold demonstration, first that it was compatible with Jewish monotheism, and secondly that it was different from pagan polytheism.[24]

There was pressure from within too. In the first place, this confusion called forth some of the earliest doctrinal controversies in the Church itself, and forced the Church to become more precise. The inner pressure demanded logical defense and intelligible explanations of the contradictory positions, especially to avert the fierce attacks of Jews and pagans. Within early Christianity, voices like "his suffering was but a make believe" were raised by Marcion, Ptolemy and the Gnostics. Marcion, for instance, absolutely denied Jesus's humanity. His Jesus was too lofty to be confined within the prison of the flesh. This was clear "Docetism" (a belief that states that Jesus only *seemed* to have a physical body and to physically die, but in reality, he was incorporeal, a pure spirit, and hence could not physically die).

The Church, while trying to defend Christ's humanity, could not itself escape from the very problem it was trying to solve, the problem of "Docetism." The Church itself had been emphasising the divinity of Jesus to such a degree that the demarcation line between his humanity and divinity were prematurely blurred. Church Father Clement of Alexandria, according to Bigg, was "near to the confines of Docetism".[25] The more the Church emphasised the hardcore divinity of Jesus using the God concept the more difficult it became to prove that Jesus of Nazareth was also the Son of God and of the same substance as God. The Church had no escape from mild Docetism and J. Moltmann confesses as such, stating that "a mild docetism runs through the christology of the ancient church."[26]

Christian Apologists and Early Church Fathers

Christianity, to prove its intellectual worth and avert the cerebral attacks of paganism, Greek philosophy and Judaism, had no choice but to be a little more precise in its teachings with regards to the relationship between God the Father and Jesus the Christ. It was difficult for non-Christian Jews and pagans to understand the assertions of strict monotheism on the one hand and the divinity of Jesus Christ, including his suffering and crucifixion as God, on the other. Christian apologists such as Justin Martyr, Theophilus, Tatian, Aristides and Athenagoras responded to this rather embarrassing situation with philosophical suppositions, to vindicate the truth of Christianity; they tried to draw a rather clear line between God and Jesus, using the then available philosophical concepts.

Justin, the most renowned of them, for instance insisted that though Jesus had come from God, he was not identical with God: "The ineffable Father and Lord of all," he says, "neither comes anywhere nor walks nor sleeps nor rises up, but remains in his own place wherever that may be, quick to behold, quick to hear, not with eyes or ears but with indescribable power."[27] Justin's God was a transcendent being, who could have not come into contact with the utilitarian sphere of man and things. To Justin, it seemed altogether absurd that such a transcendent God could be born of a woman, eat, drink and eventually be mercilessly crucified. However, strict belief in God's transcendence did not stop Justin from thinking of Jesus as a sort of divinity, and to defend Christ's relationship with God he made use of the then current Christian phraseology calling Jesus the Son of God, Logos and also the Angel. Indeed, according to him, Christ was worthy of these titles on account of his wisdom, virgin birth and because he was God's first begotten Logos: "Thou art my son; this day have I begotten thee." Jesus, the Son of God, was not like other men; he was generated in a very special way. As a fire is kindled by fire, or as a light is produced from the light of the Sun, Jesus was God born of God. He was divine, but not in the original sense; his divinity was derivative. In the words of Norris, Jesus's divinity:

> was derivative, and for that reason inferior to the one God.... In Justin's system there truly was, in the last resort, only one ultimate God. The Logos represented a slightly lower level of divinity, something between

the pure divinity of God and the nondivinity of creatures. Justin had made sense of the incarnational picture of Jesus by adopting a hierarchical picture of the world-order in which the Logos stands as a kind of bumper state between God and the world, and it is this fact that makes Justin's Christology problematic.[28]

He was a pre-existent Logos, God's agent in creation, through whom all creatures were created. Therefore, he could be called Lord and worshipped as divine but in terms of being of second rank. As Justin in one of his confessions puts it: "Thus we are not atheists, since we worship the creator of this universe [...] and that we with good reason honour Him Who has taught us these things and was born for this purpose, Jesus Christ, Who was crucified under Pontius Pilate [...] having learned that He is the Son of the true God and holding Him in the second rank, and the prophetic Spirit third in order."[29]

Justin could not have convinced his Jewish counterparts with this kind of hierarchical interpretation of the Godhead and derivative nature of divinity. Monotheism stood in his way as an insurmountable hurdle, so he adopted another approach, trying to prove that the Jewish Scriptures bore witness to two Gods: first the transcendent, supreme, unbegotten, ingenerate God, the ineffable Father, who never appeared on the earth; and second, the God of theophanies, who came down to earth on several occasions and finally became incarnate in Christ. In his Dialogue with Trypho, the Jew, he argued the matter at length:

> I will give you, my friends, another testimony from the Scriptures that as a beginning before all creatures God begat from himself a certain rational power which is called by the Holy Spirit now Glory of the Lord, again Wisdom, again Angel, again God, again Lord, and Logos. Also he called himself Captain of the host when appeared to Jesus the Son of Nave in the form of a man. For he can be called by all these names since he serves the Father's will and was begotten of the Father by will.[30]

and:

> when my God says 'God went up from Abraham,' or 'the Lord spake unto Moses,' and 'the Lord came down to see the tower which the sons of men had built,' [...] you must not imagine that the unbegotten God

himself came down or went up anywhere [...] Therefore not Abraham nor Isaac nor Jacob nor any other man saw the Father and ineffable Lord of all and of Christ himself as well, but they saw him who according to his will was at once God, his Son, and the angel who ministered to his will, and who it pleased him should be born man by the Virgin; who also was fire when he spake with Moses from the bush.[31]

As the passage just quoted indicates, to Justin, Christ was the Logos, the divine reason, the second God of the Old Testament theophanies, begotten before the creation of the world, who became incarnate in the historical person of Jesus of Nazareth. Justin also called the *Logos* the servant, the angel, the apostle. Grillmeier observes that:

> In calling the Logos the servant, the apostle, the angel of the absolutely transcendent Father, Justin gives him a diminished transcendence, even if he does not make him a creature. He compares the Logos with Herms, the Logos-interpreter of Zeus [...] There is a *deus inferior* subordinate to the *theos hypsistos.*[32]

Other apologists, such as Tatian and Hippolytus, followed Justin in his ideas of God's transcendence, ineffability, immutability and otherness while maintaining his Logos Christology.

J. N. D. Kelly underlines the two most important points that were common among all the Apologists:

> (a) that for all of them the description 'God the Father' connoted, not the first Person of the Holy Trinity, but the one Godhead considered as author of whatever exists; and (b) that they all, Athenagoras included, dated the generation of the Logos, and His eligibility for the title 'Son', not from His origination within the being of the Godhead, but from His emission or putting forth for the purposes of creation, revelation and redemption. Unless these points are firmly grasped, and their significance appreciated, a completely distorted view of the Apologists' theology is liable to result.[33]

The Apologists clearly portrayed the Logos as required for the work of creation in subordination to God the Father. They also manifestly limited the Logos as compared to God Himself, to safeguard the indispensable idea of monotheism. There were residuals of Middle Platonism in this Logos interpretation of the Apologists. The Logos was understood in relation to the cosmos and the world to stress God's absolute transcendence, invisibility and unknowability; Almighty God was too transcendent to directly deal with men and the world. The Logos, a product of God's creative will, was a subordinate mediator, a derivative god. The idea of subordination was fortified by the close linking of the creation of the world with the procession of the Logos, and then by the scheme of salvation or man's redemption through his intermediate agency.

Church Fathers, like Tertullian (160–220) and Origen (185–254), clearly maintained the Apologists' position in regards to Christ's relationship with God. Tertulian, accepting Justin's mediatorial idea of the Logos, differentiated between God and Jesus, the Word, by arguing that "by him who is invisible, we must understand the Father in the fullness of his majesty, while we recognize the Son as visible by reason of dispensation of his derived existence."[34] Tertullian, in his treatise *Against Praxeas,* explained that the Logos first existed in God as his Reason and then was "made a second" to God, or "uttered" as the Word through whom all things were made. In Tertullian we see a crystal clear line of demarcation between God the Father and the Logos, emphasising the mediatorial and secondary character of the Logos and his "derivation and portion", to use his terms, from the father's divine substance. He observes that "With regard to him (the Logos), we are taught he is derived from God and begotten by derivation so that he is Son of God and called God because of the unity of substance."[35]

God's transcendence and *monarchia* is preserved, as the Son uses the powers and the rule given to him by the Father, and will return them to the Father when the world comes to an end. The Father is the guarantee of the *monarchia,* the Son comes in at second place whilst the Spirit is assigned third place. Tertullian's trinity is not metaphysical but economic or dynamic in nature. Only the Father remains the eternal transcendent God, while the other two entities proceed from the *unitas substantiae* because they have a task to fulfill. His concept of unity is also not mathematical; there is no subdivision within the Godhead. It is more philosophical, more organic as there is a constructive integration within the Godhead of the will and the persons. It is Tertullian who introduced the concept of 'person' in Christology, arguing that the triune God is one in substance and different in person: "You have two (Father-Son), one commanding a thing to be made, another making it. But how you must understand 'another' I Have already professed, in the sense of person, not of substance."[36]

Origen also emphasised the derivative, intermediary and secondary role of Jesus. He equated the procession of the Logos from the Father with the procession of the will from the mind. The act of will neither cuts anything from the mind nor causes division within it. Origen differed from Justin and Tertullian in saying that the Logos was the eternal self-expression of God and was of the same substance as God: "The Father did not beget the Son once for all, and let him go after he was begotten but he is always begetting him."[37] Origen's idea of the eternal generation of the Logos did not mean that he had made the Logos equal with God. In his treatise *Against Celsus* he clearly differentiated between the Logos and God by making the Logos subordinate to God and thereby declaring him in some sense less than God and a "second God". McGiffert, commenting on Origen's Logos Christology, observes that there exists a marked subordinationism in Origen because he was "always more interested in the subordination of the Son to the Father than his oneness with him."[38] All in all, Origen's Trinitarian scheme is thoroughly Platonistic Subordinationism. Kelly observes that:

> The unity between Father and Son corresponds to that between light and its brightness, water and the steam which rises from it. Different in form, both share the same essential nature; and if, in the strictest sense, the Father alone is God, that is not because the Son is not also God or does not possess the Godhead, but because, as Son, He possesses it by participation or derivatively.[39]

Bigg observes that:

> We shall however wrong Origen, if we attempt to derive his subordinationism from metaphysical considerations. It is purely Scriptural, and rests wholly and entirely upon the words of Jesus, 'My Father is greater than I', 'That they may know Thee the only true God', 'None is Good save One'.[40]

Logos, then, is of secondary rank and merits secondary honour. This being the case, Origen does not permit the worship of any generate being such as Christ, but only sanctions worship of God the Father, to whom even Christ prayed. The prayers offered to Christ are meant to be conveyed to the Father through the intermediary agency of Christ. God transcends both Christ and the Spirit as they transcend the realm of inferior beings. The Son and Spirit are God as related to creatures but:

> from the viewpoint of the ineffable Godhead He is the first in the chain
> of emanations. This conception of a descending hierarchy, itself the
> product of his Platonizing background, is epitomized in the statement
> that, whereas the Father's action extends to all reality, the Son's is limit-
> ed to rational beings, and the Spirit's to those who are being sanctified.[41]

Irenaeus (202) and Clement of Alexandria (150-215) were perhaps more traditionalists than philosophers. They did not look for intellectual interpretations to denote the relationship between the Father, the Son and the Holy Spirit, preferring instead to rely on traditional terminology over philosophical concepts. For both the Logos, who had become incarnate in Jesus Christ, was no less than God himself. In his famous treatise *Against Heresies,* Irenaeus argued that the Logos existed eternally with God, did not begin to be God's Son at any particular point in history, and that the salvation and redemption of a sinful humanity could not have been attained except through God in the flesh humbling himself to the point of death. Lord Jesus Christ, the Logos of God, adopted human conditions so that humanity might become what he himself was. "How can they be saved unless it be God who wrought out their salvation on earth? And how shall man be changed into God unless God has been changed into man?"[42] In other words, the Son of God was made Son of Man so that humans could become sons of God. This guaranteed man's immortality like that of the Logos so that the "corruptible might be swallowed up by incorruption and the mortal by immortality" (1 Corinthians 15:53-54).

For Irenaeus to think of the Logos in derivative terms, and to subordinate him to God or to think of him as another being as the Apologists did, was detrimental to his saving work and hence impossible. He identified the Logos or the Son with the Father completely: "For the Father is the invisible of the Son, but the Son is the visible of the

Father."[43] In short, the Logos is God but God revealed and not God unapproachable, inaccessible and apart from the world.

Clement of Alexandria, like Irenaeus, was a moralist rather than a systematic theologian. He adopted an almost identical course in determining Jesus's relationship with God. In his view Jesus was neither derived nor a secondary or subordinate divine being to God, rather he was fully divine, God in his own right. In the tenth chapter of his *Protrepticus* Clement calls Jesus "the truly most manifest God."[44] Bigg observes that "Clement's mode of statement is such as to involve necessarily the Unity, Equality, and Eternity of the First and Second Persons. It has been asserted, that he hardly leaves sufficient room for a true distinction of Hypostasis."[45]

We can conclude this part of the discussion by noting that until the second century AC, the Christian God Paradigm in general and the doctrine of Christ's Person were not fixed but rather flexible, fluid and confusing. The ideas of subordination, and the derivative and secondary rank of Christ were common among thoughtful Christians such as Justin and Origin. On the other hand, traditionalists as well as the orthodox Church, if we can possibly use this term for purposes of convenience, inclined more towards the Unity, Equality and Eternity of Christ, and that on a par with God the Father. The latter was not without its inherent confusions and problems, and was moreover a form of possible Docetism. The Christian masses were unable to understand the syncretism between the strict monotheism of the Jews and the pagan mystery concepts of the Greco-Roman world. The Church synthesis of the mutually exclusive philosophies was artificial and arbitrary leaving many people confused and disgruntled.

The Monarchians

From the start, the belief that Christ was a god was common among many Christians, especially the Gentiles. There were many who felt it degrading to assign a secondary or subordinated position to Jesus, and thought it deeply offensive to place another God alongside with or over him, assuming that this would diminish their salvation. So they contended that Jesus was the same and only God who had created the universe, and that he had become flesh to die for their sins. There exist traces of such tendencies among Christians during Justin's times and he makes explicit references to groups such as these in his *Apology*. Writing in the early third century Hippolytus of Rome observed, "Cleomenes and his followers declare that he (Christ) is the God and Father of the universe."[46] They were later called "Modalist Monarchians".

J. N. D. Kelly well summarises "Modalistic Monarchianism" as follows:

> This was a fairly widespread, popular trend of thought which could reckon on, at any rate, a measure of sympathy in official circles; and the driving-force behind it was the twofold conviction, passionately held, of the oneness of God and the full deity of Christ. What forced it into the open was the mounting suspicion that the former of these truths was being endangered by the new Logos doctrine and by the efforts of theologians to represent the Godhead as having revealed Itself in the economy as tri-personal. Any suggestion that the Word or Son was other than, or a distinct Person from, the Father seemed to the modalists (we recall that the ancient view that 'Father' signified the Godhead Itself was still prevalent) to lead inescapably to blasphemy of two Gods.[47]

It was Praxeas (c. 210) and then Noetus, both of Asia Minor, who gave this belief a regular theological touch around c. 200. They argued that the whole of God was present in Jesus. It was Sabellius (c. 215) who became the most vocal and important theologian of the movement. Their position was quite simple; there is no God but the one creator and sustainer of the world as stated in the Scriptures, and Christ was God, that creator whom people call Father. They made use of passages of Identity such as "I and the Father are one" and stressed the absolute likeness and identity of Jesus with God. Hippolytus quotes them saying:

> there exists one and same Being, called Father and Son, not one derived from the other, but himself from himself, nominally called Father and Son according to changing of times; and that this One is that appeared [to the patriarchs], and submitted to birth from a virgin, and conversed as man among men. On account of his birth that has taken place he confessed himself to be the Son to those who saw him, while to those who could receive it he did not hide the fact that he was the Father.[48]

Epiphanius quotes Sabellians as saying "Do we have one God or three?"[49] If God is One, then the words of Isaiah 44:6 applied also to Christ: "Thus says the Lord, the King of Israel and his Redeemer, the Lord of hosts: I am the first and I am the last; beside me there is no God."

It is hard to verify details concerning the exact position and terminology of Sabellius, as most of the surviving documents are over a century later. It seems that Sabellians, as they were called, were interested in monotheism. They accused orthodox Christians, as Tertullian reports, of polytheism: "they accuse us of preaching two and three Gods while they claim that they are worshippers of one God."[50] As a result, Tertullian gave them the name "Monarchians," which has clung to them to this day. Historically they are called the "Modalist Monarchians."

This extreme position and preciseness with regards to Jesus's relationship with God may have been an offshoot of orthodox teachings and underlying ambiguity. As Harnack observes: "many facts observed in reference to the earliest bodies of Monarchians that come clearly before us, seem to prove that they bore features which must be characterised as pre-Catholic, but not un-Catholic." [51] Worshipping Jesus with absolute titles like Lord and explicitly calling him God could have led anybody to eradicate the distinction between Jesus and God. We are told that phrases such as "God is born," "the suffering God," or "the dead God" were so widespread among Christians that even Tertullian, for all his hostility to the Modolist Monarchians, could not escape using them. The main difference between the two parties is that of precision and systematisation. The Modalist Monarchians systematised the popular Christian belief in Christ in a clear and precise manner. It was a bold step towards giving a precise theological color to the rather ambiguous Christian devotional language. The Church could not accept it because of its dangerous implications; it was nothing but naive corporealism and patripassianism. Though it safeguarded Jesus's deity as well as monotheism, the objectives for which the Church had been aspiring, the Church could not approve of it in such bold terms because of its subtle implications. Linwood Urban observes that "if the whole of God is present in the historic Jesus, the *transcendence* of God is nullified. The Pre-Nicene solution asserts that there is part of God which is not incarnate, and so allows for God to transcend his presence in Jesus."[52]

In his work *Against Praxeas* Tertullian explains the reason, arguing:

> How is it that the omnipotent, invisible God, whom no man hath seen or can see, who inhabiteth light inaccessible...how is it, I say, that the Most High should have walked at evening in paradise seeking Adam,...

unless these things were an image and a type and an allegory? These things indeed could not have been believed even of the Son of God, had they not been written; perhaps they could have not been believed of the Father even had they been written. For these persons bring him down into Mary's womb, place him at Pilot's tribunal, and shut him in the tomb of Joseph. Hence their error becomes evident [...] Thus they believe that it was always one God, the Father, who did the things which were really done through the Son.[53]

Tertullian's passage is sufficient to pinpoint the underlying theological complexities. The anthropomorphic and corporeal passages of the Old Testament had played an important role in the triune interpretation of divinity. God was also known to be transcendent, for Greek philosophy would have made mockery of an anthropomorphic or any other conception of God as rudimentary or paganistic. The secondary, derivative divine being of the Platonism scheme was initially helpful in preserving God's absolute transcendence and avoiding accusations of being pagan. On the other hand, this kind of notion of divinity was not adequate for the purposes of salvation. Common believers preferring their own salvation over and beyond God's transcendence sacrificed Him at the altar of their sins. This tension is intrinsic to the entire history of Christology, as will be seen in forthcoming discussions.

Given that God's transcendence and ineffability was at stake, the defenders of orthodoxy except Zephyrinus, the bishop of Rome, condemned this group of Monarchians as heretics. Then formally, in the sixth-century Synod of Braga, orthodoxy decreed that:

If anyone does not confess that the Father and the Son and the Holy Spirit are three persons of one essence and virtue and power, as the catholic apostolic church teaches, but says that [they are] a single and solitary person, in such a way that the Father is the same as the Son and this One is also the Paraclete Spirit, as Sabellius and Priscillian have said, let him be anathema.[54]

In order to preserve God's transcendence and stability, observes Urban, "Trinitarians were ready to give up the divine simplicity. Trinitarians assert that, although God is one and simple in most respects, there are some in which he is Triune."[55] The Monarchian anthropomorphic position has continued to surface even after its condemnation, for throughout Christian history "men have been frequently condemned for denying the deity of Christ but rarely for denying the distinction between the Father and the Son. To deny the former has generally seemed unchristian; to deny the latter only unintelligent."[56] In spite of strong opposition Modalism - the crystal-clear anthropomorphic concept of God - remained widespread, especially among the simple-minded and ordinary Christians. It was shared, as McGiffert observes, "by the majority of the common people and was in harmony with the dominant piety of the age 'What harm am I doing in glorifying Christ?' was the question of Noetus and in it he voiced the sentiment of multitudes."[57] St. Augustine, Thomas Aquinas, and many other leading medieval theologians, had a modalist leaning. In modern times Friedrich Daniel Ernst Schleiermacher, Carl Barth and Carl Rahner have shown clear modalist tendencies.

Dynamic Monarchianism

Meanwhile, another kind of Monarchianism became current in the East and the West, and it took the question of Jesus's relationship with God to the other extreme. In the West Theodotus (c. 190), a leather-worker, taught that Jesus was a man, born of a virgin as a result of God's special decree through the agency of the Holy Spirit. His virgin birth did not make him a god or a divine being. God tested his piety for a period of Jesus's earthly life, and then let the Holy Ghost descend upon him at the time of baptism; God had a purpose for him and equipped him for that vocation. Jesus became the Christ at the time of his baptism and as a result of his vocation, but not due to his heavenly nature or divinity. Additionally, Jesus excelled all humanity in virtues and became an authority over them, but his adoption in no way or form diluted his humanity or made him God; he always remained an obedient servant of God. Theodotus was afterwards characterised as the founder of the God-denying revolt, adoptionism. The adoptionists made use of the biblical monotheistic passages, the Gospel passages of distinction and subordination and finally the crystal-clear Gospel passages that emphasize Jesus's feeble humanity and earthly nature. They also were also able to strike a balance between the transcendence of God and human salvation through Christ's redeeming death. Their solution was not adequate for the Orthodoxy, though; such an understanding of Jesus, observes Urban, "preserved the simplicity of God, but at the price of unfaithfulness to the tradition."[58]

In the East this movement was significantly revived under the leadership of Paul of Samosata, the bishop of Antioch and Queen Zenobia of Palmyra. Bishop Paul enjoyed authority, almost like a viceroy, and used his political influence to expound his theological views concerning Christ. He observed that Jesus did not have an essential divine nature; his nature was pure human, as he was a man from beneath, not from above and having divine substance. Jesus had a normal human birth and grew into knowledge and wisdom. The Logos of God inspired him from above and dwelt in him as an inner man. Jesus did neither lose his humanity nor his human nature, which always remained the dominant nature in Jesus. It was polished, civilised and guided by the Logos. The union of the Logos and Jesus was not a union of substance, or a merger or diffusion of natures, but rather that of will and quality. Mary did neither bear nor deliver the divine Logos, but the human Jesus, just as other humans. Moreover, Jesus the man was anointed at baptism with the Spirit from above and not the Logos. Jesus was special in the sense that he lived under the constant divine grace of a very special degree. His uniqueness lay in his union of disposition and will and not in the unity of his substance or nature with God. As Jesus advanced in the manifestation of goodness and submission to the will of God, he became the:

> Redeemer and Saviour of the human race, and at the same time entered into an eternally indissoluble union with God, because his love can never cease. Now he has obtained from God, as the reward of his love, the name which is above every name; God has committed to him the Judgment, and invested him with divine dignity, so that now we can call him "God" [born] of the virgin.[59]

Likewise, we are allowed to talk of his preexistence in connection with his goodness and in the sense of the prior degree of God. It is clear that Paul did not believe in the divine nature of Jesus. On the other hand, in addition to his adoptionism, he sought to prove that the assumption that Jesus had the divine nature or was by nature the Son of God was detrimental to monotheism as it led to duality in the Godhead. He became God but somehow, as says, Paul Tillich, "he had to deserve to become God."[60] Paul banished from divine service all Church psalms that expressed in any sense the essential divinity of Christ. Consequently, Paul was condemned at a Synod of Antioch held in 268, two earlier synods having failed to take action in the matter. He was declared as heretical because he denied Jesus's pre-existence and his unity of substance with God; in other words, his proper divinity.

Though both types of Monarchianisms were condemned as heretical, in different ways they challenged and pushed the orthodoxy to look into the immense difficulties involved in their understanding of the transcendence and unity of God, and attempt to clarify said understanding in intelligible terms. The orthodox Fathers insisted upon their concept of the relative unity of God by holding on to their Logos Christology. By the end of the third century the Logos Christology became generally accepted in all parts of the Church and found its place in most of the creeds framed in that period, especially in the East.

Arianism

Arius (256–336) brought the genuine concerns into public, and in doing so echoed the anxieties of the masses. Arius, a presbyter from Alexandria, was a man of mark. He brought the debate regarding Christ's nature, and his relationship to God, to the public and caused vehement excitement. Dorothy Sayers has neatly paraphrased the impact of Arius' views:

> "If you want the logos doctrine, I can serve it hot and hot:

God beget him and before he was begotten he was not."[61]

Arius maintained that God is one both in substance and in person. He is the only eternal and unoriginated being. The Logos, the pre-existent being, is merely a creature. There was a time when he was not and then was created by the Father out of nothing. What is true of the filial relationship is true of Jesus the Son and God the Father. The Father existed before the Son. The Son Jesus was created by the Father from a substance which was non-existent prior to Jesus's creation. Arius, observes Norris:

> was a firm believer not only in the unity of God but also in a doctrine of divine transcendence which saw God's way of being as inconsistent

with that of the created order. Logically enough, therefore, his doctrine of the Logos was so formulated as to express two convictions: first, that the Logos cannot be God in the proper sense; second, that the Logos performs an essential mediatorial role in the relation of God to [the] world. He taught, accordingly, that the Logos belongs to the created order but at the same time that he is quite superior creature, ranking above all others because he was brought into being by God "before the ages" to act as the agent of God in creation.[62]

Arius used scriptural evidences such John 14:28, where Jesus categorically stated that the Father is "greater than I," and John 17:20-26 where Jesus encouraged the disciples to become "one as we are one." Arius contended that the disciples could not have been one with God or Jesus in terms of embodying the divine nature or substance, but in will. Likewise, the unity of the Son with the Father was that of will and not of divinity or substance. Additionally, 1 Corinthians 8:5-6 was quoted to differentiate between God and Christ.

In Arius' words:

> The Father alone is God, and the Son is so called only in a lower and improper sense. He is not the essence of the Father, but a creature essentially like other creatures...or unique among them. His uniqueness may imply high prerogatives, but no creature can be a Son of God in the primary sense of full divinity.[63]

God is perfect, but the Son of God advances in wisdom and knowledge, and hence is changeable. The Son can be called Logos, but is to be sharply distinguished from the eternal impersonal logos or reason of God. The essence of the Son is identical neither with that of God nor with that of human beings. The Son, who became incarnate in Jesus, is the first of all creatures and hence higher in order than any other being, whether angels or men; Jesus did not have a human soul. "The soul of Christ was the Logos; only his body was human. As a consequence all that he did and suffered was done and suffered by the Logos."[64] Because of what he did during his earthly life, maintaining unwavering devotion to the divine will, the Son was given glory and lordship and would even be called "God" and worshipped. But to identify him with God's essence is to commit blasphemy. "So stark a monotheism," observes Pelikan, "implied an equally uncompromising view of divine transcendence."[65] Arius then was, as we can conclude with Bright, "speaking of Him as, after all, only the eldest and highest of creatures; not denying to him the title of God, but by limitations and glosses abating its real power."[66] In spite of the fact that Arius had a high view of Jesus's humanity, so much so that he denied his human nature and emphasised a mild incarnation even allowing him the title "God", his position was rejected by the Church because he denied Jesus's full divinity. The Church felt that Arius had at once affirmed and nullified the divinity and humanity of Christ.

This "half-god" (to use Tillich's term) theology of Arius was rejected by the champions of the orthodox Logos Christology, and finally defeated as heresy.

This inherent tension between the transcendental views of Godhead and redemption through the sacrificial death of God was the source of both parties' concerns. The Arians somehow preferred the transcendence of God over their own divinisation and presumed redemption. The official party could live with this tension and make sense of it by artificial bandages and irrational presuppositions. That is what was achieved by Athanasius in the Council of Nicaea – arguing against Arius and his doctrine of the distinct Christ – and the Logos Christology was rendered victorious over its opponents once and for all. In 325 AC, Emperor Constantine convened and presided over the Council of Nicaea in order to develop a statement of faith to unify the church. The Nicene Creed was written, declaring that "the Father and the Son are of the same substance" (homoousios). And "when the Logos Christology obtained a complete victory, the traditional view of the Supreme deity as one person, and, along with this, every thought of the real and complete human personality of the Redeemer was condemned as being intolerable in the Church."[67] All the bishops were required by Constantine to sign the creed, "it was made clear that this was necessary for everyone wishing to retain the episcopal rank."[68] Constantine used the Council as a propaganda tool and encouraged unity. "The emperor followed up with letters of his own announcing that 'unity of faith, sincerity of love, and community of feeling in regard to the worship of Almighty God' had been obtained in the council, and urged his Christian brethren to accept the actions from it as 'indicative of the

Divine Will."[69] Even though Arius was condemned as an arch heretic and treated as such for centuries, his sincere concerns for Christianity and his genuine insights into scriptural passages and monotheistic transcendental history could not be denied.

Francis Young argues that "Arius was not himself the arch-heretic of tradition, nor even much of an inquirer; rather he was a reactionary, a rather literal-minded conservative who appealed to scripture and tradition as the basis of his faith."[70] Many of the earlier Alexandrians had also held most of the views propagated by Arius. His transcendental conception of God had close affinities with Athenagoras, and his subordinationism belonged to the Origenist tradition. He was not as much interested to demote the Son as much as to exalt the Father. Further, Lucian of Antioch, a canonised Saint of the Catholic Church, held Christological views very similar to Arius, the main difference being that earlier Christian leaders had not resorted to the use of vicious witch hunters like Athanasius. Arius's Trinitarian scheme was as hierarchical as that of Origen. Athanasius's accusation was that Arius had brought the Logos down from heights of lofty divinity to the level of creatures, whilst Arius had constantly emphasised that the transcendence of God had been compromised by the attribution of physical processes to Him such as generation and emanation. In reality Arius had done nothing new, aside from synchronising and systematising earlier transcendental concerns in an open and coherent form. Moreover, he had forced the orthodoxy out of their comfort zone to make them face realities they were neither pleased nor ready to encounter.

The reaction of the orthodoxy was proportionately damaging; they accused Arius of violating Scripture, yet failed to notice they had done the same. Further, they were forced to adopt the non-scriptural, and utterly philosophical as well as paradoxical term, *homoousios* [of the same substance] to exclude Arius's views. We may conclude with F. Young that:

> Indeed, the popularity of his biblical solution to the tension between monotheism and faith in Christ is beyond dispute; and there is no reason to doubt Arius' sincerity or genuine Christian intention. Though his opponents attributed his popularity to deception, it is more likely that it was a response to one who was enthusiastic in his pursuit of [the] true meaning of the Christian confession.[71]

Traditional Christianity has been evading real and searching questions regarding its notions of transcendental monotheism and its understanding of the person of Christ. In the name of mysteries and paradoxes, it has long confused many rationally oriented believers. Arius brought these genuine concerns into the public sphere, and in doing so echoed the anxieties of the masses; this was the real source of his popularity. He might still have many followers today, even among contemporary Christian believers, laypersons and the clergy alike. C. S. Lewis speaks of Arianism as "one of those 'sensible' synthetic religions which are so strongly recommended today and which, then as now, included among their devotees many highly cultivated clergymen."[72] In short, Arius was one of those adventurous yet cultivated souls who had tried to locate and find a solution to the unsolved problem of Christ's relationship with Almighty God using precise exposition and clarity of thought; factors which to the Church, would destroy the 'mystery' of incarnation. This mystery was maintained by the Council of Nicaea which we will now explore in a little more detail.

The Council of Nicaea

The Arian controversy caused division in the church; the emperor feared that this rift would split the Roman Empire, whose favoured religion was Christianity. In June of 325 AC Emperor Constantine summoned the general assembly of bishops from all parts of the empire to meet at Nicaea (present-day Iznik in Turkey). There are extant several lists of the bishops who responded to the Emperor's call (from 195 to 300).

St. Athanasius was the most prominent figure in the Arian controversy; he spent over forty years of his life defending the equality of Jesus Christ with God Almighty against the half-god theology of the Christian Arians and the Jesus-is-not-God notions of the non-Christians. St. Athanasius has been highly regarded by the early Church as the Father of Orthodoxy. Frances Young gives a different view of the Saint, observing that "the enhanced role of Athanasius at Nicaea is one feature of the 'legend of Athanasius' which rapidly developed. This 'good tradition' has affected all the main sources, for Athanasius' own apologetic works were a primary source for the historians."[73] She further argues that:

> Alongside this 'good tradition' however, there are traces of a less favoura-
> ble estimates of Athanasius current among his contemporaries. Certain-

ly he must have been a politician capable of subtle maneuvers; the first seems to have been in his own election, which was definitely contested, may have been illegal, and looks as though it was enforced. There seems to have been a pitiless streak in his character - that he resorted to violence to achieve his own ends is implied by a good deal of evidence.[74]

For Athanasius, the central objective of the Christian religion was "Redemption," and he subordinated every other thing to this objective. Archibald Robertson finds Athanasius's greatness in this all-pervasive view of Christ's redemption:

> Athanasius was not a systematic theologian; that is, he produced no many-sided theology like that of Origen or Augustine. He had no interest in theological speculation, none of the instincts of a schoolman or philosopher. His theological greatness lies in his firm grasp of soteriological principles, in his resolute subordination of everything else, even the formula *homoousia* [identical in nature, consubstantial], to the central fact of Redemption, and to what the fact implied as to the Person of the Redeemer.[75]

According to Athanasius 'Salvation' or 'Redemption' demands incarnation, "the salvation was possible only on one condition, namely, that the Son of God was made in Jesus so that we might become God." In his *De Incarnatione et Contra Arianos* he discussed the matter at length:

> For in speaking of the appearance of the Saviour amongst us, we must need speak also of the origin of men, that you may know that the reason of his coming down was because of us, and that our transgression called forth the loving-kindness of the Word, that the Lord should both make haste to help us and appear among men. For of his becoming incarnate we were the object, and for our salvation he dealt so lovingly as to appear and be born even in a human body. Thus, then, God was made man, and willed that he should abide in incorruption.[76]

Hence the:

> Son of God became the Son of man in order that the sons of men, the sons of Adam, might be made sons of God. The Word, who was

begotten of the Father in Heaven in an ineffable, inexplicable, incomprehensible and eternal manner, came to this earth to be born in time of the Virgin Mary, Mother of God, in order that they who were born of earth might be born again of God, in Heaven.[77]

The Son does not have any beginning; eternally the Father had the Son, "the beginning of the Son is the Father, and as the Father is without beginning therefore the Son as the Father's [...] is without beginning as well."[78] It seems that Athanasius was not much concerned with the philosophical implications of what he was saying; he was just a preacher. His concept of the Son's origin in the Father does imply the Son's beginning and in a way subordination which he emphatically denied. Athanasius presumed more and rationalised less. He assumed that the Son was of the same substance of the Father, and was exactly like the Father; the Father was the light and the Son was His brightness.

Jesus, then, is the Logos, the Son of God from eternity, uncreated, ungenerated, of the very nature and substance of the Father. McGiffert observes that it was:

> not necessary according to Athanasius that Christ should be personally identical with God, that he and God should be the same individual, but it was necessary that he and God should be of one substance or essence. To be equal with God or at one with him in will and purpose was not enough. He must actually possess the very nature of God himself.[79]

It is interesting to note here that Athanasius, like all the other Fathers, insisted upon the ineffable, invisible nature of God the Father. To him God was not apprehensible to anybody in His ontological or expressive nature, but apprehensible only in his works and manifestation through Christ.

This idea of Christ being God and that in the Son we have the Father was not new or original with Athanasius. He was sincerely following the age-old tradition of Orthodoxy. Athanasius did differ, however, with Origen and the Apologists in completely denying subordination, adoptionism, and any significant distinction between the Son and the Father. In doing so, he landed in Modalism and was accused of Sabellianism by his opponents. It is difficult to defend Athanasius of this accusation. If in the Son we have the full and proper Godhead, the true and proper nature and substance of God, and in the Virgin Mary the "Mother of God" then what in the world could be more corporeal and anthropomorphic (Sabellianism) than this conception of the deity? F. Young observes that:

> On many occasions, Athanasius's exegesis is virtually docetic and seems to us forced and unnatural. All is subordinated to the purpose of showing that the Logos in himself had all the attributes of divinity, e.g. impassability, omniscience, etc. The texts implying weakness or ignorance he explains as merely referring to the incarnation-situation. At one point, Athanasius even goes so far as to say... he imitated our characteristics.[80]

Seemingly, Athanasius maintained that Jesus had withheld his divine omniscience and acted as if he were a man due to our human limitations. This Docetic tendency encouraged him to describe Jesus in terms which clearly limited his humanity. It was faith and salvation which led Athanasius to this point in asserting Christ's proper and complete divinity but he, as Harnack puts it, "in making use of these presuppositions in order to express his faith in the Godhead of Christ, *i.e.*, in the essential unity of the Godhead in itself with the Godhead manifested in Christ, fell into an abyss of contradictions."[81] It simply was, to use Harnack's term, "an absurdity." But:

> Athanasius put up with absurdity; without knowing it he made a still greater sacrifice to his faith – the historical Christ. It was at such a price that he saved the religious conviction that Christianity is the religion of perfect fellowship with God, from being displaced by a doctrine which possessed many lofty qualities, but which had no understanding of the inner essence of religion, which sought in religion nothing but "instruction," and finally found satisfaction in an empty dialectic.[82]

In the Council of Nicaea, the creed originally presented by Eusebius of Caesarea, a supporter of the Logos Christology was accepted- with certain additions. The will of the Emperor was the decisive factor. Constantine was not so much interested in establishing the truth of theology as he was in political harmony and power; in pursuit of this he was willing to accommodate any creed or theological position which ensured political stability and tolerance. Kelly is correct in observing that there is thus "a sense in which it is unrealistic to speak of the theology of the council."[83] Constantine was so influential that R. L. Fox could write of him that "among his other innovations, it was Constantine who first mastered the art of holding, and corrupting, an international conference."[84] Constantine himself, his relationship to Christianity and his conversion are controversial subjects to this day. It is tempting to agree with Kelly, who observes that:

> the status of the Nicene creed was very different in the generation or so following the council from what we many have been brought up to believe. One is perhaps tempted to sympathize with somewhat radical solution of the problem provided by that school of historians which treat the Nicene symbol as purely political formula representative of no strain of thought in the Church but imposed on the various wrangling groups as a badge of union.[85]

It was neither the Holy Spirit nor the ecumenical synod of around three hundred bishops who steered the Council proceedings; it was the emperor and his iron fist rule. This was the decisive factor, though lip service and occasional reverence was shown to them.

Unfortunately, later traditional Christianity gave a great deal of significance and authority to the Council's decisions and terms whose religious nature seemed more inclined to political fervour and combatting Arianism than anything else. The Nicene Creed begins:

> We believe in One God, the Father Almighty, Maker of all things both visible and invisible: And in one Lord Jesus Christ, the Son of God, Begotten of the Father, Only-begotten, *That is, from the Essence of the Father*, God from God, Light from Light, Very God from Very God, Begotten, not made, *of one essence with the Father*; by whom all things, both in heaven and earth, were made; Who for us men and for our salvation came down, and was incarnate, and became man, suffered, and rose again the third day; ascended into heavens; cometh to judge the quick and dead. And in the Holy Spirit.[86]

Then it goes on to say:

> But those who say, once He was not, and – before He was begotten, He

was not, and – He came into existence out of what was not,' or – That the Son of God was a different "hypostasis" or "ousia" or – that He was made,' or – is (was) changeable or mutable are anathematized by the Catholic and Apostolic Church of God.[87]

The central phrase of this fundamental Christian confession is *homoousios,* meaning of one substance with the Father. Though obviously a theological term, it was not exactly an adequate theological solution. It was a layman's solution to pin down a pure and stark divinity for Christ without much precision, explanation and rationality. It neither preserved the boundaries between the transcendent God and Christ by an emanative scheme of a hierarchal emanative Trinity, as affected by the early Platonist Fathers, nor kept the mystery of its secret locked in its box. Rather, it brought the redemptive Monarchian scheme into the public sphere and in confidently touted clear terms. Consequently, it was accused of being Sabellianism along with its defenders, Athanasius and Marcellus. Disputing it vigorously, Arians argued that such an analogy and identity was absolutely inappropriate to the relationship between God and the Logos, putting forward three reasons to substantiate their position: (1) God the Father was self-existent, unoriginated, eternal while the Son was produced by the Father. Therefore, the Father and the Son could not be fully equal. (2) The Father was neither begotten nor was begettable while the Son was begotten and begettable. (3) The Father had begotten the Son, the God, while the Son had not begotten another Son. How could the unoriginated Father and the originated Son be equal? Arian reasoning was logical, rational and systematic. That of the traditional Apostolic Fathers, such as Athanasius, on the other hand was illogical and confusing, their answers self-contradictory. Their doctrine made the Son both unbegotten and begotten, unbegotten as part of the whole of Deity, yet begotten of the Father as a relationship within the Trinity. A. Harnack rightly argues that there is "in fact, no philosophy in existence possessed of formulae which could present in an intelligible shape the propositions of Athanasius."[88] The same can be said of subsequent Christian Trinitarian thought at large.

The Council decided to favor the unintelligible, self-contradictory doctrine of Christology at the expense of clear precision and logic. All bishops present subscribed to this formula with the exception of two, Theonas of Marmarika and Secundus of Ptolemais, along-side Arius. Arians were condemned and called "Porphyrians", and their works ordered to be burned because, in the words of Julius of Rome, "For theirs was no ordinary offense, nor had they sinned against man, but against our Lord Jesus Christ Himself, the Son of the Living God."[89] The Emperor gave his final approval asserting that, "what satisfied the three hundred bishops is nothing else than the judgment of God, but most of all where Holy Spirit being present in the thought of men such as these and so ripe in years, made known the Divine will."[90] A majority of modern traditional Christian schol-ars view these historical dogmatic developments as an illustration of "how the Holy Spirit brings about a gradual increase in the Church's actual consciousness of the mysteries revealed by Jesus Christ."[91] A. Harnack, on the other hand, views them as an outcome of a lack of understanding and education, "As regards the composition of the Council, the view expressed by the Macedonian Sabinus of Heraclea (Socr. 1. 8), that the majority of the bishops were uneducated, is con-firmed by the astonishing results. The general acceptance of the res-olution come to by the Council is intelligible only if we presuppose that the question in dispute was above most of the bishops."[92]

The same can be said of subsequent Christian Trinitarian thought at large; The Trinitarian formula was - and remained - unintelligible, self-contradictory and irrational. It was also against the original, sim-ple, ethical and monotheistic message of Jesus of Nazareth. To claim a pure, hard-core divinity for the Son, forgetting the true essence and transcendence of God the Father and ignoring the terrible inconsisten-cies of this approach, was mind-boggling. This approach looked upon the Father not as the Father but as the Father of the Son, Jesus Christ. The ethical gospel of Jesus was completely lost in the metaphysical contortions of the Trinity and the labyrinthine discussions of the di-vine substance and persons which had endlessly followed, tragically to the detriment of the Church and the loss of souls. Andrew Fair-bairn rightly laments that the "Church, when it thought of the Father, thought more of the First Person in relation to the Second than of God in relation to man; when it thought of the Son, it thought more of the Second Person in relation to the First than of humanity in relation to God [...] The Nicene theology failed here because it interpreted God and articulated its doctrine in the terms of the schools rather than in the terms of the consciousness of Christ."[93]

He concludes, observing that:

The division of the Persons within Godhead had as its necessary result the division of God from man, and the exaltation of miraculous and unethical agencies as the means of bridging over the gulf. The inadequacy in these cardinal respects of the Nicene theology would be inexplicable were we to regard it as a creation of supernatural wisdom or the result of special Divine enlightenment; but it is altogether normal when conceived as a stage in the development of Christian thought.[94]

The Person of Jesus Christ

It was - and always has been - the Christian desire to attain redemption through the atoning death of Christ that has led them to proclaim and maintain the deity of Jesus Christ. At the same time, there has always remained the question of Christ's humanity. It was impossible to deny this humanity for according to the Gospels, Jesus had been a historical reality. Once the Church, over various gradual attempts, had finally arrived at the conclusion that Jesus was God and fully divine, they were faced with the issue of how to in some way reconcile this divine/human unity, to strike a balance between and interpret the relationship. The difficulty of regarding Christ as both divine and simultaneously human led some to Docetism (that he really was God and his humanity was just a mask) and others to Adoptionism (that he was adopted by God as baptism). The recognition of an absolute, pure divinity for Jesus made the problem more acute and insistent. Just a few decades after the Council of Nicaea the pendulum swung completely in the other direction. Focus now was no longer on the pre-existence of the Son or the relationship of God the Son to the Father, but rather the relation of God to man in the person of the historical Jesus. The God incarnate formula of the Council was considered too metaphysical to be an intelligible part of real human history; if Jesus was indeed God incarnate then what was his real nature, human or divine? Human history had no parallel to explain this incarnational paradigm, so how could humanity understand it in logical human terms?

It was Apollinaris (d. 390), bishop of Laodicea and a close friend of

Athanasius, who proposed a somewhat rational solution to this complex problem. He took the long-accepted Alexandrian Christology of the Word-flesh to its logical limits. As mentioned earlier, to Athanasius and the Nicene Creed the absolute divinity of Christ was considered essential to ensure redemption, and it was strongly held that only the true Son of God could reveal God to man. Adhering to this Word-flesh Christology, Apollinaris argued that this act of redemption could not be possible without the deification of the man Jesus Christ. Therefore, he contended that Jesus had only one theo-anthropic or divine-human nature. At the point of incarnation, the Logos, a divine spirit or mind, was united with the human body and soul of Christ to become thence onwards the active personal element in Jesus's being while relegating the human element, comprised of the body and soul, to a secondary or passive level. The frankly acknowledged presupposition of this argument is that the divine Word was substituted for the normal human soul in Christ. Apollinaris believed that if the divine was separated from the human in Christ, salvation would be imperiled, so he emphasised the deity of Christ and the unity of his person through a merger of the human with the logos making the human element glorified. How he reasoned could humans be baptized in Jesus's name and redeemed by his atoning death if he were just an ordinary man?

In Harnack's words, Apollinaris "merely completed the work of Athanasius inasmuch he added to it the Christology which was demanded by the Homousia of the Logos. They both made a supreme sacrifice to their faith in that they took from the complicated and contradictory tradition regarding Christ those elements only which were in harmony with the belief that He was the Redeemer from sin and death."[95]

But it was widely felt that Apollinaris had safeguarded the divinity of Jesus on account of his humanity. The Cappadocian Fathers, the two Gregories and other churchmen opposed him, criticising his Christology for failing to meet the essential condition of salvation and atonement, i.e., the unity of the human rational soul, the seat of sin, with the Logos. In his famous phrase Gregory Nazianzen argued that "what has not been assumed cannot be restored; it is what is united with God that is saved."[96] Apollinaris was condemned as heretical at the second council of Constantinople in 381.

On the other hand, the representatives of the Antiochian school challenged "Monophysitism" or Apollinarianism with their scientific

Christological dogma. In general, the Antiochians' interest in Jesus was more ethical than redemptive; they viewed in him a perfect ethical and moral example. Jesus could have not been a perfect ethical model had he not been a complete human being with free will and a genuine human personality. The Antiochian school, argues Kelly, "deserves credit for bringing back the historical Jesus."[97] Diodorus of Tarsus and then Theodore of Mopsuestia, like Paul of Samosata, advocated a moral union "unity of grace and will" rather than unity of substance and nature. Their Christology conformed to the "Word-man" scheme rather than the Alexandrian "Word-flesh" scheme.

Theodore emphasised the perfect humanity of Christ: "A complete man, in his nature, is Christ, consisting of a rational soul and human flesh; complete is the human person; complete also the person of the divinity in him. It is wrong to call one of them impersonal."[98] Opposing Monophysitism, he argued: "One should not say that the Logos became flesh but one should say 'He took on humanity.'"[99] To conform his views to that of the Logos Christology and Nicene doctrine of Christ's proper divinity, he had no choice but to assert Christ's two natures: one of a complete human, the other complete divine, each with a full personality and all qualities and faculties that go therewith. None of these persons or natures mixed with the other: "The Logos dwelt in man but did not become man; the human was associated and united with the divine but was not deified."[100] Their association and closeness was essential for salvation but not so close as to render it irrelevant to man as man or to involve the unchangeable, immutable Logos in the suffering of the cross. He further argued that while the scripture distinguishes the natures, it at the same time stresses the unity between them. Therefore, he argued, "we point to difference of natures, but to unity of Person" or in other words "the two natures are, through their connection, apprehended to be one reality."[101]

As we see, Theodore emphatically denies the transformation or transmutation of the Logos into flesh. He also held that the divine nature did not change the human nature. Jesus, having human nature, by grace and free will could follow the divine nature. Therefore, one could say that Mary gave birth to God. This clearly was a metaphorical rather than substance designation.

Theodore's opponents rejected this theory as leading to a "monster with two heads", a being with two personal centers and a combination of two sons.[102] Theodore denied this as mere accusation, but to McGiffert "to all intents and purpose he was doing so."[103] Cyril of Alexandria singled him out for attack, and since the Fifth General Council of Constantinople in 533 he has been labeled as a Nestorian before Nestorius.

Theodore's is another reflection of the contradictory nature of the New Testament writings. On the one hand they emphasise transcendental monotheism, and Jesus's feeble humanity and subordination to God Almighty, whilst on other occasions they seemingly attribute a kind of divine status to Jesus, especially in the Pauline and Johannine writings. The traditionalists, bent on attaining salvation through the redemptive death of Jesus and their own union with divinity, have inclined towards the Johannine interpretations and pushed them to their limits. The rational believers have always been worried about the danger this approach poses to transcendental monotheism and ethical piety. Christianity is the name and product of these antithetical and diametrically opposed tendencies, as well as concerns. Many innocent and sincere believers have had to pay for the contradictory nature of their scriptural writings. Nestorius is a good example of this theological nightmare.

The controversy regarding the person of Christ came to a head-on collision in the fifth century when Nestorius, a younger member of the Antiochian school, became bishop of Constantinople (428). He protested against the very common tendency among the masses, especially among the monks in the neighbourhood of the capital, to exalt the Virgin Mary as "Mother of God" or theotokos. "God cannot have a mother, he argued, and no creature could have engendered the Godhead; Mary bore a man, the vehicle of divinity but not God. The Godhead cannot have been carried for nine months in a woman's womb, or have been wrapped in baby-clothes, or have suffered, died and been buried."[104]

H. Chadwick observes that "nothing caused so much scandal as a remark of Nestorius that 'God is not a baby two or three months old.'"[105] Nestorius held that she should either be called 'mother of the man Jesus's or 'mother of Christ'. His objection was to the transference of human attributes to the divine Logos. He emphatically denied that the Logos participated in the sufferings of the human nature of Christ.

Nestorius believed that Jesus had two natures. He maintained that before the union of the man and the Logos in Jesus, the man was a person distinct from the Logos. Then "He who is the similitude of God has taken the person of the flesh."[106] After the union these two separate persons retained their identity: "There the person exist not without ousia, nor here again does the ousia exist without the person, nor also the nature without person, nor yet the person without ousia."[107] His watchword was that "I hold the natures apart, but unite the worship".[108] He, following Theodore of Mopsuestia in his two nature Christology, held that "when we distinguish the natures, we say that the nature of the Divine Logos is complete that His person also is complete [...] [likewise we say] that man's nature is complete and his person also is complete. But when we consider the union, we say there is one person only."[109] Nestorius argued that after incarnation there resulted a new person, namely the person of Jesus, of which the Logos and man were two component parts. He believed that for true redemption, the second Adam must have been a real man. Kelly observes that "it was all-important in his eyes that the impassability of 'the God' should be preserved, and that 'the man' for his part should retain his spontaneity and freedom of action. Hence, though speaking on occasion of a 'union'..., the term he preferred was 'conjunction'..., which seem to avoid all suspicion of a confusion or mixing of the natures."[110]

To Nestorius it was a "perfect," "exact" and "continuous" union. Unlike the Alexandrian Christological view that upheld "hypostatic or natural" union, his view of union was "voluntary." By this he meant "the drawing together of the divine and human by gracious condescension on the one hand, and love and obedience on the other. As a result of their mutual adhesion, Christ was a single being, with a single will and intelligence, inseparable and indivisible."[111] Addressing his opponent Cyril of Alexandria he said "I said and affirmed that the union is in the one person of the Messiah [...] but thou [actest] in the reverse way, because thou wishest that in the two natures God the Word should be the person of the union."[112] Nestorius was anathematised by the Fifth Ecumenical Council at Constantinople (533) under Emperor Justinian I for his supposed heresy of the two natures and two persons.

Cyril in his letter of 430, which was used as one of the sources in the Council, had already written 12 anathemas which were specifically pointed towards Nestorius. The main three points directed to Nestorius were: "(1) If anyone does not confess that Emmanuel is God in truth, and therefore the holy Virgin is *theotokos* – for she bore in the flesh the Word of God became flesh – let him be anathema. (2) If anyone does not confess that the Word of God the Father was united by hypostases to the flesh and is one Christ with his own flesh, that is, the same both God and man together, let him be anathema. (3) If any one divides the hypostases in the one Christ after his union, joining them only by conjunction in dignity, or authority or power, and not rather by coming together in a union by nature, let him be anathema."[113]

Cyril's position emphasised a physical or a metaphysical unity of the divine and human nature in Christ. It paid lip service to human nature and considered the incarnate nature of God as the real one in the historical Jesus. His formula, "out of two natures, one" left no room to doubt that the Logos God had assumed humanity. Hence, it can be said that "God is born", that "God suffered", if only in addition to, "according to the flesh". He also insisted that "since the holy Virgin gave birth after the flesh to God who was united by *hypostasis* with flesh, therefore we say that she is *theotokos*.[114] Cyril championed the popular theological position and won the wide support of the masses. This was a victory of the worship of Mary, as the mother of God quite widespread in Christian circles of his time. Cyril used his popularity and political clout to mercilessly suppress all opposition to his position. He not only deified the human Jesus but also brought God to the womb of the very human Mary, thus obliterating all possibilities, confusions and mysteries, so far vaguely maintained by the Church, between the transcendent God and the human Jesus. It was not his theology or spiritualism but his skill at political maneuvering that won him support against an otherwise more spiritual and sincere Nestorius. In Campenhausen's view Cyril "was not greatly concerned with the truth; outwardly, however, he continued to play the part of the anxious, thoughtful leader who refuses to take action for reasons of purely personal spite, leaving the first steps to his best friends and go-between."[115] It was due to Cyril's efforts and political genius that Nestorius was made guilty of heresy and deposed in the general Council of Ephesus (431) under Emperor Theodosius II but, the final settlement was reached at the Council of Chalcedon.

It becomes evident that traditional Christianity, for the sake of salvation and redemption, has always intended to crucify God and denied all efforts to make the crucifixion the suffering of a mere human being. This is crystal-clear corporealism and could not have been maintained on the basis of speculative theology or any logical effort alone. It required the backing of the state, and exploitive and political power to suppress all rational and curious inquiries, made available to several traditional Logos-flesh theologians. Further, this act of blaspheming God, to use Nestorius' term, could not have been done by the Holy Spirit as always claimed by so-called Orthodoxy, but rather by the political powers of secular and at times pagan emperors.

In conclusion, it is worth quoting the famous passage from Nestorius, who wrote: "It is my earnest desire that even by anathematizing me they may escape from blaspheming God [and that those who so escape may confess God, holy, almighty and immortal, and not change the image of the incorruptible God for the image of corruptible man, and mingle heathenism with Christianity [...] but that Christ may be confessed to be in truth and in nature God and Man, being by nature immortal and impassable as God, and mortal and passable by nature as Man – not God in both natures, nor again Man in both natures. The goal of my earnest wish is that God may be blessed on earth as in heaven]; but for Nestorius, let him be anathema; only let men speak of God as I pray for them that they may speak. For I am with those who are for God, and not with those who are against God, who with an outward show of religion reproach God and cause him to cease from being God."[116]

The words of Nestorius speak for themselves. How in the world can someone who considers Mary to be the mother of God, accepts that the Logos God spent nine months in the womb of a woman, grew like a baby, harbored complete human needs, and died on the cross, deny accusations of heathenism? This is the true challenge and struggle of popular Christianity. F. Young pays homage to Nestorius in the following words: "It was a great Christian who wrote those words. There have been many who were prepared to die as martyrs for what they believed to be the truth, but Nestorius was prepared to live cursed and consigned to oblivion, as long as God was not dishonoured [...] In tribulation he showed a greater generosity of spirit than many who have received the name saint rather than heretic."[117]

The Council of Chalcedon
The decisions of the general Council of Ephesus did not settle the issue of the person of Christ. Just fifteen years after the agreement patched up in 433, quarrel broke out again in 448 when Eutyches, Archimandrite of a monastery in the neighbourhood of Constantinople, vehemently opposed Nestorianism or the Antiochian party's "inspired

man" Christology in favor of Cyrillianism or the Alexandrian God-man Christology. It is hard to determine Eutyches' original doctrine due to lack of proper historical documentation. It is clear though that he maintained the absolute unity and merger of the divine nature into the human nature of Jesus at his birth. He vehemently repudiated the two natures' tenet in the incarnate Son and declared them non-scriptural. Although he never claimed that Jesus's flesh was from heaven, he nevertheless refused to accept that it was consubstantial with humanity. Flavian, successor to Proclus, condemned him as Apollinarian. Many modern historians argue that Eutyches was not a theologian, but a confused thinker obsessed with salvation through Christ. To guarantee salvation he ended up upsetting the tenuous balance required in connection with Christology.

Eutyches, however, appealed his condemnation. Dioscorus of Alexandria accused Flavian of requiring a test of orthodoxy other than the Nicene Creed, and Emperor Theodosius II summoned a council to meet at Ephesus in August of 449 to decide the matter. Pope Leo of Rome declined to participate in person but dispatched on June 13, 449 his famous Dogmatic Letter, or *Tome*, to Flavian, clearly condemning the "One Nature after the Union" doctrine of Eutyches. This letter was carefully phrased to shun Nestorianism on the one hand and Eutychianism on the other. But Nestorius, writes Chadwick, "reading the Tome in his lonely exile, felt that the truth had been vindicated at last, and that he could die in peace."[118] Leo's Tome was never read to the synod. Under imperial power Eutyches was immediately rehabilitated, and his orthodoxy vindicated. The confession of two natures was anathematised. Leo's letter, which was suppressed in this so-called "Robber Synod" or "Latrocinium" (Brigandage) of Ephesus, was approved at Chalcedon; in fact, the letter became decisive for the outcome at Chalcedon. The opportunity for this was provided by the death of Theodosius on July 28, 450. Marcian succeeded to the throne and cemented his position by marrying the late emperor's sister Plucheria; Marcian and Plucheria were sympathisers of the Two Nature doctrine. The Pope persuaded them to summon the council to annul the theological work of the Robber Synod. Originally planned for Nicaea, the council was transferred to Chalcedon. The proceedings of this important Council opened on October 8, 451.

The Fourth Ecumenical Council, which was actually the most largely attended synod of antiquity, solemnly approved the Nicene Creed as the standard of orthodoxy, canonised Cyril's two letters and Leo's Tome, and finally, under the imperial pressure of Emperor Marcian, approved the following formula: "Following the Holy Fathers we all with one consent teach men to confess one and the same Son, our Lord Jesus Christ, the same perfect in deity and perfect in humanity, God truly and man truly, of a reasonable soul and body, of one substance with the Father in his deity, and of one substance with us in his humanity, in all things like unto us without sin; begotten before the ages of the Father in his deity, in the last days for us and for our salvation born of Mary the Virgin, the mother God, in his humanity; one and the same Christ, Son, Lord, only begotten, acknowledged in two natures, without confusion, without change, without division, without separation; the distinction of the natures being by no means taken away because of the union, but rather the property of each nature being preserved, and concurring in one person and one hypostasis, not divided or separated into two persons but one and the same Son and only begotten God Logos, Lord Jesus Christ; as from the beginning the prophets and the Lord Jesus Christ himself taught us concerning him, and the creed of the Fathers handed down to us."[119]

By this formula the Council asserted against Nestorianism the unipersonality of Christ and asserted against Eutychianism Christ's possession of two natures, divine and human, each perfect and unchanged. As mentioned earlier, the victory was political rather than theological. Grillmeier observes that "it was only under constant pressure from the emperor Marcian that the Fathers of Chalcedon agreed to draw up a new formula of belief."[120] Kelly observes that "the imperial commissioners, in their desire to avoid a split, had to exert considerable pressure before agreement could be reached."[121] W. A. Wigram writes that the Council "failed to command respect, because it was imposed for political reasons, by a government that, as was too often the case, was making a fetish of uniformity. The verdict was, and was felt to be, a "government job" and not a free decision of the fathers of the Church. Had Theodosius lived longer, the Council would not have been held at all, and its decision was given, as things were, largely through the votes of Bishops who had gone with Dioscurus at Ephesus, and who shifted round readily to the opposite side as soon as it was clear what line the Emperor was going to take.[122] He further observes that "in large districts, the Council was rejected at once, and in none, save only in Rome, was there any enthusiasm for its doctrine. For more than a century, however, the antagonism felt for it was admitted to be that of a party in the Church, and not that of a separatist body. The word "heretic" was not applied to those who rejected Chalcedon, even by the Bishops who persecuted them. They were called "Distinguisher," or one may say "Nonconformists."[123]

The critics of Chalcedon like Timothy (surnamed Aelurus, 477) and Philoxenus, on the other hand, honestly believed that "in their ignorance the so-called Fathers who had assembled to define the faith 'had ordained nothing other than that the impure doctrines of Nestorius should be received and preached in all the Churches of God.'"[124] To them the Council "so separates, and personalizes, what is divine and what is human in Christ that the hypostatic union is dissolved, and its place taken by a mere conjunction of the divine Logos and a Man."[125] Likening themselves to the tribe of Judah they parted company with the orthodoxy. "For how could they, who alone were worthy of the title 'orthodox', offer obedience to a Council which had caused Israel to sin? Nay, a curse lay upon that Council, and upon all who agreed with it, forever."[126] Therefore, with the passage of time the old theological controversies surfaced again and again. Monophysites once again asserted their old claim of Jesus having one nature and one theanthropic will, or monothelitism. Orthodoxy opposed this trend and in 680 at the third council of Constantinople (the sixth ecumenical council), under the iron hands of Emperor Constantine Pogonatus, was able to get its doctrine of 'dyothelitism' approved. By this doctrine the idea that Christ had two wills, one divine and one human, was officialized and has remained the orthodox position ever since, both in the East and the West.

At Chalcedon, and later at Constantinople, the human element of the picture of Christ was saved. Grillmeier argues that "if the person of Christ is the highest mode of conjunction between God and man, God and the world, the Chalcedonian 'without confusion' and 'without separation' show the right mean between monism and dualism, the two extremes between which the history of christology also swings. The Chalcedonian unity of person in the distinction of the natures provides the dogmatic basis for the preservation of the divine transcendence, which must always be a feature of the Christian concept of God. But it also shows possibility of a complete immanence of God in our history, an immanence on which the biblical doctrine of the economy of salvation rests."[127]

The Chalcedonian formula had attempted to solve a long-standing Christological problem but in no way, shape or form did it provide logical or intelligible categories to satisfactorily answer the questions of Jesus's person or inner relational difficulties. In point of fact, it was more presumed than explained that Christ was at once a complete God and a complete man. What type of man he was when he did not have the sinful nature was neither addressed nor resolved? His humanity was neither a complete humanity like that of ordinary human beings, nor his divinity like that of the Father. The whole thing was in fact a hodgepodge of presumptuous confusion rather than rational theology.

Commenting on the significance of Chalcedon Paul Tillich observes: "To understand the steps in the christological doctrine, always keep in mind two pictures: (1) The being with two heads, God and man, where there is no unity; (2) The being in which one head has disappeared, but also humanity has disappeared. The one remaining head is the head of the Logos, of God himself, so that when Jesus acts, it is not the unity of something divine and something human, but it is the Logos who is acting. Thus all the struggles, all the uncertainties, the despair and loneliness, which the Gospels present, were only seemingly experienced by Jesus, but not really. They are inconsequential. This was the danger in the Eastern Development. The fact that this danger was overcome is due to the decision of Chalcedon."[128]

The figure of two heads with unity is as strange as both the other discourses mentioned by Tillich. It is more unintelligible and exposed to more subtle questions and curiosities than even the Docetic or Monarchian positions. It is impossible to logically determine the demarcation line between God and Man while insisting upon their unity, as the traditional dogma asserts. For instance, who determines when God in Jesus is acting and when the man in Jesus is steering his actions? There is neither proper guidance nor any specific formula given by the Scriptures. The Holy Spirit has been so often suppressed or evaded by emperors and Church politicians alike that claims of his abstract providence have no real meaning in this regard. Is the figure dying on the cross the human Jesus or Jesus as God? If God, then which God other than himself was he crying out to? If the figure dying was Jesus the man, then salvation is not complete. The Chalcedonian formula is full of theological contradictions.

Nevertheless, despite its inherent weaknesses the Chalcedonian concept of a unified being with two heads or natures (human and divine) has remained the official doctrine of Christian Orthodoxy to the present day. The contemporary theologian E. Brunner writes: "The Jesus Christ shown to us in the Scriptures accredits Himself to us as the God-Man. One who meets Him with that openness to truth which the Bible calls 'faith,' meets in Him One who, in the unity of His Person, is both true God and true Man. It would be good for the Church to be content with this, and not wish to know more than they can know, or more than we need, if we are to trust Him and obey Him as we should."[129]

"If you can't resolve the problem, simply accept it at face value" - this is faith at the expense of human logic and intellectual precision.

Now, if the person of Christ consists of two natures, two wills, but in reality is identical with the divine nature and knowledge rather than the human nature, then one is fully justified in querying, as Maurice Wiles does, as to how genuine this humanity is and "how genuinely human is so qualified a human will?"[130] Moreover, this doctrine of the absolute unity of the person and two natures, or unipersonality, faces a number of other crucial challenges. Most are logically obvious. For instance, who is actually doing the speaking and to whom? The narratives of Jesus praying to God, calling upon him with words such as "My God, My God" etc. make no sense. Is he appealing to himself? Even if we accept that it was Jesus's human nature that was engaged in acts of prayer such as these, was it the Person of Jesus calling the Person of Christ? Surely the idea of one calling out to the other indicates at the very least a split in the unified personality? As a unity both would have the power to alleviate the suffering so why cry out in agony? Further, being unified, surely the Godhead would have also suffered the agonies of Crucifixion. At which point we have to ask ourselves who actually died on the Cross? If it is claimed that the human element of Christ suffered on the Cross, then how in the world can salvation, redemption, and atonement be achieved, for the divine element would have to be present, the *raison d'etre* for the whole Christological myth and for which it has been brought into existence?

The world has yet to see a theologian or a philosopher who can resolve these contradictions and explain in intelligible terms the Chalcedonian doctrine of Christ's person. Brunner contends that "the aim of this doctrine is not that it may solve the mystery of Jesus. We know that when we confess Him as God-Man, and must so confess Him, we are saying something which goes far beyond anything we can understand."[131] W. Bright, after strongly defending the outcome of the Council of Chalcedon, finally admits, "after all, if Christ is believed in as One, yet as both truly God and truly Man – however little we can comprehend the relation thus created – that belief is all that the Chalcedonian terminology implies: to hold it is to be at one with the Fourth Council."[132] J. S. Whale reaches the same conclusion, observing: "Of course, an explanation of Christ's person must always be beyond our reach if by 'explain' we mean 'put into a class'. Jesus is inexplicable just because he cannot be put into a class. His uniqueness constitutes the problem to be explained. It is impossible to describe him without becoming entangled in paradoxes. The great merit of Creeds is that they left the paradox as such."[133]

The illogical, the impossible, the contradictory cannot be justified in the name of paradox, this is an insult to human intelligence; Faith is the exposition of Truth, and must be substantiated by facts, it cannot create them. To hide behind the smokescreens of mystery, blind faith, mysticism, spirituality and/or the Spirit's providence etc. is to make nonsense of scripture and simply create awe for that which pays homage to a primitive, superstitious mentality. Furthermore, it is the prerogative of faith that it is made available to all and not just a select few, able to understand the intellectual contortions of mystery-based doctrines. In reality, the history of the Trinitarian dogma is so saturated with political intrigue, the overriding needs of the State, exploitative elements moving through the corridors of power and so on, that actual scripture seems to have paid second fiddle to political expediency. And the monolithic impress of the doctrine has existed for so long that the whole is now taken for granted. The fact of the matter is that in the Trinity, we have either the exposition of illogical truth or, what dare not be comprehended, heresy and theological scandal of the greatest magnitude; there is no in between. We conclude here with the remarks of McGiffert who observes that "the problem is metaphysical and purely speculative. Except by those interested to trace the formation of the particular dogmas involved, the whole Trinitarian and Christological development might be dismissed as unworthy of notice were it not for the profound religious difference that underlay it."[134]

The Christian Church preserved these illogical and irrational dogmas of Trinity, incarnation and justification or salvation through the
atoning death of Jesus Christ. They became the unique hallmarks of
the Christian faith and tradition, maintained and imposed - but seldom understood - by the Church and emperors. Most of the emperors
presided over the religious councils and synods with politics of unity
in mind; these politicians were not theologians but somehow, they decided the true doctrine and orthodoxy through their imperial powers.
They rebuked bishops, exiled popes and sanctioned priests. They solid-
ified political powers and punished dissent by convening councils. The
monarchs monopolised political power while the Church supervised
the spiritual realms. The early Church had no hesitation in assigning
to Jesus full-scale divinity including the designation of absolute divine
titles, actions, attributes and functions; this ascription of divinity did
not cause many problems as long as the faith remained confined to
Christians interested solely in the salvation. It was God and God alone,
and nobody less than Him, who could have brought salvation to the
humanity engulfed in sin. And this is the implication we get from the
oldest surviving sermon of the Christian Church after the New Testament writings: "Brethren, we ought so to think of Jesus Christ as of
God, as of the judge of living and dead. And we ought not to belittle
our salvation; for when we belittle him, we expect also to receive little."[135]

Trinitarian and Christological Models

Since the Council of Nicaea there have been at least three competing
Trinitarian models and five Christological paradigms (with multiple
subdivisions and off shoots) vying for acceptance in the Christian community. They are Modalism (one-self divinity), Adoptionism (hierarchical divinity) and Social Trinitarianism (three-selves divinity). The
Arian Adoptionism was declared heretical from the fourth century onward, while the Orthodoxy has mostly swung between Modalism and
Social Trinitarianism. For example, St. Augustine's Psychology Trinity
model is in essence Modalism, and the Cappadocian Fathers are the
founders of the Social Trinity model.[136] Chalcedonian orthodoxy has
swayed between Modalism with some Docetic tendencies and Social
Trinitarianism with some tri-theistic propensities.

A generic definition of Modalism could be that it emphasises the
divine unity, indivisibility and ineffability by dissolving the other two

persons of the Trinity into One God as mere modes or aspects. The three persons are not equally and eternally co-existent but merely three successive revelations, manifestations or modes of One God's activities. Modalism could further be divided into following three sub-categories: Sequential Modalism (God always exists in one of his modes), Eternally Concurrent or Maximally Overlapping Modalism (God eternally exists in all of his modes) and Partially Overlapping Modalism (sometimes God exists in more than one of his modes).[137] The Western or Latin Church has mostly inclined towards one-self divinity. As seen above, in the modern times many leading Christian theologians such as Friedrich Schleiermacher, Karl Barth and Karl Rahner subscribe to this virtual modalism.

On the other hand, the Social Trinitarians focus more upon the distinction, autonomy and divinity of the three persons of the Trinity as three selves. The Persons are one thing but different objects, distinct individuals of the same kind, meaning God the Father, Son and Holy Spirit are distinct divine individuals but identical in Godhead, distinctive divine persons united in loving relationship. Social Trinitarians argue that identity is relative; persons or things can be different in certain aspects of their existence, while similar or identical in other aspects. For instance, John, Paul and Mark are different persons united in the sameness of humanity; likewise, the three persons of the Trinity are distinctive persons having independent autonomous consciousness, knowledge, will, centers of activities and freedom, but they are united in the divine essence. It is a divine society, a uni-personality composite of three persons rather than being One Person (God). As the Son is begotten of the Father and the Holy Spirit proceeds from him, both the Son and Holy Spirit carry the substance of the Father and are identical to him. Therefore, God the Father is God, Son is God and Holy Spirit is God but they are not three Gods but one God. This is a "classic example of the absurd lengths to which metaphysics can go."[138] The Social Trinity model very often degenerates into tri-theism or subordinationism. The Social Trinitarians branch out into multiple theories and models such as Functional Monotheism, Trinity Monotheism, Group Mind Social Trinitarians and many others. In the Antiquity, the Cappadocian Fathers Social Trinity and in the modern times the majority of Anglicans, Protestant and some Catholic theologians subscribe mostly to three selves Trinity. Both the Modalists and

Social Trinitarians believe in Jesus's divinity, incarnation, crucifixion, redemption and worship.

It is the nature of the Trinitarian doctrine that it can never be verbalised without contradictions. One can never say that Paul is tall and short at the same time; likewise, the begetter and the begotten can never be co-eternal and co-equal, but this is what the Orthodoxy insisted upon. There are crystal clear puzzles of personal identity, and problems of identity and constitution, in both models of the full God Trinity. This is in addition to the fact the New Testament is silent about the Trinity and its corollaries. There are twofold and threefold passages and patterns in the New Testament, but none of them substantiate the later Church Council's lofty Trinitarian claims of co-eternity and co-equality. Both Modalism and Social Trinity models are mere conjectures full of puzzles, contradictions and theological jargon. Dale Tuggy observes that "no theory in either camp evades the triune pitfalls of inconsistency, unintelligibility, and poor fit with the Bible. These two main approaches appear to be hopeless, and I argue that appeals to "mystery" are no way to avoid the difficulties at hand."[139] William Alston states that "it is a well-known fact, amply borne out by the history of the discussion of the topic, that as soon as one goes beyond the automatic recital of traditional creedal phrases one inevitably leans either in the direction of modalism-the "persons" are simply different aspects of the divine being and/or activity-or tritheism-there really are three Gods, albeit very intimately connected in some way."[140]

Consequently, the entire history of the Christian doctrine is filled with controversies, anathemas, logical impasses and unintelligible jargon. The charges of Modalism and tri-theism at times are both levelled against the same person; for instance, St. Augustine is accused of both Modalism and tri-theism by different theologians, and the same is true for the Cappadocian Fathers. It is extremely difficult to tow the tight line between the one-self and three-self Trinitarian models and avoid theological and rational impasses. A slight move towards the one-self model lands one in Modalism and a slim lean towards the three-self model verges on tri-theism. Mystery, paradox, self-contradiction, impasse and unintelligibility are the hallmark of the orthodoxy. The Christological paradigms also suffer from the same confusions, contradictions and unintelligibility.

The Christology defines Christ and his relationship with other persons of the Trinity, cosmos and man. Docetism insists upon Christ's divinity at the expense of his humanity; Modalist Monarchianism is very close to Docetism in this respect. Sabellianism, Noetianism and Patripassianism all contend about Christ's divinity while ignoring his humanity. Adoptionism, or Arianism, focuses upon his humanity at the expense of his full divinity. Separationism understands him to be two distinct beings, the human Jesus and the divine logos or Christ. They are further divided into those who emphasise his divine nature at the expense of his human nature and those who highlight his human nature at the expense of his divine nature. The Antiochenes' two nature Christ is a good example of the Separationists. It culminated into two further extremes. Nestorianism argued that Jesus had two natures (persons) in one body; the two natures were completely distinct and separate. Mary was not the mother of Logos or divine Christ but of the human Jesus. The Monophysites went on the other extreme, and held that Jesus had two natures before incarnation and that Mary carried the divine Christ, who had dominated the human nature of Jesus after the union. Therefore, after the merger Jesus had only one divine nature. Nestorians focused upon Jesus's humanity while the Monophysites insisted upon his divinity. The Chalcedonian Orthodoxy incorporated various elements of the contending parties and created a compromising synthesis; they held that Christ was full man and full God at the one and same time, but in one person and not two persons. Christ was always God but he also became man at incarnation. This creedal compromise was against the dyophysite tendencies of Nestorian and the School of Antioch, who insisted upon two natures and two persons. It disagreed with the Monophysites in arguing that two natures were hypostatically united in one person without submerging into one nature. The Chalcedonian formula was more of a political compromise and less of theology. No wonder that a logical mind like Augustine had no escape from contradictions. "Thus the Father is God, the Son is God, the Holy Spirit is God; the Father is good, the Son is good, the Holy Spirit is good; and the Father is omnipotent, the Son is omnipotent, and the Holy Spirit is omnipotent; but yet there are not three gods, nor three goods, nor three omnipotents, but one God, one good, and one omnipotent, the Trinity itself."[141] Keith E. Yandell calls it the most brutal and inexcusable error in counting.[142] Augustine, like the Orthodoxy, was clearly vacillating between modalism and tri-theism. In his

Trinitarian formulations he was contradictory, confusing and at times tri-theistic but mostly modalist.

A well-known contemporary evangelist Millard Erickson frankly states that "there is a fundamental difficulty that lies at the heart of the discussion of the doctrine of the Trinity: The doctrine seems to be impossible to believe, because at its very core it is contradictory."[143] John Hick notes that the "orthodoxy has never been able to give this idea any content. It remains a form of words without assignable meaning. For to say, without explanation, that the historical Jesus of Nazareth was also God is as devoid of meaning as to say that this circle drawn with a pencil on paper is also a square. Such a locution has to be given semantic content: and in the case of the language of incarnation every content thus far suggested has had to be repudiated."[144]

The problem with traditional Christian belief is that it is irrational and contradictory to the core; it uses impossible and mutually antithetical categories to explain the logic and rationality of its dogmas. According to V. A. Harvey, "in contrast to all other texts, it sets aside our present critically interpreted experience when it comes to interpreting the New Testament. It assumes that in this case alone what our critically interpreted experience tells us is 'impossible' is not only possible but probable and certain."[145]

According to Hick's understanding, the doctrine of "Incarnation" is a mythological idea and literally not true at all. No Christian should be asked to accept the outmoded theological and philosophical theories of the third and fourth centuries. Like every other myth, incarnation was introduced to "evoke an attitude." The real significance of Jesus does not lie in his divinity or incarnation but in his example and model. It is through his model that humanity can find God in their lives. Jesus to Hick is the "sufficient model of true humanity in a perfect relationship to God."[146] The 'Traditionalists' reject this interpretation because in this solution "the Person of Jesus has no constitutive significance."[147]

What is Salvation?

In Christianity salvation is deliverance from the state of human decadence, sin and its consequences through the redemptive act of Christ.[148] Presence of a cosmic danger and delivery from that pending calamity through a saviour is intrinsic to the Christian concept of salvation. The New Testament verb for salvation is *sozo* (occurs more than 100 times).[149] It revolves around the meanings of "deliver," "save" and "rescue". The noun *soteria* stands for salvation while the personal noun *soter* denotes saviour and redeemer. The word group describes the fact that salvation is not intrinsic but extrinsic to humanity. Humanity needs a cosmic power to deliver itself from the state of sin and its miseries; man is so wretched that he cannot do it by himself. Jesus is that cosmic intervention, the Saviour (Luke 2:11; Acts 13:23) - the salvation is spiritual, universal and at the same time personal. Christians are those who accept Jesus as their Saviour and Christianity is a faith that invites humanity to attain salvation through the name of Lord Jesus Christ, the Saviour. God the Father has sent his only begotten Son to bring salvation (John 3:17; 1 John 2:2). Thus, Jesus is "the Saviour of the world" (John 4:42; 1 John 4:14). Jesus knows his sheep, and the sheep must believe in him and follow his commands; in return, they will receive redemption, forgiveness and cleansing. Jesus will keep the sheep safe to the end (John 6:39; 10:29) and give them the gift of eternal life (John 3:16-17, 36; 1 John 2:25; 5:11, 13).

It is pertinent to note that the beginning point of salvation is belief in Lord Jesus Christ as Saviour and the act of human cleansing ensues. Self-purification and moral reformation are not the foundation of Christian salvation, rather they are automatic consequences of faith in Christ. The gift of eternal life is also not the result of human efforts but of divine grace.[150] Therefore, salvation is selective, predestined and in a sense arbitrary. It was God who bestowed the gift of salvation upon the sinful by forgiving them (Acts 13:26, 46; 28:28; Eph 4:32; Col 2:13) and reconciling them to Himself (Rom 5:10; 2 Cor 5:18-19). In this scheme human potential, capacities and participation is minimized to maximise the divine initiative, incentive, role and grace. The human role is limited to accepting the offered salvation by intellectual assent called faith, and the rest is given. Paul's statement is emphatic: "For by grace you have been saved through faith. And this is not your own doing; it is the gift of God, not a result of works, so that no one may boast. For we are his workmanship, created in Christ Jesus for good works, which God prepared beforehand, that we should walk in them." (Eph. 2:8-10) The human assent automatically transfers human sins and inequities to Christ the Saviour, and his atoning death redeems that. The sacrificial act is historical; the blood is already shed, and the price of salvation is already paid. The Christian believer just partakes in it through faith, and the good life follows inevitably. Therefore, faith is fundamental to salvation while good deeds are fruits and hence supplementary. The fruits follow the root and stem and are not preceded by them. Likewise, good works are the fruits of faith and grace and not the cause of Christian redemption. They are the proofs of Christian unity with Christ and regeneration. It is often said in the Christian circles that "Christ is the ground of our salvation, faith is the instrument of our salvation, and works are the fruit of our salvation. We are justified by grace alone through faith alone in Christ alone."

It is a collective redemption, though dispensed through individual faith. Personal participation of man in this scheme of salvation is minimal to the core. Faith and grace are far more significant than the supplementary human efforts. This is the Gospel, the good news that via the bodily sacrifice of Jesus Christ the sin, Satan, death, divine wrath and spiritual bondage were replaced with eternal bliss and glory (Heb. 2:10, 2:14-15, 9:26-28; 10:18). The Christian soteriology is absolutely Christo centric. Christ forgives sins both in his earthly as well as celestial life. Therefore, right relationship with God through Christ eliminates sin and oppression of cosmic forces, ushering in salvation. The New Testament puts the point in a nutshell: "If you confess with your lips that Jesus is Lord and believe in your heart that God raised him from the dead, you will be saved," (Rom. 10:9). This simple set of beliefs does not deserve to be the bedrock of salvation. Divine grace is the seed bed of salvation. The fact that the word "grace" occurs close to 100 times in Paul's epistles alone is sufficient to suggest that God's unmerited grace is the sole source of salvation in both the worlds.[151]

Human Depravity

Christianity is unique in its concept of sin and redemption.[152] It makes Adam and Eve responsible for the human wretchedness and depravity, deeming it necessary to cleanse the sinful state of man through the redemptive death of Christ, the second person of the triune God. The Bible insists that every individual succumbs to evil and experiences estrangement from God; the intrinsic moral corruption leads to forfeiture of salvation and punishment through hellfire. Man is lost due to his fallen nature. Before the fall man was capable of not sinning and dying, but after the fall he is doomed to sin and die. The first human Adam committed the sin and brought upon humanity the curse of estrangement. Jesus, the Son of Man has come to reconcile humanity with God and get it out of its utter destruction. (Luke 15:11-32; 19:10) Paul took this concept of human depravity to the next level: "you were dead in your transgressions and sins, in which you used to live." (Eph. 2:1) Lust, greed and impurity of all sorts were given as the proofs of moral bankruptcy. The alienation, guilt and condemnation were the result of one sin, the original sin of Adam. "The judgment followed one sin and brought condemnation," (Rom 5:16), and "the result of one trespass was condemnation for all men," (Rom. 5:18). And so "we were by nature objects of wrath" (Eph. 2:3b). All humans were captives of Satan (2 Tim 2:26; 1 John 5:19), and "slaves to sin" (Rom 6:16-17, 20). Their original humanity, the reflection of God's image, was tainted by the sin of Adam and hence deformed, degenerated and defaced. Jesus, the Son of God, was not tainted by the sin of Adam. This sinless divine being took upon the human flesh to become the Son of Man. The incarnation did not cause him to sin as he did not have a human father. He did not inherit the fallen nature and its unrestrained propensities to sin. Consequently, Jesus was a perfect man except in sin. That was what made him a perfect sacrificial agent. Therefore, man is at a loss to reconcile with the wrathful God by himself. He needs a cosmic intermediary who is Jesus Christ, "Christ served as a form of blood sacrifice, expiating sin through his blood. (Rom. 3:25) The only way out of man's predicament is the belief in the substitutionary atoning death of Christ. (John 8:24). The unbelievers are unsaved and consigned to eternal punishment. (Matt 10:28; 23:33; Luke 12:5) This perdition is the result of their refusal to accept God's offer of grace and salvation.

In Christianity there is a tension between the assured salvation and the need to do righteous deeds. The source of Christian tension is the New Testament.

Due to its multiple authors, the New Testament seems to present a variety of soteriologies like its multiple Christologies. The Synoptic Gospels emphasise good works while the Gospel of John, along with Paul's letters, focus predominantly upon faith and grace. The Synoptic scheme of salvation is far stricter than the Jewish and Muslim laws. It takes morality to a higher level of love where ritualism and legalism is replaced with spiritualism and love. Not only sexuality but the thought of it is considered evil. (Matt. 5: 2-30) Not only the murder but the thought of hate is nipped in the bud. (Matt. 5: 21-26) Matthew

6 is a grave warning to show off ritualists. Matthew 7 is a reflection of the golden rule. "Do not judge, or you too will be judged. For in the same way you judge others, you will be judged, and with the measure you use, it will be measured to you. Why do you look at the speck of sawdust in your brother's eye and pay no attention to the plank in your own eye?" (Matt. 7:1-3) The Jesus of the Synoptic Gospels wants his followers to obey the commands; the first and foremost commandment of loving God and loving the neighbour is the essence of this version of Christianity. (Mark 12:28-29) The remnants of this trend are found even in James 2: 14, where it states: "What good is it [...] if someone claims to have faith but has no deeds? Can such faith save them?" To James it is foolish to separate deeds from faith: "You foolish person, do you want evidence that faith without deeds is useless?"

The work-based salvation scheme was adopted by Pelagius (d. 419) and his disciple Caelestius (d. 431). They insisted that the divine grace amounted to human reason, conscience and freedom of choice implanted in humanity at creation. Man is capable of attaining salvation by his efforts; the divine grace is an inducement to righteous life in accordance with God's commandments and through the example of Jesus Christ. The 18th century enlightenment figures and contemporary rationalists and liberal Christians tow the same line, a scheme closely resembling to the Islamic sense of salvation. The Church declared this trend a heresy, first at the Synod of Carthage (418) and later at the Council of Ephesus (431) and followed instead the Augustinian interpretation of faith and grace,[153] as explained above.[154] The Semi Pelagians such as John Cassian (d. 435), Duns Scotus (d. 1308), William of Occam (d. 1349), and Gabriel Biel (d. 1495), who argued that the original sin only diminished the human capacity not destroying it completely, were also sanctioned. Their belief that grace was supplemental to faith and actions was severely chastised by the Church. Their efforts to steer a middle course between Pelagianism and Augustinianism by emphasising the freedom to choose, human responsibility and accountability and by denying the arbitrary, unconditional election and effectual grace were hampered by the orthodoxy.

Medieval Catholicism tried to emphasise good works, embodied in Church sacraments, giving them a relative significance of congruity in the salvation scheme. The Council of Trent (1547) tried to highlight the human ability to freely act and cooperate with the divine grace but was charged by Martin Luther and other Reformers as semi Pelagianism. The Augustinian trend, represented by the Reformers, insisted that the human rational abilities were the results of God's common grace. The unmerited favour of salvation was God's special grace, given only to the believers in Christ and through Christ. St. Augustine's dictum that "free will is sufficient for evil, but it is of no avail for good unless it is aided by Omnipotent Good,"[155] and that "the human will does not attain grace through freedom, but rather freedom through grace"[156] became the standard interpretation of human free will and divine grace in the centuries to come. The slogan that "outside the church there is no salvation" became an accepted doctrine. Martin Luther emphasised upon utter human wretchedness, sheer inability to attain salvation except through eternal election and predestination of God, unmerited grace and an absolute worthlessness of human efforts, works and sacrifices. His dictum that "Grace is given freely to those without merits and the most undeserving, and is not obtained by any efforts, endeavors, or works, whether small or great, even of the best and most virtuous of men, though they seek and pursue righteousness with burning zeal"[157] made law and good works antithetical to grace and faith. The Calvinists, Anglicans and Evangelicals all insist upon the grace at the expense of good works and human efforts.

Original Sin or Original Forgiveness?

The whole Trinitarian, incarnational and substitutionary sacrificial scheme is promoted to atone for the so called "Original Sin" or later human inequities.[158] Adam and Eve sinned against God by eating from the forbidden apple. They were punished and thrown out of the Garden. Both sincerely repented for their sin and paid the price by living an earthly life markedly different from the ideal heavenly life. Consequently, the loving God forgave them. The traditional Christianity seems inclined to promote that Almighty God is not loving enough to forgive the original sin in spite of sincere repentance by Adam and Eve. Its God is so bound by the demands of justice that He had to make all humans responsible for the unintended mistake of Adam and Eve. Even the cruelest of the world dictators would not punish entire nations for the sins of a few; doing so constitutes a collective punishment repudiated by the very human Geneva Convention. The Trinitarians, in a sense, end up accusing God of collective punishment, unrelenting wrath, lack of mercy and forgiveness just to dream that Jesus was God. They are anxious to crucify God to secure their wishful salvation. Instead of sacrificing their human immoralities they seem willing to sacrifice God at the altar of their desires. What type of justice is this?

Moreover, the original sin was against God Himself. God could have forgiven that sin (as he did according to the Quran) without punishing Himself. He did not have to die a painful death to excuse his sinful creatures. Dying an agonising death on the cross does not demonstrate Mercy or Omnipotence. Moreover, there were countless human beings who lived and died before Jesus's crucifixion, many of them were righteous people like Abraham, Moses and Isaiah. They must have been suffering torment in Hellfire before Jesus's alleged crucifixion. Why did God not sacrifice Himself soon after the Original Sin was committed to alleviate unnecessary human sufferings? Why did he wait so long to atone for the human sins? What difference did God's suffering death made to human destiny and sinful nature? Human beings are still sinning; sin has neither subsided nor ceased to exist since Jesus's crucifixion. Even those who claim to have received Jesus such as born-again Christians, Ministers, Priests and Cardinals live with the same sinful nature and do commit sins. The blood has already been shed, yet the sin is unabating. There are good and bad people in every faith community, and Christians are no exception. What did God accomplish by dying on the cross? God does not do things in vain.

The transcendental, monotheistic, Semitic consciousness of Prophet Jesus got lost in the gentile pagan world. The gentile-oriented vocabulary of Paul and John degenerated into Trinitarian jargons. Jesus's simple message of "Love your God and love your neighbour" was transformed into a mystery religion. Two millennia of theologians and philosophers have not been able to make sense of this incomprehensible Trinitarian arithmetic. To Thomas Jefferson, this "paradox that one is three, and three but one, is so incomprehensible to the human mind, that no candid man can say he has any idea of it, and how can he believe what presents no idea? He who thinks he does, only deceives himself. He proves, also, that man, once surrendering his reason, has no remaining guard against absurdities the most monstrous, and like a ship without rudder, is the sport of every wind."[159]

Trinity or Tri-theism?

The Trinity means different things to different schools of Christian thought. The Cappadocian Trinitarian paradigm is considerably different from the Augustinian model. There are countless unresolved issues inherent in both of the classical models. Is the internal unity of three persons a social unity or unity of substance? Are the three persons of Trinity the three individual modes of existence of the one and same God, consisting in their mutual relationship, or does it refer to three distinct individuals, separate centers of consciousness, three self-conscious personal beings? In both scenarios the question remains the same. On the cross (Matt. 27:46), is God calling upon Himself for help or is one independent person of Godhead calling upon another independent person of Godhead for help? In the first scenario it is "Modalism" or "Docetism", a total absurdity. Why would God call upon his own self for help? In the other scenario it is a "vulgar tritheism", to use Karl Rahner's term, or at least "Subordinationism" i.e., a lesser god is seeking a higher Gods' help.

The traditional Christians always claim that the orthodox conception of the Trinity does not promote three gods, but they do not substantiate their claims with logical arguments. The Trinity is usually explained as one Being, God, who exists in three distinct persons that are identical in essence. But one wonders how come it does not promote tri-theism and, in reality polytheism? God the Father is an independent and sovereign God with autonomous intellect and will, God the Son is an independent sovereign God with autonomous intellect and will and God the Holy Spirit is also an independent sovereign God with autonomous intellect and will. They are three distinctive persons with distinctive modes of consciousness, existence, will, intellect and roles who share a generic divine essence. They are not dependent upon each other but are equally Gods in their own right. The Father is not the Son and the Son is not the Holy Spirit. How come this is not tri-theism? Additionally, the one Being God is either the aggregate of the three collective essences i.e., a complex entity made up of three smaller parts or each one of the three is possessor of full essence of the divinity and Godhead is three times over. In the first instance there will be four Gods (divine quaternity and not trinity), with the fourth God higher than the three constituent elements as the aggregate Being is superior in essence and luminosity than the individual three Gods. In the second scenario, there are three independent Gods with full personal divine essence, which differentiates one person from the others plus an intensified shared generic divine essence. Again, there is a fourth entity the three times over of the individual Gods. It places the three persons in the genus "deity" while each one of them in a different species from that of the other two. There is no escape from tri-theism or polytheism in any of the above scenarios as both present the dilemma of plurality of persons and essence in the Being, God. This social Trinity scheme clearly degenerates into personalistic tri-theism. One wonders about the whereabouts of oneness of God in the threeness of the divine society where the threeness seems more real than the oneness. The example of John, James and Peter being human persons sharing a generic humanity is irrelevant; John is a human being and not the humanity, John's person is a reflection of his upbringing, culture and circumstances and nobody would call John "a humanity." Likewise, each person of the Trinity is a person, a God and not the Godhead. The Godhead is an aggregate of the three persons.

The fact of the matter is that, like ancient Christian Fathers, none of the contemporary conservative theological approaches seem able to solve the central problem of Christian theology; the relationship of Jesus Christ's person with the transcendent, indivisible, impassable, unique, eternal and One God. These may be good speculative works, or guesses, but are definitely not satisfactory solutions. Whether one accepts the ultra- Cappadocian movement's social Trinity or Barth's union Trinity one is still left unable to detach the Trinity from tritheism and corporealism. The incarnation of God in the human figure of Christ, whether in one mode of His existence or through one person of His Godhead, are crystal clear cases of corporealism. The difficulty lies in the insistence that traditional Christianity almost always places upon the person of Christ as being divine, the Second Person of the Trinity, and equal in all respects to God whilst simultaneously claiming Jesus's humanity as being equal in almost all respects (excepting sin) with mankind. This position is paradoxical, contradictory and defies logic. A fundamental tenet of Christianity, it nevertheless has little, if any, appeal to modern rational thought and as such is unintelligible to modern man who scrutinises particulars with rigorous criteria. Many modern Christian scholars and theologians do not seem ready to deny or denounce traditional claims, yet are at a loss as to how to prove their validity - or even reasonability - to the contemporary mind. Forced to resort to circular arguments, they make claims without logically substantiating them and in doing so repeating, in many cases, opinions either discussed in early centuries or discarded as heretical. In neither case can the charges of anthropomorphism, corporealism and, in certain cases tritheism, be denied. The source of this paradox lies in the Neoplatonic interpretation of the New Testament writings.

The Medieval Christian God paradigm then was supernatural, mysterious and hierarchical. The Holy Trinity was supreme and at the head of the heavenly pyramid. The Earth was a reflection of the heavenly hierarchy. The Church, the earthly representative of Jesus Christ, was Lord over earthly pyramid. Lower beings were subordinated to higher realms. Submission to monarchs, civil magistrates and clergy was integral to the Trinitarian theological model. The social order of Christendom was hierarchical. The natural order was also hierarchical.

St. Thomas Aquinas synthesised Aristotle's principles inherent in nature as divine powers installed by God to cooperate and assist him in the works of providence. "God *cooperated* with natural powers in a way that respected their integrity while accomplishing his purposes."[160] The concerns that such cooperation with natural phenomena and man would make God dependent upon them and jeopardise his absolute sovereignty were mitigated by the interpretation that nature and man were under God and served divine purposes. God participated in nature intrinsically through participating beings and not extrinsically as Supreme Lawgiver impressing natural laws on matter.[161] The nature was sacramentally expressing higher being of God as man was expressing God's providence through obedience to Church sacraments.[162] Nature and man were immanently divine sharing in the incarnation of Christ, the man God. S. F. Mason well summarised the medieval Trinitarian hierarchical world view. "Such a scheme was a particular manifestation of the general medieval view that the hierarchy of natural things was ordered triadically at every level - classes, orders, genera, species, and individuals within those species. All of the beings of the universe fell into one or other of three general classes - those that were wholly material, such as minerals, plants, and animals, those that were wholly spiritual, such as the angelic beings, and those that were mixed, namely human beings. Each group and sub-group divided triadically. Thus there were animals of the land, the sea, and the air, men of labour, men of prayer, and men of war, according to early medieval versions, or labourers, burghers, and nobles, with a separate ecclesiastical triadic hierarchy, according to late medieval versions, whilst above mankind were three triadic orders of angelic beings, and at the head of the scale of all beings in the universe was the supreme Trinity."[163]

Unitarian ideology, whether religio-political or scientific, was severely punished. The divinity, nature, cosmos, social order, human body and Church were all hierarchical. Even the human body was Triadic and Trinitarian. It had the natural, vital and animal spirits in it. It had three physiological fluids (two kinds of boolds and a nervous fluid). Liver was the source of dark red blood, heart of whitish red blood and brain the seat of nervous fluid.[164] Any discussion of divine simplicity, human equality, natural or body unity were banned and persecuted. Medieval Christendom was a persecutory society persecuting Unitarianism in social order, natural cosmos and human body. Independent scientific research, republican political ideology and Unitarian theology were taboos.

The supernatural incarnational theology and Bible were used as the foundational stones for the absolute political theology and hierarchical social order. A divinely appointed political order was made essential to direct man and his world. The world was divided into sacred and profane. The sacred was the realm of spirituality supervised by the priests and clerics while the profane was directed by the kings and magistrates. The depraved man needed constant supervision otherwise evil, anarchy and oppression would prevail. Man, his rights, freedoms, participation in the affairs of society, culture and government were all trampled in the name of depraved fallen nature, evil disposition and uncivilised manners. The democratic and republican political models of Greco Roman world were replaced with the absolute Church and state. Man was merely a recipient of divine grace facilitated through the good offices of the Church and monitored by the monarchy. It was an absolutely top down system of religious and political theology. God, cosmos, salvation and redemption were too complicated and mysterious for a common person to understand. Therefore blind imitation of the Church was the only way out. The society was organised based upon this supernatural worldview.

Chapter 2

Some Manifestations
of Roman Christianity

Roman Christianity manifested itself into supernaturalism, antinomianism, irrationalism, absolutism and persecutions. These devastating elements were to become the legacy of Roman Christianity to the medieval world. In the previous chapter we have focused mostly on Christian supernatural, hierarchical and paradoxical world view. This chapter will address the socio-political and moral fallouts of such a world view.

Antinomianism

There are multiple salvation schemes offered by the Gospel writers. Matthew insists that a strict moral code can bring about the salvation: "In the same way, let your light shine before others, that they may see your good deeds and glorify your Father in heaven. Do not think that I have come to abolish the Law or the Prophets; I have not come to abolish them but to fulfill them. For truly I tell you, until heaven and earth disappear, not the smallest letter, not the least stroke of a pen, will by any means disappear from the Law until everything is accomplished. Therefore anyone who sets aside one of the least of these commands and teaches others accordingly will be called least in the kingdom of heaven, but whoever practices and teaches these commands will be called great in the kingdom of heaven. For I tell you that unless your righteousness surpasses that of the Pharisees and the teachers of the law, you will certainly not enter the kingdom of heaven." (Matt.16-20) Salvation without good works is foolhardy: "Therefore everyone who hears these words of mine and puts them into practice is like a wise man who built his house on the rock. The rain came down, the streams rose, and the winds blew and beat against that house; yet it did not fall, because it had its foundation on the rock. But everyone who hears these words of mine and does not put them into practice is like a foolish man who built his house on sand. The rain came down, the streams rose, and the winds blew and beat against that house, and it fell with a great crash." (Matt. 24-27) Observing the Law and following the commandments are integral to this scheme of salvation: "Why do you ask me about what is good?" Jesus replied. "There is only One who is good. If you want to enter life, keep the commandments." (Matt. 17; also Lk. 18:18-25) Here the focus is upon good deeds rather than the faith; faith without good works is deceit. Faith is trusting God's will and providence through moral submission. Morality is antithetical to sin; it eliminates rebellion and inculcates resignation. The love and fear of God purifies hearts, minds and actions. Righteous deeds are the effect of true faith and intrinsic to divine pleasure. M. Martin observes "It is not clear according to these gospels [Synoptic] if belief in Jesus is either sufficient or necessary for salvation. Some of the pronouncements of Jesus indicate that much more is involved and, indeed, that even exemplary moral conduct independent of faith can be sufficient."[165]

There are other passages which require renouncing everything to follow Jesus (Matt.19:24-30; Mk 10:29; Matt. 20:15). "Thus, according to the synoptic Gospels, salvation is a two-track affair. It can be obtained through adhering to a strict moral code that few can follow or by following Jesus. This second track is also difficult but in a different way. It involves great personal sacrifice but not the rigors of following a strict moral code."[166]

St. Paul's Christocentrism

Contrary to the Synoptic, both John and Paul are insistent upon faith rather than moral code. For John, Jesus is the only way to salvation; his salvation scheme is Christocentric. "Jesus answered, "I am the way and the truth and the life. No one comes to the Father except through me. If you really know me, you will know my Father as well. From now on, you do know him and have seen him." (Jn.14:6-7; 3:16-36) John is more centered upon believing in Jesus than the good deeds; the moral reformation is the fruit and not the foundation of salvation. "One is saved only by believing in Jesus, which seems to involve some spiritual rebirth that may involve an ethical transformation in which one manifests the love that Jesus manifested for his disciples. There is no suggestion in John that Jesus had narrow, sectarian goals of salvation as there is in parts of the first three Gospels. On the other hand, John, like the synoptic Gospel writers, threatens punishment. He indicates that the wrath of God will rest on anyone who disobeys the Son of God."[167]

Paul, on the other hand, has no regards for good works, commandments or the Law at all. His salvation scheme is absolutely faith-based and antinomian: "For we maintain that a person is justified by faith apart from the works of the law." (Rom. 3:28; 5:1-2; 6:12-16) There is no salvation except through faith. The work-based salvation was in the Old covenant, and The New Testament, ushered through the redeeming works of Jesus, has nullified and superseded the Old Testament - now only the New Covenant is applicable. "Before the coming of this faith, we were held in custody under the law, locked up until the faith that was to come would be revealed. So the law was our guardian until Christ came that we might be justified by faith. Now that this faith has come, we are no longer under a guardian. So in Christ Jesus you are all children of God through faith, for all of you who were baptised into Christ have clothed yourselves with Christ." (Gal.3:23-27)

Some scholars maintain that Paul was a self-contradictory inconsistent thinker, making conflicting statements about justification by faith and also by works. His legal Jewish background was transformed into Christocentrism in light of his personal experience, but it did not completely disappear. For example, E. P. Sanders and H. Raisanen quote Romans 2: 6-10 as an example of Paul's conflicting views.[168] "God 'will repay each person according to what they have done'. To those who by persistence in doing good seek glory, honour and immortality, he will give eternal life. But for those who are self-seeking and who reject the truth and follow evil, there will be wrath and anger. There will be trouble and distress for every human being who does evil: first for the Jew, then for the Gentile; but glory, honour and peace for everyone who does good: first for the Jew, then for the Gentile. For God does not show favouritism." (Rom. 2:6-10) But others find him an intelligent theologian with a consistent soteriology: "This justification by works does not contradict Rom 3:20, for it is not an attempt to earn salvation by works as in the latter passage, nor is Romans 2 speaking of perfect obedience. What Paul has in mind are works which stem from faith and the work of the Holy Spirit [...] such obedience is not the result of self-effort but the work of the Holy Spirit, and that such obedience is not the earning of salvation by good works but the result of faith."[169] There might be a bit of tension in Paul's mind about the significance of works but his overall salvation scheme, unlike the Synoptic, is absolutely faith-based. Faith is conforming to Jesus's mind and trusting his redemptive works.

This is how the early Church viewed itself, preferring the Pauline salvific scheme over and beyond the Synoptic. Justification by faith became the cherished orthodox position, though its contours were initially not determined. "However, it is unclear exactly what besides belief it involves. Even when one concentrates only on the cognitive dimension of faith there are unclarities. The creeds seem to demand belief that defines Orthodox Christianity, everything from the Virgin Birth to the Second Coming, from the Resurrection to the Incarnation. On the other hand, John seems to demand only belief in the Incarnation while Paul seems to demand only belief in the Resurrection. Neither John nor Paul, unlike the creeds, demands belief in the Virgin Birth or the Trinity."[170]

Paul, the Lying Spouter

Paul's antinomian salvation scheme was Gentile in nature. It was antithetical to the Jewish orientation of many original disciples of Jesus, such as James, but congenial to the Roman mystery cults. It emancipated Christianity from the yoke of Judaism and its cumbersome laws, and allowed for new faith freedom, independence and new directions. It opened new and vast horizons for the Christian faith by colouring it with a Roman outlook. Justification by faith was a common trope among the mystery cults. It suited the cultural milieu of the Romans, at the expense of the Palestinian Christians. That is one of the reasons that St. Paul did not enjoy universal acceptance during the first three centuries after Jesus's departure. His version of Christianity was too radical and alien to the Jewish Christians; to the Jerusalem Church Paul was "the Lying Spouter" or "Scoffer"[171] who perverted the original egalitarian message of Jesus for political gains. Calvin Roetzel observes that "in the generations after his death Paul was 'for the most part unintelligible'. But even when he was intelligible he was often either misunderstood or despised. In the late first or early second century, for example, the letter of James challenged Paul's gospel of justification by faith alone without regard to works (2:24). Around AD 200, the *Kerygmata Petrou* (*Proclamations of Peter*) vilified Paul as the enemy, a helpmate of the evil one, and an impostor preaching a false gospel. It attacked his legitimacy, calling him a liar for claiming an apostolic commission that came directly from Christ in a vision. If

Paul were a true apostle, Peter continues, he would not contend with 'me,' "the foundation stone of the church." (*Clem. Hom.*17.19.1–4) While many suspected him of using dark, magical arts, others either were unacquainted with his letters or simply ignored them."[172] Certain third century anonymous treatises such as "A False Proselyte," "Messenger of Satan" or "Persecutor of Faith" are enough to show the sense of negativity harboured by some Jewish-Christian opponents of Paul. G. Bornkamm has shown that "even in his own lifetime his opponents considered him as apostle without legitimation and a perverter of the Christian Gospel. In the subsequent history of the early church, too, there were two very different judgments. For a considerable period he continued to be sternly rejected by Jewish Christians as antagonistic to Peter and James the brother of the Lord; in these circles people did not even stop short of ranking him with Simon Magus, the chief of heretics (Pseudo-Clementine)[...] Even when, as in Acts, he was hailed as a great missionary or, as in the Pastorals, an attempt was made to preserve his teaching, and when in other parts of early Christian literature voices were raised in his honour, the lines along which theology evolved were different from his."[173]

Some early Christians believed that Paul was a Roman spy working for the hegemonic designs of the imperial forces to quell the initial Christian agitation. His antinomian salvation scheme was lax and detrimental to the Christian cause. Believing in his doctrine of grace-based salvation was giving a lie to Jesus's work-based salvation. Such antagonism was widespread, especially in Palestinian circles. Robert Eisenman states that "we can get an inkling of these by reading between the lines in his letters and comprehending the doctrines about him in the Pseudoclementines and materials of similar orientation. Paul was obviously being mocked by some - within the Church not outside it - as 'the Man of Dreams', 'Lies', or 'Lying', or what was also characterised in a parallel parlance as 'the Enemy.'"[174]

Eisenman shows from within Paul's writings that Paul and his soteriology were severely chastised by James and other Jewish Christians demanding explanations from Paul. Paul was quite cognizant of these charges and was certainly worried. "This is confirmed tangentially by Paul's defensiveness with regard to such epithets, as evidenced at the end of his testimony in Galatians to his all-important meeting with Peter and James in Jerusalem (Gal. 1:20 and 4:16). It is neither accidental nor incurious that exactly where he comes to speak of 'James the brother of the Lord' and in 2 Corinthians, the Hebrew 'Archapostles', that Paul feels obliged to add: 'Now before God, (in) what I write to you, I do not lie' or, again, 'I do not lie.' This will not be the only time that Paul will via refraction refer in his defensiveness to 'the Liar' epithet evidently being applied to him by some *within* the Movement not outside it. It is, as just noted, connected to the all-important 'Enemy' terminology, known to have been applied to him in later Jewish Christianity or Ebionitism."[175] Paul was frequently scolded for personal moral laxity and theological aberrations. He was well aware of the pervasive nature of these allegations, and found it essential to rectify the situation. "There are some eight other indications of this 'Lying' epithet in the Pauline corpus alone."[176] In Roman 9 Paul insists that "I speak the truth in Christ—I am not lying, my conscience confirms it through the Holy Spirit." (Romans 9:1-2) Eisenman observes that "Paul uses this 'Lying' terminology at several other crucial junctures in his letters, particularly in Romans 3:4-8 and 9:1, where he speaks about wrongful accusations concerning himself, circumcision, the Law, and how by 'telling the Truth' he has made himself 'a curse from Christ' to his opponents."[177]

Jame's Work-based Salvation Scheme

James's works-based salvific scheme represents the opposing trend. The Book of James is "indeed the most un-Pauline book in the New Testament."[178] James insisted: "Do not merely listen to the word, and so deceive yourselves. Do what it says. Anyone who listens to the word but does not do what it says is like someone who looks at his face in a mirror and, after looking at himself, goes away and immediately forgets what he looks like. But whoever looks intently into the perfect law that gives freedom, and continues in it—not forgetting what they have heard, but doing it—they will be blessed in what they do." (James1:23-25) For him a faith without good deeds is useless: "What good is it, my brothers and sisters, if someone claims to have faith but has no deeds? Can such faith save them? Suppose a brother or a sister is without clothes and daily food. If one of you says to them, "Go in peace; keep warm and well fed," but does nothing about their physical needs, what good is it? In the same way, faith by itself, if it is not accompanied by action, is dead [...] You foolish person, do you want evidence that faith without deeds is useless?" (James 2:14-20)

Faith is the trustful acceptance of God's will, and not spiritual arrogance or moral laxity. Submissive virtues such as humility, resignation, perseverance, modesty and chastity are integral to the true faith. "Who is wise and understanding among you? Let them show it by their good life, by deeds done in the humility that comes from wisdom. But if you harbour bitter envy and selfish ambition in your hearts, do not boast about it or deny the truth. Such 'wisdom' does not come down from heaven but is earthly, unspiritual, demonic. For where you have envy and selfish ambition, there you find disorder and every evil practice. But the wisdom that comes from heaven is first of all pure; then peace-loving, considerate, submissive, full of mercy and good fruit, impartial and sincere. Peacemakers who sow in peace reap a harvest of righteousness." (James 3:13-18)

Gerald Rendall observes that in "dealing with faith and works, his aims, his interest, his inspiration are wholly ethical: doctrinally, the whole cast of his mind is conservative; he stands upon the ancient ways; earnestly, devoutly steeped in 'the traditions of the fathers,' and deriving thence his terms and his ideals; on the ethical side he remains loyal to Judaism, as interpreted and to some extent more indeed than he perceived-revised by the authoritative genius of Jesus Christ."[179] James's definition of faith is altogether different from the Pauline's, as well as the later Church definition. His faith does not entail the creedal details or cosmic implications; it is the simple cause and foundation of morality and not opposing to good works, "nor does 'faith' involve prescribed forms of thought or creed or institutional observance: the two terms are not antithetical, but complementary, companion outputs, related as cause and effect--as germ and fruit-'faith' the antecedent, 'works' the consequent; effect is the one sure evidence of cause, and without cause effect is impossible. 'Show me thy faith apart from thy works, and I by my works will show thee my faith' (ii .I8)."[180] James's work based soteriology is in line with the Jewish understandings of the law and morality; its functions are ethical rather than theological. His Jesus is a perfect teacher and not a perfect Lamb, "the person of Jesus does not suggest to him any need for theological reconstruction or advance. So far as they retain ethical authority and value, the old forms and words suffice; he has no inclination to alter or reinterpret the term 'faith,' provided only that it functions ethically, that it works, that it yields practical results. Throughout there is no suggestion of broaching or confuting any new doctrine of 'faith,'"[181] The Jerusalem Church under the leadership of James alleged that Paul's faith-based scheme of salvation was an invention, a pagan grafting on the simple message of Jesus, a recipe for moral disaster and hence an enigma to Jesus and his message. The fears James and others had of it degenerating into moral depravity soon came true.

Spiritual Arrogance

The faith-based assurance of salvation has the potential of sinking into spiritual arrogance and moral decay; after all, why should a person worry about intricacies of the Law and morality if one could attain salvation only by faith? That is what the Neoplatonic philosopher Porphyry of Tyre (234-305 AD) argued about: "If it is true that a rich man who has kept himself free from the sins of the flesh-murder, thievery, adultery, cheating and lying, fornication, blasphemy-is prohibited from getting any sort of heavenly reward, what use is it for rich men to be good? [And if the poor are the only ones destined for heaven] what's the harm in in their committing any offense they like?"[182] What is the need to go through strenuous moral code while the Kingdom and Eternal Life can be guaranteed by faith in incarnation, resurrection or redemption? Morality without law is obsolete; everything immoral is permissible in the absence of law. This scheme of salvation has serious flaws and can potentially lead to hedonism and all sorts of immoral acts. It is too lax and boastful. It is against the justice, goodness and morality of good God. It is totally irrational that the good God will grace the immoral and incestuous believers with eternal bliss just because they happen to believe in the atoning death of Jesus Christ. A faith void of good actions is useless and corruptive. This is exactly what happened in the Christian community of Paul's times. "Without the constraints of the Jewish law, such Christians reasoned, anything is possible; and as the Christian is saved by grace and faith rather than by works, anything is permissible. Given the terms of his message to the churches, Paul cannot really dispute such logic. But its practical consequences in primarily gentile congregations must have been obvious to him from an early date."[183] The philosophical conclusion that now we are saved and that 'all things are lawful' was "being taken far too far."[184]

For instance, the Church of Corinth became so boisterous about guarantees of salvation through the redemptive works of Christ that they tolerated evils such as incest and whoredom. Paul himself was dismayed at the outcome of his salvific scheme becoming a laughing stock of his fellow Christians in Jerusalem and pagans elsewhere. His strong admonitions in 1 Corinthians 5 against such unprecedented immorality are witness to this historical reality. Paul states that "It is actually reported that there is sexual immorality among you, and of a kind that even pagans do not tolerate: A man is sleeping with his father's wife. And you are proud! Shouldn't you rather have gone into mourning." (I Corinthian 5:1-2) Moral perversions were the results of undue spiritual assurances and lofty promises. The promised spiritual and eternal kingdom through faith was relapsing in lewd abyss of indecency.

David Garland explains that "The Corinthians appear to take undue pride in identifying themselves as [...] spiritual ones; 2:13, 15; 3:1; 14:37) [...] Paul's discussion of this case of incest is interwoven with his concern about the spiritual swaggering of the Corinthians (4:18; 5:2).The key issue in this section is not Paul's need to reassert his authority over the community with a show of force. The root problem is their spiritual arrogance combined with moral laxity [...] Paul wants to puncture their inflated arrogance, to shake them out of their blasé attitude toward this sinful conduct, to purify the community of the contagion, and to create a situation that drives home the seriousness of the man's sin and his need for repentance."[185]

Unfortunately, Paul's salvation scheme was vague and sumptuous. It did not delineate the need to avoid sin, do good deeds and repent while overly emphasising the true faith in the atoning death of Christ. His poetic and reassuring salvation vocabulary was unintelligible, elusive and misleading. The result was unbridled hedonism. The first-century Roman pagans were already accusing Christian faith of self-indulgence, lack of patriotism, irrationality and immorality, and the Jerusalem Church had already made Paul's soteriology responsible for moral decadence. Paul could not afford such a laxity of the Corinthian community anymore. "Paul's concerns center on the moral stigma that such a sin, 'a kind not found even among pagans,' casts on the faith. This statement is not an exaggeration for rhetorical effect [...] This behaviour is an affront to the moral consciousness even of benighted pagans, who, as far as Jews were concerned, were the epitome of moral depravity because they did not know God (1 Thess. 4:5) [...] many Gentiles were already prone to believe the worst about Christians (cf. Suetonius, *Nero* 16 'a group of people belonging to a new and malevolent fanaticism [*superstitionis*]'). Paul did not want to give unbelievers any excuse for their unbelief (10:32–33; 9:19–23; cf. Phil. 2:14–15; 1 Thess. 4:12), but this behaviour would provide hostile outsiders with material evidence for their suspicions."[186] The Church was supposed to be the teacher of righteousness and decency; any deviant behaviour torpedoed the Church's moral authority and good reputation. But if the moral standards of the Church sank below even the vulgar pagans, then there was something fundamentally wrong with their understanding of faith and grace. The spiritual confidence must lead to moral orientation and not to egregious sins. Additionally, "it would also further undermine Paul's missionary efforts, which, according to Acts, were already under attack by the conservative wing of the Jerusalem church. In Galatia, the troublers appear to have maintained that Paul's gospel of grace inevitably led to outbreaks of immorality. If news of this evil arrived in Jerusalem and if it were believed that Paul in some way fostered or condoned it, his relationship with Jerusalem Christians would have eroded even further."[187]

It seems that the sketched Corinthian promiscuity was a lingering problem. Paul had previously written to them in admonition but in vain. "I wrote to you in my letter not to associate with sexually immoral people - not at all meaning the people of this world who are immoral, or the greedy and swindlers, or idolaters. In that case you would have to leave this world. But now I am writing to you that you must not associate with anyone who claims to be a brother or sister but is sexually immoral or greedy, an idolater or slanderer, a drunkard or swindler. Do not even eat with such people." (I Corinthian 5: 9-11) Francis Downing observes that others' interpretations of their Christian faith in Cynic terms were "too radical for Paul, even though he himself may initially have prompted such a reading, by his own words and lifestyle. Some people were indeed reaching conclusions Paul could not countenance at all, and, still worse, they were acting on them, in a wide range of relationships. There was incest (1 Cor 5.1–2), there was talk at least of resort to prostitutes (1 Cor 6.12–20) and objections were being raised against formal marriage (1 Cor 7.1)."[188]

The Corinthians might have considered themselves spiritual kings and inheritors of the kingdom of God, as Paul had repeatedly preached to them, but their contemptible behaviour was sufficient of a proof that they in reality were beastly. Many New Testament scholars "link such bravado to the Corinthians' theological confusion about their freedom, expressed in the slogan 'All things are permitted' (6:12). As self-appointed 'spiritual ones' they may have imagined that 'they could break every canon of decency and yet be without sin' [...] They may even have viewed this particular case as evidence of the man's newfound maturity and freedom in the new age [...] He may have convinced himself and others that 'sexual behaviour was spiritually irrelevant' [...] and that he was now above any social taboos. He was endowed with knowledge (1:5; 8:1), reigned as one of their spiritual kings (4:8), and could judge all things but be judged by no one (2:15–16a). Such serious theological confusion may explain why Paul does not respond to this case more compassionately and encourage the Corinthians 'to restore such a one in a spirit of gentleness' (Gal. 6:1)."[189] Paul's teachings were fluid enough to possibly have caused such moral confusions, otherwise Christians at Corinth would have not been doing these abominable acts so openly and defiantly. Their laxity was the logical conclusion of their understanding of justification by faith only; why would someone worry about self-restraint, self-discipline and sobriety when all things were already permitted? Gordon Fee comments that "it is this lack of a sense of sin, and therefore of any ethical consequences to their life in the Spirit, that marks the Corinthian brand of spirituality as radically different from that which flows out of the gospel of Christ crucified."[190]

The same lack of ethical concerns and spiritual arrogance were responsible for the widespread problems related to prostitution. Paul pinpoints that perverted theological presumptions were behind such immoral practice. "'I have the right to do anything,' you say—but not everything is beneficial. 'I have the right to do anything'—but I will not be mastered by anything. You say, 'Food for the stomach and the stomach for food, and God will destroy them both.' The body, however, is not meant for sexual immorality but for the Lord, and the Lord for the body [...] Do you not know that your bodies are members of Christ himself? Shall I then take the members of Christ and unite them with a prostitute? Never! Do you not know that he who unites himself with a prostitute is one with her in body?" (1 Cor. 6:12-16) Garland states that "in this unit Paul takes aim at the problem of πορνεία (*porneia*, sexual immorality), which in this context refers to sex for hire, its root meaning in Greek. Have some Corinthian Christians consorted with prostitutes and justified their behaviour with twisted theological reasoning expressed in snappy sound bites? The majority of recent interpreters think so. They assume that the lines 'All things are permissible to me' and 'Food is meant for the belly and the belly for food, and God will destroy both one and the other' were Corinthian shibboleths bandied about to sanction lewd behaviour with prostitutes [...] 'Every sin that a man commits is outside the body,' as another Corinthian slogan used to exonerate such conduct. Paul cites these slogans to debunk them."[191] Fee observes that "apparently some men within the Christian community are going to prostitutes and are arguing for the right to do so. Being people of the Spirit, they imply, has moved them to a higher plane, the realm of spirit, where they are unaffected by behaviour that has merely to do with the body. So Paul proceeds from the affirmation of v.11 to an attack on this theological justification."[192]

Paul, throughout the Epistle, seems to rectify the misperceptions connected with his theology of justification by faith only. Some Christians have understood that their conversion to the new faith and acceptance of Lord Jesus Christ as the saviour has saved them from the eternal punishment and guaranteed them spiritual bliss. Body, to them, was something temporal which would mix with the dust after death. Therefore, no acts of physical immorality would jeopardise their salvation or destroy their spiritual unity with Christ. Paul was debunking such a twist in this section of the Epistle. "The Corinthian pneumatics' understanding of spirituality has allowed them both a false view of freedom ('everything is permissible') and of the body ('God will destroy it'), from which basis they have argued that going to prostitutes is permissible because the body doesn't matter. Paul's response to this is in three parts: (1) In vv. 12-14 he argues directly against their false premises, in v. 12 against their distortion of Christian freedom, and in vv. 13-14 against their misunderstanding of the nature of the body. In v. 13 he makes the basic assertion that controls most of the rest of the argument: 'The body is for the Lord, and the Lord for the body,' which is demonstrated by the resurrection—both Christ's and ours (v. 14)."[193] So by emphasising the resurrection Paul is closing the loopholes created by his own soteriology. Initially he must have not thought of these potential loopholes in his new age and spiritual kingdom theology. He was using the plugins to thwart the immoral potentials and realities of his antinomian attitude. There were no built-in safeguards and mechanisms to withstand the pressures of human lustful impulses. This patchy work was no alternate for a long trodden, well built and amply safeguarded salvific scheme via righteousness and morality. Paul had opened the can of worms through his justification by faith theology, and the malice spread all over.

R. J. Hoffman rightly contends that "factionalism, gluttony, competition for the outpouring and demonstration of spiritual gifts (charismata) in the form of prophecy and ecstatic utterance (I Cor. 11-15) cannot have been limited to Corinth, however. The epistle attributed in the New Testament to Jude and written in the last years of the first century indicates the pestiferousness of the problem well after Paul's valiant efforts to curb ecstaticism and sexual license in certain congregations."[194] Jude exhorted that "Woe to them! They have taken the way of Cain; they have rushed for profit into Balaam's error; they have been destroyed in Korah's rebellion." (Jude 11) Hoffman notes that "the references clearly point to internal disarray and perhaps to a growing libertinism within the churches: Cain typified treachery, lust, avarice, and self-indulgence for first-century writers; Balaam's error (Numbers 22-24) was covetousness and the corruption of the young; the reference to Khora's rebellion (Num. 16.1-34; Josephus, *Antiquities*, 4.2.), is to the enemies of Moses who were thought to have descended live into Sheol. The last of the references would indicate that the source of the troubles is a group of agitators who advocate pleasure in the here and now as a part of their love feasts: 'They concern themselves with the things of the flesh and thus corrupt themselves' (Jude 10)."[195]

Christian Libertinism

Sexual perversions were the direct results of Pauline disdain for the Jewish Law, human flesh and justification by works. His insistence that the current order was corrupt and could be rectified only through the redeeming blood of Christ made self-mortification attractive and self-indulgence and moral laxity a real possibility. Paul's eschatology of the new kingdom and, replacement of old order with the new spiritual order, was one of the main sources of the Christian libertinism. The law was abolished, the atoning blood was already shed, the faith in Lord Jesus Christ's redemptive works was established, the new kingdom had ushered and the spiritual transformation had already taken place. To Paul, the Eucharist as the direct union with the divine body was the source of this spiritual transformation; therefore, the believers were already elevated to the highest spiritual realms- there was no need for any further moral restraints. Physical joy and temporal bliss was an offshoot of such a spiritual energy. Pauline salvationism was a moral conundrum well spread all over the Gentile Christian world, "salvationism had imprinted itself on the Christian church at Corinth by the fifties of the first century; by the end of the century, the author of the letter attributed to James offers an already archaic solution-the doing of works (2.14)-as an antidote to the salvation-by-faith doctrine advocated by Paul in his desperate attempts to bring the churches under moral control."[196]

The influence of Roman mystery cults added fuel to the fire. By the beginning of the second century the Eucharist's immortality mania was akin to the mystery cults' enthusiasm for initiates' immortality. By then the pagan mystery rites were strongly embedded in the Christian churches. The physical union with Lord Jesus Christ and ensuing supposed divine energy was translated into physical excesses; the Christian feasts were known to the authorities as the places of over-indulgences. This is clear from the report of the Younger Pliny to the emperor Trajan, written around 111 AD; Pliny reports that "rumors of Christian excesses were widespread throughout Asia Minor and were doubtless linked in the popular mind with the nocturnal forest rites of the Bacchae. Described by Livy during the reign of Augustus (27 B.C.E.-14 C.E.) these rites were thought to include drunkenness, the defilement of women, promiscuous intercourse, and assorted other debaucheries. Pliny had heard this much and more about the clandestine practices of the Christians including suggestions that they occasionally sacrificed and ate their young and indulged in ritual incest at their love banquets."[197] The modern hedonistic perversions were envisaged by the first and second century Gentile spiritual enthusiasm.

The Latin rhetorician Marcus Cornelius Fronto (100-166?) highlights the Christian congregation's moral engrossments in the following words: "Already—for ill weeds grow apace—decay of morals grows from day to day, and throughout the wide world the abominations of this impious confederacy multiply. Root and branch it must be exterminated and accursed. They recognize one another by secret signs and marks; they fall in love almost before they are acquainted; everywhere they introduce a kind of religion of lust, a promiscuous 'brotherhood' and 'sisterhood' by which ordinary fornication, under cover of a hallowed name, is converted to incest. And thus their vain and foolish superstition makes an actual boast of crime. For themselves, were there not some foundation of truth, shrewd rumour would not impute gross and unmentionable forms of vice."[198] These were the words of a pagan who had seen and known the Roman sexual perversions of his time. Fronto continues: "On a special day they gather in a feast with all their children, sisters, mothers-all sexes and ages. There, flushed with the banquet after such feasting and drinking, they begin to bum with incestuous passions. They provoke a dog tied to the lampstand to leap and bound towards a scrap of food which they have tossed outside the reach of his chain. By this means the light is overturned and extinguished, and with it common knowledge of their actions; in the shameless dark and with unspeakable lust they copulate in random unions, all being equally guilty of incest, some by deed but everyone by complicity."[199]

The second-century Christian apologists such as Justine Martin, Tertullian and many others were aware of these practices. For instance Epiphanius points to a sect called the Phibionites, who "unite with each other [sister and brother] in the passion of fornication [...] The woman and the man take the fluid of the emission of the man into their hands, they stand, tum toward heaven, their hands besmeared by uncleanness, and pray (saying) 'We offer to thee this gift, the body of Christ,' and then they eat it, their own ugliness, and say: 'This is the body of Christ and this is the Passover for the sake of which our bodies suffer and are forced to confess the suffering of Christ.' similarly also with the woman when she happens to be in the flowing of the blood, they gather the blood of menstruation of her uncleanness and eat it together and say, 'This is the blood of Christ.'"[200] The anti-Jewish, anti-law and anti-constraint feelings were so widespread among the Gentile Christians that libertinism became the hallmark of some Christian communities. Even though the Roman society was inundated with sexual promiscuity somehow the Christian violations were considered the worst of all perversions. The early pagan anti-Christian polemical works highlighted these brazen violations. "The earliest literary polemic against the Christian associations was thus directed against the antinomian and libertine congregations of the new religious diaspora."[201]

On the other hand, the Christian leadership struggled to disassociate Christian faith from the failings of some of its members. For instance, the Apologists contended that the Christian salvation scheme did not permit the sort of behaviour attributed to some Christian sects. Christianity inculcated hope, love, charity and sharing but not immorality; promiscuous members were to be tried as criminals rather than Christians. Justin Martin strongly pleaded: "We demand that those accused to you be judged in order that each one who is convicted may be punished as an evildoer and not as a Christian."[202]

It is difficult to gauge the extent of the supposed abuses of Christian spirituality, but even after the passage of almost two centuries the Christian leadership was engaged in defending the Christian faith against such invectives. Tertullian argued that "not two hundred and fifty years have passed since our life began yet the rumors that circulate against us, anchored in the cruelty of the human mind, enjoy considerable success."[203] In his *Apology*, Tertullian mentioned that to his day Christians were considered 'the most criminal' of all men.[204] They were mistreated and randomly accused of heinous crimes of immorality.[205] "Yet it ought just as much to be wrung out of us (whenever that false charge is made) how many murdered babies each of us had tasted, how many acts of incest he had done in the dark, what cooks were there— yes, and what dogs." Oh! the glory of that magistrate who had brought to light some Christian who had eaten up to date a hundred babies!"[206] The Christian was considered "a man guilty of every crime, the enemy of gods, emperors, laws, morals, of all Nature together.[207] Tertullian protested that their faith was intentionally vilified, "in reading the charge, why do you call the man a Christian, why not a murderer too, if a Christian is a murderer? Why not incestuous? Or anything else you believe us to be? Or is it that in our case, and ours alone, it shames you, or vexes you, to use the actual names of our crimes?"[208] He lamented the fact that the name Christian was being despised to the extent that all sorts of promiscuities were automatically shifted to him as soon as a person was known to have converted to Christianity.[209] "If the Tiber reaches the walk, if the Nile does not rise to the fields, if the sky doesn't move or the earth does, if there is famine, if there is plague, the cry is at once : "The Christians to the lion.""[210]

Tertullian clarified that "we are a body knit together by a common religious profession, by unity of discipline, and by the bond of common hope. We meet together as an assembly and congregation, that, offering up prayer to God as with united force we may wrestle with him in our supplications [...] We pray for the emperors, too - for their ministers and for all in authority, for the welfare of the world, for the prevalence of peace and for the delay of the final consummation. We assemble to read our sacred writings [...] In the same place also exhortations are made, rebukes and sacred censures are administered... Though we have our treasure chest, it is not made up of purchase money [...] Our gifts are, as it were, piety's deposit. For they are not taken and spent on feasts and drinking bouts and eating-houses, but to support and bury poor people, to supply the wants and needs of boys and girls destitute of parents, and of old persons confined to the house."[211] He continued that "As the feast commenced with prayer, so with prayer it is closed. We go from it not like troops of evildoers nor bands of vagabonds, nor to break out into licentious acts, but to have as much care for our modesty and chastity as if we had been at a seminar on virtue rather than at a banquet."[212]

Tertullian did not deny the possibilities of Christian mystery's abuses by some Christians but insisted that the righteous outcomes were greater than the misdemeanors. Hoffman observes that "Tertullian's description of the *agape* does nothing to exclude the possibility of abuses, and indeed his analogies - the feasts of the Apaturia, the Bacchae, the Attic mysteries, and the cult of Serapis - suggest that the feasts were often marred by explosions of enthusiasm. These were to be tolerated on Tertullian's reckoning because the banquets, despite their cost, benefited the needy and because Christians were entitled (like the Megarians) 'to feast as though they were going to die on the morrow.' In any event, it is obvious from the direction of his argument that outsiders were fond of pointing out inconsistencies in the Christian public attitude toward pagan 'licentiousness' and their private indulgences in wine and song."[213] In spite of the widespread stereotypes Tertullian, like the other Apologists, also claimed that only the Christians were good, innocent, moral and saved because they had the divine message, guidance and grace. "We, then, alone are innocent. What is surprising in that, if it must be so? And it must be. Innocence we have been taught by God; in its perfection we know it, as revealed by a perfect teacher; faithfully we keep it as committed to us by one who reads the heart and cannot be despised. It was but man's opinion that gave you your idea of innocence, man's authority that enjoined it. So your rule of life is neither complete nor does it inspire such fear as to lead to true innocence."[214] The Christian blood multiplies due to God's grace. "But go to it! my good magistrates; the populace will count you a deal better, if you sacrifice the Christians to them. Torture us, rack us, condemn us, crush us; your cruelty only proves our innocence. That is why God suffers us to suffer all this [...] We multiply whenever we are mown down by you; the blood of Christians is seed."[215]

It is evident from the above discussion that the Pauline doctrine of grace and justification by faith was at times taken to its logical conclusions by some Christians, landing them into free spirit, enthusiasm, antinomianism and hedonism. Orgies, excessive drinking and unrestrained sexuality were already part of some mystery cults. They were copied by some Christian factions in the name of spiritual unification and merger with the divine. Many contended that the sin was eliminated by the death of Christ, and humanity had already been reconciled with God. Christ had become one with the believing Christians through Eucharist; the new spiritual kingdom had been established, the old laws were abolished and a new era of grace and salvation was ushered by the Crucifixion. Good works and morality were not as important as the faith in the redeeming works of Christ; therefore, no sin whatsoever could take that faith and grace away from a sincere believer. Christ was in them, and with them even when they sinned.

The Church tried its utmost to curb such tendencies in the name of Christ's love and mind, but mostly in vain. The Church's vilification of human passions such as sex, and its stress upon celibacy and chastity did not stop those adventurous souls from perversity who took the spiritual assurances of divine grace to its limits. They considered the Church's interference in their personal lives as an extension of Church's hunger for power and control. Moreover, the medieval Church used allegations of orgies and hedonism against some free spirit dissenters such as the twelfth-century Waldensians, Fretacelli, Catharism and sixteenth-century Brethren of the Free Spirit or Ranters. Not all were hedonists; some had genuine concerns about the Church's abuses and persecutions. It is quite possible that the Church authorities might have been exaggerating the hedonistic charges against the dissenters to label them with the worst possible crimes. That is not to say that there were no immoralities in the dissenters; Thomas Gale's observations about Brethren of Free Spirit are genuinely valid. He states that "it is possible to affirm that this sect was a sort of gnosis intent upon individual salvation, a system of self-exaltation often amounting to self-deification, which concluded in an aberrant form of mysticism and anarchy. What distinguished the Free Spirit from other medieval sects is total amoralism. The core of the heresy of the Free Spirit (which did not form an organised church) lay in its adherents' attitude toward themselves: they stressed the desire to surpass the human condition and become godlike, and they believed they had attained so absolute a perfection that they were incapable of sin, a conviction that often could lead to antinomianism. It was thus permissible to do whatsoever was commonly regarded as forbidden, and, in particular, such antinomianism commonly took the form of sexual promiscuity. Eroticism, far from springing from a relaxed sensuality, possessed above all a mystic and symbolic value of spiritual emancipation. Adultery too was regarded as a transcendental means of affirmation or liberation. Moreover, for the elect, sexual intercourse could not under any circumstances be sinful, so that they were able to indulge in promiscuity without fear of God or qualms of conscience."[216]

Christopher Hill maintains that sexual perversion and spiritual emancipation were anticipated by the grace-based theology of both Luther and Calvin. "This sounds very shocking, but it is worth reminding ourselves that Luther had preached Whatsoever thou shalt observe upon liberty and of love, is godly; but if thou observe anything of necessity, it is ungodly. 'If an adultery could be committed in the faith, it would no longer be a sin.' And Calvin had said that 'all external things [are] subject to our liberty, provided the nature of that liberty approves itself to our minds as before God'. The consciences of believers may rise above the Law, and may forget the whole righteousness of the Law.' Calvin hedged such phrases about with safeguards; but we can see how easily his doctrine toppled over into Antinomianism. Sir Thomas Overbury was consciously caricaturing when he described his Precisian as one who 'will not stick to commit fornication or adultery so it be done in the fear of God'. But it was very near the knuckle. All that was needed was assurance of election, of Christ within you. 'Suppose a believer commit adultery and murder,' mused Tobias Crisp; still he 'cannot commit those sins that can give occasion to him to suspect that if he come presently to Christ, he would cast him off'."[217]

Ranters and other free-spirited Christians had taken the Pauline mystical ecstasy and enthusiasm to its brink in the early seventeenth century, just like the Corinthians did in Paul's lifetime. The Pauline vocabulary of the old and new, the curse of Adam, sin and commandment and the justification by grace were readily implied to construct a hedonistic outlook. "For Ranters Christ in us is far more important than the historical Christ who died at Jerusalem, and 'all the commandments of God, both in the Old and New Testaments, are the fruits of the curse. Since all men are now freed of the curse, they are also free from the commandments; our will is God's will."[218] John Bunyan (1628-1688), the author of *Saved by Grace* who explained the "Saved by Grace" as "redemption from the curse of sin, which oppresses the poor sinner with the fears of everlasting burnings; while it elevates the body, soul, and spirit, to an exceeding weight of glory—to the possession of infinite treasures, inconceivable, and that never fade away"[219] insisted that the Ranters had turned the grace of God into wantonness and that "they lacked a conviction of sin."[220]

Lawrence Clarkson, the seventeenth-century "Seekers" preacher, argued that "there is no such act as drunkenness, adultery and theft in God [...] Sin hath its conception only in the imagination [...] What act so-ever is done by thee in light and love, is light and lovely, though it be that act called adultery [...] No matter what Scripture, saints or churches say, if that within thee do not condemn thee, thou shalt not be condemned."[221] The slogan that "If men 'believe sin, death and the curse to be abolished they are abolished. They that believe on Christ are no sinners'"[222] was common place in sixteenth-century England. Clarkson developed this theme further: "'None can be free from sin till in purity it be acted as no sin, for I judged that pure to me which to a dark understanding was impure: for to the pure all things, yea all acts were pure.' 'So that see what I can, act what I will, all is but one most sweet and lovely [...] Without act, no life; without life, no perfection.'"[223] The Ranters' spiritual arrogance was akin to the Corinthians' boastful theology, and their antinomian mysticism was sin mania. J. F. McGregor notes that the "Ranter Prophets were mystical antinomians: mystical in their claim to have become one with God; antinomian in denying the reality of sin to the believer."[224] Clement Hawes observes that "as adepts of the doctrine of salvation by free grace alone, the Ranters made a point of public drinking, smoking, and blaspheming."[225] Hill observes that the "Blasphemy Act of 9 August 1650 was aimed especially against the Ranters' denial of 'the necessity of civil and moral righteousness among men,' which tended 'to the dissolution of all human society. It denounced anyone who maintained him or herself to be God, or equal with God; or that acts of adultery, drunkenness, swearing, theft, etc. were not in themselves shameful, wicked and sinful, or that there is no such thing as sin 'but as a man or woman judgeth thereof'. The penalty was six months' imprisonment for the first offence, banishment for the second, the death of a felon if the offender refused to depart or returned."[226]

In conclusion, the Pauline concept of grace and justification by faith has the potential of degeneration into antinomianism and hedonism. The Orthodoxy's insistence upon this dogma as the essence of Christianity has not warded it off against such possible abuses. Actually there is no built in mechanism within the Christian soteriology as well as theology to safeguard the Christian faith against such violations. This is the natural and logical outcome of insistence upon justification by faith at the expense of good works. The history is a witness that this dogma has caused undue enthusiasm and mania to some believing Christians resulting in hedonism and promiscuity.

Anti-Rationalism

In addition to hedonism, Christianity was also charged with lack of rationalism. As seen in the previous chapter, the Christian concepts of a triune God, incarnation and redemption were more supra rational and emotional than rational. These unintelligible dogmas were imposed by the imperial powers rather than the power of logic and reason. No logic could prove the incarnation of Almighty and Omnipresent God into the body of a feeble man and in the womb of a frail woman, and nobody could properly explain the deification of the man Jesus to the extent of total equality with God the Almighty. No human formula could describe the Holy Trinity in terms comprehended by human mind. No reason could fully grasp the two natured Christ, a historical man with limited knowledge, means, capacities and accomplishments and at the same time infinite God with unlimited knowledge, power and authority. Reconciling the suffering Jesus with the Omnipotent Christ was a theological nightmare. In fact, the entire scheme of Christian salvation and metaphysics looked artificial, arbitrary, legendary and mythological. The so-called Christian mysteries were already known to many Roman mystery cults. In spite of that the Christians claimed that theirs was a unique mystery and a specially gifted religion. In brief Christianity was so primitive and supra rational that it was ridiculed as archaic, illogical and irrational faith even by the ancient pagans.

For instance, the 2nd century pagan philosopher Celsus made a transition from moral to intellectual attacks on Christianity. As mentioned in previous chapters, he harshly mocked Christianity for its irrational dogmas and unsophisticated theology. His multipronged philosophical assault was recorded and responded to by Origen, the second century Church Father. Celsus vehemently attacked the Christian concept of the Deity and dubbed it as thoroughly irrational.

Celsus argued that the Gospels attributed qualities and actions to Jesus which were totally alien to divinity. God Almighty was powerful and irresistible while Jesus was not; God was full of knowledge and wisdom, while Jesus was so short on ideas that he could not explain his mission and identity even to his close confidants. His behaviour was also not godly. "Look at your god: How can you regard him as a god when as a matter of fact he was not eager to make public anything he professed to do? After he had been tried and condemned and it had been decided that he should be punished, where did we find him? Hiding-trying to escape. And was he not even betrayed by those whom he was silly enough to call disciples? If he was a god, is it likely that he would have run away? Would he have permitted himself to be arrested?"[227]

Jesus supposedly came to save humanity, heal hundreds and feed thousands but only a handful of individuals (a total of twelve disciples) believed in him. Then his disciple Judas sold him for pennies, Peter denied him thrice and the others abandoned him all together. Even gang leaders, robbers and military generals enjoy more loyalty and command more respect than Jesus, the supposed god. "Most of all: Would a god –a saviour, as you say, and son of the Most High God-be betrayed by the very men who had been taught by him and shared everything with him? What an absurdity you have chosen to make a doctrine: no general worth his salt could have broached betrayal by the thousands he led; not even a robber chieftain captaining a crew of brigands would have been handed over by those whom he had tried to lead. But Jesus! He was betrayed by those closest to him, those under his authority, and he ruled neither like a good general, nor did he command the respect of his followers even to such a degree as robbers feel for their chief."[228] Jesus lacked power, eloquence and charisma of a normal human leader rest aside the God Almighty.

The Christian writings were mythical and contradictory. They were irrational and legendary, employing mutually exclusive categories and illogical plots to demonstrate monumental tasks such as incarnation.

They were intellectually dead as the death of their hero, "the writings of the disciples contain only those facts about Jesus that put a flattering face on the events of his life. It is as if someone were saying out of one side of his mouth that a man is righteous, while admitting at the same time that the man is an evildoer; or, put differently, showing a man to be a murderer while saying he is holy; or while saying he is risen, proving him to be dead; and then-above it all-claiming that he predicted it! You admit that Jesus suffered and died (rather than saying, as you might, that he appeared to endure suffering). Yet what evidence do you point to suggest that he anticipated this suffering? And if he was at some point a dead man, how can he have been immortal?"[229]

Unlike the Omniscient and Omnipotent God, Jesus was ignorant about the future. Had he known the future he would have not been betrayed or mercilessly crucified. He, like any common sense person, would have warded off dangers. "It seems to me that any god or demon-or for that matter, any sensible man-who foreknew what was going to happen to him would try very hard to avoid such a fate. I mean, if he foreknew both the man who was to betray him and the man who was going to deny him, it would seem they would have feared him as God, and knowing what he knew, that the one would not betray him or the other deny him. Of course, as you tell the story, they both betrayed him and denied him without any thought for this at all. If people conspire against a man who anticipates their conspiracy and tells them of it to their face, such traitors commonly turn away from their treachery and are thereafter on their guard. But I conclude that these things did not happen to Jesus because they were foretold. That is quite impossible. No, the very fact that they happened suggests the opposite: namely, that they were wholly unexpected. He had not predicted them. It is impossible to think that those who had already heard of their behaviour from Jesus would have carried out their intentions."[230] The Divinity and naivety do not go together.

Additionally if he was the Omnipotent God and allowed such debacles to happen then he was a cheat, a conspirator rather than being an honest god. "But perhaps," you will argue, "he foretold all these things by virtue of being a god and knowing the hearts and minds of his followers. And what he foreknew must come to pass. If it is thus the case that these things happened according to his divine intention and with his foreknowledge, we must also conclude that Jesus the god led his own disciples and prophets-those with whom he ate and drank-so far astray that they became evil and treacherous. But if he was a god, ought he not rather to have done good to men? Especially to those who followed him? In my book, a man who shared meals with another man would not intend him to betray him, especially if the first was a god! Are we then to say, as your doctrine teaches, that God himself was the conspirator-that God ate with men, only to turn his disciples into traitors and evildoers?"[231]

If he knew his noble mission of saving the humanity then why would he cry on the Cross? Does God cry, show remorse and possess all other human weaknesses? "The things that happened to Jesus were intensely painful. It must have been impossible for him to have prevented them from being so. But if it is true that he foreknew what was to happen-indeed intended it from the start, why is he represented as lamenting and wailing, and supplicating God to make him strong in the face of death. Why does he cry: 'Father, if only this cup could pass by me!' A fine God indeed who fears what he is supposed to conquer."[232] This was against the noble character of a hero rest aside a god with cosmic redeeming designs. Porphyry of Tyre repeated the same argument a century later.[233]

Celsus, Porphyry and Christian Mysteries

Celsus argued that these monstrous contradictions were neither mysteries nor paradoxes but proofs of Gospel's human origins, deceptions and untruthful nature. "It is clear to me that the writings of the Christians are a lie, and that your fables have not been well enough constructed to conceal this monstrous fiction. I have even heard that some of your interpreters, as if they had just come out of a tavern, are onto the inconsistencies and, pen in hand, alter the original writings three, four, and several more times over in order to be able to deny the contradictions in the face of criticism."[234]

This was a theme which Porphyry would repeatedly exploit to refute the Christian claims of historical authenticity. "The evangelists were fiction writers-not observers or eyewitnesses to the life of Jesus. Each of the four contradicts the other in writing his account of the events of his suffering and crucifixion."[235] He noticed that the Gospels' accounts of Jesus were so contradictory that they seemed to represent multiple people. "Based on these contradictory and secondhand reports, one might think this describes not the suffering of a single individual but of several!"[236]

Jesus was neither a true messiah nor a true god; his stories were nothing but fabrications, and the so-called Old Testament prophecies about his coming and mission were a jungle of fanciful constructions. "These same prophecies could easily be applied to a thousand others besides Jesus [...] the one who is to come (the Messiah) will be a great prince; he will be the lord of this world, and the leader of nations and armies. From this it is obvious that the prophets do not anticipate a low-grade character like this Jesus-a man who is able to make himself the son of a god by trickery, deceit and the most incredible stories. A true son of God, like the sun that illuminated the world by first illuminating itself, ought first to have been revealed as a true god. The Christians put forth this Jesus not only as the son of God but as the very Logos-not the pure and holy Logos known to the philosophers, mind you, but a new kind of Logos: a man who managed to get himself arrested and executed in the most humiliating of circumstances."[237] Celsus compared the Greek concept of Logos as the first principle of creation, wisdom and power with the Christian concept of Logos full of contradictions, shortcomings and weaknesses, to show that the same terms carried two different connotations. It was scandalous to use a loaded term such as Logos for a frail and feeble person like Jesus.

Jesus's helplessness, weakness and impatience were antithetical to the Christian claims of his divinity. Even the common people with some valour show resistance to their abusers, but Jesus was too meek to stand up to his abusers. He "could not counter even the opposition of men, or avoid the disaster that ended his life in disgrace. According to your tales, the man who sentenced him did not suffer the fate of a Pentheus by going mad or being torn to pieces; rather, Jesus permitted himself to be mocked and bedecked with a purple robe and crowned with thorns. Why did this son of a god not show one glimmer of his divinity under these conditions? Why did he refuse to deliver himself from shame-at least play the man and stand up for his own or for his father's honour? But what does he say when his body is stretched out on the cross? 'Is this blood not ichor such as flows in the veins of the blessed?' When thirsty, he drinks greedily from a sponge full of vinegar and gall, not bearing his thirst with godly patience."[238]

Christians wanted the entire human race to believe in Jesus's divinity while he himself had been at a loss to convince anybody of his godhead in his own life time. How could he be considered god after such demoralising events? Neither his life nor his death was worthy of some divine qualities, let alone full divinity. "Have you forgotten that while he lived this Jesus convinced nobody-not even his own disciples- of his divinity, and was punished shamefully for his blasphemies? Were he a god he should not have died, if only in order to convince others for good and all that he was no liar; but die he did-not only that, but died a death that can hardly be accounted an example to men. Nor was he free from blame, as you imagine. Not only was he poor, he was also a coward and a liar as well. Perhaps you Christians will say that having failed to convince men on earth of his divinity, he descended into hell to convince them there. In all of these beliefs you have been deceived; yet you persist doggedly to seek justification for the absurdities you have made doctrines."[239]

Suffering an enigmatic death could never be the proof of one's divinity, as Christians contend, otherwise every condemned robber and convicted murderer would be an angel or a god. This was not good news, a divine mystery or a paradox. It was nothing but simplemindedness and naivety - a myth created, transmitted and propagated on the authority and testimony of the traitors. "If the central doctrine of Christianity bears testing, why should we not wonder whether every condemned man is an angel even greater than your divine Jesus? I mean, why not be completely shameless and confess that every robber, every convicted murderer, is neither robber nor murderer but a god? And why? Because he had told his robber band beforehand that he would come to no good end and wind up a dead man. Your case is made the harder because not even his disciples believed in him at the time of his humiliation: those who had heard him preach and were taught by him, when they saw he was heading for trouble, did not stick with him. They were neither willing to die for his sake nor to become martyrs for his cause they even denied they had known him! Yet on the example of those original traitors, you stake your faith and profess your willingness to die."[240]

The myth of atoning death and resurrection of the cult saviour was commonplace in the Roman world. The mythological accounts of Jesus's crucifixion and resurrection were no proofs of his divinity. Building a case of a feeble man's hard divinity on such shaky grounds was nothing short of a scandal. "I suppose you will say that the earthquake and the darkness that covered the earth at the time of his death prove him a god, and that even though he did not accept the challenge to remove himself from the cross or to escape his persecutors when he was alive, yet he overcame them all by rising from the dead and showing the marks of his punishment, pierced hands and all, to others. But who really saw this? A hysterical woman, as you admit and perhaps one other person-both deluded by his sorcery, or else so wrenched with grief at his failure that they hallucinated him risen from the dead by a sort of wishful thinking. This mistaking a fantasy for reality is not at all uncommon; indeed, it has happened to thousands."[241] The Gospel stories lacked analytical, rational and historical moorings; the myth was only good for the mythical mind.

Jesus supposedly showed many miracles to the unbelieving Jews in an effort to convince them of his mission and divinity. Resurrection after the death would have been the most conclusive proof of his mission and divinity. He should have appeared to the unbelieving Jews rather than the half-crazed women. "Jesus were trying to convince anyone of his powers, then surely he ought to have appeared first to the Jews who treated him so badly-and to his accusers-indeed to everyone, everywhere. Or better, he might have saved himself the trouble of getting buried and simply have disappeared from the cross. Has there ever been such an incompetent planner: When he was in the body, he was disbelieved but preached to everyone; after his resurrection, apparently wanting to establish a strong faith, he chooses to show himself to one woman and a few comrades only. When he was punished, everyone saw; yet risen from the tomb, almost no one."[242]

Porphyry repeated the same argument after a century: "Why did this Jesus (after his crucifixion and rising as your story goes) not appear to Pilate, who had punished him saying he had done nothing worthy of execution, or to the king of the Jews, Herod, or to the high priest of the Jewish people, or to many men at the same time, as for example to people of renown among the Romans, both senators and others, whose testimony was reliable. Instead he appeared to Mary Magdalene, a prostitute who came from some horrible little village and had been possessed by seven demons, and another Mary, equally unknown, probably a peasant woman, and others who were of no account."[243] He concluded that "this silliness in the gospels ought to be taught to old women and not to reasonable people. Anyone who should take the trouble to examine these facts more closely would find thousands of similar tales, none with an ounce of sense to them."[244]

The Christians used contradictory, mutually exclusive and absurd arguments to prove that Jesus was divine. Disbelief was not a proof of godhead. It was claimed that Jesus wanted to be unnoticed, kept his true identity hidden and at the same time all these splendid claims were made about him, "they contradict themselves, condemning the Jews for failing to recognize the Christ. If he wanted to be unnoticed, why was the voice from heaven heard, declaring him the Son of God? If he did not want to be unnoticed, then why was he punished and executed? At the very least it would seem that he would want his followers to know why he had come to earth. But your Jesus does not let his followers in on his secret, and thus occasions their disbelief. This is not my own guessing: I base what I say on your own writings, which are self-refuting. What god has ever lived among men who offers disbelief as the proof of his divinity? What god appears in turn only to those who already look for his reappearance, and is not even recognized by them. The sort of god, you should answer, who piles empty abuses on his hearers by threatening them with woes for misunderstanding things which were never made plain to them. What is plain is that this Jesus was a mere man."[245] It was an irony that the plain humanity was merged into a vague divinity to create an unprecedented and unintelligible monster.

Multiple Christianities

Celsus argued that there were multiple Christianities and multiple Christologies, but none of them presented an idea but absurdities. "The religion of the Christians is not directed at an idea but at the crucified Jesus, and this is surely no better than dog or goat worship at its worst."[246] He maintained that the Christian "belief rests on no solid foundation."[247] Celsus repeatedly alleged Christianity of stupidity and slow-wittedness. To him irrationalism and primitiveness were the hallmarks of Christian doctrines. "I assume to be the case when I consider their vulgar doctrines. I doubt very much that any really intelligent man believes these doctrines of the Christians, for to believe them would require one to ignore the sort of unintelligent and uneducated people who are persuaded by it. And how can one overlook the fact that Christian teachers are only happy with stupid pupils-indeed scout about for the slow-witted."[248] He insisted that Christians were against professionalism and skills resorting instead to nonsensical claims of miraculous healing and charlatanism: "the Christian teachers warn, 'Keep away from physicians.' And to the scum that constitutes their assemblies, they say 'Make sure none of you ever obtains knowledge, for too much learning is a dangerous thing: knowledge is a disease for the soul, and the soul that acquires knowledge will perish."[249]

The Christians had turned a feeble man into a god; such a mythology was neither unique nor new. There were plenty of such mythologies far older than Christianity. Why to replace the ancient with a newer more absurd one? "I emphasise that the Christians worship a man who was arrested and died, after the manner of the Getae who reverence Zamolxis, or those Sicilians who worship Mopsus, the Aracarnanians who worship Amphilochus, or the Thebans who worship Amphiarus and the Lebadians who worship Trophonius. The honour they pay to Jesus is no different from the sort paid to Hadrian's favorite boy, Antinous. Yet they brook no comparison between Jesus and the established gods, such is the effect of the faith that has blurred their judgment. For only a blind faith explains the hold that Jesus has of their imagination. For they stress that he was born a mortal-indeed, that his flesh was as corruptible as gold, silver, and stone. By birth, he shared those carnal weaknesses that the Christians themselves regard as abominable. They will have it, however, that he put aside this flesh in favor of another, and so became a god. But if apotheosis is the hallmark of divinity, why not rather Asclepias, Dionysus, or Herakles, whose stories are far more ancient? I have heard a Christian ridicule those in Crete who show tourists the tomb of Zeus, saying that these Cretans have no reason for doing what they do. It may be so; yet the Christians base their faith on one who rose from a tomb."[250]

Stephan Goranson notices that "Celsus attacked Christianity not only for philosophic reasons, but also because he was alarmed about social consequences of the spread of Christianity."[251] Celsus argued that the Christian theology and outlook was rashly uncivilised. "Their injunctions are like this. 'Let no one educated, no one wise, no one sensible draw near. For these abilities are thought by us to be evils.' But as for anyone ignorant, anyone stupid, anyone uneducated, anyone who is a child, let him come boldly? By the fact that they themselves admit that these people are worthy of their God, they show that they want and are able to convince only the foolish, dishonourable and stupid, and only slaves, women, and little children."[252] He further observed that the Christian arguments were frivolous, unconvincing and senseless. They could not be proven in the presence of the least educated person; they were mere claims with no rational basis and made sense only to the senseless, heedless and mindless. "In private houses also we see wool-workers, cobblers, laundry-workers, and the most illiterate and bucolic yokels, who would not dare to say anything at all in front of their elders and more intelligent masters. But whenever they get hold of children in private and some stupid women with them, they let out some astounding statements as, for example, that they must not pay any attention to their father and school-teachers, but must obey them; they say that these talk nonsense and have no understanding, and that in reality they neither know nor are able to do anything good, but are taken up with mere empty chatter. But they alone, they say, know the right way to live, and if the children would believe them, they would become happy and make their home happy as well."[253] The same enthusiasts are dumbfounded in the presence of the least educated. "And if just as they are speaking they see one of the school-teachers coming some intelligent person, or even the father himself the more cautious of them flee in all directions; but the more reckless urge the children on to rebel. They whisper to them that in the presence of their father and their schoolmasters they do not feel able to explain anything to the children, since they do not want to have anything to do with the silly and obtuse teachers who are totally corrupted and far gone in wickedness and who inflict punishment on the children. But, if they like, they should leave father and their schoolmasters, and go along with the women and little children who are their playfellows to the wool dressers shop, or to the cobblers or the washerwoman's shop, that they may learn perfection. And by saying this they persuade them."[254] Porphyry could not agree more. [255]

Celsus noticed an inherent contradiction in the Christian dogmas of sin and salvation; the Christians claimed that only the pure of heart can receive the grace of God essential to understanding and digesting the mysteries of incarnation, crucifixion and resurrection. Masses were unable to understand the mysteries due to their fallen nature, sins and tainted reason. Faith in God's grace and revelation was prerequisite to understanding the mysteries. It was not that one understood the mysteries and then believed in them, it was the other way around; one was asked to believe to understand. Likewise, one was required to have a pure heart to receive the grace, and then was told that their sins were forgiven as a result of their faith. The pure of heart were already moral people. Celsus argued that "those who summon people to the other mysteries make this preliminary proclamation: Whosoever has pure hands and a wise tongue. And again others say: Whosoever is pure from all defilement, and whose soul knows nothing of evil, and who has lived well and righteously. Such are the preliminary exhortations of those who promise purification from sins. But let us hear what folk these Christians call. Whosoever is a sinner, they say, whosoever is unwise, whosoever is a child, and, in a word, whosoever is a wretch, the kingdom of God will receive him. Do you not say that a sinner is he who is dishonest, a thief, a burglar, a poisoner, a sacrilegious fellow, and a grave-robber? What others would a robber invite and call?"[256]

Celsus argued that divine incarnation required change of status; the divine realms were infinite, while the natural realms were finite. A merger of the infinite with the finite demanded change of nature, status and composition, therefore incarnation made God changeable, which was not appropriate to divine majesty. "God is good and beautiful and happy, and exists in the most beautiful state. If then He comes down to men, He must undergo change, a change from good to bad, from beautiful to shameful, from happiness to misfortune, and from what is best to what is most wicked. Who would choose a change like this? It is the nature only of a mortal being to undergo change and remoulding, whereas the nature of an immortal being to remain the same without alteration. Accordingly, God could not be capable of undergoing this change."[257]

Furthermore, as mentioned previously in the "Original Sin or Original Forgiveness?" chapter, incarnation and crucifixion jeopardised divine justice and love. Porphyry stated that "if a father is wicked, then the sins of the father must not be attributed to his children."[258] Was God not able to control even the first of his creation?[259] He instead punished the innocent progeny of Adam for his shortcomings. But what kind of punishment? "When a man was angry with the Jews and killed them all, both young and old, and burned down their city, they were completely annihilated; yet (they say) when the supreme God was angry and wrathful he sent his son with threats-and suffered all kinds of indignities."[260] God's justice would not allow punishing billions of innocent children for the crime of their distant forefather. And why did Jesus come to only save the Jews living in one corner of the world, and not the entirety of humanity? "Furthermore, if God, like Zeus in the comic poet, woke up out of his long slumber and wanted to deliver the human race from evils, why on earth did he send this spirit that you mention into one corner?

He ought to have breathed into many bodies in the same way and sent them all over the world. The comic poet wrote that Zeus woke up and sent Hermes to the Athenians and Spartans because he wanted to raise a laugh in the theatre. Yet do you not think it is more ludicrous to make the Son of God to be sent to the Jews?"[261]

Celsus concluded his treatise by stating that "I bring these accusations against the Christians, and could bring many more (which I refrain from doing); I affirm that they insult God; they lead wicked men astray, offering them all sorts of false hopes and teaching them to hate what is truly good-saying that they should avoid the company of good men."[262] Christianity "is nothing more than a debased and nonsensical version of the myth of Deucalion, a fact I am sure they would not want to come to light. As it stands, the story is really one for the hearing of small children."[263] Some reasonable Christians resort to allegory to make some sense out of nonsensical scriptural material but cause more confusion than clarification, "among the Christians, embarrassed as they ought to be by such stories, take refuge in allegory!-as they are, all in all, very stupid fables. On the other hand, some of the allegories I have seen are even more ridiculous than the myths themselves, since they attempt to explain the fables by means of ideas that really do not fit into the context of the stories."[264]

Celsus also attacked Christian exclusivism, isolationism and a sense of undue exceptionalism. That was a recipe for anarchy and chaos. "If everyone were to adopt the Christian's attitude, moreover, there would be no rule of law: the legitimate authority would be abandoned; earthly things would return to chaos and come into the hands of the lawless and savage barbarians; and nothing further would be heard of Christian worship or of wisdom, anywhere in the world."[265]

One can see that the pagan Celsus was at a loss to reconcile Christian dogmas with human reason. He maintained that the pagan polytheism was a bit more rational than the Trinitarian monotheism of the Christians. The pagans did not worship the idol or the statue; they used it as a runway to take the spiritual flight to the One and Only Supreme God. The idols, pictures or statues were nothing but a material aid for the spiritual flight.[266] Christians, on the other hand, brought down God into the womb of a frail woman[267] and then crucified him so that they could attain salvation. Their tri-theism was worse than the pagan sense of monism, pantheism and monotheism. "The God of the philosophers need not resort to such preposterous designs."[268] The Christians had exalted a feeble man to the heights of divinity truly blurring the boundaries between God and humanity, "if the Christians worshiped only one God they might have reason on their side. But as a matter of fact they worship a man who appeared only recently. They do not consider what they are doing a breach of monotheism; rather, they think it perfectly consistent to worship the great God and to worship his servant as God. And their worship of this Jesus is the more outrageous because they refuse to listen to any talk about God, the father of all, unless it includes some reference to Jesus: Tell them that Jesus, the author of the Christian insurrection, was not his son, and they will not listen to you. And when they call him Son of God, they are not really paying homage to God, rather, they are attempting to exalt Jesus to the heights."[269] Celsus insisted that the Christians played a second fiddle to God Almighty, and in reality, exalted their Jesus to the forefront. Porphyry argued the same: "Such images-such as those of animals and those in temples-were erected by ancient peoples for the sake of evoking the memory of the god. They were created so that those who saw them would remember the god or would take time out to perform ritual cleansings, or to make easier the act of prayer, whereby each person supplicates the god for the particular things of which he has need."[270] He continued, saying: "Even if someone among the Greeks were silly enough to think that gods dwelled in statues, his idea would be more sensible than that of the man who believes that the Divine Being entered into the womb of the virginal Mary to become her unborn son-and then was born, swaddled, [hauled off] to the place of blood and gall, and all the rest of it."[271] Celsus also condemned Christian understanding of a powerful and rebellious Satan as a dualism. "What makes the Christians' message dangerous, Celsus writes, is not that they believe in one God, but that they deviate from monotheism by their 'blasphemous' belief in the devil. For all the 'impious errors' the Christians commit, Celsus says, they show their greatest ignorance in "making up a being opposed to God, and calling him 'devil,' or, in the Hebrew language, 'Satan.'" All such ideas, Celsus declares, are nothing but human inventions, sacrilegious even to repeat: "it is blasphemy [...] to say that the greatest God [...] has an adversary who constrains his capacity to do good." Celsus was outraged that the Christians, who claim to worship one God, "impiously divide the kingdom of God, creating a rebellion in it, as if there were opposing factions within the divine, including one that is hostile to God!'""[272]

Celsus demanded a rational and logical approach to religion and spirituality. His logical approach to religion and morality was not acceptable to the Church. The Christian craze for guarantees of eternal salvation had brought them to an intellectual *cul de sac*; they were in a logical quandary. Origen, perhaps the most logical among the Early Church Fathers, compiled a long and systematic rebuttal of Celsus's charges in his famous treatise *Contra Celsum*. In spite of a rational mind and philosophical disposition, expertise and the encyclopaedic nature of his knowledge and epistemological abilities, Origen could not avoid theological impasses. Origen's insistence upon the utter transcendence of God was a response to the penetrating attacks of Celsus but in vain. In the words of Grillmeier, "the hour had come for the birth of speculative theology, of theological reflection, of *theoligie savante*. The confession of Jesus Christ as the Son of God, the *novum* of Christian faith [...] demanded of Christian theology a twofold demonstration, first that it was compatible with Jewish monotheism, and secondly that it was different from pagan polytheism."[273] The task was an impossibility because the mutually exclusive categories defied rationalisation and reconciliation. Origen's derivative Christology, secondary divinity of Christ and refutations of the literal Church Trinitarian formulations casted him orthodoxy, landing him in the fold of heretics.

It has been a Christian problem, from the very beginning, that their concept of God was satisfactory neither to the Jewish monotheists nor to the pagan polytheists. The Christians assimilated many pagan ideas to make Christianity palatable to pagans but their struggle to maintain the unity of Godhead and plurality of persons landed them in a no man's land. Throughout Christian history they have suffered from the same dilemma of how to uphold Jesus's divinity while simultaneously maintaining his full humanity. There was no escape from contradictions; they have always tried to keep the secret in the box. Whenever the need arose, and figures like Origen tried to be more precise and less vague, they were condemned by the Church.

On the other hand, even pagan philosophers such as Celsus condemned Christianity as an absurd system of contradictory dogmas and anti-social ethos. Celsius accused Christians of claiming to follow an abstract, ahistorical and legendry King Jesus Christ while evading the authority of a historical Roman king and state laws, the source of their welfare and wellbeing. Origen responded to Celsus's allegations of sociopathy in the following words: "Celsus exhorts us also to accept public office in our country if it is necessary to do this for the sake of the preservation of the laws and of piety. But we know of the existence in each city of another sort of country, created by the Logos of God. And we call upon those who are competent to take office, who are sound in doctrine and life, to rule over the churches. We do not accept those who love power. But we put pressure on those who on account of their great humility are reluctant hastily to take upon themselves the common responsibility of the church of God. And those who rule us well are those who have had to be forced to take office, being constrained by the great King who, we are convinced, is the Son of God, the divine Logos. Even if it is power over God's country (I mean the Church) which is exercised by those who hold office well in the Church, we say that their rule is in accordance with God's prior authority, and they do not thereby defile the appointed laws."[274]

Later on Christianity changed its stance towards the Roman Empire. Emperor Constantine co-opted Christianity, and the Christians lent their support to the empire; it did not resolve their intellectual and rational dilemma, but gave them backing of the state. The state support enhanced their political and economic standings. Constantine donated lands and other monetary benefits to the Church; his decision to remove capital from Rome to Byzantine in 326-330 made the Roman Bishop virtual ruler of the Italian peninsula. Heather Campbell observes that "between the legalisation of Christianity by Constantine about 313 and the adoption of Christianity as the legal religion of Rome by the emperor Theodosius I in 380, Christian communities received immense donations of land, labour, and other gifts from emperors and wealthy converts. The Christian clergy, originally a body of community elders and managerial functionaries, gradually acquired sacramental authority and became aligned with the grades of the imperial civil service. Each *civitas* (community or city), an urban unit and its surrounding district, had its bishop (from the Latin *episcopus*, 'overseer'). Because there had been more Roman *civitates* in the Italian and provincial European areas, there were more and usually smaller dioceses in these regions than in the distant north and east."[275]

The Church authorities claimed that in reality, Constantine handed over the ruler ship of Latin West to the Church and left for the East to establish his authority there. Constantine, they argued, "so greatly exalted the Roman Church that he handed over the imperial insignia to Saint Sylvester, pope of that city, and withdrew to Byzantium and there established the seat of his realm. This is why the Church of Rome claims that the western realms are under its jurisdiction, on the ground that they had been transferred to it by Constantine."[276] This claim was refused by the temporal authorities, who argued that Constantine himself handed over the West to one of his sons and not to the Church.

Additionally, wealth and property came to the Church from multiple sources. The Church's wealth and property was an endowment and hence inalienable. "By law this was inalienable, and as time passed it increased greatly; at Rome it was soon enormous. Emperors financed magnificent buildings; Christians in general gave not only bread and wine for the Eucharist, wax and oil for lights, and food or money for the clergy and the poor, but treasures of plate and precious stones; and not only things but land. Land flowed in from gifts and legacies, including the clergy's private property; it came to be taken for granted that the livelihood of bishop and clergy, help for the poor, and upkeep of church buildings were paid for partly by income from land."[277]

It was under the auspices of Roman Empire that Christianity penetrated deep into distant areas of Europe. "By winning recognition as the religion of the state, it added a new basic factor of equality and unification to the imperial civilisation and at the same time reintroduced Middle Eastern and Hellenistic elements into the West. Organised within the framework of the empire, the church became a complementary body upholding the state. Moreover, during the period of the decline of secular culture, Christianity and the church were the sole forces to arouse fresh creative strength by assimilating the civilisation of the ancient world and transmitting it to the Middle Ages."[278]

Christianity reached its political climax during the reign of Justinian (482-565), who ruled the Byzantine Empire from 527 to 565: "Subjects of Justinian were left in little doubt that they lived in a Christian state."[279] The Church and State were completely fused - Peter Brown observes that "Christian preaching upheld the authority of the ruler. Christian prayers, publicly offered at every liturgy, secured the safety of the empire. The divinely ordained 'harmony' of Church and State, which Justinian had proclaimed in his legislation, was more than a rhetorical flourish. It grew from the ground up in 680 cities. Ecclesiastical and secular were inextricably mixed through the collaboration of the bishop and clergy with the local elites in order to handle the day-to-day business of government. The bishop was now a principal agent in the communication between the capital and the provinces. Imperial edicts on matters as thoroughly secular as the control of banditry would be received by the bishop and read out to the local council in the bishop's audience hall adjoining the Christian basilica. They would be posted on the walls of the church. In Gerasa (Jerash, Jordan), it was the bishop who built and ran the local jail."[280] The state supplied the Church with financial, administrative and political means to help it maintain peace, order and harmony. That is what "Severus, the patriarch of Antioch, told a local bishop in no uncertain terms in around 515: bishops were there to keep the cities going. '"It is the duty of bishops to cut short and to restrain the unregulated movements of the mob [...] and to set themselves to maintain good order in the cities and to watch over the peaceful manner of those who are fed by their hand.'"[281]

The Church anti-rational theology needed the iron fist of the emperors to subdue the opposition, and the emperors needed the Church to support their monarchial and dictatorial designs. They forged an alliance, and together ruled the masses through coercion and suppression. The divine right monarchy and salvation through the Church were the ideologies created to realise the allied goal.

Christianity and State

Like the multiplicity of the New Testament Christologies and Soteriologies, there are multiple exousiologies in the New Testament. Jesus's relationship with and attitude towards state, civil power structures and religious authority is complex. Some contemporary New Testament scholars argue that Jesus saw the state and authority as corrupt, ungodly, devilish and unwanted.[282] He resented the local Jewish and greater Roman authorities,[283] rebuked them, resisted them and was finally crucified by them as a rebel. "In [...] Jesus's face-to-face encounters with the political and religious authorities, we find irony, scorn, noncooperation, indifference, and sometimes accusation. Jesus was no guerrilla. He was an 'essential' disputer."[284] He came to usher a new era of spiritual kingdom where the true authority belonged to God, and not to Mammon or king. He also defied the power structures of his time in resurrection, sending a clear message of powerlessness to the so-called powerful authorities. Jesus despised the worldly authorities and had nothing to do with them. He was not a guerrilla, or violent rebel bent upon overthrowing the existent power structures, but a scornful activist who resented the notion of worldly authority in his humiliation and death. For instance, Jacques Ellul and John Howard Yoder argue that Jesus did not eliminate the corrupt power structures, but he broke their claims to sovereignty and for this reason was killed by them.[285] "Jesus was an enemy of power but that he treated it with disdain and did not accord it any authority. In every form he challenged it radically. He did not use violent methods to destroy it."[286] Ellul discusses Jesus's temptation in Matthew 4:8-9 and Luke 4:6-7 to demonstrate Jesus's rejection of the worldly kingdoms. "The reference in these texts, then, is to political power in general ("all the kingdoms of the world") and not just the Herod monarchy. And the extraordinary thing is that according to these texts all powers, all the power and glory of the kingdoms, all that has to do with politics and political authority, belongs to the devil. It has all been given to him and he gives it to whom he wills. Those who hold political power receive it from him and depend upon him."[287] The Synoptic Gospels make it clear that Jesus and his original disciples scorned the worldly authority as a satanic impulse. "We may thus say that among Jesus's immediate followers and in the first Christian generation political authorities - what we call the state - belonged to the devil and those who held power received it from him. We have to remember this when we study the trial of Jesus."[288] The experience of Jesus and his community with the Hasmonean and Herodian dynasties was bad. Jesus hated the division and destruction brought by the civil war and uprising. Therefore, "the first Christian generation was globally hostile to political power and regarded it as bad no matter what its orientation or constitutional structures."[289] This group of scholars sees the command "render unto Caesar" as something not positive but scornful and sarcastic.[290] The context of Mark 12:13 shows that the Pharisees were well aware of Jesus's hostility to Caesar.

The Book of Revelation substantiates such reading of the Synoptic; the book is totally anti-political authority.[291] The similitude of two beasts is telling: "It takes up a theme of the later prophets, who depicted the political powers of their time as beasts. The first beast comes up from the sea. This probably represents Rome, whose armies came by sea. It has a throne that is given to it by the dragon (chs. *12-13*). The dragon, anti-God, has given all authority to the beast. People worship it. They ask who can fight against it. It is given 'all authority and power over every tribe, every people, every tongue, and every nation' *(13:7)*. All who dwell on earth worship it. Political power could hardly [...] be more expressly described, for it is this power which has authority, which controls military force, and which compels adoration (i.e., absolute obedience). This beast is created by the dragon. We thus find the same relation [...] between political power and the *diabolos*. Confirmation of this idea that the beast is the state may be found in the fact that at the end of Revelation (ch. 18) great Babylon (i.e., Rome) is destroyed. The beast unites all the kings of earth to make war on God and is finally crushed and condemned after his main representative has first been destroyed."[292] The second beast is depicted as a mediator and facilitator of the first. The Roman Empire's military as well as civil machine perpetuated its hegemony. "The second beast rises out of the earth [...] It makes all the inhabitants of the earth worship the first beast [...] It seduces the inhabitants of the earth. It tells them to make an image of the first beast [...] It animates the image of the beast and speaks in its name [...] It causes all, small and great, rich and poor, free and slave, to receive a mark on their right hand or on their forehead, so that no one can buy or sell without having the mark of the beast *(13:12-17)* [...] an exact description of propaganda in association with the police."[293] The Book of Revelation is a strong rebuke of worldly powers embodied in the Roman Empire and its enthusiastic local cronies; it prophesize's their ultimate destruction. "What is promised is the pure and simple destruction of political government: Rome, to be sure, yet not Rome alone, but power and domination in every form. These things are specifically stated to be enemies of God. God judges political power, calling it the great harlot. We can expect from it neither justice, nor truth, nor any good only destruction."[294] That is why early Christianity was absolutely hostile to worldly authorities and those who supported them. Elaine Pagels observes that "to John's dismay, the majority of Jews, and later Jesus's Gentile followers as well, would continue to follow 'the beast' and to flirt with 'the whore' called Babylon, that is, with Rome and its culture. Instead of sharing John's vision of the imminent destruction of the world and preparing for its end, many other followers of Jesus sought ways to live in that world, negotiating compromises with Rome's absolutist government as they sought to sort out, in Jesus's words, what 'belongs to Caesar' and what 'to God.' Realizing this, John decided that he had to fight on two fronts at once: not only against the Romans but also against members of God's people who accommodated them and who, John suggests, became accomplices in evil."[295] Therefore, the early Christians completely disdained the Roman Empire and its Jewish and Christian supporters.

This anti-authority trend is modern and is usually espoused by the Christian left. It has resulted from the Holocaust and many other modern human disasters, such as World War II.[296] Many conscientious Christians cannot accept the fact that the governments and religious authorities that were responsible for such barbarism, and are still wreaking havoc on humanity, deserve their unqualified obedience. The liberal and socialist leaning readers of the New Testament have severely chastised the Church and its scripture for overcautious, imbalanced and dangerous stances regarding the state and order. These irritants have used several methodologies and tactics to rescue the New Testament from the grips of absolute submission and pacifism.[297] The "Resistant Readers" have used the intertextual, evaluative and interpolative moves to discard the affirmative readings of many New Testament passages bidding absolute submission especially the Pauline corpus.[298] N. T. Wright, Peter Oaks, P. Stuhlmacher, J. D. G. Dunn, J. A. Fitzmyer and many other modern New Testament scholars read a great deal of anti-imperialism in the Gospels in general and in the Pauline Epistles in particular.[299] Their resistant Jesus and liberation theology is at odd with the official Catholic and Protestant understandings of Jesus and Paul. Seyoon Kim, after thoroughly analysing the anti-imperialist's readings of Paul, concludes that "our examinations of 1 Thessalonians, Philippians, Romans, and 1 Corinthians in interaction with some representative 'anti-imperial' interpreters have confirmed that in those epistles there is no warning about the imperial cult and no message subversive to the Roman Empire."[300] Kim argues that Paul's theology of justification by faith and new kingdom has no political implications whatsoever. "Paul does not consider the church eventually replacing the Roman Empire in this world. Nor does he project any political, social, and economic program with which the King and Lord Jesus Christ will rule this world for more adequate justice, peace, freedom, and well-being than those of the Roman Empire."[301]

Kim notes a series of violations in the anti-imperial readings of Paul and dubs them arbitrary, artificial and contradictory. "Thus, there is no anti-imperial intent to be ascertained in the Pauline Epistles. All attempts to interpret them as containing such an intent [...] are imposing an anti-imperial reading on the epistles based merely on superficial parallelism of terms between Paul's gospel preaching and the Roman imperial ideology, while the texts themselves clearly use those terms to express other concerns. Several attempts have turned out to suffer from grave self-contradiction. Some have betrayed their arbitrariness or desperation by appealing to the device of 'coding,' that Paul coded his real anti-imperial message in politically innocuous language or in anti- Jewish polemic."[302] This evaluation is substantiated by the fact that the anti-authority vigilantes are neither cohesive nor united on the exact context and possible interpretations of these passages. There is no consensus whatsoever about what exactly these texts mean. The "Resistant Readers" agree on the end but are divided over the means to get there. Consequently there are multiple pictures of a revolutionary, resistant or anarchist Jesus that have emerged as a result of Christian disapprovals of modern warfare and calamities.[303] Bernard Lategan states that "the situation in which the reader finds him- or herself and the experiences (s) he has had with authorities and the exercise of power are the real shapers of our engagement with this passage (Romans 13:1-7)."[304] The problem is compounded by the fluid nature of the New Testament and at times opposing tendencies of its writers. This "embarrassing" diversity of pictures, ideals, concepts and interpretations of Jesus Christ has led some to conclude that "everyone who writes a life of Jesus sees his own face at the bottom of a deep well."[305] The modern anti-imperial and anti-state readings of Paul and Gospels stand in the face of Christian history and tradition.

Unqualified Submission to Authorities

In the past, over the centuries Jesus's trial and crucifixion were interpreted as a voluntary submission to the temporal authorities. Jesus presented himself to the Roman court and accepted the crucifixion as a token of submission to their authority. This was further substantiated by his statement reported by both Mark and Matthew in which he clearly differentiated between God and Caesar, the two realms of authority. "Then Jesus said to them, 'Give back to Caesar what is Caesar's and to God what is God's.'" (Mk. 12:17; Matt. 20:21) Jesus also told the persecuting Pilate that his authority was from God. The idea of unqualified submission to human authorities, even at time of persecution, was augmented by the Pauline treatment of the subject. The early Church, from Constantine's times onward, and both the Catholic and Protestants down the centuries have all accepted this interpretation of the New Testament as official and have always acted upon it. Therefore the doctrine of absolute submission to the worldly authorities is considered religious, official and orthodox.

The Pauline corpus is the most precise, pinpointed and unequivocal proponent of such a submission, and Pauline literature envisaged at least three fundamental declarations regarding the structures of earthly existence. Firstly, that it was God's plan to have rules and regulations to conduct human life on earth; the existence of norms and laws necessitated power networks and structures. Secondly, that these power structures had rebelled against God due to their fallen nature. They have absolutised their relative powers and assigned themselves a place far higher than what they deserved as finite creatures. Instead of encouraging people to submit to God, they forced them into their slavery. In spite of their fallen nature and rebellion, state institutions were still needed for social order and security. Therefore, God allowed them to function under his providence. Thirdly, submitting to them ensured a relatively smooth human discourse essential for life and society. Consequently, human authorities were an extension of divine providence sanctioned by God; submission to them in reality was a submission to God.[306] Paul was highly interested in peace and order, and provided religious undergirding for a stable society. In Roman 13:1-7 Paul clearly equated obedience to higher authorities with divine submission; to Paul, the social structures and institutions were not the aggregate or a sum total of those individuals who composed them. They were the whole while the individuals were the parts, and the whole was bigger than the parts. There was no self-indulgence or self-determination; it was absolutely predetermined by God. The whole was constructed and defined by the power higher than man, meaning God. Consequently, the political, social, moral and legal authorities were not manmade but rather God-made, and hence absolute submission to them was divinely ordained. The Epistle of Paul to Romans 13:1-7 clearly laid down the fundamentals of Paul's exousiology. "Every person must be subject to the governing authorities, for no authority exists except by God's permission. The existing authorities have been established by God, so that whoever resists the authorities opposes what God has established, and those who resist will bring judgment on themselves. For the authorities are not a terror to good conduct, but to bad. Would you like to live without being afraid of the authorities? Then do what is right, and you will receive their approval. For they are God's servants, working for your good. But if you do what is wrong, you should be afraid, for it is not without reason that they bear the sword. Indeed, they are God's servants to administer punishment to anyone who does wrong. Therefore, it is necessary for you to be acquiescent to the authorities, not only for the sake of God's punishment, but also for the sake of your own conscience. This is also why you pay taxes. For rulers are God's servants faithfully devoting themselves to their work. Pay everyone whatever you owe them—taxes to whom taxes are due, tolls to whom tolls are due, fear to whom fear is due, honour to whom honour is due." (Rom. 13:1-7)

This passage has the contours of divine right monarchy and absolutism cherished by the later Christian communities. It is crystal-clear in its aims and implications. It is not a prayer or supplication to honour a king; this is a complete theology of state and order, with its own established reasoning and parameters. E. Bammel notes that "taken together this amounts to a fairly extended theology of order which goes far beyond the acclamation or prayer for the king."[307] God is the sole authority in the world, and nothing happens without his permission and plans. Paul's doctrine of absolute predestination is at full play here. Kings, monarchs and magistrates are voluntarily appointed by God, and do not have the capacity to usurp authority from him; this is in conformity with the overall theology of the Bible. C. M. Stam states that such an absolute submission to worldly authorities is the overall scriptural axiom. "It is true that we are living under 'the dispensation of the grace of God' (Eph. 3:1-4), but we are also living under the dispensation of Human Government. This dispensation, instituted in Noah's day (Gen. 9:5, 6), has never been brought to a close. *God ordained human government,* holding man responsible for the life of his brother. The decree: 'Whoso sheddeth man's blood, by man shall his blood be shed' (Gen. 9:6), makes man responsible even to execute capital punishment and this, of course, includes all lesser penalties. More than this: the particular 'powers that be' are God-ordained. Generally God

117

gives nations exactly the kind of rulers they deserve. Some of these are wicked and immoral, 'the basest of men,' yet they are 'ordained of God' (Dan. 4:17) and responsible to Him. To the pagan and arrogant Nebuchadnezzar, Daniel said: 'the God of heaven hath given thee a kingdom, power, and strength, and glory'" (Dan. 2:37) [...] Our Lord said to Pilate: '[...] Thou couldst have no power at all against Me, except it were given thee from above [...]' (John 19:11)."[308]

Obeying the rulers is equal to obeying God, and resisting them is tantamount to resisting God. Christianity is no politics. "Paul does his utmost to combat all political inclinations among the Christians. He not only exhorts his readers in passing to be loyal to the state (as he does later; Phil. 1: 2 7), but he takes up and gives concrete reference to formulae of basic affirmation of the state, which could be understood by both Jews and Gentiles."[309] This is the duty of each soul. Civil and political revolt or unrest is divinely proscribed and punished. "Thus earthly rulers may be arbitrary or oppressive or corrupt, but God says: 'Be subject,' just as He directs the wife to be subject to her husband, the child to his parents, the servant to his master. Abuse of authority in any of these cases does not change the established order of God, for without such order all would be chaos. This is not the popular philosophy of the day, but it is the path to harmony and to man's greatest happiness. The affirmation that we are responsible to obey only 'reasonable' laws leaves the question of subjection open to each man's interpretation. This philosophy has driven many a nation to anarchy."[310]

It is evident that many believing Christians do not qualify their submission to the authorities with any qualification or reservation. Charles Hodge comments that "this is a very comprehensive proposition. All authority is of God. No man has any rightful power over other men, which is not derived from God. All human power is delegated and ministerial. This is true of parents, of magistrates, and of church officers. This, however, is not all the passage means. It not only asserts that all government...*authority*) is... derived from God, but that every magistrate is of God; that is, his authority is *jure divino*."[311] He further states that "We are to obey magistrates, because they derive their authority from God. Not only is human government a divine institution, but the form in which that government exists, and the persons by whom its functions are exercised, are determined by his providence. All magistrates of whatever grade are to be regarded as acting by divine appointment; not that God designates the individuals, but it being his will that there should be magistrates, every person, who is in point of fact clothed with authority, is to be regarded as having a claim to obedience, founded on the will of God."[312]

The Hierarchical Universe

God has created a hierarchical universe. There are various levels of authority and submission, and they must all be obeyed. "In like manner, the authority of parents over their children, of husbands over their wives, of masters over their servants, is of God's ordination. There is no limitation to the injunction in this verse, so far as the objects of obedience are concerned, although there is as to the extent of the obedience itself. That is, we are to obey all that is in actual authority over us, whether their authority be legitimate or usurped, whether they are just or unjust. The actual reigning emperor was to be obeyed by the Roman Christians, whatever they might think as to his title to the sceptre."[313] There is only one exception; there is no obedience due to the worldly authorities if they require idol worship. "But if he transcended his authority, and required them to worship idols, they were to obey God rather than man. This is the limitation to all human authority. Whenever obedience to man is inconsistent with obedience to God, then disobedience becomes a duty."[314]

God has established the political power structure to reward the good and punish the evil. "In Verses 3, 4 the apostle makes an important statement that is true of law enforcement in general, whether under a dictatorship or a democracy. Rulers, he says, are not a terror to good works, but to evil. They seldom bother the law abiding citizen, but the law-breaker must always be looking over his shoulder. Thus, he continues, if you do not wish to be afraid, do what is good, but if you do what is evil '*be* afraid,' for he does not carry 'the sword' in vain. Indeed, 'he is *the minister of God*,' all unwittingly, 'a revenger to execute wrath upon him that doeth evil' (Ver. 4). Do not forget [...] that under God you can sleep restfully at night because of the police force that God has ordained. Even in this day of political and social upheaval, as evidently in Paul's day, these basic observations are true."[315] Submission to all law enforcement agencies is submission to God.

Civil authorities have a religious role in implementing God's plan for peace, order and security. God is the creator of an orderly cosmos.

The political and civil authorities are a prototype of the divine realms in creating order in the temporal society. To participate in society building activities is a must for believers. "Christians are bound not only to be obedient to those in authority, but also to perform all social and relative duties."[316] Therefore, the authorities must not be obeyed only to avoid punishment but as a willing submission to God's bigger plans, for the sake of one's conscience. "we should be subject to government, not only for fear of wrath but 'for conscience' sake' (Ver. 5), i.e., out of obedience to God."[317] Paying taxes is an expression and recognition of the civil authorities' divine prerogative. Therefore, the authorities must not be despised but rather respected as God's servants. "Those who, in our day, complain of corrupt government and assume the prerogative to decide whether or not they should pay taxes should reflect that Paul lived under the wicked Nero and his corrupt administration and *he* bids us to pay our taxes (Vers. 6, 7), and our Lord, also living under pagan Rome, taught His disciples to pay their taxes (Matt. 22:16-21; 17:24-27). This is *God's Word* on the matter. God is not a God of confusion, allowing everyone to do what is right in his own eyes; He is a God of order, and under the present conditions, considering man's fallen state, it is best that the masses 'be subject unto the higher powers,' and this responsibility devolves especially upon God's own people."[318]

The above discussed Pauline passage is generic, universal and unqualified. Any qualification, whether spiritual or temporal, will be arbitrary and artificial. It does not differentiate between good and bad, Christian or non-Christian, monarchial or democratic, consultative or dictatorial power structures; it demands and encourages an absolute submission to the higher authorities whosoever they are, just because the authorities' power are bestowed by God. "It is clear that this passage (vers. 1, 2) is applicable to men living under every form of government, monarchical, aristocratical, or democratical, in all their various modifications. Those who are in authority are to be obeyed within their sphere, no matter how or by whom appointed. It is [...] the powers *that be*, the *de facto* government, that is to be regarded as, for the time being, ordained of God. It was to Paul a matter of little importance whether the Roman emperor was appointed by the senate, the army, or the people; whether the assumption of the imperial authority by Caesar was just or unjust, or whether his successors had a legitimate claim to the throne or not. It was his object to lay down the simple principle, that magistrates are to be obeyed."[319] Any relativity, qualification or restriction on their power will be superfluous. This passage is a coherent, well-crafted and well-organised argument about a single subject: "the need for submission to governing authorities."[320]

Paul initially had preached the transitory nature of this world and coming of a new spiritual era, a new creation and a new age. We have discussed above the intentional or unintentional fanatic and enthusiastic implications of Paul's theology of grace and kingdom. Paul wanted to stifle such an enthusiasm and extremism by insisting upon obedience and congeniality to existing power systems and institutions, such as the government.[321] The inauguration of a new age of grace and salvation does not necessitate rebellion against existing modes of authority; spiritual arrogance must not lead to anarchy, revolt and civil disobedience. Charles Hodge expands upon the historical and contextual reasons for Paul's insistence upon unqualified submission. "Obedience is not enjoined on the ground of the personal merit of those in authority, but on the ground of their official station. There was peculiar necessity, during the apostolic age, for inculcating the duty of obedience to civil magistrates. This necessity arose in part from the fact that a large portion of the converts to Christianity had been Jews, and were peculiarly indisposed to submit to the heathen authorities. This indisposition (as far as it was peculiar) arose from the prevailing impression among them, that this subjection was unlawful, or at least highly derogatory to their character as the people of God, who had so long lived under a theocracy. In Deuteronomy 17:15 it is said, 'Thou shalt in any wise set *him* king over thee, whom the Lord thy God shall choose; *one* from among thy brethren shalt thou set king over thee; thou mayest not set a stranger over thee, which *is* not thy brother.'"[322] The early Jewish Christian community was always prone to agitation due to the Old Testament theology and existing political reasons. "It was a question, therefore, constantly agitated among them, 'Is it lawful to pay tribute unto Caesar, or not?'" This was a question which the great majority were at least secretly inclined to answer in the negative. Another source of the restlessness of the Jews under a foreign yoke, was the idea which they entertained of the nature of the Messiah's kingdom. As they expected a temporal Prince, whose kingdom should be of this world, they were ready to rise in rebellion at the call of every one who cried, "I am Christ." The history of the Jews at this period shows how great was the effect produced by these and similar causes on their feelings towards the Roman government. They were continually breaking out into tumults, which led to their expulsion from Rome, in 68 and, finally, to the utter destruction of Jerusalem. It is therefore not a matter of surprise, that converts from among such a people should need the injunction, "Be subject to the higher powers."[323] The early Christians' spiritual and political experiences and resultant disdain for the political authorities added to the fuel of Jewishness. "Besides the effect of their previous opinions and feelings, there is something in the character of Christianity itself, and in the incidental results of the excitement which it occasions, to account for the repugnance of many of the early Christians to submit to their civil rulers. They wrested, no doubt, the doctrine of Christian liberty, as they did other doctrines, to suit their own inclinations. This result, however, is to be attributed not to religion, but to the improper feelings of those into whose minds the form of truth, without its full power, had been received."[324] Due to these multiple reasons Paul insisted that the existing power structures were divinely ordained and must be conformed to. They embodied the will of God by rewarding goodness and punishing evil.[325] This was an extension of Jesus's command of rendering unto Caesar what was due to Caesar. "Thus when Paul directs his Christian readers to render rulers their dues - 'taxes to whom taxes are due, revenue to whom revenue is due' - he may not be quoting, or even recalling, Jesus's words but he certainly reproduces their intention, albeit in a less inflammable atmosphere."[326]

To Paul, God stood behind these authorities. Therefore their obedience was obedience to God. Paul used both positive and negative methods and appeals to stress the point of absolute submission. "This is an obvious inference from the doctrine of the preceding verse. If it is the will of God that there should be civil government, and persons appointed to exercise authority over others, it is plain that to resist such persons in the exercise of their lawful authority is an act of disobedience to God."[327] Hodge notices that "there is a ground, therefore, in the very nature of their office, why they should not be resisted."[328] One might think that the rulers have attained authority through power struggle and violence. But in reality they came through the agency of God. They were useful, benevolent and needed, and hence divinely ordained and appointed. "'Government is a benevolent institution of God, designed for the benefit of men; and, therefore, should be respected and obeyed."[329] The disobedience of government would bring temporal as well as eschatological punishment.[330] Rulers had an appointed role of maintaining order, both a positive and negative role. God punished evildoers through the punitive agency of rulers; it was surmised that temporal laws were in a sense extension of divine moral laws.[331] That is why conscientious obedience to them was required. Moo explains that "conscience" refers to "believer's knowledge of God's will and purpose."[332] Hodge explains that "subjection to magistrates is not only a civil duty enforced by penal statutes, but also a religious duty, and part of our obedience to God. *For wrath, i.e.* from fear of punishment. *For conscience' sake, i.e.,* out of regard to God, from conscientious motives. In like manner, Paul enforces all relative and social duties on religious grounds. Children are to obey their parents, because it is right in the sight of God; and servants are to be obedient to their masters, as unto Christ, doing the will of God from the heart."[333]

Therefore, political and civil submission should be done not as a practical expediency but as an insight into God's providential ordering of history. Paying taxes is also part of this conscientious attitude. The rulers are servants of God, and their service is ultimately sacred.[334] This demand of Paul is identical to Jesus's command of rendering unto Caesar what belongs to Caesar. The plain and simple meaning of the passage is that Christians are always required to do whatever their governmental leaders tell them to do no matter what the situation is.[335]

Paul's Legacy of Pacifism

M. Borg and J. D. Crossan, after analysing the context of the epistle, argue that Paul made an extremely wrong judgment and set off a dangerous and devastating trend to ward off the potentials of Christian violence against the Roman authorities. "We can now see what is Paul's concern in 13:1–7 when it is replaced within its fuller context of 12:14–13:10. It is, of course, about taxes and revenues demanded by Rome but precisely about refusing them violently, about the specter of violent tax revolts among Christians. It is something that appalls him so much that—in rather a rhetorical panic—he makes some very unwise and unqualified statements with which to ward off that possibility."[336] Paul left a legacy of absolute pessimism, pacifism and abuse of powers; the individual and his freedom were dissolved in the absolutist societal whole. It allowed tyrants to manipulate and suppress their subjects in the name of religion, spirituality and morality. Such an abuse was a wrong expression and manifestation of divine predestination. The loving God did not determine that infinite numbers of people arbitrarily suffer due to his providence. For centuries countless communities' freedoms, rights and dignities were compromised in the name of divine prerogatives. The demand of unqualified submission to the rulers as expressions of divine submission was perhaps the rashest legacy of Paul for coming generations, "insofar as this could and would be taken as a general and unqualified principle, it is one of the most imprudent passages in all of Paul's letters. Looking back on how it has been used throughout Christian history, Paul might surely wish he had never written it."[337] E. Bammel encourages sidelining Paul's theology of submission, "whatever its biblical theological significance may be and however great the momentum it gathered in church history has been, in an account of the Pauline view of the state Romans 13 must be given its place rather in a side aisle than in the nave."[338] Paul in reality Hellenised Christianity; the idea of an absolute submission even to the persecuting evil dictators was a paganisation of Christianity.

In addition to the Pauline Epistles, absolute submission to worldly authorities seems to be one dominant trend in the New Testament writings. 1 Peter 2:13-17 stresses the same absolute submission in the following manner: "For the Lord's sake submit yourselves to every human authority: whether to the king as supreme, or to governors who are sent by him to punish those who do wrong and to praise those who do right. For it is God's will that by doing right you should silence the ignorant talk of foolish people. Live like free people, and do not use your freedom as an excuse for doing evil. Instead, be God's servants. Honour everyone. Keep on loving the community of believers, fearing God, and honouring the king." (1 Peter 2:13-17)

There is a consensus among the New Testament exegetes that the passage is almost identical to Romans 13:1-7 in exhorting total submission to the authorities. The only difference is that it lays more emphasis upon the practical political implications of disobedience rather than the positive command of obeying the authorities for their God given right. The famous New Testament commentator C. J. Ellicott explains the passage in the following self-explaining words: "Second prudential rule, subordination. Literally, to every human creation, i.e., to every office or authority which men have established. It is not only to ordinances of directly Divine institution that we are to submit. Mind that he does not say we are to submit to every law that men may pass. This passage is most directly modelled on Romans 13:1, et seq., where the reason assigned for submission is the same as that in John 19:11, viz., that ultimately the authority proceeds from God Himself. Here, however, the thought is quite different. They are to submit, but not because of the original source from which the authority flows, but because of the practical consequences of not submitting. It must be done 'for the Lord's' (i.e., Jesus Christ's) 'sake,' i.e., in order not to bring discredit upon His teaching, and persecution upon His Church. This difference of treatment, in the midst of so much resemblance, shows that at the date of St. Peter's letter there was much more immediate cause for laying stress on political subordination. St. Paul, writing to the Roman Church, urges submission to Claudius, because the Roman Jews (among whom the Christians were reckoned) were often in trouble and expelled from the city of Rome (Acts 18:2); St. Peter, writing in all probability from the Roman Church, urges submission to Nero and the provincial governors because 'ignorant and foolish men' were beginning to misrepresent the Christian Church as a kind of Internationalist or Socialist conspiracy."[339] Reinhard Feldmeier observes that "subordination is commanded in view of relations with those of higher status upon whom the Christians are dependent—either the Christian community in its totality (upon the state authorities) or as members of a societal status group (as slaves upon their masters, as wives upon their husbands)—in order to minimize areas of friction."[340]

Like Romans 13, 1 Peter is also criticised for its demand of unqualified submission to the authorities. Many New Testament scholars, especially the Germans, consider such an attitude of pacifism a perversion of the original message of Jesus and his disciples. "This textual unit is often made into a reproach for 1 Peter. It is accused of falling away from the freeing message of Jesus; one sees in it the making of religion to an instrument for the stabilisation of existing hierarchies. Balch sees here the liberation theology of Exodus and of the 'early rural Palestinian Jesus movement' perverted into repression: 'Pointedly phrased, whereas the commands in the Torah protect slaves, the NT exhortations are repressive, and this reflects the cultural change from the Mosaic story of salvation to Greek politics.' Even such a level-headed exegete as Eduard Schweizer believes one must detect here the beginning of the paganisation of Christianity."[341] The left-leaning reactionaries try to import their contemporary norms and values into the culture of Peter and Paul, to eradicate the theological foundations of modern Christian pacifism. Their progressiveness is ill-disposed to dislodge either the historical authenticity of the epistles or religious authority of both Paul and Peter. For centuries, the Church had accepted this trend as authentic, orthodox and exemplary to avoid persecution, tumult and chaos; Peter laid the foundation for such an attitude. "The rulers of the Roman Empire with the Caesar at the top are to be obeyed, but 'for the sake of the Lord.' With respect to this Lord, however, remarkably the point of reference is not one of a Lordship of Christ paralleling an earthly rule, but of his unjust suffering that is explained in 2:21ff. 'Following his footsteps' (2:21) is necessary to do good even within societal power structures under which Christians suffer. To the degree that this obedience is based upon the reference to Christ it also thereby implicitly is limited."[342] Peter does not explain away the limits of obedience to prevent misunderstanding of Christian freedom and to avoid possibilities of threatening conflicts. He does put a positive face to the ordering function of the state as divinely ordained. It is evident that the radical stance of Revelation had not caught on by the time of 1 Peter, and the writer was predisposed to state and orderly society. "Subordination under the authority of the state was already presented in 2:13 as a consequence of the connection to the Lord and thereby an active decision. This is here now yet again stated more precisely by means of the insertion of the concept of freedom, which does not play a role for Paul in the context of Romans 13:1-7. First Peter stresses that recognition of the state is not a 'knuckling under' to the superior force that contradicts Christian freedom; rather the freedom of the believers proves itself in that, in obedience to God, it fits in with the state power structure as being in its essential nature a good order."[343] Peter seems to be reacting to the pagan allegations that the Christians were a fifth column in the Roman Empire, as seen above in the case of Celsus; He wants to pacify the Christian community of Rome so as to avoid the allegations of disloyalty and possibilities of persecution. His passage is a little vague but equally emphatic about the absolute submission to the rulers.

In view of the above quoted New Testament texts and its overall orientation, S. Kim argues that there is nothing anti-imperial in the Pauline or other New Testament writings. The reception history and

Church use of these texts "runs decidedly against an attempt to read a counter-imperial message out of them."[344] Consequently, the early Christian community and Church voluntarily submitted to the Roman Empire and participated in its wellbeing. Adolph Harnack had shown that the early Church definitely showed its loyalty and submission to the Roman Empire by "instituting prayer for the emperor and the state as a firm element in their worship service, as well as by obeying the governing authorities and paying taxes punctually."[345]

Clement of Rome's prayer in his epistle to the Corinthians (95 AD) exemplifies such a loyal and submissive attitude. "[...] while we render obedience to your almighty and most excellent name, and to our rulers and governors on earth. You, Master, have given them the power of sovereignty through your majestic and inexpressible might, so that we, acknowledging the glory and honour which you have given them, may be subject to them, resisting your will in nothing. Grant to them, Lord, health, peace, harmony, and stability, that they may blamelessly administer the government which you have given them. For you, heavenly Master, King of the ages, give to the sons of men glory and honour and authority over those upon the earth. Lord, direct their plans according to what is good and pleasing in your sight, so that by devoutly administering in peace and gentleness the authority which you have given them they may experience your mercy."[346]

Tertullian (160-220 AD) is another example of expressed loyalty and submission to the Roman rulers. In spite of refusing to worship the Caesar as God, Tertullian assures them Christian submission and loyalty as second only to God. "For we, on behalf of the safety of the Emperors invoke the eternal God, the true God, the living God, whom the Emperors themselves prefer to have propitious to them beyond all other gods. They know who has given them the empire they know, as men, who has given them life; they feel that He is God alone, in whose power and no other's they are, second to whom they stand, after whom they come first, before all gods and above all gods."[347] Tertullian tows the traditional Christian line of divine providence and divine right monarchy, and considers Caesar second only to God Almighty. In *Apology 33* he states that "we must needs respect him as the chosen of our Lord. So I have a right to say, Caesar is more ours than yours, appointed as he is by our God. He is mine; and so I do more for his safety, not only because I seek it from Him only who can give it; or because I who ask am one who deserve to receive; but also because I set the majesty of Caesar below God and the more commend him to God to Whom alone I subordinate him."[348] Tertullian quotes scriptures to authenticate his submission to and supplications for the emperor. He "specifically refers to the exhortation in 1 Tim 2:1-2, clearly expressing the fear that if the empire is shaken, Christians would also be caught up in the disaster *(Apology* 31). Then, alluding to 2 Thess 2:6-8, he suggests that Christians need to pray 'for the emperors, and for the whole estate of the Empire and the interests of Rome,' because the Roman Empire is the force that delays the onset of 'the great force which threatens the whole world, the end of the age itself with its menace of hideous suffering' *(Apology* 32). Finally, echoing Jesus's teaching in the Sermon on the Mount [...] Paul's teaching in Rom 12:14-21; 1 Cor 4:8-13, Tertullian argues that Christians should not be treated as enemies of Rome, as they are benevolent people who are forbidden to wish anybody evil or practice retaliation, but instead taught to love their enemies, so that they persevere even with the most savage persecutions without engaging in rebellion, passive or active."[349]

The early Christians did not find any anti-state or anti-empire messages in the New Testament writings. They were masters of Greek language and well aware of the persecuting society of their time; had there been any anti-imperial or anti-monarchial teaching in the New Testament, it would have not escaped them. The New Testament, especially the Pauline literature, was in reality staunchly pro-imperialist. The pro-monarchial epoch reached its climax in the fourth century, when the Church practically applied its principles to Constantine's empire. Constantine was declared the ideal emperor through whom God delivered his suffering people and exalted them to the helms of worldly affairs. The concept of absolute submission was practically implemented during Constantine's time, without any constraints of faith or fears of persecution. Christians were a voluntary and welcomed submission; it was a reflection of their understanding of the heavenly kingdom. In 336, Eusebius of Caesarea in his speech at the thirtieth anniversary of Constantine's reign hailed Constantine in the following flattering words: "The only- begotten Logos of God reigns as co- ruler with His Father from ages which have no beginning to infinite ages which have no end. Likewise His friend [Constantine], who derives the source of imperial authority from above and is strong in the power of his divine calling, rules the empire of the world for a long period of years. And as the Preserver of the universe orders the heavens and earth and the celestial kingdom according to His Father's will, so His friend, by leading those whom he rules on earth to the only- begotten Logos and Saviour renders them fit subjects of His kingdom. Again, He who is the common Saviour of mankind, by His invisible and divine power, drives away those rebellious spirits which once flew through the earth's air and fastened on men's souls, like the good shepherd drives savage beasts far away from his flock. And likewise His friend, armed against his enemies with standards from Him above, subdues and chastens the open adversaries of the truth by the law of combat. He who is the pre- existent Logos, the Preserver of all things, imparts to His disciples the seeds of true wisdom and salvation, and at once enlightens and gives them understanding in the knowledge of His Father's kingdom. His friend, acting like an interpreter of the Logos of God, seeks to recall the whole human race to the knowledge of God, proclaiming clearly so that all might hear and declaring with a powerful voice the laws of truth and godliness to all who dwell on the earth. The universal Saviour opens wide the heavenly gates of His Father's kingdom to those whose course leads there when they depart this world. The other, emulating the divine example, has purged his earthly dominion of every stain of impious error, and invites holy and pious worshippers within his imperial mansions."[350]

Eusebius and Constantine

Eusebius clearly equated Constantine with the heavenly Christ and laid down the Christian foundations for divine right monarchy by depicting Constantine's powers as divinely ordained. This was in line with the Pauline treatment of the subject as discussed earlier. David M. Gwynn observes that "Eusebius' rhetoric may be exaggerated, but his presentation of Constantine as the ideal Christian ruler was hugely influential on medieval and Byzantine concepts of the relationship of Church and State and the divine right of kings."[351] Here in Eusebius the two traditions, the prophetic and Hellenistic, merged to realise the divine mission of heavenly kingdom on Earth, a historical manifestation of Christian eschatology. The Roman emperor had put on the divine garment to serve as the divine vicegerent upon the earth. R. A. Markus observes that "Eusebius, for instance, had not only utilised the prophetic interpretation of the scriptures to endow Constantine with a divine mission in history; he also mobilised Hellenistic ideas of kingship to create an image of the Christian ruler as the reflection and counterpart in the visible world of God's invisible *logos*. The emperor became an intermediary between the terrestrial empire and the heavenly kingdom, the representative and agent of the latter placed at the head of the former. In his own person, the ruler was the point at which human affairs were drawn into the cosmic order. Similar ideas underlay conceptions of kingship such as those of Themistius and Synesius. They became especially influential in Constantinople. Eusebius only gave Christian form to widely current ideas."[352]

The Roman idea of man as the crown of God's creation and the king being the crown of humanity, and hence possessing more divinity, was implied by Eusebius to create an amalgamation of Roman and Christian ideas, to be emulated by coming Christian generations. This neo-Platonic philosophy of cosmic order was later adopted and expanded upon by St. Augustine. In the early part of his life Augustine believed that "society is a reflection of a higher, intelligible order of reality. More often, and more clearly, Augustine asserts that social arrangements have their due place in an overriding order which embraces them. 'What is more horrible than the public executioner? Yet he has a necessary place in the legal system, and he is part of the order of a well-governed society.'"[353] The order in human society is part of the cosmic harmony and hence an important step towards reconciling God with humanity. "Order, for Augustine, is 'that which, if we follow it in our lives, will lead us to God.' Being part of the all-embracing order in the world, human society is one of the stages of man's advance towards God. Hence the importance of ensuring that the social order really does conform to the divinely established order of the universe."[354]Augustine advocated a staunch predestination where human free will was absolutely dissolved to emphasise an overarching divine omnipotence.[355] He maintained that "in denying the power of the will he was only repeating what Paul had said long before ('"I do not do what I will, but I do the very thing I hate. [...] I can will what is right, but I cannot do it'"; see Romans 7:15-25)."[356] For him every minute detail of the cosmic order was designed, planned and executed by God. Augustine held that the human society was a reflection of Divine realms. The celestial realms were orderly, and the terrestrial realms had to conform to the celestial order. Unfortunately, due to fallen nature and original sin, man's capacities were hampered; man suffered from caprices, greed and selfishness, causing imbalance and disorder in society. God, to maintain justice and order, had appointed rulers to realize a relative order in the world. "The state operates in this world, and most of its citizens are (and always will be) those sinful men [...] In any earthly state a small number of the citizens may be men who have been converted by God's grace; since these men have died and been born anew, their loves, their aspirations, and their behaviour are completely different from those of the great mass of the unredeemed. However, as long as this world lasts, there will never be a society or a state made up solely or even predominantly of the saved. Since the two cities are inextricably bound together until the Last Judgment, every earthly state will be composed primarily of sinners, with perhaps a scattering of saints living in their midst. The political and legal system must, therefore, be set up and operated on the assumption that it is dealing with fallen men."[357] He insisted that "the whole human race, including the redeemed, remains wholly incapable of self-government [...] Recalling in the *Confessions* his own experience, Augustine instinctively identifies the question of self-government with rational control over sexual impulses."[358] He argued that he was knocked off by his libido at the age of sixteen, and his friends were amazed at his enslavement; the sexual impulses did not submit to his rational self but totally defied it. "The single desire that dominated my search for delight was simply to love and to be loved. But no restraint was imposed by the exchange of mind with mind, which marks the brightly lit pathway of friendship. Clouds of muddy carnal concupiscence filled the air. The bubbling impulses of puberty befogged and obscured my heart so that it could not see the difference between love's serenity and lust's darkness. Confusion of the two things boiled within me. It seized hold of my youthful weakness sweeping me through the precipitous rocks of desire to submerge me in a whirlpool of vice."[359] This was due to Adam's fall; being the son of Adam, man had no choice but to submit to his lust and libido. Likewise, the fallen man was under the yoke of original sin incapable of rational decisions, self-control and self-government. Augustine elaborated upon this powerlessness through the struggles he had with his own conflicting will. "I sighed after such freedom, but was bound not by an iron imposed by anyone else but by the iron of my own choice. The enemy had a grip on my will and so made a chain for me to hold me a prisoner. The consequence of a distorted will is passion. By servitude to passion, habit is formed, and habit to which there is no resistance becomes necessity. By these links, as it were, connected one to another (hence my term a chain), a harsh bondage held me under restraint. The new will, which was beginning to be within me a will to serve you freely and to enjoy you, God, the only sure source of pleasure, was not yet strong enough to conquer my older will, which had the strength of old habit. So my two wills, one old, the other new, one carnal, the other spiritual, were in conflict with one another, and their discord robbed my soul of all concentration."[360] Augustine completely denied human free will, and placed the entire blame of hedonism and conflict upon the sin of Adam. He insisted that Adam was initially granted freedom in the Garden but he misused it, and this freedom landed him in the wilderness of earthly life, marked by subjugation to carnal desires. Adam had no freedom after the first abuse of his free will; currently all children of Adam suffer from bondage and slavery to their caprice and lust. "In my own case, as I deliberated about serving my Lord God (Jer. 30: 9) which I had long been disposed to do, the self which willed to serve was identical with the self which was unwilling. It was neither wholly willing nor wholly unwilling. So I was in conflict with myself and was dissociated from myself. The dissociation came about against my will. Yet this was not a manifestation of the nature of an alien mind but the punishment suffered in my own mind. And so it was 'not I' that brought this about 'but sin which dwelt in me (Rom. 7: 17, 20), sin resulting from the punishment of a more freely chosen sin, because I was a son of Adam."[361]

The early Church Fathers had advocated that human beings were born with free will; man made his own decisions based upon his rational capacities, and mastering one's own will was considered the best way to attain morality. Augustine turned that capacity upside down. Elaine Pagels noted that "the desire to master one's will, far from expressing what Origen, Clement, and Chrysostom consider the true nature of rational beings, becomes for Augustine the great and fatal temptation: 'The fruit of the tree of knowledge of good and evil is personal control over one's own will' (proprium voluntatis arbitrium)."[362] Therefore, both rationality and morality were missing in man due to the original sin; man was at war with himself, and the internal anxiety, conflict and struggle manifested itself into societal conflict. Consequently, all men, whether Christians, believers or non-believers, were at a loss to control themselves in any given social set up. They were prone to internal strife and in fighting, and could never stop disrupting the order, peace and stability of society, hence they needed an external powerful body such as the government to control the mayhem. Pagels observed that "Augustine concludes that humankind has wholly lost its original capacity for self-government. Augustine draws so drastic a picture of the effects of Adam's sin that he embraces human government, even when tyrannical, as the indispensable defense against the forces sin has unleashed in human nature. His analysis of internal conflict, indeed, leads directly into his view of social conflict in general. The war within us drives us into war with one another — and no one, pagan or Christian, remains exempt. So, he explains, 'while a good man is progressing to perfection, one part of him can be at war with another of his parts; hence, two good men can be at war with one another.'"[363] Augustine insisted upon a strong Church and a powerful government with full-fledged executive authority; they served as the physicians to the sick society. A physician was not to worry about the likes and the dislikes of the patient, but to do what was best for him. Likewise, the Church and state should not worry about public opinion but implement the imposing discipline for the wellbeing of the given society. "Augustine tends, consequently, to discount the patients' opinions. It is the physician's responsibility not only to administer to sick and suffering humanity the life-giving medication of the sacraments, but also to carry out, when necessary, disciplinary procedures as a kind of surgery."[364] Michael Gaddis noted that "Augustine frequently justified religious coercion with reference to the "good physician" who must inflict pain in order to save the patient. In a sermon of 404 we find a metaphor that is not just medical but specifically ophthalmological: "Imagine a man, blinded by a certain darkness [...] The doctor [says to him]: 'I am about to apply some stronger eye-salves, which will wash away the darkness from you, and from their harshness you will feel some pain. But it is necessary for you to bear this health-giving pain *[dolorem salubrem]* patiently, and not to push away my hands anxious and unable to bear the discomfort [...] I warn you that you will suffer something troublesome together with the increase of illumination.'"[365]

Augustine and Theology of Governance

Unlike his predecessors, Augustine promulgated a theology of essential governance. The Church Fathers, such as John Chrysostom, had required the state to direct the pagans while leaving the believing Christians to their voluntary high moral standards. To Chrysostom, Christians needed the Church's spiritual guidance and not the strict supervision of the state. Even the state itself needed the spiritual supervision and guidance of the Church. Augustine modified that stance, requiring both the Christians and pagans to accept the yoke of the state; he espoused a powerful centralized government with absolute executive powers even over the bishops. This change of theological outlook was made possible by the political milieu of Augustine. The emperors by his times were no more anti-Christians persecuting the believers, but mostly the children of Mother Church, lending their powers and armies to implement the Church doctrines, creeds and policies. "Let us consider first how the conflicting views of Chrysostom and Augustine might sound to their contemporaries. By the beginning of the fifth century Catholic Christians lived as subjects of an empire they could no longer consider alien, much less wholly evil. Having repudiated the patronage of the traditional gods some two generations earlier, the emperors now sometimes used military force to help stamp out pagan worship. Furthermore, the two sons of Theodosius the Great, reigning since his death in 395 as emperors of East and West, continued their father's policy of withdrawing patronage from Arian Christians and placing themselves wholly in alliance with the Catholic bishops and clergy. An earlier generation of Christian bishops, including Eusebius of Caesarea, deeply impressed by the events they had witnessed and convinced that they lived at a turning point in history, had hailed Constantine and his successors as God's chosen rulers."[366] Augustine saw an ushering of a new era, the realisation of the promised divine kingdom upon earth. The pious emperor stood at the top of this kingdom with absolute legislative and executive powers. There was no division of power between the Church and state; the state was all in all, because the state served the purposes of the Church. Augustine laid down the theological foundations for an absolute divine right monarchy. "The mature Augustine offers a theology of politics far more complex and compelling than any of its rivals. Chrysostom claimed that imperial rule is unnecessary for believers, but Augustine insists that God has placed everyone, whether pagan or priest, equally in subjection to external government. Yet Augustine's reasoning diverges sharply from the naive endorsement of Constantine's court theologian, Eusebius. Augustine's dark vision of a human nature ravaged by original sin and overrun by lust for power rules out uncritical adulation and qualifies his endorsement of imperial rule. That same dark vision impels him to reject Chrysostom's more optimistic premise that imperial power is necessary for pagans, but, in effect, superfluous in the lives of pious citizens. Augustine, on the contrary, places secular government at the center of human society, indispensable for the best as well as the worst among its members. For a Christian, civic obligations rank second, certainly, to one's obligation to God (or, as this usually meant in practice, to the church). Yet apart from direct conflict of interest, even the bishop must render appropriate obedience to secular authority."[367]

Augustine got on well with the Roman authorities of his time; he had exploited their authority to persecute the Manichaean and Donatists, and provided them with a political theology to legitimise their claims to absolute power over their subjects. Augustine insisted that Adam was placed in the Garden to teach him the lesson of submission; Adam saw firsthand the consequences of his freedom. Augustine curtailed human liberties and rights with his theology of human depravity due to the sin of Adam. His contention that the humans lacked any capacity whatever for freedom of choice absolutely limited the definition of human liberty and rights. He made restricted human liberty palatable to the governing institutions with whom he wholeheartedly identified. God wanted slavery and submission, while the Serpent tempted Adam with seductive lure of liberty. The forbidden apple symbolised personal control over one's will. God never intended humanity to be truly free; Adam was always meant to be placed upon the earth. God placed him temporarily in the Garden to prove to him by his own experience that his good was truly in slavery, slavery to God in the first place and then to his appointed agent, the emperor in the second place. Augustine's theology of power was very suitable to both the Church and state. His insistence upon absolute human wretchedness due to the fall and human incapacity to govern themselves, lying helplessly in need of external intervention, validated the essential need for both the temporal and spiritual authorities with absolute powers. His dogma of religious and temporal coercion justified the papal and monarchial absolutism

135

at the expense of human dignity, individuality, freedom and rights. The Pope and emperors were excited by the political efficacy of his doctrine of human depravity and fall and the need for outside grace. They graced Augustine with sainthood and perpetuated his legacy as the most orthodox doctrine to serve their own agendas of absolute hegemony. They agreed upon the power sharing mechanism by dividing man and his surroundings into spiritual and temporal, the spiritual for the Church and the temporal for the state. Man consisted of two entities, the soul and body, and God provided guidance for both; the Church fostered the soul while the government directed the body. "Indeed, in a somewhat simple-minded way he could comment on Paul's command to obey the powers [...] by explaining it in terms of the duality of soul and body: since we consist of both and require the things we need for bodily sustenance in this life, we must be subject to the government. For it is its business to procure these. It is not its business to concern itself with the soul."[368] That was the area of the Church, as said.

Augustine was well aware of the aspired social ideals and the grounded realities. Man yearns for wholeness, fulfilment, peace, rest and tranquility but the realities of human conditions were very different from the ideals. "The condition of man consequent on Adam's fall does not allow for the achievement of the harmony and order in which alone man can find rest. Tension, strife and disorder are endemic in this realm. There can be no resolution, except eschatologically. Human society is irremediably rooted in this tension-ridden and disordered *saeculum*."[369] After the fall of Rome in 410 AD by Alaric, Augustine was disgruntled with geopolitics[370] and lost the enthusiasm for heavenly city and divine kingdom he earlier had. "The fall of the eternal city on 24 August 410, which was of greater symbolic than political importance, provoked a discussion of divine providence in history, and debate whether Christianity was about to bring about the collapse of the Roman empire. Against this ferment of argument Augustine began to write 'a large and arduous work', *magnum opus et arduum*, the *City of God*, developing themes which had already appeared in *True Religion* which he wrote as a layman, but now set in an altogether grander perspective."[371] Augustine used this opportunity to stress more upon the need for a powerful government, contending that the City of God needed a strong and powerful state to maintain its security and to protect its inhabitants. The weak Roman administration led to

Rome's demise and desecration of its people; therefore, a strong state was a prerequisite to human safety and stability. "He granted that only a strong government could assure people of peace and enable them to live without fear of social disorder. Roman law, which he knew quite a lot about, he treated with deep respect as indispensable for the coherence of society. One should not, for example, simply take the law into one's own hands when confronted by a bandit. Law and government are necessary because of the distortion, greed, and anti-social corruption in the human heart."(Chadwick, Augustine, p. 109)

The Empire's political uncertainties and Donatists' upheaval in Hippo added to the fuel. "From the late 390s Augustine's political thinking was dominated by this repudiation. Never again did he consider the institutions of society and government as agencies concerned with helping men to achieve the right order in the world. Their task was now to minimise disorder. This is the meaning of Augustine's insistence that political authority is not natural to man, but a result of his sinful condition. Here, again, he was reaching back to an old Christian tradition. According to this tradition, the purpose of the state and of its coercive machinery was to deal with the disorganisation and conflict resulting from the Fall: to prevent men from devouring each other like fish."[372] There was no delusion of self-determination or individualism or democracy in Augustine. His trust in human capacities and goodness was minimal; man was uncontrollable if left to himself, and needed an authoritative hierarchical arrangement to keep him in bounds. That hierarchical system was the state with its multiple agencies. Just like Paul before him, Augustine's understandings of human conditions and weaknesses necessitated an agency like the government, to be ruled by an authoritative king who enjoyed pious humility. Therefore, the state was an extension of divine providence and wisdom. "A man is humble before his rulers because he is humble before God. His political obedience is a symptom of his willingness to accept all processes and forces beyond his immediate control and understanding. Thus he can even accept the exercise of power by wicked men. In this, Augustine's view of obedience is strictly analogous to his view of illness, another phenomenon plainly beyond man's control and constantly frustrating his intentions. What does he do, he once wrote to a friend, when he feels depressed, and cannot preach well? *Flectamurfacile nefrangamur*—'let us bend easily lest we be broken' [...] The Christian obeys the state because he is the sort of man who would not set himself up against the hidden ways of God, either in politics or in personal distress."[373] The true spirituality was never accomplished in chaos. The healthy soul required a healthy body. Man needed order in life to reach God and that order came through the agency of state. Therefore, state was a vehicle of pilgrimage to God. The government did not make a person good but it could assist a man in shunning the unlawful and undesired behaviour. "In his later remarks on the purpose and scope of human legislation the emphasis shifts towards stressing this external character of the law. It cannot make men good, but it can secure public order, security, the rights of property. Stated more generally, its purpose is to help in avoiding conflict and to maintain the 'earthly peace.'"[374] In Henry Chadwick's words state was helpful "if not getting one to heaven, at least hedging the road to hell."[375]

It is evident that Augustine's exousiology was conditioned by his theology. His world view containing the original goodness of God, original sin of first man, fallen nature and its corollaries, human depravity and justification through faith and grace led him to believe in absolute human wretchedness and brutality. His man was neither capable of self-discipline nor self-control, and needed an external agency to force him into conformity with law. Augustine's historical experiences substantiated his fears. The Donatists and other countless heretics remained checked as long as the Roman state was able to control them, and the Catholic Church was supreme due to imperial support. The same Donatists and pagans were attacking Catholic Churches and monasteries once the Roman state was unable to protect the Church's interests. The Vandals and Visigoths of Spain had besieged Carthage and Hippo, while the German Goths had ransacked Rome and forced its inhabitants to cannibalism. The political upheavals were sufficient enough to highlight the need for a strong and powerful empire. Man was too wretched to behave morally without the authority and power of a governing state. "The great need here, in Augustine's sombre vision of the nasty brutishness of man in his fallen condition, was for bulwarks to secure society against disintegration. In its coercive machinery the state turns human ferocity itself to the limited but valuable task of securing some precarious order, some minimal cohesion, in a situation inherently tending to chaos."[376] The state was God's historical providence; therefore, a Christian was required to participate in the state activities to help and facilitate a relative order in the temporal world. So, the concern for the earthly city was a concern for the heavenly city; the eternal city was the toiling field for Church while the earthly city was the area of the state. The eternal city could never be established without the powerful arm of the earthly city, so the state and Church were mutually interdependent, needing to work together to realise an interconnected common goal i.e., the peace, order and security in the society. There was no separation of Church and state; there was no Church without a state, and the Church needed a strong state to perform its duties of the heavenly city and spiritual kingdom. Augustine was the true father of an absolute divine right monarchy and the Church, the two joined together in their duty to direct humanity in both the spiritual and temporal realms. His absolutism did not know any bounds, and his man had no freedoms or rights whatsoever. This bleak theology of physical and mental slavery was welcomed by the Church and state, at the expense of the masses. It inculcated a sense of perpetual guilt and powerlessness in the people, and they allowed themselves to be subjugated by the religious and political authorities. The Church and state were held supreme in every aspect of human life and existence.

Later generations adopted Augustine's simple and straightforward interpretations of the Church and state's mutual interdependence, and Augustine was the bridge between the late Antiquity and the medieval ages. He became the most influential philosopher and figure in the medieval Christendom, revered both by the monarchs and the bishops. Emperors were given the divine right authority to rule with absolute legislative and executive powers, and were amply used as the political arms of the Church, exploiting the bishops to galvanise support for their imperial designs. The Byzantine Empire and the Carolingian dynasty, along with all the later Holy Roman Empires and secular monarchies owed their theological foundations and political mooring to Augustine. His concept of state was absolutely monarchial without any hint of constitutionalism, consultation or counsel of the general masses. The rights were not unalienable but granted by the monarch, and their duties were also determined by the emperor. The monarch was the shadow of God upon the earth; absolute submission to him was a divinely-ordained responsibility of every soul. Augustine was also the founding father of religious coercion and persecution in Christianity.

He provided scriptural foundations for persecution of heretics and pagans by the Christian authorities.

Christianity and Persecutions

The Christian Church has been known for its persecutions of heretics. Heresy is derived from the Greek word *hairesis,* which means both 'deliberate choice' and 'sect.' The term had no negative connotation in the Greco Roman culture. The Jewish historian Josephus used the term to describe multiple sects that existed in the Judea province of his time. The Roman authorities used the same term to dub St. Paul as a schismatic (Acts 24:5; 28:22) and St. Paul used it to denote division and schism (1Corinthian 11:18-19). Perez Zagorin states that "the New Testament authors tended to conceive of heresy not in the older sense of philosophical schools or their opinions, but mainly as the fomenting of divisions and sects among Christians through the propagation of false and evil opinions. This impression is further confirmed by such passages as Paul's warning in his letter to the Romans to avoid those who 'cause divisions and offences contrary to the doctrine which ye have learned' (Rom. 16:17); and his beseeching the Corinthians in the name of Christ 'that ye all speak the same thing, and that there be no divisions [*schismata*] among you' (1 Cor. 1:10).13 The evidence of the New Testament, therefore, makes it clear that Christians of the first and second centuries were already being taught to think that heresy signified erroneous and evil beliefs contrary to the apostles' and the church's teachings and was related to schism or the creation of divisions in the Christian communities."[377] Although the idea of heresy is found in the New Testament, no concept of punishment, coercion or silencing is attached to it. Coercion against the heretics was the creation of later orthodoxy. "Systems of religion that require the faithful to adhere to a strict standard of belief and/ or worship generally produce a concomitant idea of heresy, understood as an error in matters directly related to the truths of one's confession."[378]

There was no such heresy in the Christianity of the first century, as there was no established orthodoxy, New Testament Canon, Catholic or Orthodox hierarchical Church, Pope or a set of orthodox doctrine. The Roman Empire generally tolerated a number of religious sects, and Tertullian and Justin Martyr cited this pluralism and toleration to ask for leniency against the Christians. The early Christian communities were quite divergent, with differing doctrines, rituals and practices; the term heresy was mostly used to denote differing points of view and opinion. As seen above, St. Paul had condemned divisiveness and plurality among the Christian community, and Apologists such as Justin Martyr and Tertullian had sanctioned the radical tendencies of numerous Christian sects as heretical. There was no indication of physical or economic punishment. Between 150 AD and 204 AD, when Irenaeus the bishop of Lyons died, Christian polemics against heretical sects had gotten some momentum due to pagan's assault upon the Christian faith, as seen above. The Christian leadership was forced to define the parameters of the Christian faith, and explain its teachings and doctrines in intelligible terms. Irenaeus was perhaps the first Church leader to exclude the dissenting sects from the Church of Jesus Christ, asking for their persecution and destruction. No such persecution or expulsion was possible, as there was no hierarchical church at that time, or a state to implement it. He also emphasised the need to establish the boundaries of a catholic (meaning universal) and orthodox official Church. By his time the process of identification and differentiation was on its way, and this process of identification and exclusion lead to an early sense of orthodoxy. Still, there was no orthodoxy in the sense that a set of doctrines and practices were accepted by all the Christian communities, and there was no universal definition or agreement about the Trinity, the true divinity or the nature of Jesus even among the Church Fathers such as Justin Martyr, Tertullian and Origen. Origen's statement makes clear the tremendous diversity: "Since so many of those who profess faith in Christ disagree with one another not only on little and minimal things but truly also on many great and important ones [...] it is necessary first to define that which is certain and the rule of faith, [and] *only then to inquire about other things.*" [379] He advised Heracleides, a church leader, that "your church must not differ from the other churches in opinion because you are not the false church."[380] Sabrinho notes that "the bewildering diversity in Christian thought and practice presented a constant dilemma to theorists and intellectuals in early Christian communities."[381]

As seen above, Pagans such as Celsus had assaulted Christianity for hedonism and irrationalism, and demanded its leaders to come out of the box and face the world with logic and reason. The Apologists' efforts were a response to this piercing assault. Their new "interest was fueled both by Christianity's need to achieve 'intellectual respectability' as it parted ways with Judaism and confronted pagan philosophy and by a perceptible change in the social and intellectual makeup of early Christian communities, which were growing more socially diverse and attracting better-educated believers."[382] In spite of multiple efforts they were at a loss to establish the orthodoxy. Therefore, throughout the third century the orthodoxy and doctrines were fluid. "The impossibility of defining orthodoxy, then, was part of the challenge theology posed to Christian leaders. The notion of orthodoxy rested on a paradox. On the one hand, it referred to a set of ideas and symbols that were believed to represent or embody absolute, eternal, immutable truths about God, humanity, and the universe. On the other, these ideas and symbols were always provisionally true, their meaning malleable and constantly changing, or, as the believer would have understood it, never revealed in their entirety. As a body of knowledge, orthodoxy was perpetually in flux, its meaning deriving from the continuous collective effort of many people to elucidate scripture. The truth could be revealed only through sustained inquiry and debate, and, thus, it was alive and moving in the community."[383]

Constantine and Christian Unity

The efforts to unite Christians upon a unitary Christian doctrine about Jesus and his relationship with God had to wait till 325 AD when Emperor Constantine struggled to rein in the warring bishops in the Council of Nicaea. Initially, Constantine was not inclined towards coercion or persecution of heretics, and encouraged dialogue and toleration for the sake of unity. In 324 he stated: "My own desire is, for the common good of the world and the advantage of all mankind, that thy people should enjoy a life of peace and undisturbed concord. Let those, therefore, who still delight in error, be made welcome to the same degree of peace and tranquility which they have who believe. For it may be that this restoration of equal privileges to all will prevail to lead them into the straight path. Let no one molest another, but let everyone do as his soul desires. Only let men of sound judgment be assured of this, that those only can live a life of holiness and purity, whom thou callest to a reliance on thy holy laws. With regard to those who will hold themselves aloof from us, let them have, if they please, their temples of lies: *we* have the glorious edifice of thy truth, which thou hast given us as our native home. We pray, however, that they too may receive the same blessing, and thus experience that heartfelt joy which unity of sentiment inspires."[384]

In 325 he entertained the idea of reasonable punishment to wake up the heretics' conscience and enlighten them with the truth of God. These punishments were mostly financial and social rather than physical, and his intent was more imperial than theological; he wanted peace, security and unity within the empire. Edward Gibbon observes that the "edict of Milan, the great charter of toleration, had confirmed to each individual of the Roman world the privilege of choosing and professing his own religion [...] was soon violated; with the knowledge of truth, the emperor imbibed the maxims of persecution; and the sects which dissented from the Catholic church were afflicted and oppressed by the triumph of Christianity. Constantine easily believed that the Heretics, who presumed to dispute his opinions, or to oppose his commands, were guilty of the most absurd and criminal obstinacy; and that a seasonable application of moderate severities might save those unhappy men from the danger of an everlasting condemnation. Not a moment was lost in excluding the ministers and teachers of the separated congregations from any share of the rewards and immunities which the emperor had so liberally bestowed on the orthodox clergy [...] After a preamble filled with passion and reproach, Constantine absolutely prohibits the assemblies of the Heretics, and confiscates their public property to the use either of the revenue or of the Catholic church."[385] Constantine exiled Arius and a few of his supporters, but did not inflict physical punishment on them. He deprived them of imperial privileges, which were showered upon the Nicene clergy.

Constantine turned the previously persecuted Christian church into an imperial Church. The wealth and power brought envy, jealousy and rivalries, and the process of identification and differentiation was intensified. David Gwynn notes that "the Christian Church was now an imperial Church, with wealth and privileges befitting the favoured religion of the empire. Although Christians were still not in the majority when Constantine died in 337, their numbers were growing rapidly and their new-found status was publicly displayed through their magnificent churches and the social prestige of their bishops. This dramatic expansion in turn drove the fundamental changes that redefined Christianity in the fourth century, from the canon of the New Testament and the rise of asceticism to the theological controversies that divided the Church. The reign of Constantine was truly a turning point in the history of both Christianity and the Later Roman empire."[386]

Constantine was a politician and not a theologian. He was unable to resolve the contradictory clauses and doctrines of various creeds. Christianity of his times was marred with internal chaos. "When Constantine made his historic alliance between the Roman state and the Christian church he had hoped, among other things, that this new, energetic and disciplined religion would buttress his unified empire with a unified faith. He was frustrated and disappointed. With the lifting of the persecutions and the gracious entry of the church into an earthly establishment, deep disagreements of doctrine and organisation all came into their own. The very tenacity that, a few years earlier, had resisted all attempts by Diocletian, Galerius and Maximinus to break the church by force was now active in its internal disputes."[387] The orthodox Nicene party excommunicated Arius, but Constantine figured out that the leader of the Nicene party St. Athanasius was a troublemaker; it was said that he was against the whole world. In the Council of Constantinople, Constantine exiled him and restored the orthodoxy of Arius and his party. The theological subtleties of Logos and substance were beyond the emperor. "Constantine had no understanding of these subtleties and no patience with them. Indeed, he was little concerned with Christ at all. He had opted for the God of the Christians against *Sol Invictus* because it had seemed to offer the best promise of divine favour for the Roman state, which it was the emperor's duty to secure by the proper forms of worship. The church had been granted many special privileges by him, and in return he wanted unity in it, not continual quarrelling over hair-splitting matters."[388] Therefore, the claim of existence of a universal Catholic Church and orthodoxy during Constantine's time does not stand the scrutiny. "The Christian *oikoumen* adopted by Constantine thus contained a church monolithic and universal in name only. Diversity had been a fact of life for Christians, partly resulting from their widespread diffusion and the lack of central organisation. Even within each city, the indeterminacy of Christian authority, distributed among charismatic ascetics and confessors, scriptures, synods and communal consensus, and holders of ecclesiastical offices, gave ample room for differences to arise while also making them difficult to resolve."[389]

In spite of his efforts to restore peace and unite Christians on a unitary doctrine, Constantine did not use torture or physical coercion to rein in the so-called heretics. The theological controversies continued after his death. The West was mostly Nicene and the East mostly Arian. His son emperor Constantius II (emperor from 337-361) was pro Arian. He through a number of councils rehabilitated the Arians at the cost of the Nicene party rendering them virtually powerless. His successor emperor Julian ruled by dividing further the warring Christian factions. "So far heresy had not been actually criminalised, and the clergy ran only the risks of ejection and exile."[390] These emperors were sincere Christians, but they never forgot that they were emperors first and foremost. They used the Church to further their imperial authority, and pitched differing Christian factions against each other, ensuring that the Church would remain under control. The Church was pretty much divided till the fourth century. The Christological controversies had rocked the entire Roman Empire by the time of Theodosius, Roman Emperor from AD 379 to AD 395. Constantinople was a city where everyone was a theologian. Gregory of Nyssa observed that "this is a city where every slave and artisan is a profound theologian. Ask one of them to change some silver and he explains instead how the Son differs from the Father. Ask another the price of a loaf of bread and he replies that the Son is inferior to the Father. Ask a third if your bath is ready and he tells you that the Son was created out of nothingness."[391]

Theodosius and Edict of Salonica

Theodosius was a different kind of emperor. He was a child of the Mother Church seeing everything through the prism of his eternal salvation. As a staunch believer in the Nicene Creed, he allowed the Church to use the political arm of the state to impose Nicene Christology. Under the influence of Ambrose of Milan, he prohibited all sorts of heresies and enacted laws to punish them. In Salonica, in February of 380, Theodosius issued a decree establishing the Apostolic Creed and religion of Peter as the sole authority in his empire.[392] He further ordered that "we command that those persons who follow this rule shall embrace the name of Catholic Christians. The rest, however, whom we adjudge demented and insane, shall sustain the infamy of heretical dogmas, their meeting places shall not receive the name of churches, and they shall be smitten first by divine vengeance and secondly by the retribution of our own initiative, which we shall assume in accordance with divine judgement."[393]

This edict transformed the concept of heresy in Christianity, requiring punishment both spiritual and temporal. "The concept of heresy was transformed within the Christian tradition, however, in accordance with a second and narrower understanding, insofar as heretical 'error' came to be seen to require forms of correction and punishment, both temporal and spiritual. To the extent that heresy was singled out by Christians as an especially dangerous sort of spiritual outlook, different in nature and kind from apostasy and similar forms of infidelity, it demanded persecution and extirpation of a greater intensity than other modes of unbelief."[394] Such a strict and abusive concept of heresy was a Christian invention not found in Judaism or the early Roman laws. Arians and other anti-Nicene Christian sects were persecuted. "Theodosius had brought the law centrally into differences of the Christian faith, conflated false belief with criminal intent, and obedience to the church with obedience to the state. He had reunited the split churches, made them define orthodoxy, and then used the imperial power to recall deviants to the fold or else cut them off totally. It was thus Theodosius, as much as the Council of Nicaea, who can be considered as the historic founder of the established Catholic church."[395] Previously, dissenting actions and practices were proscribed. Theodosius extended it to intent and belief. Harbouring wrong belief was detrimental to the soul and its salvation, and saving the soul was a Christian duty. The emperor, as the chief Christian, was supposed to help the Church in saving the lost souls to ensure divine pleasure and grace for the empire. Therefore, submission to the orthodox Nicene Christology and Creed was in reality a submission to the state, and rebellion against the established official Church was tantamount to rebellion against the state. Richard Lim observes that "while Christians had long entertained a notion of orthodoxy, the state's support gave it definition and weight. How was one to identify orthodox Christians, who alone could claim considerable privileges and imperial gifts? For a half-century after Nicaea, a fixed and precise definition of orthodoxy did not yet obtain, as emperors and bishops continued to revisit the decisions of 325, but closure began to be achieved under the reign of Theodosius I: orthodox Christians held communion with named bishops; they adhered to specific short creeds; and they accepted the conclusions of designated councils."[396]

Theodosius created a new religious order, uniting the Roman imperial power closely with the Catholic Church. The Bishop of Rome was also exalted as the supreme religious authority in the empire. Perez Zagorin notes that "Theodosius was an implacable enemy of heresy, against which he issued no fewer than eighteen edicts. He proscribed various heresies by name, ordered the confiscation of churches and private houses where heretics met for worship, and deprived them of the right to make wills or receive inheritances. In the case of certain heretical sects he commanded that their members be hunted down and executed. In his attempt to enforce uniformity of belief he also instituted legislation against paganism, including a comprehensive enactment in 395 forbidding anyone of whatever rank or dignity to sacrifice to or worship 'senseless images' constructed 'by human hands,' on pain of heavy fines and other penalties. He was likewise the first emperor to impose penalties on Christians who profaned their baptism by reverting to paganism."[397]

It is pertinent to mention that the state and Church were allies; the Church landed its religious hand to extend the authority of the state, while the state exerted its power and authority to force people to submit to Church teachings. There were several kinds of dissent; some heresies were geopolitical and regional, while others were intellectual and theological. There was also opposition to the Church organisation, authority, wealth and corruptions. Initially the persecutions of heresies were often propelled by geopolitics, as the nationalistic and regional impulses were integral to the heresies, and geopolitics often drove them to the forefront.[398] Even though heresy was often defined in religious terms, it often encompassed geopolitical matters. "Heresy was understood to be religious error maintained in willful and persistent opposition to religious truth as authoritatively defined and declared by the church."[399] But as said, not all heresies were theological; some heresies were intellectual and doctrinal, while others were mostly organisational deviations. The Church persecuted both kinds with equal vigour. Until the fourth century, persecution of heretics entailed mostly economic and social sanctions, and theological formulations for the use of physical coercion were a later development. It was St. Augustine who provided the theological foundations for religious persecution and coercion. "The emperor's sanction of the use of physical force to address religious nonconformity enshrined a practice that had been selectively applied by Constantine, Constantius, and Valens. Now entitled to apply coercion against rivals, some Christian bishops such as Augustine quickly rationalised its use."[400]

Augustine and Rationalization of Coercion

St. Augustine initially believed in religious freedom and shunned religious persecution. He espoused such a belief until around 397 AD, and in an undated letter to a Donatist churchman he wrote: "I do not intend that anyone should be forced into the Catholic communion against his will. On the contrary, it is my aim that the truth may be revealed to all who are in error and that [...] with the help of God, it may be made manifest so as to induce all to follow and embrace it of their own accord."[401] Later on, he changed his mind, after seeing a great number of Donatist heretics returning to the Catholic Church as a result of imperial laws; the history changed, along with the change of Augustine's mind. Michael Gaddis notes that "thus an overtly coercive paradigm came to define the Catholic and imperial approach to the Donatist problem. Augustine's change of heart on this issue has rightly been seen as a defining moment in church history, an endorsement of muscular state intervention in matters of faith. What is important here is the reasoning behind the establishment's violence: the wielders of power, and their apologists, needed to believe in the rightness of their actions. Thus they reassured themselves that their might was applied not for selfish reasons but for the greater good of their subjects, whether or not the latter appreciated the fact. Their coercion justified itself through a disciplinary discourse: it employed calibrated violence not to destroy its targets but to chastise, reform, and even educate them. This was the violence of the center, the establishment—the emperor and his functionaries, or ecclesiastical authorities who enjoyed the recognition and support of the state and had recourse to its means of enforcement. Its motives, in theory, were not anger or vengeance but rather a paternalistic compassion. But as mildly as this approach may have sought to present itself, ultimately it depended upon a coercive power backed up by the very real possibility of violence."[402]

In around 400 AD, Augustine seemed to accept and encourage religious coercion. In a letter to Donatist bishop Parmenian, he justified use of imperial power to coerce Donatists into Catholicism. Quoting Romans 13:1-7, Augustine established the God-given right of the emperor to persecute those responsible for schism. He used Matthew 13:24-30 (parable of weeds) to authorise physical coercion against the heretics. The parable was usually interpreted as permitting religious pluralism and differing opinions, leaving the judgement to God on the Day of Judgment. Matthew clearly stated that: "The servants asked him, 'Do you want us to go and pull them up?' 'No,' he answered, 'because while you are pulling the weeds, you may uproot the wheat with them. Let both grow together until the harvest. At that time I will tell the harvesters: First collect the weeds and tie them in bundles to be burned; then gather the wheat and bring it into my barn." (Matt. 13:29-30) Augustine, however, drew from it a very different lesson: "if the bad seed is known, it should be uprooted. According to his explanation, the only reason the master left the tares to grow until the harvest was the fear that uprooting them sooner would harm the grain. When this fear does not exist because it is evident which is the good seed, and when someone's crime is notorious and so execrable that it is indefensible, then it is right to use severe discipline against it, for the more perversity is corrected, the more carefully charity is safeguarded. With the help of this interpretation, which reversed the parable's meaning, Augustine was able not only to justify the Roman government's repression of the Donatists but to provide a wider reason for religious persecution by the civil authorities."[403]

Augustine thought that the use of physical punishment and fear was a genuine method to instill terror in the minds of heretics and to bring them back into the fold of orthodoxy. Philip Schaff summarised the basis of Augustine's coercion dogma in the following words: "Evidently a change had come over Numidia, for he boasts of the multitudes who had been converted, and rejoices in the fruitful use of the secular arm for their salvation. Even Circumcelliones had become steadfast Catholics. Coercion stimulates the thoughtless and those bound by custom, and delivers these held back by fear; it is like a wholesome medicine, or the wounds inflicted by a friend. God chastens in order to better the life and to bring men to repentance. The householder instructs us to compel them to come in. Sarah and Hagar are types; so the mother Church corrects her children. Everything depends on the aim in persecution, whether it be done for oppression or for good; it is the difference between Pharaoh and Moses in their treatment of Israel. The

Father gave up the Son, and the Son gave Himself up; while Judas betrayed Him. The righteousness of the end for which one suffers alone constitutes martyrdom."[404]

Augustine argued that the Lord Jesus Christ used physical coercion to make Paul submit and believe. "He not only constrained him with His voice, but even dashed him to the earth with His power; and that He might forcibly bring one who was raging amid the darkness of infidelity to desire the light of the heart, He first struck him with physical blindness of the eyes. If that punishment had not been inflicted, he would not afterwards have been healed by it; and since he had been wont to see nothing with his eyes open, if they had remained unharmed, the Scripture would not tell us that at the imposition of Ananias' hands, in order that their sight might be restored, there fell from them as it had been scales, by which the sight had been obscured. Where is what the Donatists were wont to cry: Man is at liberty to believe or not believe? Towards whom did Christ use violence? Whom did He compel? Here they have the Apostle Paul. Let them recognise in his case Christ first compelling, and afterwards teaching; first striking, and afterwards consoling. For it is wonderful how he who entered the service of the gospel in the first instance under the compulsion of bodily punishment, afterwards laboured more in the gospel than all they who were called by word only; and he who was compelled by the greater influence of fear to love, displayed that perfect love which casts out fear."[405]

To Augustine, fear was a category of love, and absolutely permitted to save the soul from eternal condemnation. The Catholic Church, as mother, must coerce its children to follow its creeds and practices; the fear of flogging might keep the sheep together. "Why, therefore, should not the Church use force in compelling her lost sons to return, if the lost sons compelled others to their destruction? Although even men who have not been compelled, but only led astray, are received by their loving mother with more affection if they are recalled to her bosom through the enforcement of terrible but salutary laws, and are the objects of far more deep congratulation than those whom she had never lost. Is it not a part of the care of the shepherd, when any sheep have left the flock, even though not violently forced away, but led astray by tender words and coaxing blandishments, to bring them back to the fold of his master when he has found them, by the fear or even the pain of the whip."[406] He insisted that "Paul was compelled by Christ; therefore the Church, in trying to compel the Donatists, is following the example of her Lord."[407] These pastoral metaphors "allowed Augustine and like-minded colleagues to rationalise policies that forced people, willing or not, toward the good. Charity—the Christian duty to love one's neighbour—demanded no less."[408] Augustine and the Catholic Church demanded the charity of submission and reconciliation on its own terms without any regard to the neighbour and his needs of charity and reconciliation.

To reinforce his view, he quoted the parable of the feast in the Gospel of Luke (Luke 14:21-23). In the parable of the feast, Jesus is reported to have asked the disciples to compel people to come in. Augustine required forcing heretics and others to join the fold of orthodoxy. "Lord Himself bids the guests in the first instance to be invited to His great supper, and afterwards compelled; for on His servants making answer to Him, 'Lord, it is done as Thou hast commanded, and yet there is room,' He said to them, 'Go out into the highways and hedges, and compel them to come in.' In those, therefore, who were first brought in with gentleness, the former obedience is fulfilled; but in those who were compelled, the disobedience is avenged. For what else is the meaning of 'Compel them to come in,' after it had previously said, 'Bring in,' and the answer had been made, 'Lord, it is done as Thou commanded, and yet there is room?'"[409] Augustine combined the spiritual reasons with the needs of the empire to construct a comprehensive doctrine of religious coercion and persecution. The emperors had always considered peace as the foundation of imperial prosperity, and dissention as the source of divine wrath. The Catholic Church was doing nothing short of realising peace by dint of religious coercion. The Church, which was previously persecuted, was blessed by God with newly-earned imperial support; that is why employing that God-given political resource was a must. "Wherefore, if the power which the Church has received by divine appointment in its due season, through the religious character and the faith of kings, be the instrument by which those who are found in the highways and hedges—that is, in heresies and schisms—are compelled to come in, then let them not find fault with being compelled, but consider whether they be so compelled. The supper of the Lord is the unity of the body of Christ, not only in the sacrament of the altar, but also in the bond of peace."[410] Moreover, a person who did not conform to the Catholic Church and its doctrines was eternally doomed; such a ruined person had no right to enjoy this life and what it entailed. He must perish and be uprooted like the tares, "deservedly you must necessarily perish, unless you come over to Catholic unity."[411]

The Donatists had insisted that belief was personal and could never be imposed from outside. They also contended that the emperor and state had nothing to do with the church. Many of them gave their lives for their cherished beliefs. Augustine argued that the Donatists' sacrifices were not accepted, while the Church and state's persecutions were divinely approved. The right and wrong depended upon the good intentions and the right motives. "But true martyrs are such as those of whom the Lord says, 'Blessed are they which are persecuted for righteousness' sake.' It is not, therefore, those who suffer persecution for their unrighteousness, and for the divisions which they impiously introduce into Christian unity, but those who suffer for righteousness' sake, that are truly martyrs. For Hagar also suffered persecution at the hands of Sarah; and in that case she who persecuted was righteous, and she unrighteous who suffered persecution. Are we to compare with this persecution which Hagar suffered the case of holy David, who was persecuted by unrighteous Saul? Surely there is in essential difference, not in respect of his suffering, but because he suffered for righteousness' sake. And the Lord Himself was crucified with two thieves; but those who were joined in their suffering were separated by the difference of its cause."[412] Therefore the Catholic Church was right, even while persecuting heretics, and the dissenters were wrong, even as victims of the Church's persecutions. Augustine laid a strong foundation for the supremacy of the Catholic Church and its countless persecutions over the next thousand years. Zagorin observed that "in dealing with heresy, Augustine thus laid great stress on what might be called the pedagogy of fear to effect a change of heart. He did not see coercion and free will as opposites in religious choice but claimed that fear plays a part in spontaneous acts of the will and may serve a good end."[413] He continued: "In one of his most important statements on the subject, contained in a letter of 417 to Boniface, the Roman governor of Africa, he propounded a distinction between two kinds of persecution. '[T]here is an unjust persecution,' he said, 'which the wicked inflict on the Church of Christ, and [...] a just persecution which the Church of Christ inflicts on the wicked.' The church persecutes from love, the Donatists from hatred; the church in order to correct error, the Donatists to hurl men into error. While the church strives to save the Donatists from perdition, the latter in their fury kill Catholics to feed their passion for cruelty. Augustine was convinced that the coercion of heretics was therefore a great mercy because it rescued them from lying demons so that they could be healed in the Catholic fold. He rejected the objection of those who said that the apostles had never called upon the kings of the earth to enforce religion, since in the apostles' times there had been no Christian emperor to whom they could appeal."[414]

The Saint and Politics

The Saint was known for his tactics of pressure and politics in addition to his policy of religious coercion. Richard Lim observes that "the tactic that Augustine used against the Manichaeans while he was bishop of Hippo combined the pressure of rumors, the threat of coercion, an imposing episcopal presence, and the use of stenography to record the victorious proceedings for later use and for posterity; the shift in the locale of the disputations from public baths to the bishop's palace is equally suggestive of the constriction of civic dialogue."[415]

A modern reader of Augustine is at times baffled by the intolerant stances of the Saint. His interpretation of the scripture and derivative methodology seems quite arbitrary and manipulative. His fear-based love and coercion-based faith is nothing short of a scandal. His words against the heretics are piercing, and his overall language against heresy is absolutely offensive to modern sensitivies. His demands for a merger of the Church and state are dangerous, and his vision of faith and salvation is a recipe for human disaster. There is no room for religious pluralism, freedom, diversity, interfaith or intra-faith dialogue or social harmony. Instead, there is hatred, bigotry, exclusivism, persecution and totalitarianism; the irony is that all this is done in the name of love and compassion. No wonder that enthusiastic, born-again modern evangelists are so bigoted, offensive, aggressive and exclusivist. The Saint seems to have a bad legacy; had it not been for his other brilliant philosophical and mystical ideas, he would not have deserve much attention or following in the modern pluralistic world when it came to his theory of religious coercion. He was the first to theorise religious persecution and physical coercion on the bases of scriptures and religious tradition. Christians leaders who followed him had no hesitations about coercing Christian and non-Christians alike. Bloodshed and religious persecution were legalised and moralised. "Between 405 and 410 the emperor Honourius decreed a number of heavy penalties against them [heretics] that put them outside the protection of the law for their seditious actions; he ordered their heresy to be put down in 'blood and proscription.'[416] Zagorin states that "Augustine, who was not only an outstanding thinker but a man of keen and sensitive conscience, wrestled strenuously with the problem of heresy and the achievement of Catholic unity by the use of coercion. It is regrettable that one of his major legacies to the Catholic Church was the formulation of a theory of persecution founded entirely on Christian grounds and supported with numerous examples from the Old and New Testaments."[417]

The world might have not witnessed the killing, maiming, burning and torturing of countless Christians and non-Christians throughout the late antiquity and medieval world had Augustine not provided the scriptural basis for religious coercion. The medieval Inquisitions took their lead from the Saint, and did the most unholy crimes in the name of the Most Holy. The Saint might not have thought of this legacy but the outcome of his theorising has been barbaric. One also wonders about the twists and turns he gave to the scriptural parables and passages. "Yves Congar, who edited some of his anti-Donatist treatises, has expressed the opinion that the texts he relied on, such as the parable of the feast and the conversion of Paul, did not serve well for his purpose."[418]

The historian Peter Brown, who has extensively studied and written about St. Augustine, notes that Augustine was the only Church Father who had discussed the subject of religious coercion with such precision and length. "As far as I know, he is the only writer in the Early Church to discuss the subject at length [...] He went on to justify religious coercion with a thoroughness and coherence which is quite as much part of his character as is his candour: and so Augustine has appeared to generations of religious liberals as 'le prince et patriarche des persecuteurs.'"[419] Brown prefers to call the coercion doctrine of Augustine an attitude rather than a doctrine. "I should like to abandon the word 'doctrine' and substitute the word 'attitude'. We may make some progress in understanding Augustine's ideas if we treat them as an 'attitude - that is, as placed a little lower than the angels of pure Augustinian theology, and a little higher than the beasts of the social and political necessities of the North African provinces."[420] Brown shows that Augustine wrestled with the idea for a long time, debating various aspects of it while suffering internal tension and agony. "Augustine's attitude to coercion is typical of the general quality of his thought. 'This thought never appears as a 'doctrine' in a state of rest: it is marked by a painful and protracted attempt to embrace and resolve tensions.""[421] Brown also demonstrates that this was not a sudden conversion to coercion, as is often believed, but a well thought-out attitude spread over decades. Augustine had espoused such an attitude against the Manicheans some years before his outbursts against the Donatists in 405 AD. He had already used the example of Paul to validate coercion against the Manicheans. In his sermons, "especially his sermons 24 and 62, to the years 399 to 401, we can see in them nothing less than a dress-rehearsal of his justification of the coercion of the Donatists after 405. In one sermon of great charm, he had even defended the politic conformity of one leading pagan by referring to the forcible conversion of St. Paul-Paul also, had been converted *ex necessitate*, by being knocked down and blinded on the road to Damascus. This scene of divine violence had begun to exercise Augustine: he would later use it extensively in his writings after 405, both *ad hominem* and applied to the Donatists in general. Thus, in Augustine's first public work against the Donatists-the *Contra Epistolam Parmeniani*, which appeared in late 400- half of his attitude to coercion is already fully formed."[422]

Brown argues that Augustine's prophetic interpretation of human history, close interactions with the harsh theology of the Old Testament and peculiar concepts of grace and predestination played a role in his attitude towards religious coercion. "What had enabled Augustine to take up so firm an attitude? Perhaps the most profound reason is that he and his colleagues were in the enviable position of knowing why history was happening [...] What was happening around them happened *secundum propheticam veritatem*. It was a prophetic truth that the Church should be diffused among all nations: this was Augustine's main contention against the Donatists. But it was a prophetic truth on exactly the same level that the Kings of the Earth should serve Christ in fear and trembling; that the gods of the nations should be uprooted from the face of the earth, and that what had been sung, centuries before by King David, should now become manifest, as a public command, in the repression of pagans, Jews and heretics throughout the Roman Empire [...] Augustine's reaction to the suppression of paganism and to the possibility of suppressing other forms of religious dissent, is, in part, determined by the deeper change which had led him from the purely allegorical exegesis of ten years previously to a concrete vision of the fulfilment of prophecy in history."[423]

The Saint had a totalitarian vision. The unqualified imperial support for the Church, continuous retreat of paganism and scathing pursuit of the Jews and heretics by the state substantiated his dream that the kingdom of God was at hand and the new era of absolute and universal submission to the gospel was about to commence. All people and nations must praise the Lord; any deviations from the Catholic Church and its creeds were nothing short of belligerence, and needed to be uprooted. The Saint intended to expedite the kingdom by his attitude of religious coercion and reformation. This was an expression of his ultimate love for the heretics, as he wanted to compel them to enter the kingdom. But unfortunately for the heretics, he was nothing short of antichrist. They lost their personal properties, churches, jobs, businesses and at times their lives due to Augustine's attitude and doctrine.

In the final analysis the Saint, especially at the time of conflict, was not that saintly. "Augustine does not emerge from such an examination as an entirely simple figure. His charity seems to vary greatly with the degree to which he was personally in the suppression of a powerful rival. He is a sensitive and conscientious pastor up to his victory over the Donatists; but, in 420, he can appear, for an instant, as a harsh and cold victor. The whole weight of his doctrine of predestination is turned, with horrible emphasis, on the broken remnants of a great church."[424] Brown argues: "But remove the foundation of honesty for one moment from this attitude, and Augustine's phrases become fallacious, horrible and insidious."[425]

Augustine's Legacy

Unfortunately, religious coercion and persecution was Augustine's horrible legacy for future generations. Both the state and Church adopted it as an official policy without many changes or modifications. The emperors initiated persecuting laws, and the bishops made their implementation certain. William Tabbernee notes that "as champions of catholic Christianity intent on preserving the *pax Dei*, the emperors promulgated laws aimed at ridding the Empire of all those who did not conform to orthodox doctrine and practice."[426] Bishops used even human spies and informants to hunt down violators and punish heretics and their cronies; quite often their coercive technics were torturous. Even though Augustine had advised the magistrates to be watchful, the angry and enraged bishops as well as the magistrates at times went beyond fatherly chastisement. Augustine wrote: "Do not lose now that fatherly care *[paternam diligentiam]* which you maintained when prosecuting the examination, in doing which you extracted the confession of such horrid crimes, not by stretching them on the rack, not by furrowing their flesh with iron claws, not by scorching them with flames, but by beating them with rods *[virgarum verberibus]*—a mode of correction used by schoolmasters, and by parents themselves in chastising children, and often also by bishops in the sentences awarded by them [in the episcopal courts]."[427] Unfortunately the iron claws were used to furrow the flesh of heretics, and Roman soldiers attacked Donatists churches and basilicas, committing massacres of the worst kinds.[428] "Those who applied physical discipline to individuals found it fairly simple to distinguish corrective punishments from lethal. Those charged with inflicting corrective violence upon an entire society faced a much harder task in restraining its worst consequences."[429]

Roman officials were also punished and fined in cases of leniency and laxity towards heretics. Physical torture and flogging became commonplace in the empire, and capital punishments including violent deaths were a norm. "The zealots who acted in the name of God managed to convince themselves that the anger that drove their actions, and the vengeance they exacted against perceived enemies of the faith, was not theirs but God's. Thus the hubris of establishment authorities who claimed to inflict violence in the best interests of their victims found its match in the equally arrogant certainty of extremists who identified their own hatreds with those of God."[430] In the name of the Prince of Peace many individuals, congregations and sects' peace and prosperity were destroyed. The common Catholic believers were encouraged to police the society and work as disciplinarian mobs. Pagans, Jews and Christian heretics deserved no respect or consideration as they were the deniers of the Lord and Church. The crazy and criminal acts of torturous violence were justified in the name of Christ, the "words from the fifth-century Egyptian abbot Shenoute neatly express the relationship between violence and religious authority [...] They articulate a claim to legitimacy, the idea that personal holiness can justify and even sanctify an action that under other circumstances would be regarded as criminal, that zeal for God outweighs respect for worldly law and order."[431] The Holy Men (monks) were often the perpetrators of the most heinous crimes. "There is considerable evidence from a much broader range of sources, with a variety of different agendas, that violent attacks on temples and synagogues, and other clashes between Christians and non-Christians, did in fact happen on numerous occasions and in nearly every corner of the Roman world, and that monks or holy men were often involved."[432] The Christian Roman Empire was a violent and persecuting society.[433] Its saints and holy men were extremely violent, bent on implementing their version of salvation and piety over the pagans, Jews and heretics. "Key to the holy man's self-justification in such conflicts was the identification of his own agenda with God's will—so that what might seem to an unsympathetic observer as extralegal 'self-help' became instead the performance of God's work. 'Self-help' had traditionally implied independence from formal law, justified by the belief that one could not depend on that law to right a wrong. In a religious context, it offered a new justification for such independence, putting one's understanding of God's law above the law of the state."[434] Not all saints were violent but majority of them were violent. "Not every late antique saint fits this pattern—there were many who led quite peaceful lives—but holy violence formed a significant part of the repertoire of behaviour available to the holy man and comprehensible to his Christian audience. Stories of holy violence emphasis the role of the saint as embodiment of 'community values'— the community in this sense being the larger 'imagined community' of late Roman Christianity. These stories, put together with tales of martyrdom and persecution, played a key role in shaping the evolving self-definition of the Christian community, by articulating boundaries between those inside (zealous Christians) and those outside (pagans, Jews, heretics, and those who tolerated them), and by presenting models of leadership and religious authority. The holy man's attacks on enemies of the faith tell us as much about power dynamics and competition for influence within the Christian camp as they do about actual relations between Christians and non-Christians."[435] Sainthood was changed from suffering violence to inflicting violence. Perceived insult or disrespect to Christian religion, its founder and its symbols was sufficient enough to invite a violent response. "Christian zealots employed and understood violence within a broad paradigm of 'doing God's will[436].'" Augustine's pleas to minimize the violence were all ignored;[437] the zealots rather took his similitude of persecution more seriously. He had declared that the presence of heretics among the Catholics was a spiritual persecution for the Catholics.[438] "Tolerating such an evil, Augustine feared, was tantamount to endorsing it."[439] The zealots took it upon themselves to eradicate the tares from the wheat. They destroyed pagan temples, torturing and maiming the pagans. They burned Jewish synagogues. "In 388, zealous Christians set fire to a synagogue in Syrian Callinicum, apparently at the instigation of the local bishop. At about the same time, some monks burned a meeting place of the Valentinian Gnostic sect, after the Valentinians had blocked the road and interrupted their procession in honour of the Maccabees."[440] They torched Magian fire temples and ransacked the heretics' churches and monasteries. "Their acts of righteous violence helped to define that community by marking its boundaries, separating the true Christians within from the heretics, hypocrites, pagans, and Jews beyond."[441] Even the persecuting emperors, such as Theodosius, were horrified by the crimes of monks. His complain to St. Ambrose was that "The monks commit many crimes".[442] John Chrysostom himself witnessed and reported many such violent crimes.[443] The vulgar personal fight between John Chrysostom and Epiphanius, monk and bishop of Salamis was nothing short of profanity.[444] Both saints hurled profanities at each other and incited their followers to attack the opponent. In 404 John's followers were blamed for the fire which almost destroyed the great Church, nearby senate house, imperial theater and the palace.[445] The so called "bad monks" had played havocs on many occasions in so many cities of the Empire. "It is no paradox that Christian authorities glorified the holy man's divine zeal even while they did their best to restrain the excesses of actual monks. The holy man inspired ordinary Christians precisely because he never compromised in the ways that they themselves often had to."[446]

John Chrysostom and Violence

John Chrysostom, who in 379-380 wrote *In On Babylas,* an apology of Christian pacifism, could incite violence against pagans, Jews and heretics by 387 AD. In his homily to the citizens of Antioch John encouraged use of force against the blasphemers in the following strong words: "But since our discourse has now turned to the subject of blasphemy, I desire to ask one favor of you all, in return for this my address, and speaking with you; which is, that you will correct on my behalf the blasphemers of this city. And should you hear anyone in the public thoroughfare, or in the midst of the forum, blaspheming God; go up to him and rebuke him; and should it be necessary to inflict blows, spare not to do so. Smite him on the face; strike his mouth; sanctify your hand with the blow, and if any should accuse you, and drag you to the place of justice, follow them there; and when the judge on the bench calls you to account, say boldly that the man blasphemed the King of angels! For if it be necessary to punish those who blaspheme an earthly king, much more so those who insult God. It is a common crime, a public injury; and it is lawful for everyone who is willing, to bring forward an accusation. Let the Jews and Greeks learn, that the Christians are the saviours of the city; that they are its guardians, its patrons, and its teachers. Let the dissolute and the perverse also learn this; that they must fear the servants of God too; that if at any time they are inclined to utter such a thing, they may look round every way at each other, and tremble even at their own shadows, anxious lest perchance a Christian, having heard what they said, should spring upon them and sharply chastise them."[447]

Anybody not showing up for Easter services was an automatic suspect. Any informant could allege that a person harboured heretical views. Any family member could level charges of theological deviances and rest assured that the accused would be brought to task. Christendom turned into a fear-instilled society, especially for the heretics. But fear was no remedy for inner convictions; the undue pressure led to ruptures, and the coercion did not stop the heresies. There were many contending parties and heretical movements in the Eastern Roman or Byzantium Empire until the sixth century. There were over thirty creeds vying for orthodoxy in the Byzantine society.[448]

Justinian and Religious Persecution

Religious persecution, especially those of pagans and Christian heretics, had become an intrinsic part of the emperor's responsibilities by the time of Justinian. "The age of Justinian was a period of unsettling change, during which the norms of society shifted in ways hostile to the 'outsiders.'"[449] Justinian was a student of theology and a staunch

Catholic orthodox; he strove to unite the empire under one Church and orthodoxy. Tabbernee notes that "more than any of his predecessors, Justinian I (527–565) understood that uniformity of worship without uniformity of belief was not really uniformity. For Justinian, the *pax Dei* depended upon uniformity in both areas. He defined heretics as 'those who *think and worship* contrary to the catholic and apostolic church and the orthodox faith' (*Cod. justin.* 1.5.18.4)."[450] Inward and outward conformity to the Catholic Church and its creeds was required of all citizens. The united faith, with a united Church and worship, was the aspired goal of Justinian and the only source of citizenship in the empire. J. Evans notes that "'He [Justinian], finding that belief in God in former times had wandered into error and was forced to go in many directions, wiped out the paths that led to error and succeeded in placing it upon the strong foundation of one faith.... But every state with an official ideology has minorities which do not fit. They are the outsiders. In Justinian's empire, they were the Jews, the Samaritans, the pagans and heretics."[451]

The Jews fared better than the pagans and heretics due to their economic prosperity and relative unity. But still "Jews, along with Samaritans and heretics, were barred from purchasing real estate from a church: indeed a Catholic owner of any property where a church was situated might not sell, bequeath or lease it to a Jew, or even entrust it to Jewish management [...] He also legislated that the Scriptures might be read in synagogues either in Greek or the local language of the congregation, but he prohibited the use of the Mishnah, for he reasoned that Jews who understood the Holy Scriptures, unfiltered by rabbinical interpretation, would perceive that they foretold Christianity and willingly convert. Another charge [...] has it that Justinian compelled Jews to postpone the Passover Feast if it fell before Easter, and that many Jews paid heavy fines for disregarding this interdict."[452]

The pagans were hit hard by Justinian. The pagan academies of Athens were closed, their books publicly burned and their dignitaries such as Thomas the Quaestor, Phocas the Patrician and many grammarians, sophists, teachers, lawyers and physicians were imprisoned. They were given three months to recant their heresies and return to the Catholic faith, barred from politics and public offices, put under constant watch and lived under constant fear. The laws against them were loud and clear. John of Ephesus suppressed Hellenic paganism, not only in the cities but also in the countryside. In the provinces of Lydia, Caria and Phrygia, thousands of pagans were forced to accept Christianity. Pagan temples were turned into Christian churches and monasteries.[453] Evans states that "John of Ephesus [...] was sent in 542 on a rural mission to the provinces of Caria, Asia, Lydia and Phrygia, with instructions to convert unbelievers, and he claimed to have won over 70,000 souls, who turned away from the errors of their ancestors. Temples were demolished, idols, altars and sacred trees destroyed, and 96 churches were built, 55 of them paid for by the imperial purse. At Sardis, the capital of Lydia, there has been found an inscription dating after 539 which refers to pagans interned there. It may be connected with John's campaign to stamp out paganism, for he used strong-arm tactics as well as persuasion. We hear no more of paganism in the area."[454]

Justinian ordered his general Narses Persermenian to demolish the Egyptian temple dedicated to Zeus Ammon originally built by Alexander the Great and send its remnants to Byzantium. Justinian sent missionaries all over the empire, compelling people to accept Catholicism or else lose their properties and persons. Many pagans were crucified and slain with the sword, especially in Antioch and Ephesus. The historian Procopius explains that the pagans of North Africa, Asia Minor and Palestine were forced to convert to Christianity.[455] "One empire, one faith and one church" was Justinian's motto; all pagans, heretics and schismatic individual and sects were to be brought under the banner of a unified Catholic Church. The Nestorians, Monophysites, Montanists and countless others were hunted down, tortured and exiled. J. Evans notes that "by the end of 536, soldiers were scouring Mesopotamia for Monophysites."[456]

The spiritual salvation of subjects through the Catholic Church was the first and foremost concern of Justinian. He stated that "making provision for all things advantageous for our subjects, we have provided for this above all as first and most necessary before other things: that we may save their souls through all persons revering the orthodox faith with pure thought and, on the one hand, worshipping and glorifying the Holy and Consubstantial Trinity and, on the other hand, confessing and venerating the Holy, Glorious, and Ever Virgin Mary, the Mother of God."[457] It was not sufficient to just believe in the Trinity or the virgin birth of Jesus or the chastity of Mary; inner conviction that Mary was *Theotokos* (Mother of God) was as essential as the Holy Trinity. Justinian wanted to control the believers' actions, worship, conscience, minds and souls. His was an absolute totalitarian ideology. His spiritual fervor, military campaigns against Persians and countless other enemies, and his soteriological outlook led him to use austere measures against the religious non-conformists. "Yet in Justinian's reign, secular space grew narrower, the political and ecclesiastical sectors moved into closer union, and there was no safe place left for the outsider."[458]

Jews, pagans and Christian heretics were barred from schools, court jobs, public offices, inheritance and even charity; they were despised as pestilence. The traitors of the Church and Lord were the traitors of the empire. There were plenty of anti-heretic laws since the times of Theodosius, and many additional laws were promulgated by Justinian, to suppress dissent and diversity even more. "The law thus introduced applied the contents of an earlier law directed at Samaritans (1.5.17) to Montanists, Tascodrogitans, and Ophitans (*Cod. justin.* 1.5.18.3). It declared that members of the other three sects, like the Samaritans, could not have their own 'synagogue' nor could they leave property to non-Catholic heirs (cf. 1.5.17). Various further penalties, such as inability to be civil servants, teachers, or lawyers, were prescribed for 'heretics' and 'pagans' in general (1.5.18.4–6) and, presumably, these prohibitions also applied to Montanists. Any persons having embraced orthodoxy for the sake of entering one of the professions mentioned but whose wife and children were still members of heretical sects were to be dismissed forthwith (1.5.18.5). Ex-heretics could not bequeath property or gifts to heirs who were still heretics (1.5.18.5–7)."[459]

Bishops were ordered to implement the laws, both in letter and spirit, and report cases of leniency or laxity to the emperor. "The most interesting aspect of this particular law promulgated by Justinian is its conclusion which instructs bishops to bring to the attention of the governor of the province any people contravening the anti-heretical measure contained in this law (*Cod. justin.* 1.5.18.12). Bishops were also to inform the emperor of any laxity on the part of the governor in enforcing the legislation (1.5.18.12). The bishops themselves were warned that, if they did not co-operate, they would be expelled from their episcopates (1.5.18.13)."[460] The heretics and their clergy were expelled from the cities. For instance, Justinian ordered that "in regard to the unholy Montanists we ordain: that none of their so-called Patriarchs [...] bishops, presbyters, deacons or other clergy [...] should be permitted to reside in this fortunate city, but all should be expelled, lest some of the rather simple-minded persons, having heard their absurd myths and following their impious teachings, should destroy their own souls. (1.5.20.3)"[461] They were not allowed to do business in the city, and many of their shops in the vicinity of Churches were confiscated. "We do not permit them generally to transact business within the sacred boundaries, so that the orthodox faith's pure mysteries may not be heard by persons who are both polluted and unworthy of every clean and pure sound heard. (*Cod. justin.* 1.5.20.4)"[462]

Justinian was never politically correct, diplomatic or accommodative; religious diversity and pluralism were curses to him. He promulgated precise, pinpointed and strict laws to eradicated diversity and to realise unification. "Justinian had no time for religious dissent. His laws against heretics are couched in blunt, implacable prose. Their style is that of the literature of theological controversy: undiplomatic, intolerant and vituperative. Heretics were considered mad, stupid or sick. Nestorians were depraved. As in Soviet Russia, deviationism was attributed to insanity. The Manichaean heretics were deemed the most odious, and the Montanists ran them a close second. Penalties were harsh. Heretical sects had their churches and church properties confiscated and their meetings outlawed. For two types of heretical felons, capital punishment was prescribed: Manichees, and Catholics who lapsed into heresy."[463] An elaborate system of intelligence and a comprehensive network of local watchdogs was established. The commoners, officials, bureaucrats and clergy were all ordered to ascertain the implementation. "Informants were encouraged. Clergy were to scrutinise their congregations and laymen to inform on each other. If any heretic was caught holding a meeting in his house, it was to be confiscated and transferred to the church [...] The aim of Justinian's policy was one empire, one church and one orthodoxy."[464]

Justinian's era was marred with natural calamities. "A sequence of earthquakes, floods, and famine had nagged the empire from the turn of the sixth century, hitting the eastern provinces particularly hard. The situation came to a head in 542 when the Great Bubonic Plague broke out, bringing an incomprehensible level of disaster. Wherever it struck, production and business halted altogether for the duration of its presence. The survivors were left to restore 'normality,' while imperial demands continued unabated. But the plague recurred, in Justinian's reign four more times, and it deepened its toll on each occasion. When Evagrius Scholasticus wrote an account of this blight in his *Ecclesiastical History,* he stated with resignation that he wrote in the fifty-second year of the plague. The cumulative effect on population, morale, and economy was as insidious as it was disastrous."[465] Justinian connected the natural phenomenon to the pleasure or displeasure of the Lord; a severe winter or hot summer was the token of Lord's displeasure with the empire. It was thought essential to persecute and humiliate the Lord's traitors to placate his wrath. The heretics were so despised that public or state charity was forbidden of them.

Tabbernee summarises four steps taken by Justinian to curb and eradicate heresy. For instance, Montanists assemblies, clergies, books and economic interests were all targeted. "The first step was to stop Montanists assembling together for worship and other purposes. Almost all of the anti-Montanist legislation forbade Montanists to gather together. Montanists were not allowed to have their own churches, and harsh penalties were prescribed for those who convened assemblies on private property. If the owner was a Montanist or Montanist sympathiser, the property was to be confiscated; if the assembly was held on an estate without the owner's knowledge or permission, the manager or leaseholder was fined, beaten, and exiled for life. Montanist clergy or others responsible for convening such gatherings were also exiled for life. Arcadius even prescribed the death penalty for these offenses."[466]

Some laws were specifically geared towards the heretic clergy and leadership. "A second step was to eliminate Montanist leadership. Montanist clergy were expelled from cities and villages so that they would have little opportunity to convert Catholics. Arcadius, again, prescribed the death penalty for Montanist clergy found in cities. Honourius excluded them from all society. Other emperors imposed heavy fines on those who ordained or let themselves be ordained as Montanist clergy. Montanist leaders were also forbidden to baptise or celebrate the eucharist. A third step was to seek out and destroy all Montanist books so that, when deprived of its clergy, the movement would not be able to continue without them. A fourth step was to make it financially and socially unattractive, if not nearly impossible, for people to become, or remain, Montanists. A variety of laws declared Montanists intestate, denied them the capacity to inherit property, give or receive donations, make contracts, transact business, trade in slaves, or testify in law suits. The property of all convicted Montanists was to be confiscated, and Montanists were not."[467] Other heretics, such as Nestorians and Monophysites, met the same fate.[468]

The legislative measures against the heretics were quite effective. The Nestorians and Monphysites, for example, migrated towards Persia and others were gradually eliminated. "The cumulative effect of all the anti-Montanist legislative measures ultimately brought about the eradication of Montanism."[469] The state and Church united their efforts to purge the empire of Lord's traitors, and Justinian maximised them to the extent that heretical tendencies were virtually suppressed. "Justinian's campaign against the Montanists appears to have been successful. There are reports of mass suicide of Montanists as a result of his legislation (Procopius, *Hist. arc.* 11.23), and, as we have already noted, John of Ephesus wiped out the remnants of Phrygian Montanism during the latter part of Justinian's reign."[470] With the exception of the Samaritans, most heretics and pagans were virtually eradicated. Justinian would personally oversee the execution, burning and drowning of many heretics; one orthodox observer would exclaim that "the *dux* has lately become a Christian by zeal of the Christ-loving emperor."[471]

The following Christians centuries are well known for their persecution of heretics and dissenters. The medieval Inquisitions well illustrate the persecuting impulses of the medieval Church.

Some Conclusions

The above discussions illustrate that the Jewish monotheism of Jesus was paganised and Hellenised due to the socio-political influences of the Roman Empire. The resultant Roman Christianity had some unintended by products, as the synthesis of two divergent traditions was obviously not without challenges. Hedonism, antinomianism, immoralism, irrationalism, royalism and persecutionism were some of the byproducts of Christian theology, soteriology and epistemology. The accumulative effect of these byproducts was the downfall of the Roman and Byzantine Empires, culminating into the medieval Dark Ages. The Christian community at large was marred with artificial intellectualism, lack of free inquiry, philosophy and logical discourse. The Church-dominated community was instead obsessed with scriptures and Church tradition. To understand such a fanatical approach to philosophy and natural knowledge, one needs to understand the ecclesiastical mindset. The contours of that lie in the Christian theology and soteriology which emphasized the life to come at the expense of this material life.

The eternal spiritual life is far longer and significant than this fading, finite and material worldly life. Therefore, the eternal salvation constitutes the primal and fundamental objective of human life. Man with his fallen nature is intrinsically sinful and cannot achieve his own salvation. There is only one way to salvation and that is through the atoning death of Jesus Christ, the second person of Trinity, the Lord who voluntarily died for human sin. Belief in his divinity and faith in his atoning crucifixion and resurrection are the cornerstones of true salvation. The Trinity, incarnation and resurrection are mysteries and cannot be grasped by limited human reason. The only source of true faith is the revelation. God has spoken to us through His Word, Jesus Christ. The spoken word of God is preserved in the Bible. Therefore, the only thing one needs to attain salvation is the Bible. There is no need for additional thinking, sciences or knowledge. All truth, wisdom, morality and common sense are contained in the revelation, which has been given to us as a substitute to all other sciences, including physical science and philosophy. In short, to succeed one needs to understand the divine revelation, digest its precepts and live one's life accordingly. Nobody has understood the revelation more than the Early Church Fathers, as they were closest to the times of Christ. The Catholic Church or the Church is the repository of their teachings. Therefore, obeying the Church is like obeying the Church fathers and obeying them is tantamount to obeying Christ, the God. Therefore, instead of wasting time in studying the pagan Greek philosophers' writings one should study the Church traditions.

Pagan philosophers were against the spirit and letter of the revelation. Aristotle did not believe in the Divine Providence and immortality of soul; he believed in eternity of this material cosmos. Plato believed in the transmigration of souls and the Stoics and Epicureans were atheists and materialists, while the Christian faith is other worldly. What did the philosophers know or say about Lord Jesus Christ, Holy Trinity, Incarnation, Justification through Faith in Crucifixion and Resurrection? They were pagans, and hence irrelevant to a believing Christian. Actually, they were fools as St. Paul remarked: "Professing themselves to be wise, they became fools." (Roman 1:22)

167

He further stated: "Where is the wise? where is the scribe? where is the disputer of this world? hath not God made foolish the wisdom of this world? For after that in the wisdom of God the world by wisdom knew not God, it pleased God by the foolishness of preaching to save them that believe. For the Jews require a sign, and the Greeks seek after wisdom: But we preach Christ crucified, unto the Jews a stumbling block, and unto the Greeks foolishness; But unto them which are called, both Jews and Greeks, Christ the power of God, and the wisdom of God. Because the foolishness of God is wiser than men; and the weakness of God is stronger than men." (1 Corinthians 1:20-25) Consequently, understanding the revelation is of prime significance, while the foolishness of pagan philosophers is darkness and antithetical to salvation. Christianity then has its own philosophy and that is nothing else but the revelation. The Bible is self-sufficient and the Church is the sole proprietor of the Bible. In short, the Church philosophy is the divine philosophy. Faith is trusting God; questioning the faith is tantamount to losing the trust in God.

The Early Church Father St. Tertullian (160-220) converted to Christianity in around 193. The African Christian was known for his hatred of reliance upon philosophy or intellectual reasoning to determine the Christian dogmas. How could one reason that the Lord Jesus Christ was a full man and equally a full God? But the very impossibility of its comprehension is the proof of this fundamental Christian doctrine's authenticity. Tertullian seems to argue that the more unintelligible a belief is, the more likely it is true. Faith is not reason; had it been reasonable, it would have not been called faith. Moreover, human reason is tainted by the original sin. The sinful man is not capable of comprehending the truth, and it needs to rely upon God's Word. We will see resonance of such a subliminal and mystical outlook in many subsequent Christian theologians all the way to St. Thomas Aquinas and Dunn Scouts with varying degrees.

Tertullian, illustrating St. Paul's above quoted statement, puts the point in the nutshell: "[T]he Lord [...] 'chose the foolish things of the world' to confound even philosophy itself. For it [i.e., philosophy] is [...] the material of the world's wisdom, the rash interpreter of the nature and the dispensation of God. Indeed heresies are themselves instigated by philosophy. [...] The same subject matter is discussed over and over again by the heretics and the philosophers; the same arguments are involved. [The heretics and philosophers constantly ask:] Whence comes evil? Why is it permitted? What is the origin of man? [...] Unhappy Aristotle, who invented [...] dialectics, the art of building up and pulling down [by using argumentation]; an art so evasive, [...] so farfetched in its conjectures, so [...] productive of contentions embarrassing even to itself, retracting everything, and really treating of nothing! Whence spring those [...] 'unprofitable questions', and 'words which spread like a cancer?' From all these, when the apostle would restrain us, he expressly names *philosophy* as that which he would have us be on our guard against. Writing to the Colossians, he says, 'See that no one beguile you through philosophy and vain deceit, after the tradition of men, and contrary to the wisdom of the Holy Ghost.' He had been at Athens and had in his interviews [in Athens] become acquainted with that human wisdom which pretends to know the truth [i.e., philosophy], whilst it only corrupts it, and is itself divided into its own manifold heresies, by the variety of its mutually repugnant sects. What indeed has Athens to do with Jerusalem? What concord is there between the Academy and the Church? [...] Our instruction comes from 'the porch of Solomon' who had himself taught that 'the Lord should be sought in simplicity of heart.' Away with all attempts to produce a mottled Christianity of Stoic, Platonic, and dialectic composition! We want no curious disputation after possessing Christ Jesus [...] With our faith, we desire no further belief. For this is our palmary faith, that there is nothing which we ought to believe besides."[472]

Tertullian also argued against the use of free will and choices. He discouraged free inquiry and questioning, and blamed freedom of choice and human inquisitiveness for internal divisions. "Tertullian insists that making choices is evil, since choice destroys group unity. To stamp out heresy, Tertullian says, church leaders must not allow people to ask questions, for it is 'questions that make people heretics'—above all, questions like these: Whence comes evil? Why is it permitted? And what is the origin of human beings? Tertullian wants to stop such questions and impose upon all believers the same *regula fidei*, 'rule of faith,' or creed."[473]

Tertullian's words became canonical in the following centuries. They epitomised the Christian battle with philosophy, and were repeatedly quoted until the end of the middle ages - and even later. The Early Church discouraged and sanctioned even the language, rhetoric, grammar and books of pagan gentiles; nothing of the barbarians was useful to Christian mind and practice. In reality their heritage and legacy were antithetical to revelation, and hence injurious to Christian piety. The Greco-Latin barbarian traditions we absolutely shunned. Charles Haskins shows that the Church insisted that the study of Latin "be narrowly limited to the essentials of grammar which gave a practical command of the language; any further study of the ancients was at the best a waste of time, and at the worst a peril to the soul. The mere beauty of Latin style might itself be a danger for men who turned their backs on this world. St. Jerome gives an oft cited account of a vision in which an angel rebuked him for being a Ciceronian rather than a Christian."[474] Haskins notices that "the fourth council of Carthage in 398 forbade bishops to read the books of the gentiles, 'The representatives of St. Peter and his disciples,' said the legate Leo in the tenth century; 'will not have Plato or Virgil or Terence as their masters nor the rest of the philosophic cattle.' Even a small amount of grammatical study was opposed by Gregory the Great, who wrote, "I do not shun at all the confusion of barbarians. I despise the proper constructions and cases, because I think it very unfitting that the words of the celestial oracle should be restricted by the rules of Donatus.'"[475] St. Jerome's Latin translation of Bible, Vulgate, became the standard of Latin language. Latin was not studied as a language, but as a tool to understand the revelation. Consequently, the language suffered the limitations of its narrow use and was thoroughly Christianised. "Smaragdus in the ninth century wrote a grammar with the examples taken from the Vulgate instead of from the dangerous pagan authors."[476] Haskin shows that the narrow mindset continued through the later centuries and defined the true Christianisation of Christendom. "The twelfth century had the same difficulties. The so-called Honourius of Autun asks, 'How is the soul-profited by the strife of Hector, the arguments of Plato, the poems of Virgil, or the elegies of Ovid, who, with others like them, are now gnashing their teeth in the prison of the infernal Babylon, under the cruel tyranny of Pluto?' Even Abaelard inquires 'why the bishops and doctors of the Christian religion do not expel from the City of God those poets whom Plato forbade to enter in to his city of the world'; 'while Nicholas, the secretary of Bernard of Clairvaux, sighs over the charm he had once found in Cicero and the poets, and in the golden sayings of the philosophers and the songs of the Sirens.'"[477]

Cultural expressions such as poetry, eloquence and rhetoric were disdained by the ecclesiastical hierarchy. Magic, witchcraft and poetry were sanctioned on equal footing. "Guibert de Nogent regrets the Latin poets of his youth. The poets were regarded with special disfavor, being sometimes classified with magicians. Thus in the illustrations in the *HortuJ deliciarum* of Herrad of Landsberg four poets or magicians, each with an evil spirit prompting him, are placed outside the circle of the seven liberal arts. When Gratian, *ca.* 1140, prepared his *Concord of Discordant Canons,* one of the major differences which he seeks to reconcile is this very question, 'Shall priests be acquainted with profane literature or no?'"[478] The Church insisted to make Christian Scripture, tradition and piety the focus of Christendom. The ecclesiastical establishment routed out perceived barbarian sciences and cultural expressions to replace them with pure Christian knowledge and wisdom. Consequently, the Church became supreme both in spiritual and temporal capacities. Authority breeds rivalries and contentions trigger decadence. This is what happened in the later centuries.

In brief, the possible hedonistic, irrational, absolutist and coercive manifestations of Christian tradition resulted in an irrational, mythological, superstitious, guilty and suppressed society where free inquiry, inquisitive discourse, free will, freedom of choices, liberty, human rights, dissent and diversity were not only discouraged but severely punished. The society was divided between the elites, clergy and laity. The class power struggle was the norm which at times trickled down to the laity. The ignorant masses were exploited to pressurise the opposing side, but mostly the masses were kept in mental and physical slavery, in line with Augustinian theology. Christendom became a hierarchical society where class consciousness and struggles were quite rampant. Bishops were suddenly exalted, and also immediately deposed and exiled once out of the favor. Emperors often changed their allies, pitching various factions against each other to realise their imperial designs. Opposing groups were severely chastised, punished and persecuted. Pagans, Jews and countless heretics were coerced to conform to the orthodox socio-political and religious requirements. Religious dissent was punished through economic, social, legal and physical sanctions. As absolutism, irrationalism and coercion lead to tensions, anxieties, the later Roman Empire and Byzantine Empires were marred with divisions, rebellion and revolts. The state was mostly unable to meet the socio-economic needs of the subjects and resentment, resistance and agitation were commonplace. Natural disasters such as earthquakes, floods and plagues added to the irony. For instance, the otherwise effective governing structure of Justinian was at a loss to confront the multiple natural disasters which played havoc during his reign. Absolutism and authoritarianism added to the subjects' dissatisfaction. The arbitrary and authoritarian understandings of the divine realms were copied to create conforming terrestrial realms. In short, "Orthodox Christians acted on their belief about God. As they perceived God to control in an authoritarian manner, so they set about finding a way in which they, in God's name, could exercise similar authoritarian control. To that end, they built an organisation that appealed to the government of the Roman Empire by promoting uniformity and obedience. In all likelihood, these Christians altered the story of Jesus's death in order to dissociate Christianity from rebellion against Roman authority. They established criteria that made it easy to recruit large numbers of people. The early Church compromised its ideology to accommodate contemporary beliefs. It was through political maneuvering that the Church won its standing as the official religion of the Roman Empire and the accompanying secular power and privilege."[479]

Arbitrary, artificial and irrational dogmas were imposed by dint of sheer power resulting in many heresies and revolts. "The Church formulated its doctrine regarding sex, free will and reincarnation in response to early heretics. In each case, it chose ideological positions which best justified Church control over the individual and over society. The Church also developed a doctrine which justified its use of force in order to compel obedience. It was not long before the Church needed that doctrine to defend its violent suppression of heresy."[480] That doctrine was afforded by the genius of Augustine.

The overall superstitious, illogical and overpowering policies of the Church and state had destructive spiritual, social, economic and political impacts degenerating into fearful, guilty and suppressed subjects and warring factions. The civilisational aspects of the Old Roman Empire gradually faded away. "The Church had devastating impact upon society. As the Church assumed leadership, activity in the fields of medicine, technology, science, education, history, art and commerce all but collapsed. Europe entered the Dark Ages. Although the Church amassed immense wealth during these centuries, most of what defines civilisation disappeared. The western Roman Empire fell during the fifth century under repeated attacks by the Germanic Goths and the Huns while the Roman province of Africa fell to the Vandals. Many blamed Christianity. In 410 when the Christian Visigoths sacked Rome, 'the eternal city' which had held strong for 620 years, criticism of the new religion intensified. One of St. Augustine's most famous works, *The City of God*, was written as a defense of Christianity against such accusations."[481]

Some modern historians contend that the Roman Empire neither fell nor declined; rather, it transitioned into middle ages and transformed itself in to an age of spirit and vibrant faith.[482] Religious Christianity, rather than secular paganism, ruled the later Antiquity and medieval age. Contemporary historian Bryn Perkins rejects such a notion as "deceptively wrong."[483] He observes that "It is currently deeply unfashionable to state that anything like a 'crisis' or a 'decline' occurred at the end of the Roman empire, let alone that a 'civilisation' collapsed and a 'dark age' ensued. The new orthodoxy is that the Roman world, in both East and West, was slowly, and essentially painlessly, 'transformed' into a medieval form. However, there is an insuperable problem with this new view: it does not fit the mass of archaeological evidence now available, which shows a startling decline in western standards of living during the fifth to seventh centuries. This was a change that affected everyone, from peasants to kings, even the bodies of saints resting in their churches. It was no mere transformation—it was decline on a scale that can reasonably be described as 'the end of a civilisation.'"[484] He maintains that almost every aspect of civilisation was absolutely devastated. "In the post-Roman West, almost all this material sophistication disappeared. Specialised production and all but the most local distribution became rare, unless for luxury goods; and the impressive range and quantity of high-quality functional goods, which had characterised the Roman period, vanished, or, at the very least, were drastically reduced. The middle and lower markets, which under the Romans had absorbed huge quantities of basic, but good-quality, items, seem to have almost entirely disappeared."[485]

There were many reasons for the fall of the Roman Empire; some historians have given almost 210 reasons for this gradual decline. I am not contending here that Christianity was the sole reason for the Empire's demise; I am arguing that Christianity, with its superstitious and irrational theology, faith-based salvation scheme, celibacy, monasticism, asceticism, militant popes/bishops, persecuting monarchy and schismatic clerical hierarchy, greatly expedited it. To me Edward Gibbon's classical analysis of the decline and fall of the Roman Empire are still valid. His following long summarizing passage deserves our utmost reflection. "As the happiness of a future life is the great object of religion, we may hear, without surprise or scandal, that the introduction, or at least the abuse, of Christianity had some influence on the decline and fall of the Roman empire. The clergy successfully preached the doctrines of patience and pusillanimity; the active virtues of society were discouraged; and the last remains of the military spirit were buried in the cloister; a large portion of public and private wealth was consecrated to the specious demands of charity and devotion; and the soldiers' pay was lavished on the useless multitudes of both sexes, who could only plead the merits of abstinence and chastity. Faith, zeal, curiosity, and the more earthly passions of malice and ambition kindled the flame of theological discord; the church, and even the state, were distracted by religious factions, whose conflicts were sometimes bloody, and always implacable; the attention of the emperors was diverted from camps to synods; the Roman world was oppressed by a new species of tyranny; and the persecuted sects became the secret enemies of their country. Yet party-spirit, however pernicious or absurd, is a principle of union as well as of dissension. The bishops, from eighteen hundred pulpits, inculcated the duty of passive obedience to a lawful and orthodox sovereign; their frequent assemblies, and perpetual correspondence, maintained the communion of distant churches: and the benevolent temper of the gospel was strengthened, though confined, by the spiritual alliance of the Catholics. The sacred indolence of the monks was devoutly embraced by a servile and effeminate age; but, if superstition had not afforded a decent retreat, the same vices would have tempted the unworthy Romans to desert, from baser motives, the standard of the republic. Religious precepts are easily obeyed, which indulge and sanctify the natural inclinations of their votaries; but the pure and genuine influence of Christianity may be traced in its beneficial, though imperfect, effects on the Barbarian proselytes of the North. If the decline of the Roman empire was hastened by the conversion of Constantine, his victorious religion broke the violence of the fall, and mollified the ferocious temper of the conquerors."[486] He specifically highlighted the above discussed religious schism as one of the major factors that paralysed the state. "Especially did religious discord and the persecution of one sect of Christians by another, after the time of Constantine, paralyze the energies of the state, waste its strength, and open the gates of the empire to the invasions of the northern barbarians, just as the same causes, two centuries later, facilitated the conquests of the Mohammedan Arabs."[487]

Many contemporary Catholic and Protestant scholars roundly reject these prepositions, and contend that Gibbon's anti-Church and monarchy enlightenment tendencies unjustifiably made Christianity the scapegoat of his biases. That may not be true. Many modern scholars have also alluded to almost the same Christianising factors as the partial sources of the Roman's demise. A. H. M. Jones, a contemporary Catholic scholar, lambasts the economically unproductive citizens of the late empire—aristocrats, civil servants, and churchmen: 'the Christian church imposed a new class of idle mouths on the resources of the empire [...] a large number lived on the alms of the peasantry, and as time went on more and more monasteries acquired landed endowments which enabled their inmates to devote themselves entirely to their spiritual duties.'"[488] The Christian Church and its teachings greatly contributed to the military, professional, economic, and technical setbacks, internal and external.

With the Fall of Rome, the ancient civilisation and culture came to a complete halt. Scottish historian William Robertson noted that "in less than a century after the barbarian nations settled in their new conquests, almost all the effects of the knowledge and civility, which the Romans had spread through Europe, disappeared. Not only the arts of elegance, which minister to luxury, and are supported by it, but many of the useful arts, without which life can scarcely be contemplated as comfortable, were neglected or lost."[489] In the words of Bryn Perkins, "with the fall of the empire, Art, Philosophy, and decent drains all vanished from the West."[490]

The pagans put the blame squarely upon the Christians, "pagans now, not unreasonably, attributed Roman failure to the abandonment by the State of the empire's traditional gods, who for centuries had provided so much security and success. The most sophisticated, radical, and influential answer to this problem was that offered by Augustine, who in 413 (initially in direct response to the sack of Rome) began his monumental *City of God*. Here he successfully sidestepped the entire problem of the failure of the Christian empire by arguing that all human affairs are flawed, and that a true Christian is really a citizen of Heaven. Abandoning centuries of Roman pride in their divinely ordained state (including Christian pride during the fourth century), Augustine argued that, in the grand perspective of Eternity, a minor event like the sack of Rome paled into insignificance."[491] Christian apologists blamed it on human sins. "Christian apologists generally had to bat on a very sticky wicket, starting from the premise that secular affairs were indeed desperate. Most resorted to what rapidly became Christian platitudes in the face of disaster. The author of the *Poem on the Providence of God*, composed in Gaul in about 416, exhorted Christians to consider whether these troubles had been brought about by their own sins, and encouraged them to realize that earthly happiness and earthly treasures are but dust and ashes, and nothing to the rewards that await us in Heaven."[492] Still others placed the blame on the wickedness of their Christian brethren. "A little later, in the 440s, Salvian, a priest from the region of Marseille, addressed the central and difficult questions, 'Why has God allowed us to become weaker and more miserable than all the tribal peoples? Why has he allowed us to be defeated by the barbarians, and subjected to the rule of our enemies?' Salvian's solution was to attribute the disasters of his age to the wickedness of his contemporaries, which had brought divine judgement down upon their own heads."[493]

The Byzantine Empire initially thrived in the East. Its geographical location, subordinative clerical arrangements, original tolerant policies, peace with the Persians and sheer luck helped it for the next few centuries. To Perkins "it was primarily good fortune, rather than innately greater strength, that was decisive."[494] But its later absolutist political and persecuting religious policies, along with the natural disasters such as the bubonic plague beginning in 540 AD, cut its progress short. The plague, which occurred over a period of almost 54 years, claimed approximately 100 million lives in the sixth century. The Empire never recovered, but the Church flourished. "The plague had quite different impact upon Christianity. People flocked to the Church in terror. The Church explained that the plague was an act of God, and disease a punishment for the sin of not obeying Church authority. The Church branded Justinian a heretic. It declared the field of Greek and Roman medicine, useless in fighting the plague, to be heresy. While the plague assured the downfall of the Roman Empire, it strengthened the Christian church. After the plague, the Church dominated the formal discipline of medicine."[495] The Church pretty much undid the centuries of works building society, culture and civilisation. Meditation, submission, charity, love, celibacy, monasticism, otherworldliness and Church became the common obsessions. "Technology disappeared as the Church became the most cohesive power in Western society. The extensive aqueduct and plumbing systems vanished. Orthodox Christians taught that all aspects of the flesh should be reviled and therefore discouraged washing as much as possible. Toilets and indoor plumbing disappeared. Disease became commonplace as sanitation and hygiene deteriorated. For hundreds of years, towns and villages were decimated by epidemics. Roman central heating systems were also abandoned."[496] The vast network of roads went into neglect, and the losses in science, technology and philosophy were monumental. "In some cases the Christian church's burning of books and repression of intellectual pursuit set humanity back as much as two millennia in its scientific understanding."[497] The Church solely focused upon teaching the Bible and Christian tradition, at the expense of philosophy and other worldly sciences. Anti-philosophy sentiments were systematically inculcated. "The Christian church had similar impact upon education and learning. The Church burned enormous amounts of literature. In 391 Christians burned down one of the world's greatest libraries in Alexandria, said to have housed 700,000 rolls. All the books of the Gnostic Basilides, Porphyry's 36 volumes, papyrus rolls of 27 schools of the Mysteries, and 270,000 ancient documents gathered by Ptolemy Philadelphus were burned. Ancient academies of learning were closed. Education for anyone outside of the Church came to an end. And what little education there was during the Dark Ages, while still limited to the clergy, was advocated by powerful kings as a means of providing themselves with capable administrators."[498] The Church monopolised the markets and sanctioned competition doing little to encourage trade. Other than excelling in Church administration and wealth accumulation, Church authorities did little to enhance economic growth, literacy, empowerment, distribution of resources and state building. It had an overall negative effect upon culture and society. "The Church played a critical role in taking Europe into the Dark Ages. Its devastating impact was felt in nearly every sphere of human endeavour. Ironically, the one area where the medieval Church had little profound impact was in changing the spirituality of common people. While most people adopted a Christian veneer, they did not significantly change their understanding or perception of God."[499] In fact, the Church caused tremendous confusions regarding the concept of God, morality and spirituality. The Trinitarian, Incarnational scheme of salvation, the internal relations and power dynamics of the three persons of divinity, the generation of Jesus and procession of Holy Spirit from God the Father, the derivative, subordinative and secondary nature of Jesus and the Holy Spirit, the divine and human nature of Jesus, the Omnipotence of a suffering Christ, the finite knowledge of an Omniscient God, the changing nature and conditions of an infinite God, the failed mission of Jesus and the botched eternal kingdom, all scandalous theological inventions, were artificial, arbitrary and illogical. The early Christian centuries were plagued with schisms, heresies, synods and councils. In spite of constant imperial interventions and persistent supervisions the Church was at a loss to bring about doctrinal unity, comprehension and intelligibility. The entirety of Christendom, East and West, was inundated with schismatic heresies and sects. The house was fully divided and the intellectual landscape was absolutely fogged. "We can perhaps understand how easy it was for Mohammed to blow the whistle on the whole confusing game, with the simple, uncompromising assertion that God Is One."[500]

Traditional Christianity wanted to have God. But how was this possible? Paul Tillich answers: "Because of the incarnation, for in the incarnation God became something which we can have, whom we can see, with whom we can talk etc."[501] Throughout their history, Christians have been trying to save the transcendent God from corporeality, anthropomorphisms and unintelligibility, but their desire for salvation had very often resulted in the opposite. This probably was among the factors that led the Islamic version of transcendence and simple monotheism, observes K. Armstrong, to "spread with astonishing rapidity throughout the Middle East and North Africa. Many of its enthusiastic converts in these lands (where Hellenism was not at home ground) turned with relief from Greek Trinitarianism, which expressed the mystery of God in an idiom that was alien to them, and adopted a more Semitic notion of the divine reality."[502] Islam, the southern Christian reformation, was eagerly welcomed by the pagans as well as many heretical Christians in Egypt, Palestine, Levant and many other areas of the Byzantine Empire.

Chapter 3

Islam: The Southern
Reformation of Christianity

Islam as a rival faith analysed, scrutinised, dissected and finally rejected Christian supernaturalism, absolutism, dogmatism, irrationalism, antinomianism, Trinitarianism, clericalism and grace-based salvation scheme. John William Draper noticed that Islam was the "first or Southern Reformation"[503] of Christianity long before the Northern Reformation in sixteenth-century Europe.[504] To W. E. H. Lecky, Islam resolved the Christian problems of idolatry and was a total break with previous civilisational patterns. "It must, however, be acknowledged that there is one example of a great religion, reigning for the most part over men who had not yet emerged from the twilight of an early civilisation, which has nevertheless succeeded in restraining its votaries from idolatry. This phenomenon, which is the preeminent glory of Mahometanism, and the most remarkable evidence of the genius of its founder, appears so much at variance with the general laws of historic development […] one of the great characteristics of the Koran is the extreme care and skill with which it labours to assist men in realising the unseen. Descriptions the most minutely detailed, and at the same time the most vivid, are mingled with powerful appeals to those sensual passions by which the imagination in all countries, but especially in those in which Mahometanism has taken root, is most forcibly influenced. In no other religion that prohibits idols was the strain upon the imagination so slight."[505] Islam rectified Church excesses in the areas of monotheism,[506] rationalism, nomianism, monarchism, clericalism and religious intolerance. Islam introduced the rule of many instead of a few; it incorporated the largest possible numbers of people in matters of religious knowledge, socio political and civil affairs. It was a commoner's revolution against the religious and political elites. Martin Pugh notes that "Islam appeared as a purified and simplified form that super-seded Christianity. This was felt to be necessary, because Muslims be-lieved that Christians had introduced into the practice of the religion all kinds of dubious notions, elaborations and misunderstandings that had not been part of the original. Islam provided a clarification and a return to a truer, simpler, stricter form. This was a view that many Christians themselves were to welcome, especially during the Protestant Refor-mation in the Sixteenth and Seventeenth centuries (although it was to overlook the central disagreement about the divinity of Christ)."[507]

Islam brought its rival, simple, rational, natural and ethical mono-theism; human, prophetic, anti-Trinitarian Christology; natural cos-mology with direct divine sovereignty without any intermediaries, co-operating natural forces or semi quasi divinities; ethical anthropology, teleology and soteriology; rational epistemology and republican exou-siology (political thought). The ethical monotheism, rational Unitari-anism, divinely ordained natural order and design, divinely installed natural laws and divinely inspired moral laws, human, prophetic Chris-tology, virtue based salvation, human reformation, participation and initiative and final reward and punishment were so emphasised and simplified by Islam that a cursory reader of its Scripture, the Quran, would not have missed it. Islam replaced the Christian supernatural, interventionist, overly miraculous, changing, irregular, abnormal and mutable cosmos with natural, regular, harmonious, immutable, order-ly and hinged cosmos with fixed, unbroken and explorable laws. It also replaced Christian religio-political absolutism with republican plural-ism and religious freedom. Islam was the Southern Reformation of the Church Christianity.

Islam and Christian Background

Islam emerged in the backdrop of the Byzantine and Sassanid empires' geopolitical wars, and Christian sectarian conflicts. The constant geo-political conflicts intensified inter-religious polemics between the Byz-antine Christianity and Sassanid Zoroastrianism and trickled down to the Arabian Peninsula. Some northern Arab tribes worked as buffer zones between the two warring empires.[508] The two main vassal Arab tribes were both heretical Christians. The Jafnid family of the tribe of Ghassan in the present-day Golan Heights area was the vassal of Byzantine, protecting them against the nomadic attacks and supplying them with military recruits at times of wars against the Persians. "The Ghassanids […] were Monophysites,"[509] believing that Jesus has only one nature which is divine. The Sassanid client of al-Hira, the Nasrid family of the tribe of Lakham, in central Iraq, played the same role for the Persian Empire.[510] They were Nestorian Christians[511] who believed that Jesus had two distinct natures, one purely divine and the other human.[512] Mary was the mother of human Jesus and not the divine person in Jesus. These northern Arab tribes were active participants in the centuries-long continuous warfare between the Byzantium and Persian empires.[513]

The Arabs highly admired and openly appreciated the Byzantine Christian civilisation and "as a result of their direct contact with these big centers of Christianity, some of the big nomadic tribes were in the process of Christianisation. Furthermore […] many of the Arab intellectuals of the age had a considerable knowledge of Christianity. The great poet al-Nabighah is an outstanding example. Another great poet of *Jahiliyyah,* al-A'sha ai-Akbar had an intimate personal contact with the Bishops of Najran, and his knowledge of Christianity was far from being a superficial one, as his *Diwdn* shows clearly and conclusively."[514]

The southern Arab tribes of Oman and Yemen were also engaged by the two empires. There was a considerable Christian community in the Southern Arabia, especially in the Najra'n area. The Sira' historian Ibn Isha'q (d. 153/770) claimed that Christianity in Najr'an was introduced by Faymiyu'n, a Syrian brick builder[515], but did not give any date for Faymiyu'n's missionary works. The Chronicles of John of Nikiu credited a woman named Theognosta with the conversion of Yemenites in the mid fourth century[516] and there are other theories as well.[517] Robert G. Holyland notes that "in the fourth to sixth centuries Christianity made major inroads into Arabia. The church in the Sasanian realm was very dynamic and established offshoots in all the islands and coastlands of east Arabia in this period […] From the mid-fifth century Byzantium energetically promoted Christianity in south Arabia, chiefly via its ally Ethiopia, which sparked off violent clashes with the advocates of Judaism […] But it was particularly the inhabitants of north Arabia who were won over to Christianity in large numbers in this period."[518]

The Yemeni leader Himyarite[519] king Yusuf Dhu Nuwas (ruled from 517 to 525-27 CE) was a Jew[520] actively engaged in anti-Christian activities, and leaned towards the Persians.[521] The Byzantines encouraged the Christian king of Axum (Ethiopia) to invade Yemen.[522] The Ethiopian general Abraha conquered Yemen, established an independent territory for himself and tried several excursions to the Persian areas while passing through Mecca and other central Arabian cities.[523] He rebuilt the Ma'rib Dam and erected a magnificent cathedral in Sana'a.[524] He tried to conquer Mecca also to divert the pilgrimage from Ka'aba to Sana'a. The Quran refers to such a botched effort and historical incident in *Surah al-Fi'l* 105. The local Yemenis rose in rebellion against Abraha in 572 AD and, with the help of the Persian King Khusro 1 Anushirwan (r. 531–579 C.E.), overthrew his government and drove the Abyssinians out. The Yemenites mostly remained Christians (between Monophysitism and Nestorianism, though the Persians preferred Nestorians) in spite of the Persian rule.[525]

From the birth of Prophet Muhammad in 570 until 620 AD, Yemen remained a Persian territory. "All of these activities had repercussions deep in the Arabian peninsula. Most Arabian communities and pastoral groups, particularly those in the north of the peninsula, were aware of the Byzantine-Sasanian rivalry and must have been constrained to accommodate to it somehow, whether by allying themselves openly with one power or the other or by carefully trying to preserve their neutrality."[526] Barnard Lewis notes that "Persian and Byzantine culture, both material and moral, permeated through several channels, most of them connected with the trans-Arabian trade routes."[527] The Prophet's Meccan opponents, the tribe of Qurysh, were closely allied with the Jafnids and through them with the Byzantines. Izutsu argues that "it would be a mistake to suppose that the people of Mecca remained entirely uninfluenced by such a situation, if only for the reason that they, as professional merchants, travelled on business so often to these Christian centers. Besides, in Mecca itself, there were also Christians, not only Christian slaves, but Christians of the clan of Banu Asad b. 'Abd al-'Uzza."[528]

It is pertinent to mention here that Waraqah bin Nawfal, the cousin of Prophet Muhammad's wife, was a Christian. He was "well-known for his Christian religion and his good knowledge of Hebrew scripture,"[529] and was an orthodox Chalcedonian Christian. As seen above, Chalcedonian Christianity maintained that Jesus was a full God and a full man; the two natures interacted in the person of Jesus but were never compromised. Mary was the mother of man Jesus and not the God, and Jesus the man died on the Cross and not God. Therefore, in the pre-Islamic Arabia all three sects of Christianity (Chalcedonian, Nestorian and Monophysites) were existent and known. The Prophet also related more to the Christians, due to their supposed monotheism, than to the dominant dualist Persians. (Surah Rum: 1-2)

Control of the luxury goods trade from China and India to the Byzantine and Roman areas was the main bone of contention between the two empires.[530] "Rivalry over trade was a significant component of this contest. Chinese silk, Indian cotton, pepper and other spices, South Arabian incense, leather (heavily in demand by the imperial armies), and other commodities had been important items of trade for the Romans, who had even established commercial colonies in South India, and they continued to be important for the Byzantines. Silk, in particular, was prized and came via the routes known collectively as the famous 'Silk Road' through Central Asia and Iran to the Mediterranean. Goods from the Indian Ocean could reach Byzantine territory either through the Persian Gulf and the Tigris-Euphrates valley or via the Red Sea."[531]

Trade caravans passed through the narrow terrain and coastal areas of Hijaz where the two cities of Mecca and Medina were located. "The long-standing hostility between Sassanian Persia and Roman Byzantine had destroyed trade along the usual overland route from the Mediterranean to the head of the Persian Gulf. A new route was therefore sought for goods which flowed from the East, and this extended along the coastal plain of Arabia, from the seaports of Yemen whence ships plied both to India and Africa. Mecca lay in the coastal plain at a point where the north-south route intersected another major route leading to the east and the markets of Iraq. Mecca was, thus, ideally located to serve as the focus of a rich exchange."[532] Therefore, the Prophet of Islam and his early companions were not aloof from the Byzantium and Persian empires and their religions and, to Patricia Crone, Islam was a political response to the pressures generated by the two superpowers.[533] As the religion and theology were well integrated into the Byzantium state and politics, knowledge of the Byzantium Empire and its wars against heresies included some knowledge of its religion and theology.

Additionally, there was a decently-sized Jewish community in the city of Yathrib, later called Medina. Judaism was the oldest of the monotheistic traditions in the Arabian Peninsula. Some Jewish tribes made an exodus to northwest Arabia as a result of the Babylonian Exile in 597 BCE, and others followed suite due to Roman persecutions. A wave of Jewish tribes migrated to Southern Arabia after the Great Revolt in 70 AD, almost six centuries before the appearance of Islam. As the Jewish tribes lacked autonomy and mostly lived as protégés of one or another of the regional Arab tribes, they had propensities towards expressing their superiority through their patriarchal, scriptural, legal and monotheistic legacy. The Jews, by then, had produced one of the greatest legalistic traditions of all times, due to their affinity with the scripture and law. They showed expressed tendencies towards boasting about their legal legacy and monotheistic consciousness. This dialectical predilection did contribute to stir monotheistic and legalistic instincts in some native Arabs, but on a very limited level. Jews, like the Christians, were exclusivists but on the tribal grounds as the chosen people of God.

Islam claimed to have come as a grand reformative scheme to rectify the Jewish, Christian, Zoroastrian and polytheistic compromises both in religion and politics - especially the Christian theological extremes. It ushered a new era in religion, politics and society. Antony Black observes that "it was also a new beginning in the history of ideas; political thought under Islam was different to anything that had gone before. Muhammad was a *prophet* (rasul: messenger), claiming to recite whatever God told him to recite, with no human intermediary. Although he was influenced by Arab tribal custom, Judaism and Christianity, he rebelled against these, and recast their patterns in the furnace of his own revelation. Thus, the foundation of Islam was a decisive break in human thinking about politics and society."[534]

The Jewish monotheistic tradition was marred with a number of intrinsic problems. Judaic tradition was an amalgamation of anthropomorphic and transcendental tendencies.[535] The Israelites attributed a visible human form to God; indeed, a majority of mortal, human, physical and mental categories appeared to be present in the Hebrew God. God had a body; in the plains of Mamre, He appeared to Abraham in a mythico-anthropomorphic form; Abraham bowed down towards the ground, offered God water, requested Him to let him wash His feet, fetched Him a morsel of bread and God responded to Abraham's request and did eat, (Genesis 18:1-9). In the Hebrew Torah God appeared in human form, ate, drank, rested and was refreshed. For example, in a well-known biblical encounter, God wrestled with Jacob, dislocated Jacob's thigh and was even shown to be weak, unable to physically dominate Jacob, to the point of finally asking Jacob to let Him go as the dawn broke. As a result of this wrestling encounter God changed Jacob's name to Israel meaning "he struggles with God." So, the Israelites considered themselves as a God-striven nation.

Additionally, vestiges of animism, polytheism, henotheism, monolatry, national monotheism and universal and ethical monotheism, all these 'isms' were overlooked in most cases, if not sanctioned by the Hebrew Bible's writers and hence present in one way or the other, though inertly, in the Hebrew's monotheistic conceptions. The Jewish community's God was a national god who had made a special covenant with Abraham, chose his progeny through his son Isaac as His Chosen People and granted them the eternal rights of the Holy Land, the Promised Land. Very often He represented the Hebrews aspirations and national agendas, projecting in a sense their failures, dreams and fears into the cosmos. A. Lod states that "the god whom Moses sought to win over to his people was not a universal god like that of Islam: he had a proper name, Jahweh, local centers of worship, and an essential national character, he was and chose to be the God of Israel."[536] He further argues that "the Israelites, when they emerge into the full light of history [...] were not monotheists. They only worshipped one national god, Jahweh; but they believed in the existence and power of other gods: they were monolaters. But monolatry is a form of polytheism."[537] Thus in the Hebrew God what we had was not the absolute transcendent and universal God but rather an imperfect, local, national, corporeal and finite God.

The Jewish legal thought was well-developed but its political thought was rudimentary. It had a comprehensive ethnic law, but a less-developed concept of political authority, military power and sacred monarchy, due to the historical realities of being under the constant watch of alien powers. Its political thought predominantly revolved around kingship and sacred monarchy.[538] "When you enter the land the Lord your God is giving you and have taken possession of it and settled in it, and you say, "Let us set a king over us like all the nations around us," be sure to appoint over you a king the Lord your God chooses. He must be from among your fellow Israelites. Do not place a foreigner over you, one who is not an Israelite. (*Deuteronomy* 17:14-15) Monarchy was considered a gift of God.[539] (1 Samuel 9:16)

The Persian Zoroastrians believed in a dualistic theology where Ahura Mazda, the god of Light, was pitched against Ahriman, the god of Darkness, both vying for human souls through cosmological agents called angels. In Zoroastrianism, there was a clear-cut hierarchical emanation scheme of divinities worthy of worship.[540] The Zoroastrians in the Prophet's time believed in a dualistic cosmogonic theology,[541] and had a hierarchical society. They believed in a class system where the elite groups were considered closer to God than others; the Persian class system closely resembled the Indian caste system. E. Yarshater notes that the "Iranians were divided from ancient times -at least from the Achaemenian period- essentially into three classes: priests, warriors or nobles, and husbandmen."[542]

The emperor was considered the shadow of God upon the earth, and obedience to him was tantamount to divine obedience. The Persian state was an absolute monarchy, where the ruler enjoyed absolute executive, legislative and judicial powers; any challenge to or rebellion against the ruler was a taboo, thought to be punished by divine wrath.[543]

We have already discussed the details of Christian concept of God, Trinity and its various ramifications into many sectarian theologies. We have also discussed the Christian concept of the divine right monarchy and religious persecutionism. To Islam, the idea of a Triune God in all its forms and manifestations was an aberration.

Islamic Reformation of Christianity

As noted above, Islam was the "first or Southern Reformation"[544] of Christianity long before the Northern Reformation in sixteenth-century Europe.[545] It rectified Christian excesses in the areas of monotheism,[546] rationalism, nomianism, political and religious absolutism.

Islam reformed Christian Trinitarianism by restoring pristine transcendental monotheism of the Semites. It presented a simple, straightforward and logical concept of the One and Unique God. It absolutely rejected the incarnational jargon and established strict parameters to safeguard God's proper relationship with Jesus, Mary and the cosmos. Muhammad, notes William Draper, was "horrorstricken at the doctrine of the divinity of Jesus, the worship of Mary as the mother of God, the adoration of images and paintings, in his eyes a base idolatry. He absolutely rejects the Trinity, of which he seems to have entertained the idea that it could not be interpreted otherwise than as presenting three distinct Gods. His first and ruling idea was simply religious reform—to overthrow Arabian idolatry, and put an end to the wild sectarianism of Christianity. That he proposed to set up a new religion was a calumny invented against him in Constantinople, where he was looked upon with detestation, like that with which in after ages Luther was regarded in Rome."[547] Unlike Luther, Muhammad's reformation of Church Christianity was exhaustive and complete.

The Muslim Scripture insisted that one of its main purposes was to rectify the Trinitarian, Incarnational and redemptive Christian theology.[548] All problems connected to divine incarnation, diffusion or confusion were eliminated by Islamic concept of divine otherness. Draper observed that Islam was "the first or Southern Reformation. The point in dispute had respect to the nature of God. It involved the rise of Mohammedanism. Its result was, that much of Asia and Africa, with the historic cities Jerusalem, Alexandria, and Carthage, were wrenched from Christendom, and the doctrine of the Unity of God established in the larger portion of what had been the Roman Empire."[549] He further states that "this political event was followed by the restoration of science, the establishment of colleges, schools, libraries, throughout the dominions of the Arabians. Those conquerors, pressing forward rapidly in their intellectual development, rejected the anthropomorphic ideas of the nature of God remaining in their popular belief, and accepted other more philosophical ones."[550] Islam categorically rejected the anthropomorphic and corporeal concept of God embodied in incarnation, hence restoring reason and logic in place of un-intelligible mysteries, preparing the way for science and philosophy to flourish in the following centuries.

This reasoned approach to religion was made possible by reformation of Christian incarnational salvation scheme. The Christian faith by its supernatural Trinitarian interpretations had rendered Jesus so lofty, unique and transcendent that he became really irrelevant to humanity except in spiritual realms of submission and repentance. He, in his divinity, was un-approachable and inimitable. Human beings had to rise to titanic moral heights to equal his co-eternal, co-equal, sinless Godhead. In view of this unsurmountable challenge, Jesus and his moral message became irrelevant to humanity. It was so ideal, angelic and lofty that only an angelic, divine person could rise up to it or realise it. Moreover, the Christian dogma of original sin and fallen nature weakened human self-confidence and self-belief in human abilities, minimizing possibilities of human initiatives and hard work. Islam by attacking the Trinity and the original sin restored human self-esteem and provided them with a human model of excellence in man, Jesus, to pursue their moral and intellectual capacities without restraint. Islam made Christianity a rational, simplistic, moral and universal faith by removing its local, artificial, supernatural scaffolding and by connecting it with the universal, moral, monotheistic prophetic tradition of Abraham, Noah, Moses and Muhammad. This humanisation of Jesus resulted in a moral, rational and intellectual empowerment of humanity. Islam's total rejection of Trinity, original sin and redemptive crucifixion was vital to this transformation.

The Christian foundations for divine incarnation and crucifixion were demolished by denial of original sin and its replacement with the concept of original love and forgiveness. (Quran 2:37; 7:23) Islam remedied the problems related to the notion of human depravity by launching a concept of pristine human nature. (30:30) "In fact, the Quran offers an entirely different picture of the human condition. All of a sudden, the sky clears up, the darkness is dissipated, and in place of the tragic sense of life there appears a new bright vista of the eternal life. The difference between the two worldviews on this problem is exactly like the difference between Night and Day."[551] The human salvation was directly connected with human endeavors and justification by a mixture of works and grace was emphasise. (2:82) This way man was at once relieved of the shackles of supposed cosmic threats, divine wrath and redemption and arbitrary predestination. He was granted independence, innocence and freedom of choice, and empowered to self-govern, self-discipline and self-reform. They were invited to fully participate in the rough and tumble of this life, to equally share the responsibilities of his felicity. Franz Rosenthal accurately captured the essential feature of Islam when he stated that "man was seen by Islam as the center of action in this world."[552] Lawrence Rosen shows the level of trust Islam placed in the rational and moral capacities of man so that man can control his passions and destiny. "For reason to develop, however, it is important to place oneself in association with those teachers or leaders who, by the development of their own reason, can provide the context for the enlargement of one's own self-control. Thus knowledge of Holy Writ and of world affairs both serve to develop the capacity to act wisely and responsibly."[553] Instead of being left to the mumbo-jumbo of cosmic threats, divine incarnation and redemptive death of Jesus, man was encouraged to take charge of his own life and surroundings. He was to work through the ups and downs of this earthly life with rational outlook and moral bent to master his own destiny. The mediational agencies of Christ and priests were absolutely abolished. There was no inherent human wretchedness that needed cosmic interventions or divine redemptions. God was not far off from man to necessitate priestly interventions. Islam put man in direct contact with God. This was a true reformation of the Church Christianity. The Prophet of Islam was well aware of Christian supernatural dogmas and pretty conscious of his reforming scheme.

The Quran used the term "Nasa'ra" to denote all sects of Christians. "In the Quran Nasa'ra seems to apply to all kinds of Christians, Byzantine, Nestorian and Monophysite."[554] The Prophet of Islam had lifelong exposure to Christians in Mecca and Medina. The story of his childhood encounter with the Christian monk Bahi'ra on his way to Syria is known, his listening to the Najra'ni Bishop Quss in the market of Ukaz is well documented and his close ties with Waraqa bin Nawfel are already discussed. The Prophet's frequent encounters with Abyssinian Christian slaves in Mecca are also documented by Ibn Ishaq and other Muslim historians.[555] In addition to the above mentioned, "the Prophet knew a number of other individual Christians."[556] Salman Farsi, who was originally Zoroastrian, had converted to Christianity before converting to Islam. He lived for years with monks and bishops. "Of more interest is Zaid b. Ha'ritha, so close to the Prophet, who came from parents belonging to Christian tribes in the south of Syria. He was bought by Khadija and given by her to Muhammad, but the Prophet freed Zaid and thereafter treated him as an adopted son. Zaid may have had impressions of Christian teaching and discussed them with Muhammad, but he became one of the first Muslims."[557] The Prophet's first nurse Umm Ayman was a Christian from Abyssinia, and his Egyptian concubine Mariyah was originally a Coptic Christian. In addition to Waraqa bin Nawfal, "Khadija had other Christian relatives; 'Uthman b. al-Huwayrith who aimed at being 'king' of Mecca about A.D. 605 had become a Christian with Byzantine help and was related to Khadija's father."[558] The first Muslims migrated to the Christian Abyssinia and lived there for years. Some of them returned to Mecca while the others returned in the 7th year of Hijra to Medina. Also, "from the Christian centre at Najran visits were paid to Muhammad on several occasions. Twenty Christians visited him in Mecca, either from Najran or Abyssinia. It is said that when they heard the Quran 'their eyes flowed with tears and they accepted God's call, believed in him, and declared his truth'. Then they went home.'"559 The Prophet's interactions with the Christians of Najra'n are well-documented, and the Prophet personally hosted their delegation at Medina. "At the time of their prayers they stood and prayed in the mosque, the Prophet having said that they were to be allowed to do so. They prayed towards the east. There followed a long theological discussion."560 The Prophet's respect for and appreciation of the Christian Abyssinian King Negus is also well known.

The Christian presence in South and North Arabia, their political dominance in the areas surrounding the Arabian peninsula, their constant wars with the Persians, the Meccan caravan trade and constant interactions with the Yemenite, Abyssinian, Jafnid, Nasrid and Byzantium Christians, presence of learned Christians such as Waraqa, Bishop Quss and may be illiterate but devoted Abyssinian slaves in Mecca, the Prophet's close ties with individuals of Christian background and his detailed dialogues with the Delegation of Najra'n are sufficient proofs of his basic knowledge of the Christian theology and their main internal differences. The Quran has referred to many such differences and in fights between the Christians. Therefore, the claims of Western scholars such as Richard Bell and others that the Prophet was ignorant about Orthodox Christology and Chalcedonian Orthodoxy of the Byzantium and that he responded mostly to some sectarian Christian factions is not true.561 The Chalcedonian Orthodoxy was well established long before the advent of Islam though it was not the dominant trend among the Christians of Arabian Peninsula. The Quran reacted and responded to all the main Christian sects and their varying Christologies.

The Quran and Trinitarian Christology

The Quran categorically rejects the Christian concepts of the Trinity, Incarnation, division of persons in the Godhead, plurality of divinity, categorisation of Jesus as the Son of God and the second person of Trinity, co-eternal, co-equal and identical with God and its correlatives doctrines such as the original sin, fallen nature, redemption, crucifixion and resurrection. Islam denies Christ's divinity, preexistence, any mediatorial role in creation, resurrection, judgment, redemption and salvation and strictly prohibits his worship in any way or form. The categorical rejection of the Christian doctrines of Incarnation, Triune God, plural divinity, divine sonship and redemptive death is found in many passages of the Quran, in both the Meccans and Madani chapters. The Qura'n rejects the Trinitarian Christology in all its forms and categories, except the Prophet Christology. The New Testament's Angel, peculiar Messianic and Son of Man, Son of God, Kyrios, Logos and Theos all these Trinitarian Christological formulations[562] with varying theological implications are emphatically refuted. The later Trinitarian interpretations whether Modalist (one-self), Social (three-selves), Augustinian (Psychological), Cappadocian (Social), Chalcedonian (a mixture of one and three-selves), Monophysite (one divine person), Nestorian (one human person) or Mariamites (Mary worshippers), are all rebutted and systematically eliminated with logical inferences. Instead, the transcendental, Unitarian and ethical monotheism and man Christology is overly emphasised.

Monotheism is belief in One God, who is also the Only God. Jews, Christians and Muslims all claim to be monotheists. The monotheistic conception of both Judaism and Islam is Unitarian, while the Christian notion of God is Trinitarian. The strict, moral and transcendental Islamic monotheism differs from the Jewish monotheism in its focus upon divine transcendence and morality and from the Christian concept in rejecting Trinitarian and incarnational interpretations of God in all its forms and shapes.

Even though the Trinitarian theological formulations are unique to Christianity there is no consensus among the Christians about what truly constitutes the Trinity and how is it understood, explained and interpreted.[563] The tension between monotheism, monotheistic Trinitarianism, vulgar tritheism, pantheism and refined polytheism is the hallmark of the Christian tradition. One can easily find traces of all these isms in the historical unfolding of the Christian doctrine of God, and at times within the fold of broader orthodoxy. For the purpose of our limited comparison, we can divide the Trinitarian Christian thought into three main models. They are Modalism (one-self divinity), Adoptionism (hierarchical divinity) and Social Trinitarianism (three-selves divinity).

The Quran rejects all the above sketched Trinitarian paradigms. The systematic Quranic refutations of the Trinity start with rejecting the Original Sin and subsequent claims of human wretchedness, the foundation stones of incarnation and Trinitarian schemes, the sonship of Jesus, the corner stone of Christology and Christ's divinity, adoptionism, the fundamental ingredient of Arian semi-god Christology and finally both the Augustinian and Cappadocian Trinitarian models. The Quran completes its refutational scheme by denying the crucifixion to defy the claims of Christ's atoning death.

The Quran and Divine Sonship

The Quran insists upon the virgin birth of Jesus, his mission, miracles and prophet-hood but confines all his activities in the terrestrial realms as the prophet and representative of the celestial realms. (3:42-59)[564] Jesus's absolute humanity, sheer dependence upon God and outright servitude is overly emphasised. (4:171-172; 5:116-119) His virgin birth is equated with the creation of Adam. The confusing language of father/son is utterly eradicated. Jesus's moral mission in line with the universal prophetic tradition is upheld, but the murky contours of his godhead, pre-existence, angelic existence, cosmic role, incarnation, redemption, crucifixion and resurrections are all denied (4:155-158).

The Quran takes offense to the notion that a feeble historical man was elevated to the heights of divinity and embellished with attributes befitting only to the Almighty God. To the Quran this was the utmost polytheism (*Shirk*), riled and protested by the heavens and earth and unpardoned by God the Almighty. The Trinitarian arrangements were the most monstrous of all the blasphemies. (19:88-95) These strong admonitions occur in one of the early Meccan chapters of the Quran.

Sura Maryam, the chapter of Mary, revealed in the 5th year of Prophethood, is a detailed description of Jesus's virgin birth and chastity of his mother Mary. After giving a detailed description of Mary's family background, her righteousness and virgin birth of Prophet Jesus through the word of God, the Quran states: "Such was, in the words of truth, Jesus the son of Mary, about whose nature they so deeply disagree. It is not conceivable that God should have taken unto Himself a son: limitless is He in His glory! When He wills a thing to be, He but says unto it 'Be' - and it is! And [thus it was that Jesus always said]: 'Verily, God is my Sustainer as well as your Sustainer; so worship [none but] Him: this (alone] is a straight way.' And yet, the sects [that follow the Bible] are at variance among themselves [about the nature of Jesus]! Woe, then, unto all who deny the truth when that awesome Day will appear! How well will they hear and see [the truth] on the Day when they come before Us!" (19:35-38)[565] In these verses the Quran emphatically argues that Jesus was the son of Mary and not the Son of God.[566] The infinite God does not beget especially a finite human being. He is the Sustainer and Creator of Jesus and not his Father. That is why Jesus worshipped him as God and not as Father.

It is usually argued that the title "Son of God" was the beginning of Jesus' special relationship with God the Father, and hence the starting point of his divinity and lordship. J. Moltmann notes that "it is his sonship which stamps his lordship, not his lordship which gives its character to his sonship."[567] He also states that The doctrine of Jesus's divinity "grew up out of the biblical testimony to Jesus' sonship, and out of the Johannine doctrine of the Logos."[568] That is perhaps the reason that the Quran uses multiple arguments and methodologies to refute Jesus's divine sonship.

The above quoted verses reject the Christian's claims of Jesus's sonship and his role in creation. The Omnipotent God does not need any such medium for creation purposes. The Sovereign God is directly involved in all acts of creation, maintenance and expansion. Unlike Christianity, the Quran eliminates the need for emanation as well as mediation. God directly creates without any intermediary entities; his command "be" automatically translates into physical realities. The above verses also allude to Christian sectarianism and their varying interpretations regarding the true nature of Jesus (Christologies) to elucidate lack of unanimity, certainty and precision regarding the Christian doctrine within Christian circles. The Quran denounces multiple Christian sects for making such a blasphemous statement (Jesus is God) based on such whimsical and shaky foundations. In the above quoted verses, the need for a mediatorial agency, sonship, incarnation, redemption through violent death and Christ's divinity all are demolished in one shot. He is not the son of God and therefore not divine; the denial of his divine sonship is the rejection of his divinity.

There are, in addition, many other Quranic passages which address the issue of divine sonship at length. "They say: 'Allah hath begotten a son': Glory be to Him- Nay, to Him belongs all that is in the heavens and on earth: everything renders worship to Him. The Originator of the heavens and the earth: when He decreeth a matter, He saith to it:

'Be,' and it is," (2:116-17). Begetting is indicative of temporality. There was a time when God was eternally there but Jesus was not. Even the Christians accept the fact that only God the Father is unoriginated, while God the Son and God the Holy Spirit are generated or begotten by the Father. From the Quranic perspective, the heavens and Earth existed long before the historical advent of Jesus. The creation of these humungous entities was far more complicated than creation of a feeble man, Jesus, without a father. God was in control of, in communication with and in love with his creatures long before the existence of Jesus; therefore, God did not need a Son to fill the vacuum, as there was no vacuum to be filled. God knew the human conditions and dealt with them centuries before Jesus's existence. God did not need to consult, use or assign anyone to create the existence. He was and is fully in control of and in constant communication with his creatures. God is too Majestic, Glorified and Exalted to need an intermediary between Him and the cosmos. He is totally independent, autonomous and self-sufficient. He is the Sovereign. He is closer to man than his jugular vein and knows the whispering of his heart and the blinking of his eyes. It is not difficult for Him to grace Jesus with a virgin birth. He created Adam without a father and mother and created Eve from a father without mother. He completed the circle by creating Jesus from a mother without a father. This shows God's absolute power and dominion. The creation of Jesus is just like the creation of Adam. (3:59) Even the Gospels call Adam the son of God but nobody worships Adam as God or a divine person. The Old Testament conferres the same title "son of God" upon many individual and collective entities without equating them with God or assigning them any portion of the divinity.

These verses refute both the Orthodox eternal as well as the Adoptionist temporal view of Jesus's sonship. Begetting a son in eternity or in time at baptism is not befitting the Majesty of God as it does not serve any purpose or function in the cosmos. Geoffrey Parrinder and others are wrong when they try to apply these verses only to the Arains and Adoptionist Christians. Parrinder argues that "the key words are 'take to himself any offspring.' 'Take to himself' means literally to 'acquire' (yattakhidha), and so this verse denies that God acquires a son in the course of time. This had been said by Adoptionist and Arian heretics in Christianity, who said that Jesus became or was adopted Son of God at his baptism or some other moment. But the orthodox rejected this in teaching that the Son is eternal."[569] In reality, the Orthodox Christian position of eternity of the Son and equality of the Son with God the Father is more un-Islamic than the Arian adoptionism in time and half divinity of Christ. Associating Jesus with God from eternity and as equal in divinity is a greater sin than claiming his adoption in time, or conditioning his divinity with a specific purpose of redemption, as Arians contend. Moreover, the Orthodox also believe that the eternity of the Father is absolute, while the Son's eternity is relative and derivative. God the Father is the only unoriginated being, while the Son and the Holy Spirit are generated by the Father. Generation is connected with time and hence cannot be eternal like the eternity of the Father, the source of that generation; the begetter and the begotten can never be equal. Generation and derivative status are indicative of temporality and finitude rather than the divinity. The Quran confutes both the temporal and eternal sonship as something absolutely not befitting the Magnificence and Glory of God.

The Quran argues about the same point from a different perspective. It logically addresses the issues related to the plurality of persons in the godhead and their autonomy, independence and eternity. The eternity and equality require eternal authority, autonomy and dominion while the submission, dependence and humility denote servitude and derivative status. Had there been multiple equals, the cosmos would not be orderly the way it has been forever. Its order, system and continuity are proof of its unitary master. Therefore, God is One and not triune. He has no son or equal. The Quran states: "No son did Allah beget, nor is there any god along with Him: (if there were many gods), behold, each god would have taken away what he had created, and some would have lorded it over others! Glory to Allah! (He transcends) the (sort of) things they attribute to Him! He knows what is hidden and what is open: too high is He for the partners they attribute to Him." (23:91-92) Independent divinity requires autonomy, will and dominion, and autonomy requires capacity to disagree. Eternal submission and conformity are impossible with autonomy and dominion. Had there been any other god beside God, then there would have been some lapses or chaos in the universe at some stage of existence. The lack of such a precedent proves the Oneness of God and non-divinity of Christ. Here God's Omnipotence and Omniscience is emphasised in contrast to Jesus's finite knowledge, potentials and submission. It is the Son who according to the New Testament prays to the Father, submits to Him and considers himself the servant of Him and not vice versa. This is not equality or divinity; it is servitude, which is antithetical to dominion and divinity. According to the Christians, even the divine person in Jesus absolutely submits to the Father; never ever has he shown autonomy or independence. The Quranic argument demolishes the foundations of all Trinitarian models, which emphasise the distinctive nature of the three persons of Godhead. Distinction requires autonomy and independence while the Trinitarian models claim three persons' autonomy and dependence at the same time hence transitioning into logical impasse.

Another Quranic verse addresses the same matter from a different angle. "Wonderful Originator of the heavens and the earth: how can He have a son when He hath no consort? He created all things, and He hath full knowledge of all things. That is Allah, your Lord! There is no god but He, The Creator of all things: then worship ye Him: and He hath power to dispose of all affairs." (6:101-2) Here the Quran alludes to the fact that having a son through a consort is logically more plausible than a mere spiritual word changing into a historical person of divine stature, co-equal and co-eternal with God. His not having consort eliminates all logical possibilities of him having a son.

The Quran and Mariolatry

Some Christian scholars argue that the Quranic Christology is misplaced because the Quran has an erroneous understanding of the Trinity. They, since the times of Thomas Aquinas, wrongly contend that unlike in Christianity, the Quran includes Mary in the triune formula and rejects Jesus's divine son-ship only due to sexual implications.[570] The above verses of the Quran (6:101-102) are quoted to substantiate their flawed interpretations.

These verses do not directly mention the Trinity. They address the overall concept of divine plurality. The Quran refers to the Arab polytheists who believed that Allah has sons and daughters.[571] Verse 72:3 from the chapter "Jinn" refers to the Jinn and not to the Christian dogma of the Trinity. Nothing in the Quran includes Mary as the third person of the Trinity. The verse "And when Allah saith: O Jesus, son of Mary! Didst thou say unto mankind: Take me and my mother for two gods beside Allah? he saith: Be glorified! It was not mine to utter that to which I had no right. If I used to say it, then Thou knewest it. Thou knowest what is in my mind, and I know not what is in Thy Mind. Lo! Thou, only Thou, art the Knower of Things Hidden?" (5:116) does not refer to the Trinity either; it alludes to the worship of Mary as God. The worship of Mary as a goddess was quite prevalent in some Christian circles.[572] St. Athanasius of Alexandria (b. ca. 296–298, d. 373 AD), the architect of the Nicean Creed (325 AD), called Mary "the Mother of God." By the fourth century there was a common tendency among the Christian masses, especially among monks, to exalt and worship the Virgin Mary as "Mother of God" or *theotokos*. As seen previously, Nestorius, bishop of Constantinople (428 AD), cried in vain to Cyril of Alexandria (c. 376–444 AD), the Patriarch of Alexandria from 412 to 444, and to the Church in general, "Do not make the Virgin into a goddess." Nestorius observed that "God cannot have a mother [...] and no creature could have engendered the Godhead; Mary bore a man, the vehicle of divinity but not God. The Godhead cannot have been carried for nine months in a woman's womb, or have been wrapped in baby clothes, or have suffered, died and been buried."[573]

Cyril condemned Nestorius in his letter of 430 AD: "If anyone does not confess that Emmanuel is God in truth, and therefore the holy Virgin is *theotokos* – for she bore in the flesh the Word of God became flesh – let him be anathema."[574] The Fifth Ecumenical Council at Constantinople (533) anathematised Nestorius; the worship of Mary as the mother of God was quite widespread in Christian circles at that time. She was worshipped, called upon in prayers for support and venerated through Christian iconography. Sixteenth-century scholar George Sale noted: "The notion of the divinity of the Virgin Mary was also believed by some at the Council of Nice, who said there were two gods besides the Father viz. Christ and the virgin Mary, and were thence named Mariamites. Others imagined her to be exempt from humanity, and deified; which goes but little beyond the popish superstition in calling her the complement of the Trinity, as if it were imperfect without her. This foolish imagination is justly condemned in the Koran as idolatrous."[575]

Mary was also excessively revered by the Monophysite, who differed with Chalcedonian and Nestorian Christians in contending that Jesus had only one divine nature. He was the walking God on earth, which meant that he was always God. So, Mary was believed to be the very literal Mother of God and worshipped as such. Reverend W. St. Clair Tisdall wrote in his *The Original Sources of The Quran* and Edward

Gibbon in his *The History of the Decline and Fall of the Roman Empire* that Mary was worshipped "with the name and honours of a goddess."[576] Therefore, the above-quoted Quranic verse alludes to the worship of Mary as a goddess and not as a person of the Trinity.[577] The Quran condemns both exaggerated Mariology[578] and any association with God.[579] G. Parrinder has recognised this fact: "The Quran may well be directed against this heresy. It gives its support against Mariolatry, while at the same time it recognises the importance of Mary as the vessel chosen by God for the birth of his Christ."[580]

It is pertinent to note here that the Quranic Mary is the vessel of the human, created and Prophet Jesus and not the God Jesus Christ. This Quranic Mariology is totally different from the Chalcedonian, Monophysite and Pauline Mariology. With the exception of the Adoptionists, all Christian Christological formulations bring God in the womb of Mary who in reality carries the incarnate God. To the Quran, any such claim is preposterous and blasphemous.

The Quran, Modalism, Dynamic Monarchians, Social Trinitarians and Monophysites

The Quran emphatically rejects the modalist, dynamic, social Trinitarian and monophysite Trinitarian formulations. Incarnation in all forms and Trinity in all shapes are antithetical to the Quranic message.

In the incarnation jargon, St. Paul is no less a compromiser than the Monophysites. His elastic vocabulary is the source of later theological confusions. St. Paul's incarnation theology closely resembles the Monophysite Christological scheme. To Paul "God was in Christ, reconciling the world unto himself." (2 Cor. 5:19) To the Quran, this is crystal-clear *Shirk*. This equation of God with, and incarnation in, Christ is categorically invalidated by the following verses of the Quran: "They have certainly disbelieved who say that Allah is Christ, the son of Mary. Say, "Then who could prevent Allah at all if He had intended to destroy Christ, the son of Mary, or his mother or everyone on the earth?" And to Allah belongs the dominion of the heavens and the earth and whatever is between them. He creates what He wills, and Allah is over all things competent." (5:17) The argument is that the divine incarnation would have made Jesus and his mother incorruptible while they are not; both were feeble humans who died like other human beings. Only God is eternal, ever living and incorruptible.

The Quran does not get into the Christian jargon of God "*in* Christ" and God "*is* Christ." For the Quran, claims of both God *in* Christ and Christ *as* God are blasphemous. The Orthodox Christianity has always insisted that God was in Christ and that Christ was God. This unintelligible Christian jargon is not theological or philosophical sophistication but naiveté. There was a time when Jesus was non-existent and then came into being; therefore, God the Son was incomplete before his incarnation in the human Jesus. The Son is the only person of the Trinity who combines two natures (Man and God) which became possible only in time and space when the historical Jesus came into being. So, the Son became the true or complete Son only in time after not being so for a long time, which means there was a time when God was not in Christ and Christ was not God, because the historical Christ was non-existent and then God incarnated in Jesus and Jesus became God. The process of becoming is not befitting of the eternal God. The compound (Man and God) came into existent only after the historical Jesus was conceived. Creation, composition, time, space, body all are creaturely traits inappropriate to the majesty of God. The mere idea of divine incarnation in a human being and divinisation of a feeble man is antithetical to the Quranic worldview. Divinity can never be confined to or incarnated through humanity.

The Quran categorically equates such a doctrine with disbelief. "They have certainly disbelieved who say, 'Allah is the Messiah, the son of Mary' while the Messiah has said, 'O Children of Israel, worship Allah, my Lord and your Lord.' Indeed, he who associates others with Allah - Allah has forbidden him Paradise, and his refuge is the Fire. And there are not for the wrongdoers any helpers." (5:71) This Quranic passage categorically denounces the orthodox Christian claim that God was in Jesus and that Jesus was God. It especially refutes the modalist claims that Jesus was one mode or aspect of God. It also denies the Patripassianism of some early Christians such as Noetus (200 AD) and later Sabellianism[581] and Modalistic Monarchianism,[582] which claimed that there was only One God and Christ was God. Therefore, Christ was the God who created the universe and died on the Cross for human's sake. As briefly discussed earlier, to the modalists "the Son and Spirit are not distinct individuals from the Father. Either it was the Father who became incarnate, suffered and died—the Son being at most the human aspect of Christ—or else the one God sequentially assumed three roles as Father, Son and Holy Spirit in relation to his creatures."[583] They opposed the distinctions between the persons as tri-theism and insisted upon the divine unity by emphasising the absolute divinity and full Godhead of Jesus Christ as the Only God whom people call the Father. Epiphanius quotes Sabellians as saying: "Do we have one God or three?"[584] To him, God the Father and God the Son were two different modes of the same God and that God the Father suffered on the Cross because Jesus shared the same divine substance of the Father and was one aspect of the same God. This "Economic Trinity" preserved the unity of God by denying the three autonomous persons within Godhead which to the Modalists was nothing short of tri-theism. As a result, Tertullian gave them the name "Monarchians" which has clung to them to this day. Historically they are called the 'Modalist Monarchians'.

The Modalist Monarchians systematised the popular Christian belief in Christ in a clear and precise manner. It was a bold step towards giving a precise theological colour to the rather ambiguous Christian devotional language, but The Church could not accept it because of its dangerous implications. It was nothing but naive corporealism and patripassianism.

Their opponents, the Dynamic Monarchians insisted upon the full humanity of Jesus and adoption at the time of baptism. They emphasised upon Christ's love and submission to God and unity with God in will and not in substance. To them, the divine titles of Christ were honourific. In the East this movement was significantly revived under the leadership of Paul of Samosata, the bishop of Antioch. Paul did not believe in the divine nature of Jesus. On the other hand, in addition to his adoptionism, he sought to prove that the assumption that Jesus had a divine nature, or was by nature the Son of God, was detrimental to monotheism as it led to duality in the Godhead. He became God but somehow, as says, Paul Tillich, "he had to deserve to become God."[585] Paul banished all Church psalms that expressed in any sense the essential divinity of Christ from divine service. Consequently, Paul was condemned at a Synod of Antioch held in 268, two earlier synods having failed to take action in the matter. He was declared as heretical because he denied Jesus's pre-existence and his unity of substance with God; in other words his proper divinity.

Though both types of Monarchianism were condemned as heretical, they challenged the orthodoxy in different ways, pushing it to look into the immense difficulties involved in their understanding of the transcendence and unity of God and attempted to clarify it in intelligible terms.

The Monophysites resembled the Modalist Monarchians in making Jesus full God, but went to the other extreme by highlighting the autonomous divine substance of all three persons of the Trinity. So, the Father, Son and Holy Spirit were all gods in their own right leading to a sense of tri-theism. The Monophysite insistence that in Jesus there was only one nature, and that was divine, made Jesus full God and caused God the Son to suffer the pains of Cross. The only difference was that instead of the Father, they crucified God the Son. In reality the Monophysites were not very far from Orthodox Chalcedonian theology though they were more honest, frank, and intelligible than the Orthodoxy. The Chalcedonian formula differed only in ascribing to Jesus a second human nature and in insisting that only the human person of Jesus died on the Cross. The Monophysites and Modalists wondered about the validity of the Orthodox salvation, which was achieved by the crucifixion of a mere human Jesus instead of God the Christ. To them, the original sin required a divine sacrifice of cosmic proportions. As seen in the first chapter, the Orthodoxy created a monster Jesus with two natures (human and divine), arbitrarily moving between his two natures; praying to God, eating, drinking, crying and finally dying on the cross as a human but in the end looking more Godly than human. The Orthodox person of the Christ seemed to accomplish different tasks using multiple personalities. The Monophysites merged the humanity in pure divinity, while the Orthodoxy under the influence of Cappadocian Fathers maintained the two natures Christology at the expense of systematisation, intelligibility and salvation. Jesus to the Orthodoxy, in spite of the personal challenges and human weaknesses, was still a full God.

The above Quranic passage denies all claims of Christ's divinity, full godhead and worship in all its above shapes and forms. To the Quran, the Modalist Monarchians brought the entire godhead to the womb of a woman, and then crucified God on the Cross, while the Monophysites brought the full divine substance to the womb of the woman Mary and crucified the divinity, though partial, on the Cross. On the other hand, the Orthodox felt the dangers of such claims of "God bearing Mother" and "Crucified God" but did nothing to avert those dangers except inserting a comma. They just inserted a human nature along with the divine nature of Christ, making him unintelligible, incomprehensible and totally confusing. God was in Christ and Christ was God, but somehow God escaped the death on the Cross. Only the human in Christ was killed on the Cross. But the posterity did not accept such a belittling of the atoning death of the Christ and they in the end also killed God on the Cross, just like the Monarchians and Monophysites. The above quoted Quranic verse dubbed all claims of Christ's full divinity, whether Monarchian, Monophysite or Chalcedonian, as disbelief. The Quran denies the "God in Christ" theological formulation by denying the Logos Christology and sonship of Jesus. To the Quran, Jesus, the Son of Mary, was a creature and servant of God who worshipped God as a proof of his creatureliness.

The Qur'an and Augustinian and Cappadocian Models

The Quranic anti-Trinitarian statements roundly reject both interpretations of the Trinity, whether Augustinian Psychological (Latin Trinity) or Cappadocian Social (Eastern Trinity).[586] The Augustinian model of three distinct modes or aspects of one person or (water, ice, and vapour in one essence or mind, knowledge and love or memory, intellect and will in man)[587] and the Cappadocian social Trinity[588] of James, John, and Luke sharing the same human essence (unity of mind, heart and will of three persons)[589] are considered beliefs that associate partners with God, and are unacceptable to Islam. On the surface they seem identical, but deeper analysis shows that the two models are at odds with each other. The Cappadocian Social Trinity "asserts that the divine essence is a universal, and Augustine just as decisively denies this."[590] J. P. Moreland and W. Lane Craig note that "the central commitment of social trinitarianism is that in God there are three distinct centers of self-consciousness, each with its proper intellect and will. The central commitment of anti-social trinitarianism is that there is only one God, whose unicity of intellect and will is not compromised by the diversity of persons. Social trinitarianism threatens to veer into tritheism; anti-social trinitarianism is in danger of lapsing into unitarianism."[591]

The Quran rejected the Augustinian sense of Trinity because, like the Modalists, it incarnated the whole of divinity in the historical feeble man Christ with all human natural needs and weaknesses and ultimately killed God on the Cross. Moreland and Craig note that "anti-social trinitarianism seems to reduce to classical modalism."[592] The Augustinian model appears to be monotheistic, but its incarnational implications are appalling. Karl Rahner notes that the Augustinian "speculations on the Trinity result in that well-known quandary which makes all of his marvelous profundity look so utterly vacuous."[593] The Quranic verse 5:71, "they have certainly disbelieved who say that Allah is Christ, the son of Mary," refers to such a notion of utterly vacuous Trinity which mercilessly kills the whole of God on the Cross, with serious theological and philosophical implications. The equation of God with Jesus, the man born of Mary, is blasphemous to the Quran. The claim that the full divinity can incarnate in a small entity like man, go through human natural needs and finally die on the Cross is nothing short of disbelief in the Omnipotent and Omniscient Irresistible God. The logical absurdity of such a claim can be gauged from the Gospel claims that Jesus called upon God on the Cross. Was he calling upon himself? Was he the God or Father of himself? Was he subordinated to himself? Did he worship himself? These are the logical impasses which prove the deception claims of Dale Tuggy.[594]

The Quran and Social Trinity

The Social Trinity of the Cappadocian Fathers or Functional Monotheism is no less offensive to the Quran. It focuses more upon the autonomy and independence of the three persons than their unity and clearly lands in tri-theism more so than the Augustinian model. Even if John, Mark and Luke share the primary reality of being humans they are neither identical nor dependent upon each other. They are three independent instances of that reality. One of them can die or cease to exist without the other two dying. Likewise, the three persons of godhead are separate centers of consciousness and will, even if they share the primary reality called divine essence. Unfortunately, even the primary reality or the essence of the three persons of the Trinity seems to be different. From Gregory of Nyssa to Richard Swinburne, all Social Trinitarians admit that there exists a fundamental distinction between the three persons. Gregory states that "although we acknowledge the nature is undifferentiated, we do not deny a distinction with respect to causality. That is the only way by which we distinguish one Person from the other, by believing, that is, that one is the cause and the other depends on the cause. Again, we recognise another distinction with regard to that which depends on the cause. There is that which depends on the first cause and that which is derived from what immediately depends on the first cause. Thus the attribute of being only-begotten without doubt remains with the Son, and we do not question that the Spirit is derived from the Father."[595]

The three people's original natures and existences are absolutely different. The uncaused Father, the Son caused by the Father and the Holy Spirit caused by both Father and Son are totally different animals. Richard Swinburne states that "the Father is the Father because he has the essential property of not being caused to exist by anything else [...] The Son is the Son because he has the essential property of being caused to exist by an uncaused divine person acting alone. The Spirit is the Spirit because he is caused to exist by an uncaused divine person in cooperation with a divine person who is caused to exist by the uncaused divine person acting alone."[596] The primary reality, origin and substance of the three people are distinctively different. The Social Trinity in fact is hierarchical and differentiative; it entails three divinities of different statures and substances, as Justine Martin stated.[597] Each person is an instance of deity but of different kind. The Social Trinity is the cooperative society of the three unequal gods. This is nothing short of, to use Brian Leftow's phrase, "refined paganism".[598] Therefore "there is no salient difference between functional monotheism and polytheism."[599]

John Hick notes that "this form of Trinitarianism moves dangerously close to the tritheism which Islam has always feared and suspected to be the outcome of trinitarianism. And, of course, mediaeval pictorial representations of the Persons of the Trinity have often fostered a virtual tritheism at the popular level."[600] Early Muslim scholars, such as the third/ninth century Zaydī Imām al-Qāsim b. Ibrāhīm, and a little later, the philosopher Abū Yūsuf al-Kindī, pinpointed that the Christian Trinitarian formulations were tri-theistic as they identified three separate individuals with particular properties and substances.[601] Karl Rahner, John Hick and others noted the same complexities in the twenty-first century. Rahner stated that there was "the real danger in the doctrine of the Trinity, not so much in the abstract theology of the textbooks, but in the average conception of the normal Christian. This is the danger of a popular, unverbalised, but at bottom quite massive tritheism. Whenever efforts are made to think of the Trinity, this danger looms much larger than that of Sabellian modalism. There can be no doubt about it: speaking of three persons in God entails almost inevitably the danger [...] of believing that there exist in God three distinct consciousnesses, spiritual vitalities, centers of activity, and so on. This danger is increased by the fact that, even in the usual presentation of the scholarly treatises on the Trinity, there is *first* developed a concept of 'person' derived from experience and philosophy, independently of the doctrine of the Trinity as found in revelation and of the history of this doctrine. Next this concept is applied to God, and thus it is demonstrated that there are three *such* persons in God."[602]

The Orthodox Chalcedonian formula leans more towards this autonomy of the persons (independent consciousness and personalities) than the uni-personality of God or divine essence. As seen in chapter 1, and to quote Karl Rahner, the Social Trinity sets up "this divine 'essence' itself as a 'fourth' reality pre-existing in the three persons."[603] God the Father, God the Son, God the Holy Spirit and the divine essence make up four entities. Medieval Muslim scholars, such as Abu Isa al-Warraq, Abu Bakr al-Baqilani, Abu Mansur al-Maturidi and Taqi al Din Ibn Taymiyyah, argued the same point; that the Orthodox Chalcedonian Trinitarian scheme degenerated into a fourth entity.[604] The fact of the matter is that the Social Trinity lands into divine quaternity and pure polytheism because it entails that "the divine essence is an object that is somehow prior to—even independent of—the divine persons."[605] The divine essence makes a prior, bigger entity aggregate of the three smaller entities with bigger self-consciousness, mind and will. Therefore, this so called "Group Mind Monotheism" is more paganist than the Functional Monotheism. The paganism of the two groups of Social Trinitarians, the "Group Mind Monotheism" and "Functional Monotheism," is just relative. Both of them are polytheistic though "Group Mind Monotheism" is more vulgar than the "Functional Monotheism.

Karl Rahner notes that "honesty finally forces us to inquire, not without misgivings, why we still call 'persons' that which remains ultimately of God's threefold 'personality,' since we have to remove from these persons precisely that which at first we thought of as constituting a person. Later on, when the more subtle remarks of the theologians have been forgotten, we see that once more we glide probably into a false and basically tritheistic conception, as we think of the three persons as of three different personalities with different centers of activity."[606]

The third group of Social Trinitarians, the so-called "Trinity Mono-theism," is also troublesome. It maintains that "while the persons of the Trinity are divine, it is the Trinity as a whole that is properly God [...] that the Trinity alone is God and that the Father, Son and Holy Spirit, while divine, are not Gods."[607] Brian Leftow observes that "either the Trinity is a fourth case of the divine nature, in addition to the Persons, or it is not. If it is, we have too many cases of deity for orthodoxy. If it is not, and yet is divine, there are two ways to be divine—by being a case of deity, and by being a Trinity of such cases. If there is more than one way to be divine, Trinity monotheism becomes Plantingian Arianism. But if there is in fact only one way to be divine, then there are two al-ternatives. One is that only the Trinity is God, and God is composed of non-divine persons. The other is that the sum of all divine persons is somehow not divine. To accept this last claim would be to give up Trin-ity monotheism altogether."[608] To Islam, such a concept of Godhead is also an absurdity; it makes the One Godhead composite of non-gods or lesser gods/divines. The divine person's natures are different than the nature of the Godhead (Trinity) and Trinity is not the sort of things three persons are. The Trinity has more substance of divinity than the three individual persons. It also constitutes a divine quaternity of une-qual four divines, a total polytheistic absurdity.

The Quran categorically refutes this tri-theism and paganism in all its above discussed shapes and forms by verse 5:73 which states that they disbelieve who say that "Behold, God is the third of a trinity." The divi-sion of divine persons in the Trinity is nothing short of polytheism. Karl Rahner wholeheartedly recognises the validity of such Jewish and Islam-ic abhorrence towards the polytheistic Trinity, "in a history of faith and theology that has become increasingly clear and explicit, Christianity acknowledges the threefoldness of the one God and consequently faces the question from Old Testament monotheism and the faith of Islam and its theology as to whether the profession of faith in the triune God does not amount basically to an absolutely pernicious tritheism and whether the Christian acknowledgment of the oneness of God is no more than a disguise for such tritheism or (if it is not to be stated so radically) simply a doctrine that cannot really be implemented religiously and logically by someone for whom the acknowledgment of the oneness of God is not merely a proposition maintained verbally and theoretically but the very heart of his existence in theory and practice."[609]

The Social Trinitarians claim that the three persons equally share the one divine essence. The one divine essence cannot be all in one person otherwise that person will be the only full God. It is shared by the three persons. Jesus's share is one third of the total essence; therefore, he is one person of the Triune Godhead with two other equals which to the Quran is partnership and association, the Social Trinitarian Society. This is simple and pure *shirk*, dubbed as disbelief by the Quran; they disbelieve who say that "Behold, God is the third of a trinity." The Quran vehemently scorns the Orthodox Trinitarian formulations, in both its Augustinian as well as Cappadocian forms. Both the Psychological as well as Social Trinity, both Latin and Eastern Trinities are aberrations of true monotheism and not sophistication or philosophising of it.

On the other hand, C. J. Block contends that there is nothing anti-Chalcedonian or anti-Trinitarian in the Quran. The Quranic polemics are directed to the overt tri-theism of the Najarani Monophysites and not to the Orthodox Augustinian or Cappadocian Trinitarian formulas. He argues that "the Qura'nic revelations implicitly distinguish between trinitarianism and tritheism, it may be re-considered whether or not in spite of its clear unitarian leanings, the Qura'n itself is an anti-trinitarian document at all."[610] He argues that the Prophet was conversing with the Christians from the early Meccan period, but he never uttered anything specifically anti-tritheistic until he met with the delegation of Najran. To Block the above discussed verses 5:72-73 are addressed to the Philoponian tri-theistic Monophysites.[611] He further argues that "the word 'trinity' existed in spoken Arabic from the time of the Monophysite debate over the Theophaschite formula, 'One of the Holy Trinity has suffered in the flesh', from 527–36. The Ghassanids were involved in the debate, and it is unreasonable to suggest that the Arab phylarch did not have terminology in his own tongue for a Christian concept so foundational as 'trinity', especially since we know that some Arab kings had been Christians since the mid-fourth century. Shahı̂d recounts the development of Arabic as a theological language stating that, 'already in the fourth century there was an Arabic confession of faith, the Nicene Creed. In the sixth century, the Ghassanid rulers discussed theology'. Though other scripts were used to render it in writing, it is irrational to suppose that the Arabic word for 'trinity' had not been developed during the period of more than 250 years of

Arab Christianity prior to Islam."[612] But the Quran did not specifically imply or refute such a term. Block gives multiple valid historical proofs to substantiate the claim that the word "Trinity" - "*al-Thalu'th*" - was widespread among the Arab Christians.[613] He states that "it is conclusive that the term 'trinity' existed in the spoken Arabic language of South Arabia prior to both the advent of Islam and written Arabic, and would therefore have been known by Abu Ha'ritha. It is clear from the Si'ra that Christology was a major theme of Abu Ha'ritha's dialogue with the Prophet, and it is thus posited that the Arabic word for trinity, al-tha'lu'th, was used during the discussion. It was most certainly a known term during the composition of the Quran. Yet if the term 'trinity' was available in Arabic, why did the Quranic revelations produce a different term (three) to communicate 'trinity'?"[614] Therefore, the Quran clearly "responds directly to the Monophysite tritheistic doctrine by deliberately using the word 'three' instead of 'trinity' to highlight the tritheistic doctrine."[615]

Christian Apologists and Quranic Christology

It seems that Block is following the lead of Christian apologists, such as G. Parrinder, K. Cragg, Robert Morey, Richard Bell, M. Watt, P. Schaff and many others, who maintain that somehow the Prophet of Islam was ignorant about the sophisticated Christian theology[616] embodied in the Chalcedonian mystery and that he, instead of refuting the erudite Chalcedonian Trinitarian Christology, just denied the misplaced Trinity of some peripheral Christian groups or crude tri-theism of others such as the Monophysites.[617] For instance, Parrinder states that "it has often been thought that the Quran denies the Christian teaching of the Trinity, and commentators have taken its words to be a rejection of orthodox Christian doctrine. However, it seems more likely that it is heretical doctrines that are denied in the Quran, and orthodox Christians should agree with most of its statements."[618] R. C. Zaehner states that the Quran "does not explicitly deny any specific Christian doctrine except that Christ is the son of God, and this for obvious reasons [...] For, except to those well coached in Christian theology, sonship implies physical procreation and this is unthinkable in God who is a pure Spirit."[619] He Christianises the Quranic understanding of virgin birth and draws some far-fetched conclusions claiming that "the Incarnation of Christ, then, breathed from the Spirit of God, is thus regarded as an event as momentous as the original creation or the universal resurrection at the end of time. This would seem to indicate that Muhammad must, again unconsciously, be reproducing the Christian idea of Christ as the new Adam and as the 'first fruits' of the resurrection."[620] Sidney Griffith argues that the verse 5:73 "the third of three (*thālith thalātha*)", does not refer to the Trinity but to Jesus who in Syriac literature was often called 'the third of three.'"[621]

Such Christian apologists tend to impose their peculiar sense of Christology over the Quranic text; they wittingly or unwittingly do violence to the Quranic text and worldview to Christianise Islam. They daydream and inflict the Quran with their theological aspirations without much respect for the truth, analysis, context or logic of the Quran. Contrary to their tactics, the Quran lends itself to anti-Trinitarian, anti-incarnation interpretations far more easily than the circumspective and illusionary interpretations of the Christian apologetics. This fact is well recognized by many Christian scholars of Islam. For instance, David Thomas notes that the above cited two verses (5:72-73) are equally directed at the Orthodox doctrines of incarnation and Trinity. "But it is equally plausible to read this and the preceding verse, which is evidently intended as a pair with this since it begins with the same formula *(laqad kafara lladhīna qālū inna...)*, as intentional simplifications of the two major Christian beliefs in the humanity and divinity of Christ and the Trinity, simplifications that expose the weaknesses they each contain when analysed from the strictly monotheistic perspective of the Quran. Thus, q 5:72 attacks what it portrays as the eternal God [...] and the human born of Mary (q.v.) being identical, while q 5:73 attacks the notion that God could have partners in his divinity. The teaching in this verse is certainly that Christians place other beings alongside the true God."[622] Therefore the Christian apologists' circumvention of the Quranic anti-Trinitarian arguments is ill-fated and ill disposed. The modern apologists hide behind the smoke screens of God's ineffability and mystery to evade logic and intelligibility like The Cappadocian Fathers.[623] Their "theology of the incomprehensible generation"[624] and "incomprehensible unity of the incomprehensible and yet irreducible distinct divine persons"[625] is truly irrational and has been incomprehensible for the past two millennia. But Jesus' origination from God and birth through Mary are time-bound events and hence comprehensible. Jesus, the originated Son of Mary can never be equal to God the

Originator. He is too accessible and comprehensive and not ineffable. Moreover, the incarnation of divine person in Jesus was either before the conception or after the delivery. The Orthodoxy argues that the incarnation took place before the birth, while the Adoptionists contend that it happened at the time of Jesus' baptism. To the Chalcedonian Orthodox, the unity of the two persons in Jesus was complete. This makes the Orthodox incarnation scheme disgraceful to God making him go through the difficulties of birth and pains of crucifixion which, even to their own doctrines is impossible for God. The above Quranic references to Jesus and Mary's human weaknesses and needs allude to this preposterous possibility. The Quran does not put limits to what God cannot do, it just describes the things which are so inappropriate that God's Majesty does not allow Him to do.

Bishop Kenneth Cragg is wrong when he states that "to believe that God stooped to our need and weakness is not to make God less, but more, the God of all power and glory."[626] The all-powerful God does not need to go through human ordeals to forgive or reconcile man to himself. He can do it with full glory and magnificence without descending from His majesty to the womb of a woman or crying for help on the Cross. Islam does not differentiate between God in Himself (Immanent Trinity) and in relation with the world (Economic Trinity).[627] Karl Rahner's twofold division of Trinity is artificial. The contemporary Apologetic's efforts to equate such a categorisation with the Islamic concepts of *Tawhid al-Dha't* (Ontological Unity) and *Tawhid al-Afa'al* (Unity of Actions) is totally out of place.[628] Such claims of Paul of Antioch and other medieval Christian apologists were well refuted by the Muslim scholars.[629]

The Islamic Unity of God's essence and actions does not cause any division of persons or actions within the Godhead, while the Trinity in its various forms does result in the division of persons and their distinctive functions, properties, attributes, wills, knowledge, consciousness and personalities. The three persons of the Trinity are not the same in every aspect of their existence, properties and actions, as shown above. The claims of three person's unity in the divine substance are arbitrary and unintelligible. Had they possessed the same divine substance then they would have been identical in every aspect of their existence, powers, abilities and functional autonomy but they are not by the Christian's own admission. God the Son can never originate the

210

Father or the Holy Spirit. God the Father never prays to God the Son or calls upon him during stress. God the Father or the Holy Spirit never incarnate in a human being, only the Son does. They are distinctive persons with distinctive functions, properties, attributes, powers, wills and consciousness. They seem to have independent and autonomous personalities with distinctive functions, natures and substances. The Islamic sense of Unity of God's essence and actions is totally different than all the Trinitarian formulas.

The ninth-century Muslim scholar Abu Isa al-Warraq noted these diverging realities and distinctions between the three persons of the Trinity. God the Father is what God the Son is not and God the Son is what God the Holy Spirit is not. The distinctions are too obvious to be ignored in the name of divine essence. Abu Isa al-Warraq noted that "the named members of the Trinity are all and each distinct in their existence, and so the problem occurs of how they can be said to remain identical when one of them is involved in the action of Incarnation that the others are not."[630] As seen above, neither God the Father nor God the Holy Spirit incarnate and take upon human flesh. Only Jesus is said to have incarnated in the human flesh, hence having two natures: one divine and other human. David Thomas comments that al Warraq "has a radically different understanding from his Christian opponents, shared with Muslim theologians in this and other periods, that something that can be named is an entity with its own unique characteristics that distinguish it from other things. Thus, in the back of his mind in this discussion lies the assumption that the Christian concept of the Godhead involves four separate beings, the substance and the three hypostases; he has, in fact, raised this issue in the first part of his refutation of the Christian sects."[631] This well-versed Muslim polemicist argued that "because the doctrine of the Incarnation states in plain terms that it was the Son who united with the human nature of the Messiah, then this hypostasis must be different in some manner from the others. So, the contradictions within Christian doctrines arising from the concurrent insistence that the hypostases are identical in their common substantiality can be drawn out."[632]

Therefore, three persons of the Trinity denote three different gods rather than the simplicity or unity of One God; otherwise Christ will be his own Father as well as his own Son, an absolute sophistry.[633] Likewise the Trinity cannot be equated with Islamic sense of God's actions.

In Islam God's actions are not only three but countless. Also, His attributes are not three but infinite. There is no comparison between the Islamic concepts of the Unity of Essence and Actions with Karl Rahner's Immanent and Economic Trinity[634] or Islamic concept of divine attributes with the God the Father as Life, the Son as Speech and the Holy Spirit as Knowledge.[635] In Islam, the divine attributes are of God's essence and not separate from his being; they are infinite in numbers. On the other hand, the Christians confine them to only three attributes outside of God's being, with distinctive person, functions and roles. The Muslim scholars from the early Islamic periods have refuted such claims of identity and resemblance.[636] They contended that "since the doctrine entails beings who are distinct in themselves and yet uniform with each other it is rationally unsustainable, because no being can possess opposite characteristics such as these."[637]

The above two discussion amply proves that undoubtedly, the Quran condemns the Trinitarian formulation in all its forms and categories. The claims of Block and other Christian apologetics are unsubstantiated guesswork, theories and hunches. The Quranic anti-Trinitarian narrative is well trenched in the Islamic theological, legal and philosophical traditions. This is how the immediate disciples of the Prophet and later Muslim jurists, theologians and Quranic exegetes understood the Quran. The centuries-long Muslim anti-Trinitarian interpretations of these Quranic verses vouch for such a historical reality.[638]

It seems that Christian apologists are either ignorant about the depth of Quranic arguments or have a partial or perverted view of its Christology. Neal Robinson rightly observes that modern Christian apologists are mostly partial, circumspective and selective.[639] "The weaknesses of the polemical perspective are obvious. The polemicists suffer from selective vision; their vested interest in Christianity leads them to focus on certain issues while ignoring others and it prevents them from evaluating their observations impartially [...] despite the apologists' insistence on their own impartiality, their approach probably owes much to extrinsic factors."[640] He pinpoints three such factors. "First [...] there may sometimes be an element of bad faith, an underhanded and dishonest attempt to commend Christianity to Muslims by foisting on them a Christian interpretation of the Quran which they know full well does not do justice to all the evidence. Second, there is the influence of that venerable tradition within Christianity which identifies Jesus Christ as the incarnation of the *Logos* or universal cosmic Reason. The implications of that identification are that although the fullness of God's truth is only found in Jesus Christ it is nonetheless present in a piecemeal and partial fashion in the whole human race. Consequently non-Christian religions can be regarded as having an educative role in preparing men and women for the fullness of the Gospel. Third, in some writers there may be a deep seated psychological need an urge to reconcile their intuitive recognition of the validity of Muslim experience of the Transcendent with their own continued allegiance to traditional Christian verities."[641]

We cannot let them speak for the Quran. We must let the Quran speak for itself. The Quran is loud and clear about the fallacies of incarnation and Trinity. Clearly, whether the 'Holy' Trinity is composed of the Father, Jesus, and Mary (as was the case in Collyridianism) or the Father, Son and the Holy Spirit, both viewpoints are equally and categorically condemned in the Quran. Any idea of associating partners in any shape or form with the One and Only God is totally unacceptable.

The Quran calls out the Christians directly: "O People of the Book! Commit no excesses in your religion: nor say of Allah aught but the truth. The Messiah Jesus the son of Mary was (no more than) a Messenger of Allah, and His Word, which He bestowed on Mary, and a Spirit proceeding from Him: so believe in Allah and His Messengers. Say not "Three": desist: it will be better for you: for Allah is One God: Glory be Him: (for Exalted is He) above having a son. To Him belong all things in the heavens and on earth. And enough is Allah as a Disposer of affairs. Christ disdaineth not to serve and worship Allah, nor do the angels, those nearest (to Allah): those who disdain His worship and are arrogant, He will gather them all together unto Himself to (answer)." (4:171-72).

Christian apologists such as German C. Schedl and Risse have noticed that these "polemical statements of the Quran are directed towards Christian distortions and excesses, be it in the doctrine of the Trinity or in Christology; cf. the Quranic admonition 'commit no excesses in your religion!' (4.171)."[642]

The above verses (4:171-172) deconstruct Gospel of John's Word theology, Logos' pre-existence and role in the creation as well as divinity. Jesus was the created word of God and not the agent in creation or "Word" *with* God or *in* God or God in any way or form. The Christian apologetics from the times of John of Damascus[643] (675-750 AD)[644] to modern times have wrongly argued that the Quranic word and the Gospel of John's "Word" denote the same Christ.[645] For instance Daniel Madigan argues that "A satisfactory Logos-Christology gives us a first opening into a more accessible theology of the Trinity, because Muslim theology has already settled on an expression about God's Word or Speech (*kalām Allāh* in Arabic) to the effect that it is an essential attribute of God, which although it is not simply identical with God, is nothing other than divine. In the classic Arabic formulation it is *ṣifah dhātiyyah lā 'aynuhu wa-lā ghayruh*. That is a paradox which to my mind is almost identical to the one John leaves us with in the very first verse of his Gospel."[646] In spite of the good intentions Madigan is totally misleading. The divine speech in Islam is neither identical with God nor a person or entity outside God. It is an attribute of God. John's Word, on the other hand, is a distinctive entity outside or beside God and is identical with God. Additionally, to the Quran it is a life giving word "be" which gave life to Adam, heavens and the earth and none of them are divine.[647] Therefore, the Quranic concept of God's word and speech is absolutely antithetical to John's concept of the Word and later Logos Christology. They are two totally different animals.

Quranic Christology vs John's Christology

The Quran intentionally employs loaded Christian terms such as "word" and "spirit" to deconstruct them and to refute their Christological implications. Proper evaluations of these Quranic terms in their proper contexts sufficiently prove that their Christianisation by the Christian apologetics is ill-disposed and misplaced.[648] In the Quran, Jesus the word and the spirit of God is a created being and not the pre-existent Logos responsible for creation. There was a time when the Word was not and then was begotten of the God. Creation in time does not make Jesus eternal, creator or equal with God; The Originator and the begotten can never be equal.

Likewise, the term "Servant of God" is used by both the Quran and New Testament, but their implications are totally opposed. K. Cragg has noted that "Paul, in Phil. 2 is saying, in line with the Quran, that Jesus as Messiah will never consider servanthood beneath his dignity (this is the sense of *yastankifa*) but gladly embraces it as the self-expanding task of love. He makes no reservation of himself in obedience to the costly will of God. This, as Paul sees it, is the very nature of Christ's Sonship. In Surah 4:172, the same readiness in Jesus for humility is stated and saluted. But the passage sees this servanthood as the very disqualification of the notion that Jesus is 'Son'. Clearly the 'sonship' here in mind is that of pampered 'status' which will not soil a hand, lest the heir be mistaken for a menial slave. Such is not the Sonship of Jesus in the New Testament. The logic by which, for the Quran, Jesus can never be 'Son' to God is precisely the logic by which, for Paul and the New Testament, he is. Both Scriptures affirm his being gladly 'servant' to God. That is their unity. The Quran however, denies his 'Sonship' on the very grounds in which the Christian sees it to consist, namely a loving obedience to God. For the latter there is a quality of service which only the 'Son' can bring."[649] The same goes for the "word" and "spirit".

The Quranic use of the term "Spirit" is also meant to deconstruct the Christian theological excesses and exaggerations embodied in the Logos Christology, as seen in chapter 1. Leirvik notes that "it is clear also from the Quranic use of spirit that it is connected with creation (cf. about Adam in 15.29) and life-giving ability. In the Quranic perspective, Christ himself is seen as a creation of the life-giving spirit, but at the same time as a privileged vehicle of the spirit, aided by the Holy Spirit in his mighty signs (2.253)."[650] The Quranic concept of the Holy Spirit (Archangel Gabriel) and his supportive role in Jesus's mission keeps both the Spirit and Christ within the realms of createdness.

Islamic Christology is closer to the early "Servant Christology"[651]of the New Testament (Lk. 22:37) than the later Christological jargon of the Logos or Word Christology. The Quranic Christology has close resemblance to some salient features of the subordination Christology of Luke. "According to Raisanen, the Quranic picture comes close to some central features of Lukan Christology. His suggestion is that 'On the whole, Luke gives us a Christology characterised by the emphatic subordination of Jesus to God'. In all his doings and fate, Jesus is subordinated to God's permission and plan (Acts 2.22f.). He is referred to by Luke as God's Christ (Acts 3.18, Luke 9.20) and God's servant (Acts 3.13, 4.27), and no Trinitarian doctrine can be traced within the works of Luke."[652] The Quranic Christology, like its Lukan counterpart, is antithetical to John's Christology of Word with its dualistic or Trinitarian implications, at least the way John was later understood by the Church Councils. The Gospel of John also included the Lukan subordinating expressions, showing clear signs of tension between the sub-ordinating and identification passages. (John 20:17) In fact the same tension (between subordination and identification) can also be found in all the four Gospels. That tension was later exploited by the Church Fathers to construct the Trinitarian Christology preferring the identi-fication over the subordination of the Son with the Father. The Quran categorically eliminated that tension as well as all possibilities of Jesus's identification with God, and- once for all - eradicated the sources of centuries-long Christian confusions and circular reasoning.

The Quranic correctives were truly creative and precise. Leirik states that "the Quranic Christology may be taken as a creative reinter-pretation in its own right 'outside the walls', reflecting different cultural presuppositions, and breaking radically with all traces of identification of Christ with God."[653] The Quran was aware of the Christian jargon. It utilised the Christian phrases and their sequential arguments to deconstruct and nullify their wrong theological implications. David Thomas notes that "There is a curious reminiscence of the classical Christian doctrine in the immediately preceding mention of Jesus as word and spirit of God, though also a clear denial of it on the grounds that the titles hypostasised into persons of the godhead by Christians are no more than qualities to be ascribed to the human Jesus.) Like the other two, this third quranic reference to tripleness in deity is, then, really directed against associating creatures with God, though it must be taken as intended to refute the central Christian doctrine of the Trinity, and, as such, as a radical deconstruction of that doctrine in its essential formulation of three discrete beings who share in divinity."[654] He concludes, noticing that "a straightforward interpretation would be that here as in q 5:73 the Quran warns against both divinisation of Christ and Trinitarian exaggerations because no other beings should be placed beside God in divinity."[655]

In the above verses, the createdness of Jesus is highlighted, in spite of his being the word of God and a spirit from Him. As already dis-cussed, even the most Orthodox Christians accept that the Son of God was begotten of the Father and that the Holy Spirit proceeded from the Father. The creation or procession in time is against eternity. Therefore, the Son or the Holy Spirit cannot be eternal in the ultimate sense while God the Father is eternal. Even the Christian concept of their eternity is relative (in relation to the creation) and not absolute like the Father.

The Quran also argues that Jesus, the Word, Command of God and the Spirit from Him, was created in time. He cannot be the eternal part of God or united with the eternal essence of God. He cannot be the eternal attribute of God either because createdness in time and after non-existence denotes temporality. The eternal and temporal are antithetical and cannot be united, confused or diffused with one another.

Muslims, from the early 9th century onward, had employed this Quranic argument of temporality to denounce Christian claims of Jesus's divinity, sonship, incarnation as well as the doctrine of Trinity. David Thomas has well documented these early Muslim anti-Christian polemics.[656] The anti-Christian works of Abu Isa al-Warraq, Qadi Abdul Jabbar, Ibn Hazm and Ibn Taymiyyah are just a few examples of this category of theological polemics.[657] The modern Quranic exegete Muhammad Asad also tows the same lines: "In the verse under discussion, which stresses the purely human nature of Jesus and refutes the belief in his divinity, the Quran points out that Jesus, like all other human beings, was 'a soul created by Him.'"[658] This Quranic focus upon the createdness of Jesus nullifies all claims of his divinity, a central Christian dogma of all Christian denominations and sects. Therefore, the Quran is through and through anti-Trinitarian, anti-incarnation and anti-divinisation of Christ. Prophet Muhammad was not ignorant about the fundamentals of Christian theology, and the Quran is not a naïve response to the Christian excesses. The Quran is a comprehensive, systematic, willful and all-embracing refutation of the Christian excesses in theological matters. Gordon D. Newby states that "Quranic evidence indicates that, while the full range of Gospel narratives is not represented, the Quran represents particularly the Gospel of Luke quite accurately and with close readings. Recent scholarship in this area is challenging the earlier notions that the Quran portrayed only a heterodox form of Christianity and is pointing to a more mainstream pre-Islamic Christianity, albeit divided among the various Christological heresies of the day."[659]

The Quran came as a rectifier of Jewish and Christian excesses against God. The Christian tradition claimed to have believed in monotheism, but to the Quran, the Christian dogma of the Trinity and incarnation was a clear violation of the divine unity and transcendence. Hence, Allah revealed the Book (al-Quran) to His servant (Muhammad) "that He may warn those who say, 'Allah hath begotten a son': no knowledge have they of such a thing, nor had their fathers. It is a grievous thing that issues from their mouths as a saying. What they say is nothing but falsehood" (18:4-5). Their claims of Jesus's divinity and sonship are proof of their utter ignorance, "they who make such a preposterous claim have no real knowledge of Him."[660] The Prophet was asked to employ different arguments to bring the point across: "Say: 'Praise be to Allah, Who begets no son, and has no partner in (His) dominion: nor (needs) He any to protect Him from humiliation: yea, magnify Him for His greatness and glory!' (17:111). The verse refers to Christ's crucifixion experience and humiliations as antithetical to true divinity. Another passage states: "Say: 'If the Most Gracious had a son, I would be the first to worship.' Glory to the Lord of the heavens and the earth, the lord of the Throne He transcends the things they attribute to Him." (43:81-2). To the Quran, the most serious sin one can commit is the claim that God has begotten a son.

They say: "The Most Gracious has betaken a son!" Indeed ye have put forth a thing most monstrous! At it the skies are about to burst, the earth to split asunder, and the mountains to fall down in utter ruin, that they attributed a son to The Most Gracious. For it is not consonant with majesty of The Most Gracious that He should beget a son. Not one of the beings in the heavens and the earth but must come to The Most Gracious as a servant. (19:88-93).

Muhammad Asad observes that "the idea that God might have a 'son' - either in the real or in the metaphorical sense of this term - would presuppose a degree of innate likeness between 'the father' and 'the son': but God is in every respect unique, so that 'there is nothing like unto Him' (42:11) and 'nothing that could be compared with Him' (112:4). Moreover, the concept of 'progeny' implies an organic continuation of the progenitor, or of part of him, in another being and, therefore, presupposes a degree of incompleteness before the act of procreation (or incarnation, if the term 'sonship' is used metaphorically): and the idea of incompleteness, in whatever sense, negates the very concept of God. But even if the idea of 'sonship' is meant to express no more than one of the different 'aspects' of the One Deity (as is claimed in the Christian dogma of the 'Trinity'), it is described in the Quran as blasphemous inasmuch as it amounts to an attempt at defining Him who is 'sublimely exalted above anything that men may devise by way of definition.'"[661]

In addition to the above discussed anti-Trinitarian polemics in 5: 72-73, the Quran in these verses (19:88-93) alludes to Jesus's statement reported in Matthew 4:10; Luke 4:8 and John 20:17 where Jesus insists upon the worship of only One God and uses it as a springboard to refute the later Trinitarian claims. According to the Quran: "Certainly they disbelieve who say: "Allah is Christ the son of Mary." But said Christ: "O Children of Israel! Worship Allah, my Lord and your Lord." Whoever joins other gods with Allah, Allah will forbid him the Garden, and the Fire will be his abode. There will for the wrong-doers be no one to help. They disbelieve who say: Allah is one of the three (in a Trinity) for there is no god except One God. If they desist not from their word (of blasphemy), verily a grievous chastisement will befall the disbelievers among them. Why turn they not to Allah and seek His forgiveness? For Allah is Oft-forgiving, Most Merciful. Christ the son of Mary was no more than a Messenger; many were the Messengers that passed away before him. His mother was a woman of truth. They had both to eat their (daily) food. See how Allah doth make His Signs clear to them; and see in what ways they are deluded away from the truth! (5:72-76).

The Quran underscores that salvation is connected with true theological outlook (faith) and strict ethical virtues (action). The grace-based Trinitarian salvation scheme diminishes the need for human efforts, virtue and righteousness to maximize divine intervention, arbitrary grace and erratic love. The triune, Trinitarian notions of God are arbitrary, circular, paradoxical, misleading, irrational, mythological and hence eternally condemned. They compromise God's unity, sovereignty, self-sufficiency, omnipotence, omnipresence, omniscience and cosmos' unity and integrity. They lead humanity to an idolatry of divine persons and related mysterious dogmas. Anthropomorphism, corporealism, fetishism, frequent miraculous interventionism, abnormalism, supernaturalism and divine incarnation make God (the Father) and his natural laws obsolete.[662] Jesus and nature's intermediary cooperative roles make God too transcendent, aloof and irrelevant. They also make man too evil, depraved, ignorant and dependent on Church, state, natural phenomena and random grace. They confuse a believer about divisions of persons within the godhead, and dilute one's relationship with the One and Only God and with virtue. They also muddle with sincere worship of and submission to the will of One God, the essence of morality. They are antithetical to pristine teachings of historical Jesus, who directed his sole being to submission of One God and love of neighbour, and therefore deserve severe judgement.

Let us read 5:72 one more time to see the seriousness of the Quranic admonitions against Trinity. "Indeed, the truth deny they who say, "Behold, God is the Christ, son of Mary" - seeing that the Christ [himself] said, "O children of Israel! Worship God [alone], who is my Sustainer as well as your Sustainer." Behold, whoever ascribes divinity to any being beside God, unto him will God deny paradise, and his goal shall be the fire: and such evildoers will have none to succour them!" (5:72)

It is worth emphasising once more that these Quranic statements roundly reject both interpretations of the Trinity, the docetistic and monarchian, the monophysites as well as the dyophysites. They reject the Trinitarian claims of the Augustinian and Cappadocian camps. The Trinitarian theology, with its incarnational bent, is absolutely disgraceful to Almighty God and his transcendence. It brings him down to the earth and mercilessly crucifies him. It is supernatural, hierarchical and arbitrary. The same triadic hierarchy is translated into human social order and people are divided into arbitrary classes such as clergy, royalty, nobility and laity. This way, both the celestial and terrestrial realms, both divinity and humanity are compromised and corrupted. The Unity of God means unity of humanity and cosmos. The Trinitarian formula disturbs that unity by compartmentalising it and assigning different compartments to various persons of the Trinity. The Sovereign God does not need any help in any aspects of His Lordship, creation and its management. The Quran blames Christian Trinitarian dogma of blurring the transcendental realm with utilitarian sphere of want and need.

Unfortunately, the Christian Church did not pay much attention to the Quranic corrective measures and is still struggling with the intelligibility and logical formulation of the Trinitarian maze. Islam's call to return to the original, Unitarian, monotheistic and Semitic consciousness of Jesus has been met with Christian hostilities. Christianity has preserved their loyalty to the Greco-Roman legacy, at the expense of Jesus and his God. The reformation of the Christian dogma has been long due, and only the Islamic Jesus can rescue Christianity from its long history of Christological jargon and unintelligible quibbles. G. Parrinder has noted that "when the newly discovered Gnostic apocryphal writings, such as the so-called Gospel of Thomas, are examined, one may feel thankful that orthodox Christianity rejected the extremes of Neo-Platonic mysticism. But did the church keep close enough to its Biblical roots? Early Islam, thanks to its Semitic background and original isolation, was even more free from Greek speculation. Its prophetic witness to the unity of God, and in general to the humanity of Jesus and his mother, was a needful corrective which the church largely ignored. In the rethinking of doctrinal expression today Islam and Christianity can learn much from each other."[663] He further observes that "Christianity [...] has often been blind to Christ, Docetic in its view of his humanity, and impervious to the prophetic correction that Islam maintained to some dogmas."[664] It is time that the Christian leadership should pay attention to the Islamic corrective measures to its outmoded dogmas, so as to make sense to the modern mind which pays attentions to minute details and cherishes intelligibility.[665] The myth of God incarnate must give way to divine unity and transcendence, as Karl Barth, John Hick and many other Christian theologians have passionately longed for.[666]

We conclude this part of the discussion with the observation that the brief Islamic confession "there is no god but God" excludes any worship and sincere service in the absolute sense to anybody or anything other than God Almighty since everybody or everything other than God can only be a false god. The Christianity's comprehension of God had left many problems unsolved (as detailed in previous chapters) and the Quranic account came to purge the confused, adulterated, even mystical understanding of the Divine contained in i.e., ideas such as the incarnation, corporealism and physical anthropomorphism of God, that had come to prevail. Monotheistic theology is nothing new in the history of western religious traditions. Nevertheless, the radical monotheism of Islam offers distinctive solutions to the difficult and thorny problems of the nature of God, freewill and predestination, the relationship of good to evil, and of reason to revelation. Islamic insistence upon God's absolute transcendence and perfect unity is quite distinctive among the Semitic traditions. Therefore, the distinctive feature of Islam, as Richard C. Martin rightly observes, is that "Among the Western religious traditions, Islam has most insistently asserted the unity and oneness of God."[667]

Now we turn to the peculiar characteristics of the Islamic monotheism.

Tawhid: The Islamic Monotheism

In Islam God stands alone: transcendent and majestic. The faith is marked by a strict and uncompromising ethical monotheism, signifying the absolute Oneness, Unity, Uniqueness and Transcendence of God, in its highest and purest sense, and which formally and unequivocally eliminates all notions of polytheism, pantheism, dualism, monolatry, henotheism, tritheism, trinitarianism, and indeed any postulation or conception of the participation of persons in the divinity of God. Thus, it is a universal truth that mainstream Islam has always emphasised the absolute Unitarianism, transcendence and unity of God, avoiding corporeal notions and anthropomorphic images of His being. However, this understanding of transcendence is not abstract in the philosophical sense of the term, for many poetical expressions are used in the Quran to establish a kind of divine yet vague modality with regards to God, so as to make the transcendent deity immanent and live, and to allow for the provision of ample opportunities to develop a meaningful relationship with Him. The Islamic God is loving, compassionate and closer to man than his jugular vein, but transcendent and ineffable in his essence. His relationship with man is moral and teleological.

The word "Islam" means submission and peace: submission to the moral will of the One and Transcendent God, and peace with the Creator and His creatures. Islam claims to be in unison with the original messages of the prophets Moses and Jesus, but finds fault with historical Judaic and Christian notions of the deity.[668] The Hebrew Bible's anthropomorphic conceptions of Yahweh (God) and Christianity's belief in a triune God are both unacceptable to Islam, for they are viewed as having compromised God's transcendence and unity. The Islamic Scripture, the Quran, on one level, is believed to have been revealed as a corrective measure, to rectify not only the polytheistic conceptions of God but also to clarify and amend Jewish and Christian compromises with regards to God's transcendence, especially the Christian's Trinitarian violations. Islam identifies the source of this compromise in the historical adulteration of the previous revelations (both intentional and unintentional) and claims to have fixed the problem through revelation of the Quran, returning to original purity the message that had been undermined and corrupted. Islam also claims to have avoided the historical mistakes that led to the intermixing or interjection of human words with the word of God. Indeed, the faith deems historical authenticity, textual purity and solemn preservation of the original scripture, as key safeguards to guarantee and preserve the unity and transcendence of God and humanity's correct perception of Him.

Transcendence of God and the Quran

Divine unity and transcendence are the essence of the Quranic message. The Quranic concept of transcendental monotheism is simple, logical and straightforward. It is free of the Christian mysteries, paradoxes and contradictions, and nourishes reasoning and rational discourse. It is absolutely antithetical to the Christian Trinitarian theology and its lax moral implications. There is no division in the Godhead, no multiple divine persons, divine generation, procession or incarnation, no diffusion, confusion or merger of the divinity with humanity, no mysteries, paradoxes and no logical impasses. It is a simple and straightforward absolute Unitarian monotheism void of all unintelligible Trinitarian waffle and Incarnational guff. It is laid out in crystal-clear rational terms and safeguarded against all possible Trinitarian violations, from modes to attributes to persons. The Quranic concept of *Tawhid* is squarely aimed at rectifying Christian excesses.

The Quranic worldview divides reality into two generic realms, God and non-God. God is the Eternal Creator and nothing is like unto Him.[669] He has no son, equal, partner or divine society or composite Godhead. He remains forever the transcendental Other devoid of any resemblance, similarity, partnership and association. He is that unique being who can only be called the Reality and the Being as everything other than Him derives its reality, existence and being from Him. Allah, the Arabic word for God, is semantically the highest focused word of the Quran. The Quranic worldview is theocentric to the core; ontologically nothing can stand equal or opposed to Him. He always remains the transcendental Other who presides over the entire system of existence as its Master and Creator. Everything other than Him is His creature and stands inferior to Him in the hierarchy of being including Jesus and the Holy Spirit.

The second realm consists of everything other than God. It is the order of time-space, creation and of experience. Ontologically these two orders always remain disparate. The Creator neither descends to the realm of space-time and experience to be united, incarnated, diffused or confused with creatures nor can the creatures ascend to be ontologically united or diffused with the Creator. The Islamic concept of God is the absolute opposite of the Christian notion of God; ontologically God never descends to the earth, and humanity is never deified to ascend to the divine realms. God always remains the utterly sublime transcendental Other. This is the Quranic concept of divine Unity, and it is absolutely opposed to the Christian concept of Incarnation, Trinity, Unity of Godhead and Plurality of Persons and atoning death of Christ.

This unity is the thread which runs through the entire Quranic corpus as the core of the Quranic message. All Quranic concepts, ideas, and ideologies are woven together to pinpoint, elaborate, and describe this very doctrine of the Oneness, Unity, and Transcendence of God, and to encourage mankind to establish a meaningful and right relationship with Him. There is so much emphasis in the Quran upon the Oneness, Unity and Uniqueness of Almighty God that no stone seems to be left unturned to make this crystal-clear, even to a cursory reader. Moreover, the Quranic concept of "Monotheism" is neither progressive nor ambiguous. It is neither confusing nor contradictory. It is monotheistic and theocentric to the very definition of the word. It is negative, affirmative, rational, normative and self-explanatory.

The Islamic Creed

The Quranic monotheism does not start with monolatry or with the affirmations of the existence or Oneness of the Deity. It starts by absolutely negating all concepts, kinds, ideas, understandings, and illusions of divinity or godhead other than the One and the only Divine. It starts with the Credo of Islam *Lā ilāha illa Allāh*, the *shahādah* or confession, which is derived from the Quran itself. The whole Quran, observes Charles Eaton, is "a commentary on these four words, or as an amplification of them."[670] The first part of this declaration, *Lā ilāha*, negates the existence of each and any false god, and condemns false devotion, worship, and ideas of dependence upon such gods. The profession of faith (*shahādah*) is a commitment to radical transcendental monotheism.

The Arabic word *ilāh* is a comprehensive word. It stands for a number of mutually interconnected meanings. The root of this word consists of three letters i.e., *alif, lām* and *ha*. Ragib Al-Isfahānī and Mawdudi have shown the connotations of various derivatives of this word, as found in the lexicons, as follows:

1. Became confused or perplexed.
2. Achieved peace and mental calm by seeking refuge with someone or establishing relation with him.
3. Became frightened of some impending mishap or disaster, and

someone gave him the necessary shelter.

4. Turned to another eagerly, due to the intensity of his feelings for him.

5. The lost offspring of the she-camel rushed to snuggle up to its mother on finding it.

6. Became hidden, or concealed, or elevated.

7. Adored, offered worship to.[671]

These literal meanings of the word make it clear, that the word *ilāh* stands for anything awfully mysterious, concealed, frightening, extremely attractive, absorbing one's whole being, demanding absolute love, adoration, dependence, and worship. Whatever and whosoever possess these qualities, and makes human beings adore, worship, or take refuge in it or him, can be called *ilāh*. Therefore, the word can refer to any being, person, matter, or concept which attracts people's full attention and is taken as an object of worship and absolute adoration, whether out of love or fear. That is why the Quran uses the word in both positive and negative senses, meaning that it may denote the true God or a false god. It may be added that the Quran frequently uses the term for the true God. There are some verses where it uses the same term for false gods also (see for instance see 28:38; 15:96; 17:22, 17:39; 25:43; 45:23). The word "Allah" is derived from "*ilah*."

The Quran claims that the strict ethical monotheism is the hallmark of Semitic consciousness. The original Jews, Christians and Muslims worshipped the same One and Only God in the ultimate sense. The Hebrew *Elohim*, the Aramaic *Eloha* and the Arabic *Allah* are the names of the same One and Only God. Therefore, Moses, Jesus and Muhammad all worshipped the same God with identical name. They would have not applied other cultures or people's names to their God. (They definitely did not call their deity "God" as the word "god" was not part of their vocabulary. It is derived from the medieval German word "gott," a name for a Viking god.)[672] If they were to wake up today, they would definitely recognise Allah as the name of their God along with most of his beautiful names such as *Ahad*, *Rahman* and *Rahim*. These names were part of their Hebrew, Aramaic and Arabic languages, cultures and backgrounds.[673] That is why the Aramaic influenced later books of the Hebrew Bible (Old Testament), the Syriac and Arabic Bibles and the Quran all use the word *'Ilaha*, *Alaha* and *Allah* to denote the One and Only God.

Likewise, the original disciples of Jesus would have definitely worshipped Allah as Aramaic, and not Greek, was their mother tongue and religious lingo. They could have possibly understood some dialect of Greek, the language of foreign occupying Roman forces, but naturally not incorporating Greco-Roman religious terms into their sacred vocabulary. It is also obvious that they could not have worshiped "Christ" or "Trinity," as both terms were alien to them. These words were the production of later Christian centuries, as seen above. The original Nazoreans (Nazarenes) followed the Hebrew Bible, as there was no New Testament at their times. The Hebrew Bible was - and is - absolutely void of the words "Christ," "Trinity" and "Triune God". In fact, the Christians of the first few centuries would have not worshipped the "Trinity" as currently understood with loaded reverential meanings. There was no officially established Trinity, Triune God or Apostolic Creed until the Council of Nicaea in 325 AD or the well-defined doctrine of Trinity with modern connotations until the Council of Constantinople (381 AD) and in reality, until the Council of Chalcedon in 451 AD. The idea of Jesus as the perfect God and perfect man was introduced by the Council of Chalcedon. Therefore, it is safe to say that Jesus and his original disciples, along with early centuries of official Christianity, did not worship the "Trinity"; They worshipped the One and Only indivisible God of the Jews. The first part of Islamic Confession is a reflection of this historical reality. Unlike the confusing and self-contradicting Christian creeds, the credo of Islam is short, simple, straight forward and logical.

By means of the first part of the *shahādah,* the existence as well as the reality of any and every god and object of worship is absolutely negated. With an explosive "No" all allusions of multiplicity, incarnation, self-sufficiency, godhead and divinity are at once shattered. The third word of the confession *illa* is the link and isthmus between what is negated and what is affirmed. All that is denied is finally restored by the fourth word Allah. It means that there is no reality, no god, none self-sufficient except Allah, the true Reality.

The second part of the *shahādah* contains an immediate corollary on the mission and prophethood of Muhammad. It says, *Muhammadun Rasūl Allāh,* "and Muhammad is the Messenger of God." The true Reality is historically revealed through the mission and prophethood of Muhammad; Prophet Muhammad is the embodiment of the divine message and not a reflection of the divine Person.

The pronouncement of this confession is the pronouncement of God's Oneness, Uniqueness and Transcendence. Perhaps this is the reason that it has been mentioned in the Quran and the Prophetic traditions (Sunnah) more frequently than any other phrase. It has been referred to as *kalimah ṭayyibah* (sacred utterance) (14:24), *al-qawl al-thābit* (the firm word) (14:27), *kalimah al-taqwā* (utterance of piety) (48:26), *maqālid al-samawāti wa al-ard* (key to the heavens and the earth) etc. As the confession is the essence of the Islamic faith and the only token of entry into it, it can safely be asserted that the Oneness, Unity and Unicity of God is the essence of the Islamic religion. This confession is a Muslim's sublime obsession. It polarises the thought of Islam into real and non-real. It occupies Muslim thoughts and actions.

In the Quran, the Islamic unitarian formula, with its *Lā ilāha* form, occurs 41 times. This is in addition to the numerous other forms (23 different formulas) that the Quran uses to negate godhead or divinity in any form or way. The Quran states: "And your God is One God: there is no god but He, Most Gracious, Most Merciful" (2:163).[674] At another place it says: "Allah! There is no god but He, the Living, the Self-Subsisting, the Supporter of all" (3:2). The reality of divine unity and transcendence is witnessed by God and by all of His righteous creatures: "There is no god but He: that is the witness of Allah, His angels, and those endowed with knowledge, standing firm on justice. There is no god but He the Exalted in Power, the Wise" (3:18). The famous "Throne Verse" (*āyat al-Kursī*) also starts with the same confession.

"Allah! There is no god but He, the Living, the Self-subsisting, Supporter of all, no slumber can seize Him nor sleep. His are all things in the heavens and on earth. Who is there who can intercede in His presence except as He permitteh? He knoweth what (appeareth to His creatures as) Before or After or Behind them. Nor shall they compass aught of His knowledge except as He willeth. His Throne doth extend over the heavens and the earth, and He feeleth no fatigue in guarding and preserving them for He is the Most High, the Supreme (in glory)."(2:255)

The point of emphasis in the verse is clear. It is one of the countless Quranic verses that leaves no room for any confusion or ambiguity *vis-a-vis* the absolute Oneness, Uniqueness, Omnipotence, Omnipresence, Omniscience and Transcendence of God. Mawdudi explains the first part of the verse, by stating that "irrespective of the number of gods or objects of worship set up by ignorant people, the fact remains that godhead in its entirety belongs exclusively to the Eternal Being, Who is indebted to no one for His existence. In fact, He is not only self-existent, but upon Him rests the entire order of the universe. None shares either His attributes or His power and might, and no one has the same claims against creatures as He. Hence, if anywhere in the heavens or the earth someone sets up anything or anybody as an object of worship and service (*ilah*) either instead of or in addition to the One True God, this amounts to declaring war on reality."[675]

With regards to the *shahādah*'s significance, Al-Faruqi observes that "This seemingly negative statement, brief to the utmost limits of brevity, carries the greatest and richest meanings in the whole of Islam. Sometimes a whole culture, a whole civilisation, or a whole history lies compressed in one sentence. This certainly is the case of *al-kalimah* (pronouncement) or *al-shahadah* of Islam. All the diversity, wealth and history, culture and learning, wisdom and civilisation of Islam is compressed in this shortest of sentences – *la ilaha illa Allah* (There is no god but God)."[676]

In addition to the *shahādah*, the Quran uses many other formulas to highlight the Unity and Oneness of God. "Allah has said: 'Take not (for worship) two gods: for He is just One God: then fear me (and Me alone).' To Him belongs whatever is in the heavens and on earth, and to Him is the religion always: then will ye fear other than Allah?" (16:51-52). "But your God is One God: so submit then your will to Him [...]" (22:34). Prophet Muhammad is ordained to declare: "Say: What has come to me by inspiration is that Your God is One God: will ye therefore bow to His Will (in Islam)" (21:108). "Say: 'I am but a man like yourselves, (but) the inspiration has come to me, that your God is One God: whoever expects to meet his Lord, let him work righteousness, and in the worship of his Lord, admit no one as partner'" (18:110; see also 13:30; 13:36; 6:56; 6:71; 6:162; 6:163; 10:104; 13:16; 17:42, 17:53; 39:11; 39:14; 39:38; 39:64; 40:66; 41:6; 72:20).

In the famous *Sūrah al-Kāfirūn* (109), the Prophet is ordered to disavow himself absolutely from the unbelievers and what they worship other than One God. But it is surah 112 *al-Ikhlās*, "sincerity," where the Prophet is given such a comprehensive lesson of Oneness, Uniqueness, Unicity and Transcendence of God that, if one does not read from the Quran anything other than this short surah and properly apprehends its meaning, one cannot admit any doubt or confusion regarding the Quranic concept of transcendence and strict monotheism.

T. B. Irving translates the chapter of "Sincerity" (*al-Ikhlās*) as follows: "Say: 'God is Unique! God is the Source [for everything]; He has not fathered anyone nor was He fathered, and there is nothing comparable to Him.'"

Al-Ikhlās or the Chapter of Sincerity consists of four Makkan verses only. Yet, this brief construction heralds monumental implications: it emphasises God's divine Unity, Uniqueness, Self-Sufficiency, Transcendence and Purity; stands as a powerful statement against the Christian concept of a triune God – the trinity of divine Persons; acts as a profound declaration against the Son of God Christology; and demands sincere and sole worship of the One and Only God eliminating possibilities of any partnership or association with Him. It is also equal to one third of the Quran (hadith reported by Bukhari, 4628) since it explains *al-tawḥīd,* one of the three most essential doctrines of Islam, the other two being Prophethood/Revelation and the Day of Judgement.

The pagans of Mecca queried the Prophet about the lineage (origin) of Allah. As a response Allah revealed this verse "Say: Allah is Unique". The Arabic term *Aḥad* is used in this surah to indicate the Unicity of God instead of the frequently used Quranic term *waḥīd.*[677] The term *Aḥad* is much more precise than the frequently used term *waḥīd* which means "one". *Aḥad* has the added connotations of absolute and continuous unity and the absence of equals. Al-Alusī explains that the root of the word *ahad* is *waḥīd.* The difference being that *ahad* cannot be divided, distributed or analysed while *waḥīd* could be.[678] Al-Bayhaqī states that *al-ahad* is the one who does not have any similar, like or an equivalent or match while *al-wahid* means the one who has no associate or partner. That is why God Almighty gave this name to Himself... As if the verse "He begets not neither is He begotten" is a kind of explanation of the verse "He is One" and Almighty God can never be divided nor come to an end.[679]

The second verse of the chapter contains the word *al-Ṣamad,* which has been used nowhere else in the Quran except in this surah. The word itself is so comprehensive that it has been translated differently by a number of different translators. *Al-Ṣamad* is one of the "most beautiful names" of God, and its root has the primary meaning of "without hollow" or "without cleft." Allah is without mixture of any sort, without any possibility of division into parts, because in Him there is no "hollow." *Al-Ṣamad* denotes that God is unknowable, enjoying intrinsic self-sufficiency and unicity without cleft or internal division. Some have explained the word *al-Ṣamad* as meaning "The Master who is depended upon in all matters."[680] M. Asad translates it as "God the Eternal, the Uncaused Cause of All Being." He further observes that "This rendering gives no more than an approximate meaning of the term as-samad, which occurs in the Quran only once, and is applied to God alone. It comprises the concept of Primary Cause and eternal, independent Being, combined with the idea that everything existing or conceivable goes back to Him as its source and is, therefore, dependent on Him for its beginning as well as for its continued existence."[681]

The third verse of Surah *Al-Ikhlās* "He begets not, and neither is He begotten" reaffirms this unicity by categorically rejecting any multiplicity within the divine unity. It also simultaneously shatters the "daughters of God" concept, held by the polytheists of Mecca, as well as the Christian concept of the Trinity. Muslims were put on their guard during the very early stages of revelation against any association and multiplicity within the godhead, and it didn't take long for the supposed mystery of the Trinity or incarnation to be declared a betrayal of the divine transcendence, unity and uniqueness of God and a "cleft" in the godhead. It was unequivocally understood that Allah is everlasting while creatures are temporal; that no changeable circumstances effect the divine existence, ever, while creatures are changeable; that Allah is perfect while creatures are imperfect; and that generation, birth, procession, multiplication, progress and development are an absurdity with regards to Allah while intrinsic to His creatures. In sum, so wholly strict and pristine was this quality of "One" stipulated that it included total refutation of utterly human and creaturely limitations, including any notion of familial relations (father, son, daughter).

The last verse of *al-Ikhlas* dispels all possibilities of a crude anthropomorphism, corporealism and incarnation existing in relation to God. The verse is unequivocal in stating that nothing resembles God, either in His being or in His actions and attributes. This early Meccan verse at once demolishes all Trinitarian and incarnational models; all vain talk of multiple divine persons, unity of essence, nature, composite Godhead, multi-personality, all incarnational and Trinitarian Christological formulations, all Trinitarian models, every possibility of similarity, resemblance and comparison with divinity is absolutely nullified. All absolute power structures are demolished, to reserve the absolute dominion solely for God. In fact, God is the only effective power in existence; He is the absolute reality, with absolute qualities and attributes. Everything other than Him is relative and dependent upon His transcendental being for its existence, sustenance and continuity. The claims of God's absolute unity and uniqueness made in the previous verses are hereby sealed, confirmed and elaborated by this final verse "there is nothing like unto Him." M. Asad writes that "the fact that God is one and unique in every respect, without beginning and without end, has its logical correlate in the statement that "there is nothing that could be compared with Him"-thus precluding any possibility of describing or defining Him [...] Consequently, the *quality* of His being is beyond the range of human comprehension or imagination: which also explains why any attempt at "depicting" God by means of figurative representations or even abstract symbols must be qualified as a blasphemous denial of the truth."[682]

Categories of *Tawhid*

When the term *tawḥīd*[683] is used in reference to God Almighty, it means realisation of the divine unity and transcendence in all of man's actions, directly or indirectly related to God. It is the belief that Allah is One and Unique, without partner in His dominion and His actions (*rububiyyah*), One without similitude in His essence and attributes (*asmā' wa ṣifāt*), and One without rival in His divinity and in worship (*uluḥiyyah/'ibādah*).[684] The Islamic concept of *Tawhid* is so comprehensive that it closes all possibilities of Incarnation and Trinity, whether in divine essence, nature, modes, attributes or actions.

These three categories of *tawḥīd*, are sometimes referred to as *Tawḥīd al-Dhāt* (unity of the Being), *Tawḥīd al-Ṣifāt* (Unity of the Attributes) and *Tawḥīd al-Afʿāl* (Unity of the Actions). The Unity of God, according to the Quran, implies that God is the Absolute One in His person (*dhāt*), Absolute One in His attributes (*ṣifāt*) and Absolute One in His works (*afʿāl*). The Oneness of His person means that there is neither plurality of gods, nor plurality of persons in the Godhead; the Oneness of attributes implies that no other being possesses one or more of the Divine attributes in the absolute sense; His Oneness in works implies that none can do the works which God has done, or which God may do.

This comprehensive and well-guarded concept of divine unity is antithetical to the Christian notions of plurality of persons in the godhead. It eliminates the need and possibility of divine incarnation into human realms, mediatorial agencies between God and man, derivative divinities, transfer of divine names, attributes and actions to finite creatures, confusing Trinitarian, crucifixion and resurrection jargon and mysterious paradoxes. The third category of *Tawhid*, unity of names and attributes, is squarely aimed at the Judeo-Christian compromises of divine names, attributes and actions. As Almighty God is One, Unique, and incomparable in His lordship, sovereignty, and worship, He is also One and Unique in His names and attributes. In Judaism and Christianity, the conception of God is to a greater or lesser extent bound to the limitations of His creatures. As seen above, both the Augustinian one-self and the Cappadocian three-self Trinitarian models in spite of all circular reasoning, paradoxes and mysteries, end up crucifying the whole or one third divinity on the Cross. Islam emphatically proclaims that Almighty God, the Transcendent and Exalted Lord and Sustainer of all that exists, is far above possessing any of the creaturely attributes which have been ascribed to Him by man. He is not bound to any of the limitations of human beings or any other of His creatures; He has neither form nor body, nor corporeal or physical attributes, features, or characteristics. Rather, His attributes are infinite and absolute; they are far above any sort of limitations, defects, and deficiencies, such as his having a beginning or an end, begetting or being begotten, having physical dimensions, or having needs such as requiring food, rest, or procreation etc. He is the One Who gives such dimensions and characteristics to His creations, while not sharing them in the slightest degree.

The third dimension of *al-tawhīd* (Oneness of Names and Attributes) is specifically directed towards Jewish and Christian compromises of the divine transcendence. Judaism, Christianity, and Islam constitute successive moments of Semitic consciousness in their long march through history as carriers of a divine mission on earth. Identifying itself with the original pristine message sent by God to mankind, Islam as the final Revelation, notably protected from scriptural corruption, stands as a corrective element, finding fault with the Jewish and Christian conception and portrayal of God as delineated in the historical documents accepted by the two faiths as scriptures. Islam holds these documents accountable for compromising the divine transcendence and hence committing the most grievous error against the Semitic consciousness, polluting its once pure essence. As detailed in previous chapters, the biblical conception of God is anthropomorphic, corporeal and pluralistic. After criticising a number of biblical passages portraying God in anthropomorphic terms, al-Faruqi asserts that "Islam also charged that the relation Judaism claimed to bind God to "His People" straight-jacketed Him into granting them favors despite their immorality, their hardship and stiffneckedness (Deuteronomy 9:5-6). A "bound" god, bound in any sense or degree, is not the transcendent God of Semitic consciousness."[685]

Likewise, Christianity gravely misconceived the divine unity by reformulating it as a triune Godhead, using the incarnational gambit as justification to commit excesses against God and place countless limitations upon him. According to al-Faruqi the "Christians have committed themselves to divine non-transcendence so resolutely that it had become with them an *idee fixe*, enabling Paul Tillich to declare *sub specie eternitatis* that the transcendent God is unknown and unknowable unless He is concretised in an object of nature and history."[686]

Equally improper has been God talk in Christianity, including the language and terminology used to express creedal prepositions. Although Christianity has never ceased to claim that God is transcendent, nevertheless it has always spoken of Him as a real man, living in this earthly domain, walking and doing all the things men do, including suffering the agonies of death. So, to Christians, Jesus has always been both man and God. As discussed in earlier chapters, this man-God statement is inherently flawed, more of a claim than a logical preposition substantiated by rational arguments or reasonable facts. This being so, Christianity has never been able to systematically articulate the God-man dogma in intelligible terms or take a consistent position on Jesus's humanity or divinity; and not surprisingly its turbulent history has been fraught with accusations of apostasy and heresy hurled back and forth. This also explains why Christian God language has always been confusing, at best, for confusion sows confusion. When pinned down, every Christian has to admit that the God they worship is both transcendent and incarnate. Yet this claim of transcendence to al-Faruqi is "*ipso facto* devoid of grounds. To maintain the contrary, one has to give up the laws of logic."[687] In sum, a wide gulf of conceptual differences regarding the doctrine of divine transcendence exists and separates Islam from both Judaism and Christianity.

Islam emphasises that God by very definition of His reality cannot simply be a sort of supernatural or superhuman personality/being, directing worldly affairs from the heavens/soaring clouds whilst simultaneously sharing in creaturely attributes, needs, and qualities. For God is nothing less than the Creator, Originator, and Fashioner of this vast universe, the One Who keeps it functioning in accordance with His infinite wisdom, knowledge and master plans. God infinitely transcends anything which the human mind can possibly perceive or comprehend, or the senses grasp, imagine, or explain. God is far, far above any similarity or comparability with any of His creatures; this special emphasis upon the Divine transcendence is what the third category of al-tawhīd is designated for. God is One in His Names and Attributes. His Names, Actions and Attributes surpass human names, actions and attributes as much as His Being surpasses their beings. The Absolute Creator utterly transcends the relative actions and attributes of His creatures. This is implied in the first assertion of the Islamic creed that "There is no god but God." In addition to being a denial of any associates to God in His worship, rule and judgeship of the universe, it also contains a denial of the possibility of any creature representing, personifying, or in any way or form expressing the divine Being. The Quran says of God that "To Him is due the primal origin of the heavens and the earth: When He decreeth a matter, He saith to it: 'Be,' and it is." (2:117; 2:163). "There is no God but He, ever-living, ever-active" (3:2). "May He be glorified beyond any description!" (6:100) "No sense may perceive Him" (6:103) "Praised be He, the Transcendent Who greatly transcends all claims and reports about Him" (17:43). As a result of this stringent emphasis upon the divine transcendence, Muslims have been supremely careful never to associate, in any manner possible, any image or thing with the presence of the divine or with their consciousness of the divine. This fact is well reflected in Muslim discourse, speech, and writings concerning the divine. Indeed, Muslims have only ever employed the language of the Quran, and its terms and expressions, to present or describe God – the transcendental language and terminology chosen by God Himself in fact to depict Himself in the verses of the Quran.[688]

The Quran prescribes the fundamental transcendental criterion in the following verses: "There is nothing whatever like unto Him"

(42:11). "And there is none like unto Him" (112:4 which we have already had the opportunity to quote and explain in this chapter), and "knowest thou of any who is worthy of the same Name as He?" (19:65). After having established this criterion, the Quran represents God as having "the Most Beautiful Names": "Allah is He, than Whom there is no other god:-Who knows (all things) both secret and open; He, Most Gracious, Most Merciful. Allah is He, than Whom there is no other god;- the Sovereign, the Holy One, the Source of Peace (and Perfection), the Guardian of Faith, the Preserver of Safety, the Exalted in Might, the Irresistible, the justly Proud, Glory to Allah! (High is He) above the partners they attribute to Him. He is Allah, the Creator, the Originator, the Fashioner to Him belong the Most Beautiful Names: whatever is in the heavens and on earth, doth declare His Praises and Glory: and He is the Exalted in Might, the Wise." (59:22-24).

This is a passage of great sublimity; it sums up the generic attributes and names of Allah. While establishing the fundamental principle of divine otherness by the words "nothing is like unto Him," the passage institutes the basis of a possible divine modality. The One and Unique God is the most Merciful, the Compassionate. His knowledge extends to everything seen and unseen, present and future, near and far, in being and not in being: in fact, these relative contrasts do not even apply to the Absolute God. He is unknowable in His being yet knowable through His names and attributes. These beautiful names and attributes are the only source and basis of a possible divine modality. This is perhaps the reason why the Quran and Hadith have taken upon themselves to fix the boundaries of this modality to avoid confusion and excesses.

It is pertinent to reiterate that all of God's names are derived from the Quran and the Hadith; they are *tawqifiyyah,* meaning that they are preconcertedly determined either by a Quranic text or an authentic prophetic report; nothing can be added to them or subtracted from them, the reason being to confess utter dependence upon God regarding the proper knowledge of and about His being. Such sheer dependence upon the revelatory knowledge is in fact a recognition of the impossibility of knowing God, except through what He has decided to reveal to us. Another established criterion among all mainstream Muslim scholars is that God possesses all these perfections from eternity. God cannot be characterised by names insinuating that He acquired these perfections, or by blemish or bad names such as poor, cruel, cheat etc. He cannot be given any evil quality or attribute. The scholars also agree that diminutives of God's names are prohibited, as are words alluding to dual meanings, such as those conveying praise as well as condemnation. The other established criterion is that God's absolute transcendence and exalted majesty must be maintained at all costs. All ideas, concepts, imaginations, and even perceptions leading to resemblance, similarity, comparability, corporeality, and anthropomorphism must be denied of Him.

It is important to realise that the presence of some of these names and qualities in humanity does not make them resemble God. Firstly, because their presence does not make these attributes and qualities of God anthropomorphic or corporeal; and secondly because in God they are perfections and absolute, while in humanity they are imperfect and relative. God is the First and the Everlasting. These attributes are non-corporeal and are first present in Him and then in human beings. So, to describe God utilising these non-physical attributes and absolute qualities in no way makes Him similar or comparable to man. They are simply expressions which pave the way for man to try to know God as much as human limitations allow.

Consequently, all efforts should be directed towards reflecting upon the creatures of God instead of reflecting upon His essence, for there is no way that one can comprehend divine essence. "He knows what is before or after or behind them: but they shall comprehend Him not." (20:110). The Prophet pinpointed this fact by encouraging reflection upon God's creation and not upon God Himself.

In short, the Transcendent God has not the least resemblance to the limited, deficient, and imperfect creatures of His creation. Entirely out of the question is His resemblance to any and all other gods and of course their semi-human nature; deities fashioned by the minds of men, whose lack of knowledge and understanding, and need to supply the deficiencies of their own comprehension, caused such inane inventions. Contrary to this, God enjoys all attributes of perfection appropriate to His Divine Majesty and Exalted Power. Contemplation upon these and His beautiful names is the only recourse to grasp the barest glimpses of His Divine majesty.

In the light of what has been discussed so far, we can conclude that the Quranic concept of God is straightforward and self-explanatory. It consists of the absolute denial of the existence, authority, rule, sovereignty, and abilities to harm or benefit, of other gods (completely and utterly rejecting their worship and the representation of God in any way or form) whilst simultaneously restoring all these attributes and qualities in God Himself. Accordingly, God's attributes and qualities are absolute and are never connected with any physical object, body part or organ. For instance, God can speak through inanimate things such as a bush or a tree, as in the case of Moses (28:30) and in fact, "it is not fitting for a man that Allah should speak to him except by inspiration, or from behind a veil, or by sending of a Messenger to reveal, with Allah's permission, what Allah wills: for He is Most High, Most Wise" (42:51). God does not have a body. Nobody can see Him. Moses' request for a glimpse of God was answered by the following words: "Allah said: 'By no means canst thou see Me; But look upon the Mount; if it abides in its place, then shalt thou see Me.' When his Lord manifested (revealed) Himself to the Mount, He made it as dust, and Moses fell down in a swoon. When he recovered his senses he said: "Glory be to Thee! To Thee I turn in repentance, and I am the first to believe." (7:143)

The reason being that "no vision can grasp Him, but His grasp is over all vision; He is the Subtle Well Aware" (6:103). In short, the Quran has explained its monotheism in simple, logical, and intelligible terms and categories, elaborated it with additional logical ways, methods and examples and well protected this concept from possible violations. The Divine transcendence is an intrinsic part of the Quranic concept of the Deity. The transcendent God is immanent by dint of His countless absolute attributes expressed through His Beautiful Names and many other signs and manifestations throughout His creation. Moreover, the Quran makes special efforts to safeguard against all possible violations, confusions, and ambiguities, the immensely important concept of the Divine Unity, Uniqueness, and Transcendence of God. This original alertness, observes Bishop Cragg, "against all false theologies accompanies the whole elaboration of Muslim religion. It is, as it were, a supreme "Protestantism" in its very genesis, a cry of heart and a mission of will against all that violated the Divine unity or distracted men from the single direction of their love, their loyalty, and their obedience."[689] Cragg continues that the "ringing shout of praise that echoes through all Islamic ritual and dogma: *Allahu akbar*, "Greater is God," which, grammatically, is a comparative form made all the more striking by its refusal, indeed its inability, to enter any stated comparison. "God is greater" than all that could conceivably be set in any clause after "than." The idea of framing such a clause is itself unthinkable. Yet the superlative ("God is the greatest") is not preferred, for this could imply approximate equality and would, as such, be open to ambiguity, as the psalm is which declares: "He is a great king above all gods." Are we to understand that the gods exist, if only as underlings? Or do we mean that the Lord reigns in utter majesty alone? Islam has no truck with such double possibility of intention. It was not the existence of *Allah* that Muhammad proclaimed. The tribes knew Him by His name. It was His *sole* existence, negating all pluralism. God is exalted above all that might – though always impossibly – compare with Him."[690]

Tawhid, Islamic Art and God Talk

It is this notion of the absolute transcendence of God that has been reflected in Islamic art, language, and indeed so many other aspects of Islamic civilisation and culture. Islam is, and always has been, unceasingly on guard, constantly on high alert against any corporeality, anthropomorphism or any form of comparability, injecting the divine with the non-divine. Unlike Christian art,[691] Islamic art[692] has always avoided sensory images, anthropomorphic depictions or corporeal portrayals of God in all times and places. No mosque has ever contained any object, depiction or statue even remotely connected with divinity. Students of religious art are amazed to see mosques devoid of any decorative pictures, depictions or iconography, aside from lace-like Quranic verses and abstract arabesques adorning walls and ceilings. The latter are in-themselves simply motifs, designs made of stylised stalk, leaf and flower, deliberately denaturalised and symmetrically repeated to dispel any suggestion of the creaturely natural being a vehicle of expression for the divine. Al-Faruqi writes that all the "arts in Islam developed in fulfillment of divine transcendence acting as supreme principle of esthetics."[693]

The same strict precautions have been taken with regards to the Islamic language. Islamic theological discourse (God-talk) revolves strictly around Quranic terminology, despite the existence of, and in fact serving as an interface between, the tremendous geographical, linguistic, cultural and ethnic diversities that span the Muslim world. This is the objective of the Quranic dicta, "we (God) have revealed it as an Arabic Quran" (12:2; 20:113). So, any God-talk by Muslims is predominantly scriptural or Quran-talk, utilising Arabic categories, terms, literary forms and expressions peculiar to the Quran. Muslims have always avoided the use of phrases such as father and son regarding the God-man relationship. Hence, phrases such as "God the Father", "Mother of God", "Son of God", "Crucified God" or "Sons of God" or their equivalent etc., will not be found in Islamic literature. They are utterly banished from the Islamic lexicon, and religious vocabulary, to eliminate and prevent the rise of any consciousness that could lead to pernicious confusion and difficulty with regard to the essence of God, as occurred with regard to Jewish and Christian conceptions of the Divine. The Quranic transcendental axiom is uncompromising in separating the divine realm from the non-divine creaturely one. For the sake of analogy, God stands on one side of the boundary, alone and unique, whilst everything other than He stands on the other, dividing the transcendent from the natural. This is the necessary criterion of Muslim God talk, and a presupposition of God's exiological ultimacy. On the other hand, however, terms such as 'Lord', 'Master', the 'Most Merciful', the 'Compassionate', are frequently used to denote God, while phrases such as "servant" (`abd*), "mankind" (*al-nās*), "human being" (*al-insān*), "creation" (*khalq*) etc., are used to denote man and creation.

Tawhid: The Ethical Monotheism

Al-Tawhid, with all its multiplex emphasis, is not meant merely to exalt God and chant His glories. It is also not meant to claim special privity with God, enjoy special privileges in His name or assert superiority over His creatures. None of these elements are implied in the Quranic understanding of monotheism; it is a responsibility rather than a privilege. It is meant to create the proper response in man, the response that is essential to encourage man to work towards transforming the human society of time and space in accordance with divine moral rules. The unity of God leads to the unity of His creation. No superiority is granted based upon origin, ethnicity, colour, creed or financial or social status. The basic human rights of dignity, freedom, equality and justice are universally granted to all humans because of their humanity. A right relationship with God is the sole guarantee of a just and right relationship between men. A loving connection between man and his God will assure a morally equipped caring human society. On the other hand, any wrong understanding of who God is or a wrong relationship with Him will cause imbalance in man-to-man relationships. The Islamic transcendental monotheism, if understood properly and applied in spirit, can warrant an ethically balanced and caring human society. It is grounded in human responsibility, socio political and economic accountability and universal justice.

The essence of al-Tawḥid can be summarised in the following five terms: (1) Duality of reality (God and non-God) and God as the moral normativity: meaning the Being who commands (moral will of God) and whose commandments are ought-to-be. (2) Ideationality: meaning that the relationship between the two orders of reality is ideational in nature. Man can understand this relationship and its demand easily through the faculty of understanding. (3) Teleology: that the nature of the cosmos is teleological; that it is purposive, serving a purpose of its Creator, and doing so out of design. Man also has a purpose, and that is to be God's vicegerent on earth. (4) Capacity of man and malleability of Nature: since the nature of the cosmos is teleological, hence the actualisation of the Divine purpose must be possible in space and time. (5) Responsibility and Judgment: i.e., that man stands responsible to realise the moral will of God and change himself, his society, and environment so as to conform to the divine pattern. To do so is success, and to disobey Him is to incur punishment and failure. The forgoing five principles, argues al-Faruqi, are "self-evident truths. They constitute the core of Tawhid and the quintessence of Islam."[694]

Therefore, the Quranic message is squarely aimed at man and his well-being. Indeed, it calls itself "guidance for mankind" (hudan li al-nās [2:185] and numerous equivalents elsewhere). Even though the divine names and attributes are the subject of countless Quranic verses, the Quran is not a treatise about God and His nature. The divine existence is functional. He is the Creator, Sustainer and Cherisher of man and his cosmos. He has created the universe to serve man, and is keen to guide man. He loves man and cares about his salvation. Finally, He will judge man individually and collectively and mete out loving justice again for the sake of man. He has taken upon Himself that He will not forgive human violations until the man violated against is compensated for and satisfied. Izutsu presents the point in the following words: "For among all these created things "man" is the one to which is attached so great an importance in the Koran that it attracts at least the same amount of our attention as God. Man, his nature, conduct,

psychology, duties and destiny are, in fact, as much the central preoc-
cupation of the Koranic thought as the problem of God Himself. What
God is, says and does, becomes a problem chiefly, if not exclusively,
in connection with the problem of how man reacts to it. The Koranic
thought as a whole is concerned with the problem of salvation of human beings. If it were not for this problem, the Book would have not
been "sent down", as the Koran itself explicitly and repeatedly emphasises. And in this particular sense, the concept of man is important to
such a degree that it forms the second major pole standing face to face
with [the] principal pole, that is concept of Allah."[695]

Consequently, *Tawhid* is directly connected with the moral sphere
of human life. Its essence cannot be achieved without actualising its
demands of unity and universality of truth, unity, equality, and equity
among the human race, and all that has to take place here and now i.e.,
practically in human society. Al-Faruqi expresses the point succinctly:
"*Tawhid* commits man to an ethic of action; that is, to an ethic where
worth and unworth are measured by the degree of success the moral subject achieves in disturbing the flow of space-time, in his body
as well as around him. It does not deny the ethic of intent where the
same measurement is made by the level of personal values effecting the
moral subject's state of consciousness alone, for the two are not incom-
patible."[696] He further observes that "Having acquiesced to God alone
as his Master, having committed himself, his life and all energies to His
service, and having recognised His Master's will as that which ought to
be actualised in space-time, he must enter the rough and tumble of the
market place and history and therein bring about the desired transformation. He cannot lead a monastic, isolationist existence unless it be
as an exercise in self-discipline and self-mastery."[697]

This moral function of man is to justify his creation in God's moral
image, in the best of form, as the vicegerent of God on earth. Therefore, Islamic understanding of monotheism is moralistic through and
through.[698] This explains why the Quran almost always combines both
faith (*imān*) and good deeds (*amal ṣāliḥ*) together, the one reflecting the
other (2:25; 2:82; 2:277; 3:57; 4:57; 4:122; 4:173; 5:9; 5:93). The Quran
also vehemently stigmatises those who disobey God's moral will and
follow their own desires, inclinations, and moods as gods. The word the
Quran employs to denote this tendency is *hawā* (occurring 17 times),
which can be translated as "caprice or whim." "Have you seen him who

has taken his own caprice to be his god?" (25:43; 45:23). This moralistic understanding of *al-tawḥīd* along with its notion of the Day of Judgment is reflected in the very early Meccan chapters of the Quran. Such a concept of the Divinity is revolutionary and plays a vital role in Muslim life. The following early Meccan chapter (107 *al-Ma'ūn* "Neighbourly Needs"), is sufficient to give an example of the Quranic correlation of belief in God and the Day of Judgment and efforts to transform one's surroundings: "Seest thou one who denies the Day of Judgment. Then such is the one who repulses the orphan and encourages not the feeding of the indigent. So woe to the worshippers who are neglectful of their prayers, those who (want but) to be seen, but refuse (to supply even) neighbourly needs."[699] It can therefore be claimed, clearly, loudly and unequivocally, that the Quran connects human salvation with morality, and not solely with family lineage or belief in or confession of a specific set of doctrines or dogmas. Our own actions in this earthly domain define and govern our existence in the Hereafter. The Quranic message of unity diametrically opposes tribalism, racism, nationalism, ethnic discrimination, human differentiation, cultic veneration, divine domestication, trinitarianism, superstitious dogmatism and secularism. Islam is less of an orthodoxy and more of an orthopraxy.

Furthermore, the Quranic concept of monotheism is not evolutionary; it is original and universal. The Quran gives this moralistic understanding of monotheism a universal dimension by claiming that this was the same message revealed to all the prophets and nations since the beginning of time. "For We assuredly sent amongst every People a Messenger, (with the Command), "Serve Allah, and eschew Evil"" (16:36; 35:24). The message is timeless, unchanged, and universal. For instance, Noah, one of the most ancient of prophets, was sent to his people with the message: "Worship Allah! ye have no other god but Him" (7:59). All subsequent prophets and messengers of God received and communicated the same message (7:65-93). This theme occurs very frequently in the Quran.[700] The Ten Commandments given to Moses were rehearsed by Jesus on the Mount and reiterated by Muhammad in the Quran. The *Shalome* of the original Hebrews is the *Salām* and Islam of the Quran. Jesus's original message of salvation was nothing but "follow the commandments". Love your God and love your neighbour, we can therefore state, is the essence of this universal monotheistic consciousness.

We conclude this section with the claim that the Quranic Creator Paradigm does maintain a wonderful demarcation line between God and whatever is non-God by holding fast to the concept of His transcendence, uniqueness, and otherness. This concept is no bare unity or abstraction, but a vivid, alive, and demanding concept which makes God relevant to the here and now, by means of emphasising His immanence through the modality it provides by the countless Quranic verses. The modality and the language are essentially structured in such a way as to allow many possibilities of communication, without making God resemble or disappear in the world He has created. This type of transcendental concept is pervasive throughout the Quran, the authentic hadith literature, and also throughout the history of Islamic civilisation. All mainstream Muslim thinkers, even the philosophers to an extent, seem to have followed the same line: the sense of and a belief in the transcendental Deity who is mysterious, ineffable, and unknowable in His essence, but at the same time very close to His creatures by dint of His knowledge, power, mercy, and love. Direct submission to his moral commands is Islam which is the only way to attain human felicity and salvation. Moral reactions to these divine commands lead to righteous deeds, which in turn bring peace and security in the social realms. Therefore, moral reformation of man and his surroundings is the goal of Islamic monotheism and ethical monotheism, and its moral implications are the foundations of human salvation. Unlike the irrational, superstitious, mythological and antinomian Christian Trinitarian faith, the Islamic faith, with its strict ethical monotheism and work-based salvation scheme, is moralistic, rational, reformative and self-perpetuating. It is common sensical, logical and self-disciplining; it does not need the strong arm of the state to impose it. It is not afraid of being intellectually probed, rationally analysed, politically and philosophically contested and scientifically demonstrated. It is free of overburdening unintelligible mysteries and circular paradoxes. It is simple, logical, moral and practical. It guarantees human spiritual as well as intellectual satisfaction in this life and salvation in the life to come. Therefore, now we turn to the Islamic concept of salvation.

Salvation

The orthodox Christian and Islamic schemes of salvation are poles apart. Christianity is centered upon human depravity the redemptive sacrifice of Jesus Christ, eternal election, grace and faith, with human efforts and good deeds playing second fiddle. Islam, on the other hand, primarily focuses upon human actions coupled with right faith and appropriate relation with God.[701]

The salvation scheme of Islam is homocentric; it revolves around human potentials, capacities and participation in the moral reformation here and now. The salvation is personal, moral and spiritual but its fruits are collective, a just moral system. It begins with faith in One God, who assigns a moral purpose to human life and judges man based on that moral compass. Morality is a reflection of and submission to the divine commandments, and salvation is the end result of submission. Man is the moral agent and hence the main character in this saga of salvation, while God's role is functional, pedagogical and secondary. God creates man with intellectual capacities and a will to choose, gives him a working knowledge of good and bad, educates him about the good and bad consequences of his choices in both worlds and grants him freedom of choice. It is man who makes or breaks their destiny by one's choices. Therefore, man is the primary agent of salvation while God is the initiator, facilitator and dispenser of salvation. Islam on the vertical level is God's guidance (*Huda*), while Islam on the human level is submission to God's guidance. Islam on the horizontal level is success and prosperity, and on the ultimate level is eternal success or salvation. Consequently, salvation in Islam is peace with the Creator, peace and prosperity in the human society and success and prosperity in the life to come. The Quranic term for salvation is *Falah* which denotes success, prosperity and bliss. In brief salvation is a mix of divine grace and human efforts, divine grace in the ultimate sense depending upon human preparatory works.

In contrast to Christianity, the divine role in the Islamic scheme of salvation is conditional and not arbitrary or sacrificial. The Islamic salvific scheme is moral, resulting in avoidance of - and deliverance from - calamities in the terrestrial realms, resulting in ultimate deliverance from eternal sufferings in the celestial realms. Proximity to God and spiritual companionship (Paradise) are the outcomes of salvation, while chastising punishment and hellfire are the abode of those who will fail to attain salvation. Salvation is not the deliverance from bondage of sins, but from sins and their evil consequences; it is not a change of nature, but a life in conformity with the primordial pure nature. It is deliverance from the darker sides of human existence, from fear, tension, anxiety, dread, crime, greed, arrogance and guilt. Instead of protecting oneself from the undeserved divine wrath or an impending external cosmic threat, Islamic concept of salvation is directed towards the dangers from within. Man is prone to uncontrolled desires and unabating whims which land him into depravity; sin and wretchedness result from bad human choices. Salvation, then, is deliverance from the inner diseases of immorality into the fellowship of God and His grace. That grace and guidance is free for all, but ultimately achieved only by those who choose to respond to it with a contrite submissive heart. The Quran states: "Surely those who do believe and do deeds of righteousness unto them the All Merciful shall assign love." (19:96; see also 2:82; 4:173; 13:29; 16:97; 18:88; 25:70-71)

The pristine good nature of man is often veiled by the dust of lust and sin. The divine guidance is a reminder, a proof and a cleansing agent that dusts off the effects of lust and sin rendering man and his heart to God, morality and spirituality. Revelation, Prophets and even belief in God and his goodness will not bring salvation until and unless man responds to them and acts upon their incentives. Man does not get anything except the fruits of his efforts. (53:39) God's mercy, grace and assurance are the outcome of these efforts and not a prelude to them. The Quranic dictum that "But he will prosper, Who purifies himself," (87:14) summarises the above discussion well.

Individual self-purification leads to a collective just world order, the Ummah. It results in human humility, tolerance, forgiveness, devotion in prayers, charity, fear of disobedience and divine wrath, protection of sexuality, modesty, chastity, preservation of human life and rights, observance of one's pledges, fulfilment of one's promises, penance and repentance, avoidance of vain talk, remembrance of God and observance of familial ties. (Quran 25:63-77) The grace of God covers the conscious believers and their righteous actions, multiplying their rewards and granting them success in this life and the life to come. Toiling the field of worldly life and going through its rough and tumble with a sense of purpose determines the eternal bliss. God is pleased with those who labour, and unhappy with those who give to rebellion.

The Islamic salvific scheme is founded on God's grace of faith and revelation, human response to that through hard work, morality and reformation and God's ultimate grace to infinitely multiply the rewards. The finite human efforts are covered from both sides by the infinite divine grace, which is in turn conditioned by the human struggles. This way man participates in his salvation, albeit with his limited capacities. The infinite divine grace is comprehensive but not arbitrary; god and man are partners on the human reformative level, while being fully apart on the ontological level. The divine grace does not abandon man to the mercy of his human conditions while on earth. It guides him, supports his moral endeavours and graces his struggles without incarnation or confusing his surroundings with unintelligible, mysterious and miraculous interventions. Man's reason, logic and sense of justice are never challenged because they are divine gifts. They are rather heightened by the Islamic concept of salvation.

Righteousness and morality were directly connected with good deeds within the framework of Islamic devotional[702] and doctrine systems.[703] Good intention, sincerity, humility, true spirituality and God consciousness were cherished to reduce the harms of dry legalism and ritualism. All systems of Islamic life, such as socioeconomic and political, were directly connected with Islamic soteriology and human salvation, hence heightening the sense of human accountability before God rather than just the human agencies.[704] The mediational agency of bishops, priests and kings was abolished, and man was directly connected with the Omnipresent and Omniscient Loving God. (2: 186; 50:16) Equality before law and God and a strong sense of *Taqwa* (God's presence) was universally preached. Intercessions, indulgences and shortcuts were proscribed, and violations of law were treated gradually, systematically but strictly. The austere punitive methods were introduced as reformative and rehabilitative measures. Voluntary submission, responsibility and a sense of duty to higher realms were incorporated into the legal and punitive process. The community was educated to reflect upon the laws as a reformative scheme rather than an arbitrary imposition. The egalitarian Islamic laws guaranteed human rights and freedoms while simultaneously emphasising human responsibilities and mutual duties. In brief, Islam created a unique society quite different from the Greek, Persian and Christian societies. Black notes that "Muhammad set out to replace both the tribe and the state with a religious community and a moral and legal order. And he did indeed found a unique type of community, face-to-face and world-wide, relating individual to group through a unique combination of rites and ethics which, in retrospect, could have been deliberately designed to forge inter-personal bonds on a global scale. Islam provided a specific path, quite different to that taken by Egypt, the Greek poleis and the feudal monarchies of Europe, from tribalism to a wider and more structured society. The space occupied in other cultures by relatively impersonal state officials was here occupied by the Shari'a and charismatic individuals."[705]

The Quran and Human Reason

The Quran emphasised a great deal upon reflection, reasoning, logical argumentation, common sense and intelligibility. Reason and rational discourse were prized in matters of theology, cosmology, soteriology and human psychology; faith and reason were the two sides of the same coin. "The Quran assumes that humans are rational beings who are capable of critical thought, and open to persuasion. This is evident from the lengths to which it goes to appeal to people and persuade them. Furthermore, commands are rarely issued to the believers without giving the reason or underlying wisdom, and the Quran frequently exhorts people to consider and reflect, especially on the wonders of the natural world which are presented as signs of God's power and beneficence; interestingly there seems to be a reciprocal relationship between faith on the one hand and understanding or intelligence on the other."[706] Rational contemplation, deductive inferences, logical reasoning and argumentation were integral to the Quranic message. "Argumentation is a very prominent aspect of the Quran, and an inherent part of its discourse; any reader will quickly notice how frequently the text addresses protagonists, whether real or imagined."[707] Kate Zebiri defines argument as "providing reasons to the listener or reader for believing something to be the case, or for doing (or not doing) something. It will be helpful to bear in mind the classical distinction between logic and rhetoric: while logic concerns itself with the validity of arguments, in the sphere of rhetoric a good argument is one which is effective in convincing the audience, regardless of its deductive validity."[708] Unlike Christianity, the Quran used both logical and rhetorical reasoning to get its message across. The Quran was first and foremost a book of guidance, aimed at stirring a moral response in its audiences. There-fore, emotive, rhetorical and logical reasoning were mixed and merged to create an effective spiritual amalgamation. Rational discourse was a second nature to the Quran; Quranic rational arguments were so fully assimilated into larger Islamic narrative that at times they lost their separate identity. Zebiri notes that "in the classical Islamic scholarly tradition, Quranic argumentation did not become one of the branches of the Quranic sciences; a possible explanation for this is that 'reason-ing and argument are so integral to the content of the Quran and so inseparable from its structure that they in many ways shaped the very consciousness of Quranic scholars.'"[709] Rosalind Ward Gwynne agrees with such an assessment. "Muslims have so internalised patterns of reasoning that many affirm that the Quran appeals first of all to the human powers of intellect."[710]

Unlike Christian theology and soteriology, the Quranic perception of man was inherently positive. The Quran maintained that man was predominantly a rational being, capable of reasoning, understanding and comprehension. Analytical reasoning and demonstrative knowl-edge enhanced human reformative capacities. Therefore, reasoning and demonstration were among the fundamental tools of the Quranic message. "The principles of reasoning, explanation and justification are part of the intelligibility that the Quran presents as characteristic of God's creation. The very fact that so much of the Quran is in the form of arguments shows to what extent human beings are perceived as needing reasons for their actions and as being capable of altering their conduct by rational choice when presented with an alternative of demonstrated superiority."[711]

What is Reason?

Reason is an elastic term, and means different things to different peo-ple and cultural systems. Generally speaking, it denotes the human ca-pacity to make sense of things by logical means and verifying facts by common sense, experience, experiments and logic. It extends to con-structing beliefs, practices and institutions based on such a common-sensical, intelligible, understandable and expressible logic. The process itself, or the outcome or an aspect of it, could be called rationality: "reason is abstract and rationality is the exercise of reason in thought or action."[712] The logic and rationality implied here is different than the strict Aristotelian syllogistic rationality and logic of prepositions, premises and conclusions which worries more about the process and less about the validity of the conclusion drawn. Commonsensical reasoning is more inductive and less deductive. It focuses upon objectivity, common sense and universality while shunning subjectivity, particularity and sophistry.

Various cultures, traditions and ideologies have employed the same term in a number of varying but broadly related conceptual frameworks. For instance, the Greeks called it Logos, and the English word logic is derived from it. Philosophically *"logos* tends to be used in three senses: first, for the inner nature of something; second, for the theory explaining it; and third, for the verbal exposition of its theory. The Stoics developed the concept of *logos* most elaborately, but the notion was at the foundation of Greek philosophy from the beginning: There is a rational structure to the universe and its operation, this inner rationality can be understood by theory, and this theory can be expressed in speech. The most remarkable aspect of this enterprise was that it operated under very few constraints. From the beginning, Greek philosophers did not feel constrained by conventional religious views, so their systems ranged from sophisticated intellectual mysticism to unabashed materialism."[713]

For the Scholastic Christians reasons was the tool to understand and explicate the Christian doctrine. To the medieval Christians "revelation was supreme: If there was a religious doctrine that clashed with philosophy, the scholastic theologian had to work out some sort of reconciliation. To take a famous example, in the Eucharist, the bread and wine change into the body and blood of Christ – but of course they still appear to be bread and wine. It was the business of the scholastic to explain how this could be made compatible with the Aristotelian theory of material substances."[714] The Scholastics did not doubt, critically analyse or challenge the doctrine itself or its foundational categories, even though there were some logical problems with the foundational categories and premises of certain Christian doctrines. That is why these doctrines defied inner rationality, logical inferences, coherent theory, verbalisation and communication in logical fashions. The Scholastic reasoning toed the traditional theological lines and remained within the narrow framework of Christian revelation and tradition, limiting the scope of reason and its activities. Their final refuge was in mystery and paradox, as the primary defining categories of the Christian doctrines such as incarnation and Trinity were illogical, self-contradictory and arbitrary. In spite of some high caliber philosophical minds, Scholastic rationality suffered limitations, relativity and circular reasoning, due to the nature of their enterprise and its imposing boundaries.

The Enlightenment reasoning was a reaction to such authoritative theological impositions; it freed human reasoning from the shackles of Church and other forms of traditional authorities. Enlightenment reasoning referred predominantly to an individual's rational capacity to understand things and nature, independent of the inherited religious and political traditions. "Enlightenment thought is characterised by a rejection of inherited authority, whether religious or political, and by a boundless faith in the capacities of human reason when freed from the inherited fetters of religious and political authority."[715] Earlier Enlightenment figures did not intend to abolish Christianity, but to rationalise it on logical premises and deductions by eliminating unintelligible mysteries and circular paradoxes. Unlike the Scholastics, the Enlightenment thinkers stepped out of the theological and traditional boxes and challenged the foundational categories of doctrines such as the original sin, incarnation and Trinity. To them the reasonableness of the Gospel Christianity rather than the mysterious Church Christianity was the starting point as well as the goal. They replaced "the weight of dusty authorities with the simple process, accessible to all, of logical argument from clear and distinct ideas to the most complex and yet certain knowledge."[716] They cherished the Greek logos' tripartite rationality of inner coherence, logical theorising and intelligible exposition/ communication and applied it to the Christian doctrines. The reason in the nature and the universal natural reason were equally applied to religion and philosophy to make the human thought, principles, society and surrounding more in line with natural logic, reason and natural laws. Natural reason, law, logic, deduction and intelligibility were the corner stones of the Enlightenment rationality, challenging the unnatural, illogical and unintelligible elements of both the medieval religious and political traditions. They attacked the *Old Regime's* supernatural, unintelligible, absolutist and persecutory religious and political theology with natural, simple, intelligible, rational, moral and pluralistic theology. Commonsense and reason constituted the essence of the seventeenth and eighteenth century enlighteners reasonable Christianity.[717]

"The universal disposition of this Age is bent upon a rational religion," observed one Anglican cleric in 1667. All around him the clergy were agreed that the "skeptical genius" of their "knowing age" had brought to a new prominence that "church troubling" question, "how far Mens Reason hath to do in matters of Religion."[718] John Locke's "*Reasonableness of Christianity*" was the hallmark of such rationality.

The reason in the Scientific Era was predominantly connected with the empirical method, mathematical calculations and natural world and philosophy. It was closely connected with the materialistic trend in the Greek philosophy and "whatever could not be explained by the methods of empirical and mathematical natural philosophy came to be seen as unknowable, unimportant, or nonsensical, especially once the practical successes of the new science had won enormous prestige for physical science and its methods."[719] Rationality and intelligibility were closely connected with observations, experiments, empirical data and mathematical calculations, mostly confining them to the physical or material aspects of nature and human existence. Many faith-based claims were either declared nonsensical or absolutely irrelevant. The material aspects of human existence were highlighted at the expense of spiritual realms.

The Post-Enlightenment Utilitarian reason was neither spiritual nor religious or scientific. It was a socio political and economic phenomenon. For Utilitarians "the goal of all ethical, social, and political activity is the increase in the sum total of human happiness, "the greatest good for the greatest number."[720] Productivity, efficiency, progress, professionalism and profit are key elements in the Utilitarian rational discourse. Such an understanding of reason "had a certain inhumanity, some serious philosophical problems, and an insensitivity to cultural diversity. The influence of Utilitarianism has ebbed and flowed in the two centuries since, but it can be taken as representative of a post-Enlightenment Western tendency, particularly in the social sciences, to define rationality as the practical organisation of society: economic and productive efficiency, a well-organised bureaucracy, and the like."[721] Reason, efficiency, materialism and consumerism were mutually confused and submerged by this ideology.

On the other hand, Relativism brought reason to inner human realms, from the objective truths to subjective inferences. Consequently, the modern man "turned from seeking eternal rational truth to studying the nature of human subjectivity."[722] It brought morality, religiosity and truth to the human realms and disconnected them from God and universe, the absolutes. Things are right or wrong, false or true, reasonable and justified or irrational and non-justified not because of any inherent absolute principle, but because of the contextual framework giving rise to them. To the Relativists, the local norms, cultural settings, individual standards, social values and overall framework of meanings determine and supply the truth claims of any given act, statement or thing. Things are void of any contextual framework-independent vantage point or absolutes, and are relative. Relativism relativised the truth. "If truth was simply a function of where and when one lived and how one was educated, then no culture or religion was inherently superior to another; each was equally true and had to be understood in its own terms."[723]Even though it enhanced mutual social appreciation, open-mindedness and tolerance, Relativism brought the authority from above to the earth making man and his society absolutes degenerating into ethical and intellectual permissiveness.

Quranic Rationality

The Quranic sense of reason and rationality incorporates elements of the Greek logos (internal coherence, logical theorising and intelligible communication), Enlightenment features of challenging the traditional religious and political authoritative wisdom, Scholastic sense of supremacy of revelation (but only that revelation which complies with foundational rational categories, internal logical coherence and communicative intelligibility) with an understanding of compatibility between reason and revelation. It adds spiritual well-being to the Utilitarian principle of the greater good, but rejects the relativist notions of truth and morality. To the Quran, ultimate truth and morality are the absolute universals applicable to all human contexts and conditions with certain emergency-based exceptions. The Islamic sense of reason and rationality focuses more upon internal coherence, logical deduction and communicative intelligibility. A working meta-definition of Islamic rationality could be that "reason or rationality is the systematic and controlling use of beliefs, arguments, or actions based on well-grounded premises and valid arguments such that another person who has access to the same information and can understand the argument correctly ought to agree that the premises are well-grounded, that the logic is sound, and that the resultant beliefs, arguments, or actions are correct."[724] This broader definition fits very well with the Quranic perception of rationality. The Quran is big on logical argumentation, contemplation, reflection, reasoning, demonstration and intelligibility. To the Quran, man is inherently rational, and demonstrative tools and knowledge enhance man's comprehension capacities and reformative abilities. Man does the best of what he understands the most, and is convinced of its truthfulness and significance. Human understanding, comprehension and intelligibility are the key factors in molding human life on the moral spiritual lines; that is why the Quran is pretty much focused upon collective human logic, reasoning and reflection.

The Quran used deductive reasoning (3:110) (a conclusion follows the stated premises)[725], inductive reasoning (5:43) (formulation of general laws based on limited observations of recurring patterns)[726] and analogical (2:223) (reasoning from the particular to the particular) reasoning.[727] Islamic law, or *Fiqh*, is predominantly based upon *Qiyas*, or analogical reasoning.[728] The Quran has also employed multiple other rational arguments.[729] Zebiri states that "the Quran appeals to common sense or uses logical or quasi-logical arguments. A number of hypothetical arguments are of this type, for example those that draw an analogy between God's unity and earthly kingship, and point to the need for a single unified authority to ensure order: 'If there were in them [the heavens and the earth] other gods besides God, there would be ruin in both' (Q 21:22; cf. 12:39). This argument is developed elsewhere: had there been other gods, 'each god would have taken away what he had created, and each would have tried to overcome the others' (Q 23:91; cf. 17:42). The deductive reasoning in these verses leads to the conclusion that since the universe is not in chaos, it must have a single Lord. Elsewhere there is an appeal to the individual, along the lines that it is better to serve one master than many who are at variance with one another (Q 39:29)."[730]

The Quranic arguments are mostly phenomenal in nature: "the Quran contains arguments from creation, from signs, and from providence – witness the countless references to natural phenomena: the alternation of night and day, and the sun and moon in their orbits are evidence not just of God's existence and power but also of His mercy and beneficence."[731] (See 2:164; 3:190-191) The Quran claims that a rational discourse and a contemplative mind automatically lead one to God; atheism, polytheism and paganism are considered abnormal and irrational. "The pagans are depicted as fickle and irrational: when they are lost at sea, they call upon God, but when they are safe on dry land they revert to their idols (Q 29:65; cf. 6:63–4; 17:67). The attribution of daughters to God and sons to themselves is further evidence of their inconsistency and unreasonableness, while their insistence on sticking to the ways of their forefathers makes them appear stubborn and mindlessly conservative. One particular argument employed by the pagans is simply condemned as false and baseless, while the pagans themselves are depicted as dishonest and disingenuous."[732] Gwynne observes that "the Quran treats human beings as endowed with the capacity to assess arguments, weigh proofs, consider implications, and reach proper conclusions. Ideally, humans will see this capacity in each other as well and conduct themselves accordingly."[733] She has done a fascinating study of the Quranic deductive, inductive, analogical and many other kinds of logical arguments to demonstrate that the Quran is intrinsically a rational as well as rhetorical book. In chapter 6 she explores the "Quranic applications of arguments based upon comparison, including similarity, analogy, and parable. Analysis of apparent comparisons showed that very often such constructions actually mask quite different forms of reasoning, such as legal arguments, categorical arguments, and disjunction."[734] She quotes Imam al-Suyuti to enumerate the variety of rational arguments used by the Quran. "The 'Ulama' have said that the great Quran contains all types of proofs (barāhīn) and evidence (adilla): there is no type of proof (burhān) or evidence (dalāla) or disjunction (taqsīm) or warning tahdhir constructed from the entire range of things known by reason or authority which God has not articulated. But He conveyed it according to the customs of the Arabs, without the fine points of the methods of the theologians."[735] In chapter 8, using Imam al-Ghazali's short treatise on Quranic logic, al-Qistas al-Mustaqīm, and works of Najm al-Dīn al-Tufi, she identifies "examples of ten of the nineteen valid moods of the categorical syllogism"[736] used by Aristotle and leaves "open the possibility that all nineteen may be found within the sacred text."[737] This does not mean that the Quran is a book of logic, or that Greek philosophy is the standard of truth; it demonstrates the fact that unlike Christianity, the Quran gives reason and logic an extremely important position in human knowledge, understanding and conduct. "The fact that many Quranic arguments can be analysed by formal logic is in no way an assertion that Muhammad was 'influenced' by Greek or Hellenistic thought, or, for that matter, that Aristotle was a direct recipient of divine revelation. Cogent argument is a product not only of formal logical training but of intelligence, language skills, and motivation, as anyone knows who has studied logic but lost an argument to someone who has not."[738]

The Islamic rationality could very well be defined as a truth-seeking common-sense logic. Shabbir Ahktar's definition of reason does justice to this aspect of Islamic rationality. Reason is "a human capacity whose *telos* is truth; arguments are means of approaching truth. Reason is imposed on mere thought as a way to correct the errors introduced by the senses and the passions. Reason, as systematic or critical orientation, is a faculty transcending unrefined common sense. Its application yields a priori principles (of logical consistency) for guiding our understanding of sense experience. At its broadest, theoretical and practical reason is our deposit of critically organised common sense; at its core lies a kernel of widely accepted moral values and shared intellectual ideals."[739] To the Quran, the authentic revelation and reason both have the same goal of realising the truth-seeking common-sense logic, with the condition that the human reason is protected from the pitfalls of sensual whims, personal desires, passions and agendas. The reason and faith are fully compatible, as long as human reason can be guarded against the personal weaknesses by submitting man to the universally agreed morality and logic.

Reason and Revelation

Islam narrowed the gap between revelation and intellection and removed the dichotomy between *fides* and *ratio*. The source of both reason and revelation was God; therefore, true faith was not confrontational to human reason and intellect. The book of creation and the book of revelation both contained *Ayat*, the signs of God, and reflection and contemplation of both categories of *Ayat* would lead to God. Izutsu notes that "the Quranic conception may be made more understandable by a comparison with the philosophical *weltanschauung* of a modern Western philosher, Karl Jaspers who, interestingly enough, has made precisely this point one of the foundation-stones of his system. In this system much attention is paid to the problem of the symbolic nature of the world. According to Jaspers, we live at several different levels. When we leave the level of the normal, daily commonplace reason *(Verstand),* at which natural things including man appear to our eyes simply as natural things, and step into the realm of *Existenz,* we find ourselves suddenly in a strange world, standing in front of God, whom he calls philosophically *das Umgreifende* meaning something infinitely great comprising everything from above. This All Compriser keeps talking to us, not directly, but through the natural things. Things no longer exist here as natural, objective things, but they are symbols, through which the All-Compriser talks to us."[740] In other words "the world is a big book of symbols, a book which only those who live at the level of *Existenz* are able read. This would exactly correspond to the Quranic thought according to which all things are in truth *ayat* of Allah, and their symbolic nature can only be grasped by those who have *'aql* (intellect) who can 'think' *(tafakkur)* in the true sense of the word."

Reason was the common human denominator, and facilitated the processes of comprehending the divine signs, as well as leading the way to understanding the divine will embodied in morality. Unlike modern science and utilitarianism, to the Quran, rationality was intelligibility and not instrumentality or material goodness. Logical use of reason to reach one's lawful and unlawful ends was reserved for the modern social and physical scientists. The Quran reserved reason for the ultimate goals, such as the noble cause of understanding God's will in the universe and leading the way to Him through moral choices. Rationality for the purposes of morality, spirituality and eternal salvation is the hallmark of the Quranic revelation.

Intelligibility denoted that the Master had created an orderly and structured cosmos which could be understood and decoded. The cosmos, wittingly or unwittingly, submits to the universal laws of God. These universal codes could be comprehended, analysed, categorised, constructed and communicated through rational means. As man was an integral part of the cosmos and united with all men in human nature, man's personal knowledge and experience of the intelligent nature and cosmos could be turned into universal rational wholes. This far, the Quranic rationality pretty much towed the lines of Greek philosophy. It differed with the materialistic Greek philosophy in its insistence that man to cosmos relations and comprehensions could be translated into intelligible, scientific and rational terms in the realms of man-to-man relationships, i.e., morality. Greek philosophers seldom concerned themselves with religion or morality, but the Quran added the moral element to the philosophical discourse. This inter-subjective context of rationality elevated collective human reason over and beyond the subjective rationality of the individual and sophistry of passion and immorality. This intrinsic intelligibility, the *Sunnan* of Allah (3:190-191; 17:77) or universal natural laws, were to be trans-lated into inter-personal and inter-cultural relations to transform the individual and society accordingly and to limit the whimsical impulses and subjective apprehensions of the individual. The Quran heightened the collective logic and common sense over the individual subjectiv-ity; the society, and not the individual, was given the referential au-thority. The individual king, Popes, priests and individual entities such as the clergy, Church, nobility and scholarly bodies were all to follow the universal laws of morality, logic and common sense. Unintelligi-ble mysteries, dogmas, doctrines and immoral practices, no matter who the originator was, were to be discarded due the universal laws of logic and morality. The collective and universal wisdom was more significant than individual wisdom and sophistry; therefore, the divine right of monarchy and the infallibility of the Pope or Mufti, especially against the established collective wisdom and logic, were considered hoax and usurpation. Religious and political authorities were to be ex-ercised within the realms of morality, justice and common logic. These elements of the Quranic rationality were the harbingers of the 18th cen-tury Enlightenment. Just like the Enlightenment figures, the Quran rejected the religious and political traditions of its time and insisted upon individual rational capacities, freedom and liberty to access the truth. The reason did not create the truth. It just accessed the already existing truth with the use of logic and common sense.

The Quran and Qualitative Rationality

The Quran insisted upon a qualitative rather than quantitative ration-ality, making reason part of a bigger whole. Reason was not the in-dependent master of man and his surroundings, but a companion in traversing the vast creation of God. Human reason was not infinite; it suffered the finitude of its possessor, the man. Additionally, the cos-mic reality contained for more entities than man. These cosmic realities were interconnected and intertwined. Man could not behave as the only consumer, master or player in the universe; man, though very signifi-cant, was still a small part of a huge cosmic reality. Therefore, the reality was far bigger than man's epistemic constructions and conceptual abstractions of it. Like man, human reason was a part of the larger whole and not the whole itself, and the larger reality was the subject of true revelation and faith. The Islamic faith was not the sum total of rational abstractions or logical prepositions, it was a divine gift understood and enhanced by reason. By its very nature, faith had aspects which could not be limited to or comprehended by abstract reasoning or analytical inquiry, because faith dealt with material as well as spiritual realms. Some faith constructions were suprarational transcending the cognitive capacities of *Aql* (human intellect) but not anti-rational like the central doctrines of Christianity. Resurrection, paradise, hellfire, angels and many other metaphysical aspects of faith fell into this suprarational category; they limited the reason's scope, but not its freedom just like its possessor, man. Reason was like a student who needed a guide and a set of rules to grow into knowledge. The unsupervised, unlimited and uncontrolled reason was like a car without breaks and steering wheel, a formula for disaster. The unaided human reason was guided through the certain agency of universal revelation and morality and given a secondary but important role of understanding, explaining and interpreting the revelation. Unlike Christianity, the Islamic faith did not contain unintelligible, illogical, irrational and self-contradicting metaphysics and theology. Its suprarational elements were confined to the spiritual or soteriological realms; this made the work of Muslim scholastics easy and within the realms of intelligible rationality.

Rational discourse was made the handmaiden of Islamic theology, soteriology and law. The reason's role was primarily hermeneutical and not adversarial or anarchic; it helped mostly in understanding the divine intent and in constructing, formulating and defending faith claims rather than destructing them. The early Prophetic theology "relied on the exegetical use of reason in order to extract new opinions from sacred texts and thus to understand and explicate scripture and to appreciate the rationale for the Messenger's actions."[741] To the Quran, reason was the tool of comprehending, understanding and communicating the universal moral and logical principles, with the purposes of seeking and supporting the truth. Human logic and common sense were often veiled by human passions, whims, desires, senses, agendas and traditions. The revelation dusted it off with extra sensual, supra traditional, objective and moral messages to enable it see and follow the truth. Consequently, the genuine reason and ultimate truth were mutually supportive and not adversarial. Untainted reason was the human tool to decipher the greater truth and universal reality, rather than confining itself to the material or physical aspects of the natural world. The Islamic sense of reason differed with both the Christian understanding of the role of reason as well as the Enlightenment use of reason. Christianity suppressed reason under the yoke of irrational and unintelligible dogmas, while Enlightenment figures assigned it a far bigger role than its capacities. The finite human reason was at a loss to explore the metaphysical and spiritual realms on its own, and ultimately denied their existence or at least harnessed antagonistic views about them. As spirituality, metaphysics and morality go hand in hand, the ultimate result was the loss of ultimate grounds of ethical and human values. The resultant nihilism, relativism, objectivism, subjectivism, individualism, moral skepticism and many related ideologies have distanced man from God as well as from man. The Islamic conception of reason's role was a middle ground between the two extremes. It freed reason from the shackles of Christian suppression but assigned it a constructive role in defining, comprehending and communicating the collective moral and logical values with a sense of purpose, finding the truth.

The Quran denied reason's self-sufficiency and total independence, placing it under the yoke of divine revelation, but with an important role to understand and explain it. The true, authentic and certain knowledge of revelation was to be acquired through the agency of analytical reasoning. Such acquired knowledge enjoyed certitude, confidence and permanence and was elevated over traditionalism and blind imitation. Man was not infinite with infinite rational capacities, which is why he was given a finite portion of knowledge and comprehension. Man's limited knowledge was augmented through the agency of revelation, which was to be understood and reinforced through the rational discourse. This way God and man, reason and revelation were made partners in the pursuit of a just moral order, and not in the ontological realms which were beyond human comprehensions. The reason cooperated with the revelation but never superseded it. Comprehension and elucidation of revelation's practical and moral concerns were the assigned tasks of the reason. Theoretical curiosity, mythological endeavors and superstitious projects were wrong uses of the reason. Reason, like its possessor, was to serve the moral concerns of the Master rather than challenging His moral precincts or existence. The Quranic sense of reasoning was not confined to atomism or logical rationality but to human experience, spirituality and even intuition. It was not mere positivism or science, but the entire cosmos and its ultimate dimensions, that were given to the understanding and interpretations of the human reason. Man's ultimate concerns and questions about meaning were to be resolved by human reason. Spiritual and physical realms were assigned to the human mind and intellect, though spiritual concerns overrode the physical ones.

The Quran consigned a dialectical purpose to human reason, encouraging it to inquire, probe and even doubt at time the revelation and God, to finally reach the conclusions supportive of God and revelation. Reason was to refrain from cultural restrictions, bondages, myths and limitations to universalise the truth by locating the agreed upon universal values and norms in the revelation. Reason was a competent dialogue partner and dispenser of revelation, but not its master and rejecter. By emphasising the secondary, exegetical and domesticated role of reason, Islam avoided the complications and extremes of both the Christian Trinitarian mysticism and Greek philosophy's disruptive positivism. Islam's was the middle way between the Christian and Hellenistic extremes. Islam dubbed the Christian mystical and paradoxical extremes as naivety and the Hellenistic objections to revelation and moral imperatives as stemming from moral cynicism, human caprices and passions rather than from true intellectual discourse. Islam insisted upon the moral and logical universals to debunk the local, naïve and superstitious Trinitarian outlook of the Christian faith and its disastrous legal and social implications. The Quran gave far more active role to rational intelligibility in ultimate concerns than the fideistic Roman Church Fathers of late antiquity, but less than the 18th century Enlightenment figures' claims of total self-sufficiency. The resultant Islamic concepts and ideas received rational clarity and intelligibility, but within the framework of revelation. Islam's was the qualitative, rational and spiritual Enlightenment over a millennium before the English Enlightenment.

Likewise, Islam condemned the Arab polytheists for undermining the universal morals and rational concepts by localising the infinite divinity of the One and Only God. As the ineffable and Omnipotent God could not be confined to the womb of a feeble woman and body of a feeble man Jesus, likewise he could not be placed in a localised shrine or idol made of wood and stone. The localised, confined, changeable and disappearing god was no God at all. Such a rational argument was made through the inquisitive mind of Prophet Abraham; in a dialectical manner, he looked at the possibility of the star, moon and Sun as divinities. But their changeability and temporariness convinced him otherwise. (6: 7-79) He made a transition from the finitude of the celestial bodies to the infinitude of their creator, the unoriginated universal and unchangeable First cause of every caused thing. Abraham's rational discourse with King Nimrud was telling. He challenged Nimrud's claims to divinity through the movement of the Sun, claiming that Almighty God routinely brought forth the Sun from the East, let Nimrud bring it from the West, if possible. (2:258) Abraham mocked his priestly father and his idolatrous nation by crushing their idols in the temple and placing the ax on the shoulder of the chief idol, the most divine representative of their chief deity. (21:52-68) Abraham, out of abundance of inquisitive inquiry, even asked God to show him through practical experience the possibility of resurrection after death. (2:260) He subscribed to such a belief with ardent convictions after a practical experimental demonstration by God of such a possibility. Abraham was presented by the Quran as an iconoclast of human reasoning and analytical inquiry. Many other Prophets were presented as engaging in logical discourse with their people. Prophet Muhamad invited his contemporaries to rationally reflect upon his person and mission, both in individual and collective capacities. (34:46) How could he, who had lived among them for forty years and never lied or cheated anyone, lie in the name of God, the overpowering and irresistible? The Quran invited both believers and non-believers to contemplate the divine signs in the heavens and the earth, especially in the wondrous and intricate human body. (51:20-22) The Quran's emotionally-charged rational appeal was always accompanied by moral exhortations to realise ethical transformation in human life and society. The Quranic parables were also analytical, logically challenging the powers and divinities of the so-called guardian gods of the polytheists. The parable of fly highlighted the inability of the Meccan gods to create or avert the most insignificant of God's creature, the fly. (22:73) The parable of the spider and its frail house symbolised the frailty of the idols and their utter powerlessness. (29:41) The parable of the good and bad tree highlighted the flourishing nature of the good and damaging effects of the bad actions. (14:24-26) God's Omnipresence and ineffability was symbolised by the light. God as the light of the heavens and the earth was totally imminent and at the same time mysteriously transcendental. (24:25) The Quranic parables invited man to reflect upon the nature and its Master to understand the underlying universal principles. "The Islamic scripture sees itself as rationally comprehensible and egalitarian."[742]

The Quran used a plethora of styles, methods and mechanisms to make the overall message of Islam intelligible and comprehendible. It used the prophetic stories of the past - glad tidings, warnings, commands, appeals, implorations, motivations, syllogisms, deductions, parables, emotional, intellectual and revelatory arguments - and both the stick of punishment and the carrot of reward to awaken both reason and mind in man, the centre of Quran's guidance. The Quranic use of logical deductions and moral exhortation were geared towards stirring man's intellectual and emotional capacities to understand Oneness of God, unity of man and reality and the aspired voluntary transformation of human society based upon faith, knowledge, morality, virtue, rights and freedoms as sketched in the previous sections. In this way, reason played a vital role in undoing the Christian excesses in the areas of theology, soteriology and exousiology. The man-to-God, man-to-man and man-to-cosmos relations were again founded upon rational foundations; divine mysteries were consigned to the supra rational realms, but man-to-man and man-to-cosmos dimensions of human existence were brought down to human levels of understanding and comprehension. Man was encouraged to understand man and his surroundings, while shunning efforts to comprehend divine being and essence. Rather than concerning himself with theoretical conceptions of the Triune God - his essence, internal plurality and relations, mysteries of incarnation and paradoxes of crucifixion and resurrection - man was encouraged to reflect upon God's miracles in the universe and man's own wonderful body, and make a leap of submission from the orderly cosmos to the Loving Master of the cosmos. Man was invited to become God's partner in the rough and tumble of this life and, by submitting to the divine moral plans, earn his place in the proximity of God in the life to come.

It is often argued that rational discourse creeped into Islamic discussions during the theological controversies of the first century and because of the Greek philosophy. The above detailed Quranic rational approach and logical reasoning defies such claims. A. J. Arberry notes that "the reiterated and unambiguous teaching of the Koran on the two orders of revelation—God's power as seen in His creation, and God's will as disclosed to His Messengers— opened the way to a rational discussion of religious truths long before the rise of theological controversy. Indeed in respect to some particular matters debated in Mohammed's own time, such especially as the doctrine of the resurrection, the Koran itself laid down the method of argument."[743] (See Quran 50:2-11; 22:4-7) Arberry argues that the Quranic call to dialogue "call thou to the way of thy Lord with wisdom and good admonition, and dispute with them in the better way." (16:125) is a reflection of Aristotelian threefold proof scheme. "This verse would be taken to confirm Aristotle's threefold differentiation of proof into demonstrative, rhetorical and dialectical."[744] Binyamin Abrahamov shows how the Muslim theologians such as Abu al-Hasan Ali al-Ash'ari, Abu Mansur al-Maturidi, al-Ghazali, al-Razi and Ibn Taymiyyah all used the Quranic rational arguments to substantiate their theological positions.[745] It is evidently clear that the Quran has elevated reflection, meditation and rationalisation to the status of religious virtues and duties.[746] Daniel Madigan has identified thirty-five Quranic words which are specifically directed towards "perception, knowledge, understanding, clarity, and truth."[747] In reality the preservation of human intellect and reason is one of the fundamental objectives of the Islamic Shari'ah.[748]

In short, The Quran formulated the Islamic concept of God, man, society, state, cosmos and salvation on intelligible rational grounds and commanded man to fully engage in the practical concerns of life leaving aside the Christian theoretical assumptions, supernatural mysteries, paradoxical confusions, human depravity, worthlessness and evilness. Islamic rationality empowered man, increased his self-esteem, elevated his self-worth and encouraged him to participate in the religious, political and civic arena for purposes of reformation. No priest, church or monarch could impose irrational, mysterious and unintelligible ideas, dogmas and laws upon him.

Islamic Monotheism and Religious Diversity

In spite of its strict ethical monotheism and moralistic salvific scheme Islam is not an exclusivist religion; it is an inclusive faith. It relegates beliefs to the personal realms, and does not permit religious coercion in any way or form. It encourages conversation, dialogue and even intellectual disputation, but in the best possible way. It is also a missionary religion; it encourages Muslims to share their tenants with others without any indication of manipulation, pressure or compulsion. Faith is a very private and personal phenomenon, and nobody can be forced to believe in something contradictory to one's reason, logic, feelings and understandings. A manipulated, forced or distorted faith is no faith at all. True faith is tantamount to one's totality of inner being and deep held convictions; that is why it cannot be imposed from outside. It is the other way around, travelling from the inside outward. External factors can influence faith in a number of ways, but cannot create its facts or realities. That is why the Quran vehemently prohibits any compulsion in the matter of faith and religion. It encourages dialogue and rational discourse with a sense of serenity especially with the Christians. Traditional Trinitarian Christianity has compromised the ethical monotheism, divine justice and moral salvation schemes, and the resultant Christian theology and worldview has become confusing, contradictory and mythological. Muslims ought to invite them back to strict ethical monotheism and its moral corollaries, but without any pressure or coercion. Difference of opinion, religion, colour and creed can never be the justification of persecution.

As discussed, *Al-Tawḥid*, the Unity of God also means unity of God's creatures in the ultimate sense. All humans are dignified creatures of God, irrespective of their religion, colour or creed; respecting them is respecting God in a generic sense. Islamic monotheism requires Muslims to humble themselves in respecting and serving all creatures of God, including people of other faith traditions. Therefore, interfaith and intra-faith dialogues are encouraged but persecutions are absolutely prohibited.

Man is the crown of God's creation and created in his moral image. Humanity as a whole is a reflection of the divine morality and is essentially one. Man is divinely dignified and capable of imitating countless divine attributes such as love, mercy, compassion, honesty, sincerity, courtesy, reciprocity etc. to live a productive moral life. This moral function of man, justifies his creation in God's moral image, in the best of form, as the vicegerent of God on earth endowed with reason. The rational capacity enables man to understand his place in the cosmos, his relation with God and man. Man's rational and moral potentials are among the leading factors of him being the image of God and the crown of God's creatures. Consequently, God has dignified and honoured all the human beings over many of his creatures. Man's dignity is intrinsic to his humanity. Therefore, all humans are divinely dignified not because of their beliefs, practices, colours, origins or orientations but due to their humanity. Followers of other religions are divinely dignified human beings and Muslims have no choice but to respect them. Not honouring them will compromise their divine prerogative landing a Muslim in the realms of major Islamic sins.

The fundamental human rights emanate from the dual Islamic concepts of transcendental monotheism and human dignity. The objectives of Islamic Shari'ah (preservation of life, faith, property, family, reason/honour)[749] are a reflection of the God given inalienable human rights. Amina Wadud notes that "the purpose of the Quran [...] is to establish social justice. In the eleventh century, Ibn Jawziyyah agreed with this notion when he described *shari'a* [...] He asserts that the *maqasid* of *shari'a*, the goal, or ultimate intent, is justice. Justice is both a social and moral term, as well as a principle, a virtue. It is not an abstraction. It is woven throughout the entire Quran and as such becomes the basis for establishing the idea in Islam of the five freedoms or rights: life, religion, intellect, family (or genealogy) and property."[750] Civil rights - such as privacy, equality in freedom of religion, expression, socio-economic and personal choices - are natural extensions of the inalienable human rights and equally guaranteed by the Islamic law. The individual's civil rights must be maintained as long as they do not encroach upon the rights of others. Human dignity and respect are the quintessential rights of every human being. In short, the unity of God leads to the unity of His creation. All humans are equal. No superiority is granted based upon origin, ethnicity, colour, creed or financial or social status. The basic human rights of dignity, freedom, equality and justice are universally granted to all humans because of their humanity. Consequently, violations of these inalienable rights, especially due to religious reasons, are a taboo in Islam.

The Adam Connection
In addition to the common ontological origins, humans also enjoy common biological roots. They all come from a single pair, Adam and Eve, and the resultant universal brotherhood and sisterhood surpasses all narrow identities of creed, colour and ethnicity. Islam exhorts the extended Adam family to be watchful of their duties towards one another. Mutual love and respect are the most fundamental of these duties. The

Quran states: "O mankind, indeed We have created you from a male and a female and made you nations and tribes that you may know one another. Indeed, the most noble of you in the sight of Allah is the most righteous of you. Indeed, Allah is all Knowing and all Aware." (49:13) The Muslims ought to love and respect their fellow humans. Any disrespect or discrimination against them in the fundamental realms is in reality a sin against God. The Quran states: "O people! be careful of (your duty to) your Lord, Who created you from a single being and created its mate of the same (kind) and spread from these two, many men and women; and be careful of (your duty to) Allah, by Whom you demand one of another (your rights), and (to) the ties of relationship; surely Allah ever watches over you." (4:1) Any violation of the basic human rights and their civil corollaries comes under these stern Quranic warnings.

The Islamic doctrine provides for religious freedom. The Quran states, "let there be no compulsion in religion" (2:256) and "will you then compel mankind, against their will, to believe?" (10:99). "And say, 'The truth is from your Lord, so whoever wills - let him believe; and whoever wills - let him disbelieve.'"(18:29) One is as free to leave the fold of Islam as is he free to enter it. Muslim blasphemy laws were political rather than theological, intended to stop treason and not conversion. The Muslims' forced imposition of Islamic theology and abuse of blasphemy laws is a violation of the fundamental Quranic principles, as many contemporary Muslims scholars have shown.[751]

Islam mandates Muslim preservation of all places of worship: "For had it not been for God's checking some men by means of others, monasteries, churches, synagogues, and mosques, wherein the name of God is often mentioned, would have been destroyed" (22:40). Therefore, the desecration, destruction, obstruction or vandalism by Muslims of other houses of worship here or abroad is a gross violation of Islamic legal principles. Christians and others must be allowed to freely express and practice their religion in the Muslim majority contexts.

The Abrahamic Connection

Among the children of Adam, Islam closely relates with the family of Abraham. To the Quran, Abraham was a nation into himself. Jews, Christians and Muslims all subscribe to the faith of father Abraham, and are heirs to his monotheistic consciousness. Both the Jews and the Christians claim to be the descendants of Abraham through Isaac, while the Muslims trace their lineage back to Ishmael. As the children of one father, Abraham, they are a united Ummah or a family of nations. The Quranic term Ummah denotes a small or a big group of people who have something very significant in common. The three Semitic traditions have close theological, linguistic, ethnic, cultural, historical and geographical affinities. The Bible recognises these familial ties detailing God's promises to make Ishmael and his children into a great nation. (Gen. 17:20). The Abrahamic history is one of a single global family; Muslims have no choice but to respect and love their cousins, the members of Abrahamic Ummah.

The Quran depicts Abraham in generic terms such as "a submitter to God" denying his associations with narrow historical identities. Historically speaking, Judaism and Christianity both came long after Abraham, and hence he cannot be labeled as a Jew or a Christian. Unlike the Bible, the Quran describes the Abrahamic faith in strictly monotheistic terms refuting all possibilities of polytheisms. "Abraham was neither a Jew nor a Christian, but he was one inclining toward truth, a submitter to God. And he was not of the polytheists." (3:67) In light of the available biblical data, polytheism, or in extreme case henotheism, rather than monotheism seems to be a better alternative with regard to the patriarch's understanding of God. The Biblical text portrays patriarchs such as Abraham as worshipping other gods besides Yahweh. "Thus says the Lord, the God of Israel: Long ago your ancestors - Terah and his sons Abraham and Nahor - lived beyond the Euphrates and served other gods" (Joshua 24:3). The Quran emphatically and repeatedly denies the charges of polytheism when it comes to Abraham. "He was not a polytheist" is an oft repeated Quranic phrase. The children of Abraham are preferred over others not because of their blood ties to Abraham, but due to their monotheistic consciousness. They are but one theological Ummah. The Prophet Muhammad, while trying to create a multi-religious community consisting of these three faith groups in the City of Medina, actually described them as an Ummah. The Constitution of Medina is a living proof of this affinity.

The Quran calls them *"Ahl al Kitab"* - "People of the Book" -, a special designation highlighting their role in the revelatory history. The Jews and Christians are heirs to divine revelations, and still possess many of the divine truths. The divine message, revelation and truth are not the prerogative of Muslims only; Jews and Christians are partners in that. Fred Donner notes that "at this early stage in the history of the Believers' movement, then, it seems that Jews or Christians who were sufficiently pious could, if they wished, have participated in it because they recognised God's oneness already. Or, to put it the other way around, some of the early Believers were Christians or Jews-although surely not all were. The reason for this 'confessionally open' or ecumenical quality was simply that the basic ideas of the Believers and their insistence on observance of strict piety were in no way antithetical to the beliefs and practices of some Christians and Jews. Indeed, the Quran itself sometimes notes a certain parallelism between the Believers and the established monotheistic faiths."[752] The Quran challenges the Jews to follow the divinely-revealed judgments in the Torah. "But how is it that they come to you for judgement while they have the Torah, in which is the judgement of Allah? Then they turn away, [even] after that; but those are not [in fact] believers." (5:43) The Quran invites the Christians to follow the divinely-revealed truths in the Gospel. "And let the People of the Gospel judge by what Allah has revealed therein. And whoever does not judge by what Allah has revealed - then it is those who are the defiantly disobedient." (5:47)

The Quran does find faults with the textual purity of the present Jewish and Christian scriptures, and maintains that the original texts were historically compromised. The pure word of God was mixed up with human words and interpretations over the centuries. The Bible still contains the word of God as well as many divinely revealed truths such as monotheism, human accountability and moral values. One has to sift through the biblical text to locate them. The Abrahamic monotheistic legacy is common to the Jews, Christians and Muslims. The Quran invites them to focus upon this legacy. "Say, 'O People of the Book, come to terms common between us and you: that we worship none but God, and that we associate nothing with Him, and that none of us takes others as lords besides God.' And if they turn away, say, 'Bear witness that we have submitted.'" (3:6) Islam wants the children of Abraham to follow the common words and work their differences through this common heritage and framework.

They are also partners in the ultimate salvific scheme; the sincere and righteous Jews and Christians have as much claim to salvation as the righteous Muslims. The only condition is that they must stick to the primordial message of strict ethical monotheism, care about the accountability on the Day of Judgment and engage in good deeds in accordance with moral demands of ethical monotheism. "Closer examination of the Quran reveals a number of passages indicating that some Christians and Jews could belong to the Believers' movement-not simply by virtue of their being Christians or Jews, but because they were inclined to righteousness. For example, Q. 3:199 states, 'There are among the people of the book those who Believe in God and what was sent down to you and was sent down to them [...] 'Other verses, such as Q. 3:113-116, lay this out in greater detail. These passages and other like them suggest that some peoples of the book Christians and Jews-were considered Believers. The line separating Believers from unbelievers did not, then, coincide simply with the boundaries of the peoples of the book. Rather, it cut across those communities, depending on their commitment to God and to observance of His law, so that some of them were to be considered Believers, while others were not."[753] The purity of belief, intention and action is the key to God. The Loving Lord does not waste anybody's genuine beliefs and efforts.[754] The Quran states: "Those who believe (in the Quran), and those who follow the Jewish (scriptures), and the Christians and the Sabians, - any who believe in God and the Last Day, and work righteousness, shall have their reward with their Lord; on them shall be no fear, nor shall they grieve." (2:62) The exact same message is reiterated in a variety of the Quranic verses. (5:72; 22:17)

The modern Quranic exegete Muhammad Asad explains these verses in the following words: "The above passage - which recurs in the Quran several times - lays down a fundamental doctrine of Islam. With a breadth of vision unparalleled in any other religious faith, the idea of 'salvation' is here made conditional upon three elements only: belief in God, belief in the Day of Judgment, and righteous action in life. The statement of this doctrine at this juncture - that is, in the midst of an appeal to the children of Israel – is warranted by the false Jewish belief that their descent from Abraham entitles them to be regarded as "God's chosen people."[755] Muslims are but one community among multiple communities of truth seekers; they do not have monopoly over God, revelation, truth, morality and salvation.

On the other hand, a majority of classical Quranic exegetes contend that the above quoted verses refer to the believing Jews and Christians before the advent of Islam, or those Jews and Christians who converted to Islam. They also assert that these inclusive verses were later abrogated by the exclusive Quranic verses such as 3:85, "And whoever desires other than Islam as religion - never will it be accepted from him, and he, in the Hereafter, will be among the losers." Donner notes that "the notion that the early community of Believers of Muhammad's day included pious Christians and Jews is, of course, very different from what the traditional Muslim sources of later times tell us. In later Islamic tradition, right down to the present, 'Islam' refers to a particular religion, distinct from Christianity, Judaism, and others, and 'Muslim' refers to an adherent of this religion."[756]

It is pertinent to note that "Islam" in the above verse is used as a general phenomenon of submission, and not as a historical religious tradition. There is no authentic Hadith or Quranic statement to substantiate a sweeping abrogation claim either. The report attributed to Ibn Abbas is questionable. Even al-Tabari, the stalwart of Muslim exegetes, had rejected such an interpretation and its overarching implications.[757] The divine promises are not temporal but eternal. God does not specify, single out or confine his rewards to a group of people at the expense or exclusion of others; anyone who fulfils the conditions of pristine faith and does good deed will be rewarded by God, though the reward will vary in accordance with the quality and quantity of faith and righteousness.

The late Fazlur Rahman's critique of such an exclusive interpretation of the classical exegetes is not unwarranted. He observes that "the vast majority of Muslim commentators exercise themselves fruitlessly to avoid having to admit the obvious meaning: that those--from any section of humankind - who believe in God and the Last Day and do good deeds are saved. They either say that by Jews, Christians, and Sabeans here are meant those who have actually become 'Muslims'—which interpretation is clearly belied by the fact that 'Muslims' constitute only the first of the four groups of those who believe - or that they were those good Jews, Christians, and Sabeans who lived before the advent of the Prophet Muhammad - which is an even worse *tour de force*. Even when replying to Jewish and Christian claims that the hereafter was theirs alone, the Quran says, 'On the contrary, whosoever surrenders himself to God while he does good deeds as well, he shall find his reward with his Lord, shall have no fear, nor shall he come to grief.'[758]

Muhammad Abduh and Rashid Rida, the two modern Egyptian exegetes, have preceded Rahman in opening the possibilities of salvation
to the righteous Jews and Christians and in criticising the classical exegetes for their hesitation to include the righteous People of the Book
into the fold of true belief.[759] Muhammad Asad also supports the idea of
inclusion.[760] Fred Donner states that "as used in the Quran, then, *islam*
and *muslim* do not yet have the sense of confessional distinctness we
now associate with 'Islam' and 'Muslim'; they meant something broader
and more inclusive and were sometimes even applied to some Christians and Jews, who were, after all, also monotheists (Q. 3:52, 3:83, and
29:46)."[761] Barnard Lewis notes that "at first sight, this verse might seem
to treat the four monotheistic and scriptural religions as equal. While
such an interpretation is excluded by other passages in the Quran, this
verse nevertheless served to justify the tolerated position accorded to
the followers of these religions under Muslim rule."[762] Jacques Waardenburg notes that "all except the pagan Arabs can be rewarded on the Last
Day if they have been faithful to God and have acted correctly. The solution for the problem of different kinds of faith in God is thus seen to be
eschatological, at the end of time."[763] Jane D. McAuliffe observes that
"the first clear instance of Quranic approbation of Christians denies
them the stature of singularity. It compliments them in a cluster, yoked
with others in a common nod of approval. The verse links Christians
with Jews, with a somewhat mysterious group named the Sabi'un, and
yet more generally, with any who believe in God."[764]

It seems clear that the belief in One God and the Day of Judgment,
coupled with moral actions, is the bare minimum required to attain
the pleasure of God. Moral competition and righteous rivalry are the
foundations of the Quranic concept of religious pluralism and diversity. The Quran puts the point in a nutshell: "And We have revealed
to you, [O Muhammad], the Book in truth, confirming that which
preceded it of the Scripture and as a criterion over it. So judge between
them by what Allah has revealed and do not follow their inclinations
away from what has come to you of the truth. To each of you We prescribed a law and a method. Had Allah willed, He would have made
you one nation [united in religion], but [He intended] to test you in
what He has given you; so race to [all that is] good. To Allah is your
return all together, and He will [then] inform you concerning that over
which you used to differ." (5:48). It also states that "for each [religious

following] is a direction toward which it faces. So race to [all that is] good. Wherever you may be, Allah will bring you forth [for judgement] all together. Indeed, Allah is over all things competent." (2:148; see also 2:115) The Quran uses the plural (*khayrat*) meaning that there are many ways to achieve goodness and many kinds of righteousness. It exhorts the children of Abraham to compete in the matters of goodness. Kate Zebiri notes that "the Quran itself has, among scriptures, a uniquely developed awareness of religious plurality, at one point even appearing to offer rationale for the existence of competing religions."[765]

The mere existence of diverse religious communities, divine approval of their existence and encouragement to compete in the matters of goodness is a clear proof that, from the Quranic perspective, religious pluralism and inclusivism is a rule and not an exception. The Quran includes the righteous members of the Abrahamic community in the ultimate salvific scheme. "They are not [all] the same; among the People of the Scripture is a community standing [in obedience], reciting the verses of Allah during periods of the night and prostrating [in prayer]. They believe in Allah and the Last Day, and they enjoin what is right and forbid what is wrong and hasten to good deeds. And those are among the righteous. And whatever good they do - never will it be removed from them. And Allah is Knowing of the righteous." (3:113-115) It divides the People of Book into two categories: the righteous and the evil doers. The righteous among them are promised the reward. "And among the People of the Scripture is he who, if you entrust him with a great amount [of wealth], he will return it to you. And among them is he who, if you entrust him with a [single] silver coin, he will not return it to you unless you are constantly standing over him [demanding it]. That is because they say, "There is no blame upon us concerning the unlearned." And they speak untruth about Allah while they know [it]. But yes, whoever fulfills his commitment and fears Allah - then indeed, Allah loves those who fear Him." (3:75-76) God's consciousness and morality are the cornerstones of true guidance and many righteous Jews and Christians may very well attain that.[766]

Jane McAuliffe disagrees with such an understanding of the above Quranic verses. After studying seven clusters of the Quranic verses which deal with the Christians, she argues that the praiseworthy Quranic Christians are either a "small fraction"[767] of the Christian community or "neither the historical nor the living community of the people who call themselves Christians. As a conceptual idealisation, the notion of Qura'nic Christians bears very little relation to present or past sociological configurations of the Christian community."[768] In light of her extensive study of the ten Quranic exegetical works, McAuliffe concludes that "In no way [...] does Biblical Christianity remain a fully valid 'way of salvation' after the advent of Muhammad."[769] However, she also notes that "the commentators here presented represent major strands of Qura'nic exegesis but cannot be deemed to speak for all Muslims in all periods of history."[770]

As seen above, the Quran categorically disagrees with historical Christianity on the issues related to Christ's divinity, incarnation and redeeming death. The Quranic promise of salvation covers only those who believe in One and Only God and the Day of Judgment and do the good deeds, and Trinitarian jargons are excluded from such a promise of salvation. McAuliffe also notes that "what Christians term the doctrines of the Incarnation and the Trinity, Muslims have frequently excoriated as the blasphemies of divine reproduction and tritheism."[771] We can conclude this part of the discussion with Jacques Waardenburg that "the Quran direct reproaches at the Christians but explicitly or implicitly recognises positive religious values in them [...] Asking for the Quranic view of the Christian religion, one only finds texts which refute certain doctrines concerning the person of Jesus, the nature of God, and God's relationship to Jesus."[772] He further observes that "the definitive Quranic judgment of Jews and Christians appears to be eschatologically suspended. It is simply left to God's final judgment at the end of history."[773]

Additionally, the Quranic permission for Jihad is directly connected with the protection of various houses of worships and the worshippers. The Quran states: "Permission to fight is given to those (i.e., believers against disbelievers), who are fighting them, (and) because they (believers) have been wronged, and surely, Allah is Able to give them (believers) victory. Those who have been expelled from their homes unjustly only because they said: 'Our Lord is Allah.' - For had it not been that Allah checks one set of people by means of another, monasteries, churches, synagogues, and mosques, wherein the Name of Allah is mentioned much would surely have been pulled down. Verily, Allah will help those who help His (Cause). Truly, Allah is All-Strong, All-Mighty." (22:39-40) Asma Afsaruddin observes that "at first reading, Quran 22:39–40 clearly establish the reasons for engaging in armed combat (*jus ad bellum*) and, even more important for our purpose, transparently state that the objective of the combative jihad is to defend all houses of worship, and by extension all religious practitioners, when under attack. The combative jihad, according to these verses, may thus be understood to be undertaken in defense of a basic religious freedom to worship the one God, regardless of which religious group exercises it, when that freedom is violently curtailed by a hostile adversary [...] although early commentators, such as Mujahid ibn Jabr (d. 720) and Muqatil ibn Sulayman (d. 767), stayed close to the actual signification of these verses and recognised their ecumenical potential, later commentators, starting with al-Tabari (d. 923), attempted to compromise and ameliorate this potential through a variety of hermeneutic and reading stratagems."[774] The early Quranic exegete Muqatil ibn Sulayman explained that "the monasteries of the monks, the churches of the Christians, the synagogues of the Jews, and the mosques of the Muslims would all have been destroyed. All of these religious groups (*al-milal*) mention the name of God profusely in their places of worship, and God defends these places of worship through the Muslims."[775] After a detailed analysis of the pre-Crusade Muslim exegetical work's inclusive and post Crusade exclusivist interpretations, Afsaruddin concludes that "in comparison with those of their predecessors, the perspectives of al-Razi, al-Qurtubi, and Ibn Kathir clearly appear more exclusionary vis-a-vis the People of the Book and considerably attenuate the ecumenical potential of Quran 22:39–40. Their commentaries establish that by the Seljuq and Mamluk periods in the wake of the Crusades (and later the Mongol invasions) and, in the case of al-Qurtubi, by the time of the Spanish Reconquista, Muslims were increasingly fearful and on the defensive against non-Muslims. Such changing circumstances altered Muslim sensibilities, affecting the ways in which Muslims reimagined their relationships with other religious communities and found sanction for them in their readings of their holiest text. Such reimaginings are signaled by the changing conceptions of the purview of jihad/*qital* that emerge in these exegetical works."[776]

The Word of God or Jesus Connection

Among the children of Abraham Islam relates more closely to the Christians than even to the Jews, "you will find the nearest of them in affection to the believers those who say, 'We are Christians.' That is because among them are priests and monks and because they are not arrogant." (5:82) The Jesus connection is very strong between the two faith traditions.[777] Jane D. McAuliffe states that "the most striking example of Quranic praise of Christians occurs in *surat al-ma'idah* (5):82-83. These verses figure prominently in virtually all attempts to base Muslim-Christian rapprochement upon specific Quranic texts."[778] The classical Jewish stance on Jesus and his mother Mary is extremely problematic; Islam, on the other hand, believes that Jesus is the Word of God who was blessed with the virgin birth. It vouches for the chastity of his mother, his apostolic mission and ministry, his countless miracles and his redeeming actions through moral scheme of salvation. Islam differs with certain historical Christian formulations regarding the person of Christ - his nature and relationship to God, incarnation, crucifixion, atoning death and mediational function. The Christian incarnation and Trinitarian theology are stumbling blocks for Muslims. Therefore, Islam invites the Trinitarian Christians to enter religious dialogue with a rational mindset. This dialogical Islamic approach must be founded on commonalities and principles of mutual understanding and respect. The rational, historical and scriptural argumentation must be done with a sense of serenity and in an environment of respect and love. Any dialogue not based upon mutual respect and love is futile.

Islamic Nomianism

Pauline antinomian tendencies were curtailed by Islam to reinstate a reformed version of the Jewish law. The Islamic Shar'iah or law filled the moral vacuum left by the absence of a systematic Christian law. The Shari'ah was meant to realise human goodness and well-being on universal levels, and not to restrict human freedom, progress and development. It was an all-embracing way of life. "Islam, by way of contrast, set out to order personal and social behaviour in detail on the basis of a new revealed religious code, based on the Quran and the hadith (sayings of the Prophet). 'Marriage, divorce, inheritance, slavery and manumission, commerce, torts, crimes, war, taxation, and more' were all provided for by their Prophet. Early Islam differed from early Christianity in aspiring to cater for every aspect of living. The focus of Islam was its Religious Law (the Shari'a): 'living in accordance with god's law was the essence of religion [...] *shar'* (law/right) was often used to mean religion in general' [...] 'The foundation of this religion is jurisprudence', said al-Ghazali [...] 'Orthodoxy' was a juristic concept meaning correct interpretation of the Shari'a [...] Political activism stemmed from the duty of all Muslims to 'command right and prohibit wrong.'[779]

Early Muslims were fully engaged in understanding, interpreting and implementing the divine laws, while Christians were quarreling over the nature of God and Christ. In Islam orthodoxy in reality was orthoproxy; human actions and conduct were the focus of Islamic religion, and good deeds and noble conduct were required of rulers and subjects. Good character was the sole determining factor of eternal salvation and felicity. The revealed Islamic law constituted the foundation of such a noble conduct. It aspired to eliminate narrow identities and boundaries such as tribe, ethnicity, colour and creed. (4:1; 49:13) It abolished the caste systems and hierarchical social stratum. It worked towards universal humanism at the expense of narrow tribalism, social stratification, racism and elitism. Nobility was based upon piety and learning not on lineage, social status or political position. "Spiritual authority was personal, deriving from an individual's qualities, such as piety and learning [...] This was in contrast to the organisation of authority in Christianity in this period; the authority of bishops and clergy depended much more on their official position and less on personal merit."[780]

Human equality, freedom and fair dealing were emphasised at every level. (4:135; 5:8) Moral values were inculcated from the grass root. Justice was highly prized. "Good and bad were described in terms of personal relationships (trustfulness (iman), ingratitude/infidelity (kufr)). Members of the community were to possess personal honour, courage, manliness (muruwwa: *virtu*), and sidq (truthfulness, faithfulness, loyalty), and to practise hospitality. At the same time these values were given a universalist meaning. The People, it was said, were bound together by faith and justice, not, like the Arab tribes, by kinship. Islam revolutionised tribal society by catapulting the individual into the centre of social responsibility; no longer could one shelter behind the group from God. Concern for justice must override clan ties. 'Asabiyya (clannishness, group spirit) in the sense of helping 'your own people in an unjust cause' was condemned [...] What ultimately matters is not tribe, race or gender, but godliness."[781] Enjoining the good and stopping evil was made a universal human responsibility; Muslims were required to practice this commandment in accordance with their capabilities and capacities. (3:104) This moral and reformative paradigm was the essence of their religion and the purpose of their existence. (3:111) Michael Cook, in his wonderful book *Forbidding Wrong in Islam*, well elucidates the importance, history and parameters of this important Quranic principle.[782]

The Islamic law was fairly implemented to bring social order, peace and harmony through justice. The violators were dealt with iron hand without any exception. Equality before law was the cherished maxim of Prophet Muhammad and his disciples. God and justice were equated and realisation of a just social order was made the ultimate goal of Islamic society. (57:25) Human reason, conscience and common sense were armed to serve as the vanguards of justice, equality and law. Individual and communal vigilance was highly appreciated. The Quranic laws were made over and beyond human tempering guaranteeing an egalitarian and just society.

Christian antinomian tendencies were chastised and observance of law and morality was highly emphasised. Michael Cook notes that "Christianity [...] is not a law centred religion. Islam, for all its liberalisation, unmistakably remains one, and in this it is supported by the legal content of the Koran."[783]

The law and morality were embodied in the obedience of God and His Apostle. To N. J. Coulson this was Islam's supreme innovation "into the social structure of Arabia: the establishment of a novel political authority possessing legislative power."[784] The divine law, rather than the tribe or divine right ruler, was made supreme, and the divine right rulers were at once replaced by divine rules equally applicable to all. The divine rules were comprehensive and universal, producing social cohesion. "The new religion and its Law instilled a social identity that bound members together, carved them off from outsiders. A strong sense of belonging and a 'clear-cut distinction between members and non-members' were transposed onto the religious 'umma. The Law achieved this partly because it covered most aspects of behaviour, often in great detail. It replaced tribal custom while retaining the immediacy of the group in the life of the individual. The Shari'a became the skeletal structure of Islamic society which was law-governed (nomocratic) to a peculiar degree."[785] A variety of methods were used to ensure voluntary submission to law and to construct a cohesive social identity. "All this was achieved by a variety of methods, not

277

perhaps consciously designed for this end, but in some ways achieving social cohesion more successfully than the Judaic, Hellenic, Roman or Christian regimes."[786] The language, rituals, customs and many mundane aspects of life were woven together to craft a new Islamic identity. "Many ritual parts of the Shari'a, rules about the body and its functions (such as circumcision, rules about defecation, menstruation, teeth-cleaning, dietary rules and the numerous details of sexual and familial etiquette), had the effect of making members instantly recognisable to one another; of making relations between relative strangers predictable and manageable. Religious significance was attached to acts that were of no obvious utility but achieved social bonding, such as communal prayer and pilgrimage. In the Pilgrimage, Islam brought together the universal and the particular with almost Hegelian genius, as believers from all over the world came together to revere, among other things, a black rock – once a focus of local tribal worship. The relationship between insiders and outsiders was not mitigated by a theory of values universal to human beings as such; Islam was an uncompromisingly pure form of revelationism. The boundaries of the People were the boundaries of the moral universe. This was symbolised and reinforced by the Arabic language."[787]

The law contained constants and variables;[788] constants were universal and permanent "incapable of transmutation despite the changing pressures of time and social exigencies,"[789] while variables were local and changeable.[790] The Quran gave generic as well as detailed legal prescriptions.[791] The generic prescriptions, such as the principles of justice[792] and mutual consultation, allowed human interpretations, appropriations and accommodations. The detailed prescriptions, such as the family laws, daily prayers, fasting and pilgrimage, were less fluid. The legal constants allowed unity and continuity, while the variables permitted diversity and localisation. This way various local cultures, norms and customs were accommodated within the universal unity of the Islamic law and morality. Lawrence Rosen observes that "so long as fundamental Quranic precepts are not violated, local practice is seen as itself Islamic, an orientation that is vital to the emphasis in Islamic law on the local articulation of the acceptable."[793] Rosen further argues that "custom is indeed, and always has been, a source of Islamic law- but not in European sense of source which has been projected onto Islamic law, but as an integral aspect of the shari'a itself. The internal contradictions in some historical accounts of Islamic law may be resolved if one sees custom not as something attended to occasionally by certain thinkers but as a constant factor in the life of a legal system that from the outset integrated it into the legal rather than seeing it as a separate entity."[794] This attitude facilitated the spread of Islam among divergent local traditions and cultures.[795]

Islamic law and morality contained more constants and fewer variables, giving an overall Islamic colouring to a variety of cultural expressions and diversity.[796] Universal moral values were granted authority over and beyond local norms and individual interpretations. Personal prophecies, intuitions and ecstasies were prohibited. "The new society was in principle universal, and in practice commercial and 'citied' (Hodgson's phrase meaning cities were an integral part), but individuals were still removed from themselves and absorbed into the group. The result was a type of society generically different from Greek, Roman and also Euro-Christian civilisation."[797]

Righteousness and morality were directly connected with good deeds within the framework of Islamic devotional[798] and doctrine systems.[799] Good intention, sincerity, humility, true spirituality and God consciousness were cherished to reduce the harms of dry legalism and ritualism. All systems of Islamic life, such as socioeconomic and political, were directly connected with Islamic soteriology and human salvation, heightening the sense of human accountability before God rather than just human agencies.[800] The mediational agency of bishops, priests and kings was abolished and man was directly connected with the Omnipresent and Omniscient Loving God. (2: 186; 50:16) Equality before law and God and a strong sense of *Taqwa* (God's presence) was universally preached. Intercessions, indulgences and shortcuts were proscribed. Violations of law were treated gradually, systematically but strictly. Austere punitive methods were introduced as reformative and rehabilitative measures. Voluntary submission, responsibility and sense of duty to higher realms were incorporated into the legal and punitive process. The community was educated to reflect upon the laws as a reformative scheme rather than an arbitrary imposition. The egalitarian Islamic laws guaranteed human rights and freedoms while simultaneously emphasising human responsibilities and mutual duties. In brief, Islam created a unique society quite different from the Greek, Persian and Christian societies.

Islam and Divine Right Monarchy

The Christian concept of divine right monarchy was also abhorred by Islam, because it assigned sovereignty and dominion to the king. In Islam absolute dominion and sovereignty belonged to God, whose moral will was the law to be followed in human interactions, meaning "the supremacy of Shari'a."[801] "Islamic Law declares that sovereignty belongs to God; He is the Creator, and He is the Legislator. The attributes of this sovereignty can be best ascertained from the Quran where reference to God is expressed in terms that are suggestive of one or other aspects of His sovereignty; as in this declaration: 'He governs all affairs from the heavens to the earth' (35:5); 'Blessed is He in whose hand is the sovereignty, and He over all things has power' (67:1–2); or as in this command: 'Say: 'Lord, sovereign of all sovereignty. You bestow sovereignty on whom You will, and take it away from whom You please; You exalt whomever You will and abase whomever You please. In your hand lies all that is good; You have power over all things"(3:26).43 Like several others, these texts have, in fact, a direct bearing upon the political aspects; they have signified sovereignty as ultimate legal and governmental authority over the universe, life and humanity."[802]

Christianity allowed absolute sovereignty for the ruler;[803] the monarch was "*autokrater*: the one who rules by himself,"[804] not answerable to anybody for what he ordained.[805] He was the Christ on earth and hence sacred and absolute.[806] Absolute submission and fear was due to him,[807] and His authority was invincible.[808] Softness was considered the enemy of government.[809] Any attempt to disobey, disagree with or rebel against the rulers was sacrilege.[810] The Pope was also sovereign in matters of religion and faith. Contrary to that, Islam eliminated any notion of religious or political sovereignty in the absolute sense. "The nature and the meaning of sovereignty in Islam preclude the two sovereignties known in the Middle Ages (i.e. the Roman Emperor and the Pope) and the later modern absolute and non-responsible single sovereign presented by Bodin (1530–1596), Hugo Grotius (1583–1645), the creator of the law of nations in Western disciplines, Hobbes (1588–1679), or Austin (1613–1669), whose concept of sovereignty was the result of special circumstances which swept Europe in the sixteenth century."[811] Rose W. Lane lauds Islam's emancipation of humanity from the bondage of absolute monarchs by establishing individual freedom in practical affairs. Prophet Muhammad abolished both monarchial and papal authority to restore human freedom and autonomy. "There is no superior *kind* of man; men are humanly equal. The Emperor has no actual power over anyone. In Mohammed's observation and belief, a priest is no holier or more powerful than any other man, either [...] His view was that the priests corrupted Abraham's teaching when they assumed authority to rule the Jews. Christ attacked the priests, and reasserted the truth. But the Catholic and Greek priests now corrupted Christ's teaching, by claiming authority to control Christians. This showed, he said, that organisation is evil. There should be no priests. Each individual must recognise his direct relation to God, his self-controlling, personal responsibility."[812] It was this discovery of individual freedom that caused Islam to spread like a wildfire. "The knowledge that men are free swept across the known world as swiftly as Americans swept across this continent [...] All the tribes of Arabia from the Red Sea to the Euphrates declared that men are free, that there is but one God, and that Mohammed was one of the prophets. In eighty years, the world was Moslem from the Indian Ocean to the Atlantic. The Mediterranean was a Moslem lake and the western gate of the known world had a new Arabic name: Gibraltar."[813]

In Christendom, the problem related to rulers' sovereignty was compounded due to the absence of Christian religious law. The Christian faith was antinomian; with the exception of some marriage and sex rules, there was nothing much in the New Testament that could be called a law. Antony Black notes that "Christianity [...] in both the Sermon on the Mount (Matt. 5: 1-7: 29) and St Paul's epistles, explicitly rejected the idea that adherence to any law could bring anyone nearer to god. For Christians, the divine law praised in the Psalms either meant ethical conduct in general, or was a metaphor for obedience to god. Except for marriage and sexual conduct, there was no detailed religious blueprint. Consequently, in Europe a good deal of law lay quite outside the religious sphere."[814] This vacuum was filled by the secular often tyrant emperors and kings who legislated, promulgated and abrogated laws at whims. These finite laws often suffered the finitude and injustices of their promulgaters. Absolutism was a recipe for tyranny. Islam scorned such an absolute monarchy. Antony Black observes that "the principle of kingly domination (mulk) was bitterly attacked; to call a human being king was to trespass upon the divine prerogative."[815] Patricia Crone notes that "the only being to whom you could legitimately apply the awesome titles of king *(Malik)* and despot *(Jabbar)* was God. One could not question the overweening power of ultimate reality, but it was both presumptuous and rebellious for humans to claim such power for themselves, and those who did so merely branded themselves as kings in the sense of impious tyrants."[816]

In addition, Islam insisted upon human equality, universal human dignity and rights of life, property, privacy, family, religious, socio economic and personal freedoms as God given rights.[817] These fundamental rights were independent of both Church and state. Democratic values, such as mutual consultation *(Shura)*,[818] social contract *(Bay'ah)*,[819] rulers' accountability *(Muhasabah)*[820] and service-based authority, were introduced and practiced.[821] "The political system in Islam can be understood as a consultative rule, that is, rule by *shurah* (consultation). Consultation is a basic principle in all spheres of Islamic political and social systems. It is also essential for the proper function of the organs of the state, its overall activity and Islamic identity. The Quran commands Muslims to take their decisions after consultation in both public and other matters. This makes consultation mandatory, by virtue of it being the subject of a direct Quranic command as specific as those requiring obligatory prayers and tax *(zakat)*."[822] The field and scope of mutual consultation was wide open as the Shari'ah included only a small number of fixed commandments and detailed prescriptions. It's generic prescriptions as well as the non-prescribed areas allowed a wide range of human interpretations and legislation. Even the form and method of consultation was not fixed by the Quran. "The deliberate silence of the *shari'ah* about the form of consultation is suggestive of the need for continuous temporal legislation. This legislation would relate to administration and other affairs not touched upon by the *shari'ah*, as well as the affairs for which the *shari'ah* has provided only broad basic principles with no detailed laws."[823] The flexible and generic Islamic principles of governance necessitated a great deal of human participation, intellectualisation and appropriation in the form, method and direction of the state and government. "It would thus appear that the form of government, the form of consultation, the kind of legislature, and the procedures to be used all could have some alteration and adjustment from time to time without any compromise to their Islamic nature. In the view of this context, many scholars view the Islamic system of government as similar to a democratic system."[824]

It is often argued that Islam and democracy are antithetical, that the democratic system assigns sovereignty to people while Islam reserves that for God only; that is not true. The sovereign God does not descend to the earth to rule people; rather, He sends laws to facilitate justice and equality. The laws are understood, interpreted and implemented by people in conformity with their times, situations and cultures. The divine sovereignty means the sovereignty of laws, "'sovereignty' is not 'God', but it is vested in the law by God. An Islamic state is limited both by and to the law. It follows that the sovereignty of an Islamic state is practically the sovereignty of the law, and that the law limits the governmental power and regulates its functions. Limiting governmental power to the law does not imply autocracy, but implies democracy in its widest sense because the law requires consultation. In this way, the idea that 'sovereignty belongs to God' does not make the political theory in Islam differ from that in democracy but increases the elements of similarity and compatibility between the two systems."[825] Humans share in that sovereignty in their role as interpreters, facilitators and administrators of the divine laws. Islam encourages the full-fledged human participation in the matters of state and authority, but within the established parameters of the divine law and its spirit. Khatab and Bouma state: "the claim that 'God is the only legislator' does not make the Islamic system against democracy where the 'people legislate' for themselves. This is because of the fact that the *shariʿah* did not give detail on everything in this life, but kept silent on some issues, including the method of consultation and other matters at the heart of the structures and functions of state, and between state and its subjects, between the subjects themselves, and between state and other states in the world community. The silence of the *shariʿah* about these affairs is suggestive of the need for continuous temporal legislation. Muslims are allowed to legislate for affairs not touched upon by the *shariʿah*, as well as the affairs for which the *shariʿah* has provided only broad basic principles with no detailed laws. This means, first of all that all, human legislation is temporal and interpretive and not absolute. Second, in Islam, people legislate to people, as people legislate to people in a democracy. In either case, human beings will use their talent and expertise to legislate in ways suited to their situation."[826] The head of an Islamic state is its chief executive, bound by the laws like any of his subjects. The Islamic state is a constitutional form of governance rather than a divine right monarchy. J. Wellhausen calls it a theocracy founded upon the notion of justice. "The theocracy may be defined as the commonwealth, at the head of which stands, not the king and the usurped or inherited power, but the Prophet and the Law of God. In the idea of God justice, and not holiness, predominated. His rule was the rule of justice."[827]

The absolute divine right monarchy was totally abolished and the Quran/Shari'ah/law was established as an ultimate constitutional authority, over and beyond human reach. Quranic constitutional powers reserved the sovereignty and dominion for God, while giving the Caliphs derivative and secondary powers within the established parameters of the Quran.[828] The Muslim masses were thus empowered with the oversight process. The Christian clerical establishment and elitism was replaced with socio-religious egalitarianism. The Quran was the constitutional authority over and beyond the rulers, and all Muslims were required to understand and implement Quranic teachings. The authorities' executive and legislative powers were extremely limited by the constitutional powers of the Quran, and made conditional to their conformity with the universal egalitarian principles of the Quran. The Muslim obedience to state authorities was qualified. (4:59) There was no obedience to the state in the matters of disobedience to God and morality. The moral, duty bound and voluntary submission to the Islamic state with religious intent and zeal was highly encouraged. But rebellions and revolts were encouraged if the authorities crossed the limits and persistently went overboard. Mass participation in the matters of state was aspired; a communal sense of belonging to the new religious order, and a commitment to its missionary zeal was inculcated. The masses were charged with a new sense of mission and enthusiasm to galvanise the largest possible participation in the historical reformative scheme of Islam. Imperialism, clericalism and elitism, the hall marks of Christendom, were fought against with utmost vigour and courage.

The Prophet did neither allow hereditary kingship, nor did he appoint a successor; he left it to the Muslim community to choose their leader. None of the first four rightly guided caliphs appointed their successor from among the ruling families.[829] Four different methods of election were exercised by the Rightly Guided Caliphs, making the election process flexible. The presidential, parliamentarian and other possible democratic forms of government could easily be deduced from the early models. Two main characteristics, non-hereditary and public allegiance, were the hallmarks of these state models. The *Khilafah* or Caliphate was vicegerency and not a divine right monarchy.[830] The Caliph represented God's laws as understood and interpreted by the Prophet of Islam for the wellbeing of the Muslim community. Therefore, the Caliph represented God, his Prophet and people at the same time. Some members of the Muslim community revolted against the third Caliph Othman when they alleged nepotism; in the end they killed him, in spite of his magnificent past and close ties to the Prophet. The early Muslim community was truly egalitarian, with active vigilance over their rulers. The transition to the hereditary form of government was an Islamic aberration and very much contested by the Muslim community of the first Islamic century.

The greater Muslim community of Hijaz and Iraq opposed the transition from caliphate to hereditary kingship when it was practiced by Mua'wiyah bin Abu Sufyan (602 – 680 AD).[831] Mua'wiyah had accepted Islam after the conquest of Mecca and did not have enough time in the companionship of the Prophet, who died just two years after the conquest of Mecca. He was very junior to Abu Bakr and Umar in Islam. Actually, the Prophet's family under the leadership of his grandson Hussain bin Ali (626–680) was massacred in the desert of Karbala because of their strong opposition to such a transition.[832] Karen Armstrong observes that "Husain refused to surrender, however, convinced that the sight of the Prophet's family on the march in quest for true Islamic values would remind the *ummah* of its prime duty."[833] The event caused tremendous opposition to the Umayyad rule.[834]

Abdullah ibn Zubair (624–692), the grandson of the first Caliph Abu Bakr, also fought this transition with his blood and the loss of family.[835] His "was also an attempt to return to the pristine values of the first ummah."[836] Patricia Crone notes that "automatic succession within a single family was quite rightly seen as a first step towards the imperial form of government which was to culminate under the 'Abba'sids. The sources for the Umayyad period abound in calls for the election of the caliph, whether from among all Muslims, all Arabs, all Qurashi's, or all members of the Prophet's family, by consultation *(shura)*."837

The early Umayyad rulers were neither absolute monarchs[838] nor secular. B. Lewis states that "the ninth century Byzantine chronicler Theophanes describes Mu'awiya not as a King or Emperor but as a *protosymboulos,* 'first counsellor of Saracens.' This is not inept description of the nature of the authority which he exercised. The chief instrument of his government of the Arabs was the Shura', the council of Sheikhs, summoned by the Caliph or a provincial governor, with both consultative and executive functions. Associated with these tribal councils were the Wufud, delegations of tribes, together forming a loose structure based largely on the freely given consent and loyalty of the Arabs. Mu'awiya rarely commanded, but was skillful on operating through the more acceptable process of persuasion and through his personal ability and prestige."[839] The Umayyad rulers implemented the Islamic law to the best of their abilities. Armstrong observes that "The first Umayyad caliphs were not absolute monarchs [...] It would be wrong to think of the Umayyads as "secular" rulers."[840] Their administration was also multi-religious; Caliph Mu'awiya's chief secretary was a Syrian Christian.[841] Their first and fundamental mistake was the transition from the caliphate to a sort of limited monarchy, where the ruler and his family enjoyed relatively greater autonomy and privileges. Secondly, they introduced Arabism, giving tribalism and hereditary caste domination in both military and civil affairs.[842] The early Muslim community resisted even such a limited monarchy and tribalism; the first century of Islam was filled with bloodshed, due to a series of rebellions against the Umayyad's transition to a limited monarchy. The greater Muslim community always resisted the new Umayyad arrangements as an aberration to the established patterns of the Prophet and his rightly guided caliphs.[843] They insisted that the Prophet had always encouraged public participation in the matters of state and institution building. The tribal or hereditary claims to state authority were absolutely un-Islamic. The Medinian state of the Prophet was an inclusive society where all tribes, clans and religions were accommodated. Therefore royalism, kingship and monarchism, no matter how much limited, were totally against Islamic vision of state and governance.[844] Unfortunately, the Umayyads coerced the Muslim community into submission and set a wrong precedent for the coming Muslim centuries, a plague that has vulgarised the Muslim community for the past fourteen centuries. The monarchial model is the Sunnah of Umayyad's, a clan who fought Islam until they were subdued, rather than the Prophet of Islam. Monarchy is anti-Islamic, period.

In spite of secularisation of the Islamic state, the Umayyad and later Muslim dynasties were not considered divine right monarchies.

The caliphs were not divinely ordained, but usurpers of state power through force and corruption. They were true perverters of divine wisdom due to their wrong use of freedom and power. The Ulema (religious scholars) often opposed the political authorities, dubbing them un-Islamic dictators. The strong Muslim opposition to, and persistent struggles against, monarchies resulted in a unique power-sharing Muslim paradigm where the executive and legislative powers of the Caliph and state were limited by Quranic laws and scholarly engagement. The Ulema, or religious bodies, were granted powers to interpret and legislate laws, as well as oversea their implementation. The Caliph's legislative authority was especially limited through the Islamic laws, norms and practices and relegated mostly to the areas where Islamic law was silent. He headed the executive branch of the government while relegating the legislative and judiciary to the religious circles. All the three branches of the government were required to work within the framework of Islamic Shari'ah hence curtailing their executive, legislative and judiciary powers. Therefore, the Islamic caliphate was neither a divine right monarchy nor theocracy, but a limited constitutional monarchy where the powers of the caliph, *shura* or parliament and judiciary were thoroughly restricted by the Qura'nic laws and juristic principles. The Caliph derived his political authority from the fact that he was to be the chief guarantor of the Islamic law's thorough implementation. He was *Amir al-Mu'mineen*, the chief of believers.

Islam and Religious Freedom

The authority of the Islamic state never extended to faith, intentions, inner convictions and private practices, as was the case in the Roman and Byzantine Christian empires. The Islamic state's authority was limited to the outward public practices and actions of the subjects.[845] The relative outward socio-moral conformity rather than doctrinal unity was the aspired goal; religious diversity and pluralism were generally tolerated. The state was governed by the Muslim rulers but their politics was not Islamic. The Jews, Christians, Zoroastrians, Hindus and Buddhists, all religions were allowed free practice and semi-independence. The People of Book enjoyed special status among the minorities. They paid the state tax (*Jizya*) like all other religious minorities but enjoyed greater freedom and privileges. They had their own independent courts, communities, business entities, temples and Churches and hierarchical clerical establishments. Had the politics of the Islamic state been Islamic, they would have never enjoyed such independence and freedom. Christendom did not allow religious diversity or pluralism because its politics were merged with religion. The public discourse and decorum of the Islamic state was a sort of agreed-upon policy between the Islamic state and its religious minorities. Public consumption of wine, gambling and other un-Islamic activities was prohibited, while the same were allowed within non-Islamic settings and private places.

The subjects' right of privacy, personal convictions, financial, religious and familial freedoms were God-given rights independent of state, colour, creed or race. Likewise, diversity was accepted and expected within the Muslim community. There were multiple legal, theological and political schools of thought and all were assimilated and accepted, with a few exceptions like al-Khawarij, with its militant theological bent.[846] That is why religious persecutions, including Muslim heretics, were not common. Of course, there were violations and many rulers exploited the orthodoxy to punish their political opponents whether Muslims or non-Muslims. But these were exceptions and not the rule. The inclusive Muslim society was made possible due to the crystal-clear Quranic teachings and a practical model of inclusivity and diversity established by Prophet Muhammad in the City of Medina. The Constitution of Medina outlined the main contours of such an inclusive society.[847]

The Constitution of Medina

M. Hamidullah argued that "although the rules and regulations of a country can be found in a more or less written form everywhere, yet, in spite of strenuous search, I could not find any instance of the constitution of a country, as distinct from ordinary laws, reduced to writing, before the time of the Holy Prophet Muhammad."[848] Khatab and Bouma also note that "the Constitution of Medina is the first Constitution of democracy in the history of constitutional rule. Its principles were also based on the Quran and *sunnah*. Equipped with these principles the Prophet managed to establish the first Islamic state, which included people of multi-religious and several cultural backgrounds in an *ummah wahidah* (one nation) based on universal principles that constituted the Charter."[849] It incorporated some of the most significant characteristics of modern society and state. "The Constitution introduced a number of political rights and facilities to be provided by the state to all its members, Muslims and non-Muslims alike, in return for the duties. For example, the Constitution promulgated: (i) standing laws defining the rights and duties of all members, (ii) arrangements for impartial decisions on matters of right and (iii) unfailing protection of the members of the community in the enjoyment of their rights. These are the very characteristics of the political society defined by John Locke: 'a society which fails to provide these facilities is not really a political society at all, but a continuation of the state of nature.'"[850] Its forty eight articles - 53 articles according to M. Hamidullah -[851] enumerated multiple religious, social, economic and political rights and duties "including (i) the freedom of belief, that is, every community has the right to live according to its belief; (ii) the freedom of movement from and to Medina: 'whoever will go out is safe and whoever will stay in Medina is safe'; (iii) the assurance that if there is an external threat to non-Muslims, the Muslims would help them and vice versa; (iv) the assurance that both Muslims and non-Muslims are believers and would stand together to defend Medina against any attack; (v) the agreement that no one should go to war before consulting with the Prophet (article 36); (vi) the assurance that when consultation occurs the representatives of all parties should be present; (vii) the assurance that in cases of negotiation with foreign states, representatives of all parties should be present, and that negotiations should not be concluded unilaterally; (viii) the understanding that when a person acquires guilt they acquire it only against themselves; (ix) that a person is not liable for their ally's misdeeds; (x) that charity and goodness are clearly distinguishable from crime and injury; and (xi) that God is the guarantor of the truth and goodwill of this covenant."[852] Barnard Lewis states that "it is interesting to note that this first constitution of the Arabian Prophet dealt almost exclusively with the relationship of the members among themselves and with the outside."[853]

It replaced Jewish and Christian exclusivism with Islamic sense of inclusivism and diversity. The Prophet had emphasised the universal nature of revelation considering himself the culmination of that historical phenomenon; this opened the possibilities of multiple paths to salvation. "Recognising plurality, the Quran neither confines faith and salvation to Muslims, nor denies faith and salvation to other religions."[854] John L. Esposito observes that "theologically and historically

Islam has a long record of tolerance."[855] He further states that "Muslims regard Jews and Christians as 'People of the Book,' people who have also received a revelation and a scripture from God (the Torah for Jews and the Gospels for Christians). The Quran and Islam recognise that followers of the three great Abrahamic religions, the children of Abraham, share a common belief in the one God, in biblical prophets such as Moses and Jesus, in human accountability, and in a Final Judgment followed by eternal reward or punishment. All share the common hope and promise of eternal reward: 'Surely the believers and the Jews, Christians and Sabians [Middle East groups traditionally recognised by Islam as having a monotheistic orientation], whoever believes in God and the Last Day, and whoever does right, shall have his reward with his Lord and will neither have fear nor regret' (2:62)."[856]

The Jews, Christians and Sabians or Zoroastrians were given a bigger role in the salvific scheme and religious legitimacy, because they were the People of Book. Barnard Lewis observed that "the Quran recognises Judaism, Christianity, and a rather problematic third party, the religion of the Sabians, as earlier, incomplete, and imperfect forms of Islam itself, and therefore as containing a genuine if distorted divine revelation."[857] Their religious history, virtues and strengths were appreciated and their excesses were criticised. In spite of harsh criticisms of their compromises whether theological or moral, Islam never excluded them from the fold of belief and overall religious legitimacy. Tamara Sonn notes that "Muslims consider Jews and Christians to be their spiritual siblings. They are among the *ahl al-kitab*, the 'People of the Book' or 'People of Scripture.'"[858]

The Prophet always considered them fellow seekers of truth, though at times misguided due to their historical embellishments, and was very tolerant towards them. To Esposito "no such tolerance existed in Christendom, where Jews, Muslims, and other Christians (those who did not accept the authority of the pope) were subjected to forced conversion, persecution, or expulsion."[859] Even the critical Barnard Lewis accepts this historical fact: "Persecution, that is to say, violent and active repression, was rare and atypical. Jews and Christians under Muslim rule were not normally called upon to suffer martyrdom for their faith. They were not often obliged to make the choice, which confronted Muslims and Jews in reconquered Spain, between exile, apostasy, and death. They were not subject to any major territorial or occupational restrictions, such as were the common lot of Jews in premodern Europe. There are some exceptions to these statements, but they do not affect the broad pattern until comparatively modern times and even then only in special areas, periods, and cases."[860]

The Islamic differentiation process did not translate into social or political exclusion of the People of Book. It never went to the level of religious coercion or persecution. The Jews, Christians and Zoroastrians, all the People of the Book, were included in the greater community of believers, or Ummah. W. M. Watt observed that ummah predominantly meant "a religious community, until in the latest instances (none much after Uhud according to Bell) ummah is applied almost exclusively to the Muslim, Jewish, and Christian communities, or some section of them."[861] Wellhausen noted that it included all inhabitants of Medina, "The Umma embraces a wide area, the whole precincts of Medina are to be a district of inviolable peace. There are still heathen among the Ansar, and they are not excluded, but expressly included. The Jews are also included [...] It is significant that the Umma includes both heathen and Jews, and also that it consists in general not of individuals but of alliances."[862] The heathens were mostly hypocrites. M. Rodinson agreed that "the umma or community was therefore the people of Medina as a whole, presenting a united front to the outside world."[863] Michael Cook noted that "'Constitution of Medina', in which Muhammad establishes a community to which believers and Jews alike belong, while retaining their different faiths."[864] Tamara Sonn observed that Prophet Muhammad differentiated between the religious and political loyalty, which was fused by Christendom, and allowed Jews to be part of the political unity while retaining their separate religious identity. "Since religious loyalty and political loyalty were often linked, to change one's religion was tantamount to changing one's political loyalty, a potentially treasonous act. Christianity had attempted to supersede this religio-political identity. Jesus's command 'to render unto Caesar the things that are Caesar's, and unto God the things that are God's' (Matt. 22:21) could allow people to follow their religious conscience without it calling into question their political loyalty. People could be Christian in the Roman empire without being considered subversives. But the equation of religious and political loyalty was reimposed when Christianity was declared the official religion of the Roman empire. The Quran's teaching of religious freedom was a return to the ideal espoused by Jesus. It was a reassertion of the independence of religious and ethnic identity. This ethic was institutionalized in the Constitution of Medina, when Prophet Muhammad included Jews and Muslims in the same political community."[865]

All members of ummah were equally protected. Watt noted that "'the dhimmah of God is one', the meaning is presumably that the 'compact guaranteeing security' is one; and this implies (as is shown in the following clauses) that all members of the ummah are equally protected, that all are equally capable of giving protection which the whole ummah is obliged to make effective, and that they all stand to one another in the relation of protector and protected, while none is to be protected, except temporarily, by anyone outside the community."[866] Michael Cook states that "this document declares the existence of a community or people (umma) made up of Muhammad's followers, both those of Quraysh and those of Yathrib. To this community belong also the Jews, subject to the qualification that they follow their own religion. Just as important, the document establishes an authority within the community: any serious dispute between the parties to the document must be referred to God and Muhammad. From the mass of stipulations making up the rest of the document, two themes are worth picking out. One is a concern to clarify the relationship between the new community and the existing tribal structure; this is particularly apparent in the regulations regarding the payment of bloodwit and the ransoming of captives. The other is the fact that a major interest of the parties of the document is the waging of war. There are stipulations regarding the initiation and termination of hostilities, contribution to their cost, and so forth. Jews contribute, and fight alongside the believers."[867]

The Jews were given a special place in the ummah. The Charter or Constitution of Medina[868] specifically used the term "ummah" to denote the Jews. "The Jews were also not mentioned as "various tribes" but simply as Jews, indeed very respectfully, as with Christians, who are 'People of the Book,' an ethnic minority here being made equal to a majority in a brotherhood, forming one community *ummah wahidah* (one nation). Thus, the Constitution laid down the foundation of the first Islamic state of multi-tribal and multi-religious society. The objective of the various rules enunciated in the Constitution was to maintain peace and cooperation, to protect the life and property of all citizens, to eliminate aggression and injustice regardless of tribal or religious affiliations, and to ensure freedom of religion and movement. Indeed, the Constitution of Medina placed the rules of justice over and above religious solidarity, and affirmed the right of the victims of aggression and injustice to restitution regardless of their tribal and religious affiliations."[869] Carl W. Ernst states that "Medina was a polity composed of Muhammad's religious followers plus Jews and pagans, all of whom nonetheless accepted his position of leadership, at least in theory. From the beginning, therefore, it is clear that religious plural- ism was a principle accepted as the basis for a Muslim society. In this respect Muslim politics was a radical departure from the example of Christian Rome, which did not tolerate rival faiths except when certain rulers found it useful for the moment to protect a minority such as the Jews."[870] Islam allowed freedom of religion in the 7th century while Europe did not tolerate other religions, even after the 18th century En- lightenment. Ernst notes that "the essential point to be noted is that re- ligious toleration in Europe was only extended to different varieties of Christianity; non-Christian religions did not receive this concession."[871] Religious plurality in Europe is a very recent phenomenon.

Contrary to that the Constitution of Medina eliminated the narrow boundaries of ethnicity, tribe, colour, religion and creed in favor of universal humanity and values. It created a civic society irrespective of religious affiliations of its members. "The created Constitution stip- ulated that the social and political activities in the new system must be subjected to a set of universal values, collective intelligence and standards that treat all people equally. It repeatedly emphasised the fundamental nature of justice and righteousness, and frequently con- demned in different expressions injustice and despotism."[872] The Char- ter of Medina incorporated the Jews as equal citizens of the Islamic state with equal rights of property, religious freedom and economic empowerment. The participating Jews were declared one community (ummah) with the Muslims. Consequently "the Jews not only partici- pated in financing the war expenses but also took an active part in the battles; their share in the booty was equal to that of the Muslims."[873]

Some scholars such as Wellhausen and others have claimed that the Jews constituted an inferior part of the Ummah. Uri Rubin re- futes such claims. "None of these assumptions seem to be borne out by the text of the document. There seems to be no reason why the meaning of the term umma in the 'Constitution' should be different from its meaning in the Quran, the only surviving document which stems from the same period and environment."[874] Uri further states that "when looking for clues in the Quran to the meaning of this article, it is not merely the term umma which must be trailed, but rather the locution: *'umma wdhida'*! This phrase occurs in the Quran no less than nine times. In all cases with no exception it denotes people united by a common religious orientation, in contrast to people divided by different kinds of faith. The conclusion with respect to article 1 of the 'Constitution' is, therefore, inevitable. This article declares that the Muslims of Quraysh and Yathrib, as well as the Jews, constitute one unity, sharing the same religious orientation, thus being distinct from all the rest of the people who adhere to other kinds of faith. It is thereby clear that the new unity is designed to be based not only on common sacred territory but also on common faith."[875]

The Constitution declared the City of Medina as sacred. "That the main basis of' the new unity was to be a territorial one is indicated in article 39: "the inner part (jawf) of Yathrib is sacred (haram) for the people of this document. In making the territory of Medina a protected haram, Muhammad put it on a level with the haram of Mecca."[876]The physical presence of the Jews, and free exercise of their religious practices, did not violate that sanctity. The Prophet especially appreciated their common history and monotheism as the children of Abraham. There's was a territorial as well as religious unity. Eri Rubin states: "It is clear now that within the *umma wa'hida* which separated all monotheistic groups of Medina from other people, the Jews were given the position of 'umma of believers', thus being distinguished from all other monotheistic (Muslim) members of the *umma wa'hida*. Their recognition as believers provided them with the privilege to stick to their own Jewish *din* while enjoying complete protection. This was indeed a far-reaching concession on the part of Muhammad designed to win the Jews over to his cause."[877] This concession was promulgated by the Quran and it never changed. The coercive policies of the Christian state were forever replaced with the golden Quranic rule of no coercion in the matters of religion." (2:256) The State of Medina was a unique model of religious freedom, diversity and civic engagement. It was a revolutionary concept of civic government, "in this early model of an Islamic state Muhammad brought about a social transformation based upon the cultural foundation of the message of the Quran. The immediate purposes were to condition the pattern of thinking and actions of the citizens in order to fashion them into a new social and political unity, to maintain peace and cooperation, to protect the life and property of all citizens, to eliminate aggression and injustice regardless of tribal or religious affiliations, and to ensure freedom of religion and movement. All citizens of this state were to follow, as one *ummah*, the charismatic personality of Muhammad. He was the Prophet and the Ruler but not the Sovereign. Sovereignty would not rest with Muhammad or any particular group, but with the Law founded on the basis of justice and goodness, maintaining the dignity of all groups in the community."[878] M. Rodinson observed that "Muhammad's role in this extensive community was a modest one. He was simply Allah's intermediary in settling disputes and quarrels between its members. 'Wherever there is anything about which you differ, it is to be referred to Allah and to Muhammad.'"[879] Watt also noted that "his powers under the Constitution are so slight that they cannot have been much less at the beginning of his residence in Medina. All that the Constitution explicitly states is that disputes are to be referred to Muhammad [...] He is very far, however, from being autocratic ruler of Medina. He is merely one among a number of important men."[880]

Religious persecutions were absolutely prohibited; the later expulsion of the three Jewish tribes from Medina was not a religious act, but a political move resulting from their treason during the Battle of Ditches. The six or seven other Jewish tribes[881] who remained loyal to the Contract of Medina never left the City, and were treated as equal citizens of the Muslim state till the end of Prophet's life. Tamara Sonn observed that "on three occasions local tribes were believed to have violated the constitution by conspiring with outsiders against the Medinan community. They were therefore expelled (in the first two cases), or executed (in the third case). Because all three of these tribes were Jewish, some people think that the community in Medina turned against Jews. In fact, some verses from the Quran referring to incidents such as these caution the Muslims against trusting Jews and Christians. (For example, "O you who believe, do not take Jews and Christians for friends. They are friends of one another," 5:52.) However, other Jewish tribes continued to live in peace in Medina. Furthermore, the majority of verses of the Quran [...] endorse pluralism."[882] Hamidullah noted that "when the Muslims went to war against some Jewish tribes or ordered their expulsion from the city of *Madina*, not only that the rest of the tribes remained quiet, but on certain occasions they rendered military help to the Muslims; and this treaty or constitutional Act was not considered as repudiated in so far as other Jewish tribes were concerned, but was regarded as still in force."[883] The Islamic state of Medina was a multi-religious and multi-cultural pluralist state. It guaranteed religious, social, economic and political freedom to its diverse citizenry and bonded them together into a united whole. This was contrary to the often persecuting Christian Roman and Byzantine empires.

Conclusion

In brief, Islam rectified the Christian excesses in the areas of monotheism, rationalism, nomianism and religio-political absolutism. Islam considered itself a Christian reformation scheme in line with the original message of Jesus and his immediate disciples. This reformation scheme of Islam was partially appropriated, absorbed and implemented by the seventeenth and eighteenth century Enlightenment figures such as Henry Stubbe, John Toland, John Locke and sects such as Unitarians, Socinians and early Deists.

Endnotes

1   See S. Angus, *The Mystery Religions*, (New York, Dover Publications, 1975)

2   C. W. Dampier, *A History of Science and it Relation to Philosophy and Religion*, Cambridge, (Cambridge University Press, 1966), P. 61

3   Shirley C. Guthrie, Jr., *Christian Doctrine* (Richmond: CLC Press, 1968), p.223.

4   Northrop Frye, *"The Religious Vision of William Blake," Toward a New Christianity*, Thomas J. J. Altizer, ed. (New York: Harcourt, Brace & World Inc., 1967), p.40.

5   Ian R. Netton, *Text and Trauma: An East-West Primer* (Richmond: Curzon Press, 1996), p.91.

6   See for details Richard A. Burridge, *What Are the Gospels? A Comparison with Graeco-Roman Biography* (New York: Cambridge University Press, 1992), pp.271-74.

7   Charles Gore, *The Incarnation of the Son of God* (New York: Scribner's Sons, 1960), p.1.

8   Philip Schaff, *History of the Christian Church* (Michigan: W. B. Eerdmans, 1976), vol.2, p.570.

9   Joachim Jeremias, *New Testament Theology*, John Bowden, trans. (New York: Charles Scribner's Sons, 1971), p.1.

10   Robert M. Grant, *The Formation of The New Testament*, (New York, Harper and Row, 1965), p.8.

11   C. P. S. Clarke, *Short History of The Christian Church* (London: Longman, 1966), p.28.

12   John N. D. Kelly, *Early Christian Doctrines* (New York: Harper and Brothers, 1958), p.53.

13   See John D. Crossan, *The Historical Jesus: The Life of a Mediterranean Jewish Peasant*, (San Francisco: Harper Collins, 1991) p. XXX

14   Crossan, *The Historical Jesus,* p. XXX.

15   Don Cupitt, *Christ, Faith and History: Cambridge Studies in Christology*, S. W. Sykes, J. P. Clayton, eds. (Cambridge: Cambridge University Press, 1972), p.134.

16   Ibid., p.137.

17   Crossan, *The Historical Jesus*, p. XXVIII.

18   Crossan, *The Historical Jesus*, p.132.

19   Lightfoot, *History and Interpretation in the Gospels*, p.22.

20   *Commentary on the Gospel of John* (Book II), ch.2, http://www.newadvent.org/fathers/101502.htm.

21   Kelly, *Early Christian Doctrines*, p.173.

22   Quoted from Jurgan Moltmann, *The Crucified God* (New York: Harper & Row, 1974), p.89.

23   Henry Chadwick, *Early Christian Thought and the Classical Tradition* (New York: Dorset Press, 1967), p.25.

24   Alois Grillmeier, *Christ in Christian Tradition*, John Bowden, trans. (Atlanta: John Knox Press, 1975), vol.1, p.106.

25   Charles Bigg, *The Christian Platonists of Alexandria*, (Oxford, Oxford University Press, 1913), p.102.

26   Moltmann, *The Crucified God*, p.89.

27   See details in Richard R. Hopkins, *How Greek Philosophy Corrupted the Christian Concept of God,* (Springville, Utah, Horizon Publishers, 2009), p. 130

28   Richard A. Norris, Jr., ed. and trans., *The Christological Controversy* (Philadelphia: Fortress Press, 1980), p.7.

29   Kelly, *Early Christian Creeds*, p.72.

30   Quoted from Arthur C. McGiffert, *A History of Christian Thought* (New York: Charles Scribner's Sons, 1960), vol.1, p.113.

31   Quoted from McGiffert, *A History of Christian Thought.*, p.114.

32   Grillmeier, *Christ in Christian Tradition*, p.110.

33   Kelly, *Early Christian Doctrines*, pp.100-01.

34   Quoted from Norris, *The Christological Controversy*, p.114.

35   Grillmeier, *Christ in Christian Tradition*, p.119.

36   Grillmeier, *Christ in Christian Tradition*, p.125.

37   McGiffert, *A History of Christian Thought*, vol.1, p.219.

38   McGiffert, *A History of Christian Thought*, p.223.

39   Kelly, *Early Christian Doctrines*, p.130.

40   Bigg, *The Christian Platonists of Alexandria*, pp.223-24.

41   Bigg, *The Christian Platonists of Alexandria*, p.132.

42   McGiffert, *A History of Christian Thought*, vol.1, p.143.

43   McGiffert, *A History of Christian Thought*, p.144.

44   McGiffert, *A History of Christian Thought*, p.205.

45   Bigg, *The Christian Platonists of Alexandria*, p.97.

46   McGiffert, *A History of Christian Thought*, vol.1, p.233.

47   Kelly, *Early Christian Doctrines*, p.119.

48   Jaroslav Pelikan, *The Christian Tradition: A History of the Development of Doctrine* (Chicago; London: University of Chicago Press, 1971), vol.1, p.178.

49   Pelikan, *The Christian Tradition*, p.179.

50   McGiffert, *A History of Christian Thought*, vol.1, p.234.

51   Pelikan, *The Christian Tradition*,, vol.3, p.12.

52   Linwood Urban, *A Short History of Christian Thought* (New York: Oxford University Press, 1995), p.58.

53   Quoted from McGiffert, *A History of Christian Thought*, vol.1, pp.235-36.

54   Pelikan, *The Christian Tradition*, vol.1, pp.181-82.

55   Urban, *A Short History of Christian Thought*, p.59.

56   McGiffert, *A History of Christian Thought*, vol.1, p.275.

57   Ibid., p.239.

58   Urban, *A Short History of Christian Thought*, p.57.

59   Adolph Harnack, *History of Dogma*, OR, Wipf and Stock Publishers, 1997, vol.3, pp.41-42.

60   Paul Tillich, *A History of Christian Thought*, Carl E. Braaten, ed. (New York: Simon & Schuster, 1968), p.65.

61   Dorothy L. Sayers, *The Emperor Constantine* (New York: Harper & Brothers, 1951), p.119.

62   Norris, *The Christological Controversy*, pp.17-18.

63   Henry M. Gwatkin, *Studies of Arianism* (New York: AMS Press, 1978), p.24.

64   McGiffert, *A History of Christian Thought*, vol.1, p.248.

65   Pelikan, *The Christian Tradition: A History of the Development of Doctrine*, vol.1, p.194.

66   William Bright, *The Age of Fathers* (New York: AMS Press, 1970), vol.1, p.57.

67   Bright, *The Age of Fathers*, , p.57

68   Charles Matson Odahl, *Constantine and the Christian Empire*, (New York, Routledge, 2010), p. 198-199

69 Odahl, *Constantine*, p. 201

70 Frances M. Young, *From Nicaea to Chalcedon* (London: S.C.M. Press, 1983), p.64.

71 Ibid.

72 C.S. Lewis, in his Introduction to *The Incarnation of the Word of God, Being the Treatise of St. Athanasius*, Geoffrey Bles, trans. (London: The Centenary Press, 1944), p.11.

73 Young, *From Nicaea to Chalcedon*, p.65.

74 Young, *From Nicaea to Chalcedon*, p.67.

75 Archibald Robertson in his Introduction "St. Athanasius: Select Works and Letters," *A Select Library of Nicene and Post-Nicene Fathers of the Christian Church* (Grand Rapids: W. B. Eerdmans, 1957), vol. IV, p. IXXII.

76 Edward R. Hardy, C. C. Richardson, eds., *Christology of the Later Fathers*, The Library of Christian Classics (Philadelphia: The Westminster Press, n.d.), vol. III, pp.58-59.

77 Edward R. Hardy, C. C. Richardson, eds., *Christology of the Later Fathers*, p.60.

78 Quoted from Eginhard P. Meijering, *God Being History: Studies in Patristic Philosophy* (Amsterdam: North-Holland Publishing Company, 1975), p.93.

79 McGiffert, *A History of Christian Thought*, vol.1, pp.253-54.

80 Young, *From Nicaea to Chalcedon*, p.74.

81 Adolph Harnack, *History of Dogma*, vol.4, p.46.

82 Harnack, *History of Dogma*, p.49.

83 Kelly, *Early Christian Doctrines*, pp.236-37.

84 Robin L. Fox, *Pagans and Christians* (New York: Alfred & Knopf Inc., 1987), p.655.

85 Kelly, *Early Christian Creeds*, p.255.

86 Kelly, *Early Christian Creeds*, pp.215-16.

87 Bright, *The Age of Fathers*, vol.1, p.96.

88 Harnack, *History of Dogma*, vol.4, p.47.

89 Bright, *The Age of Fathers*, vol.1, p.98.

90 Harnack, *History of Dogma*, vol.4, pp.58-59.

91 George S. J. Meloney, *The Cosmic Christ, From Paul to Teilhard* (New York: Sheed & Ward, 1968), vol.1, p.99.

92 Harnack, *History of Dogma*, vol.4, p.51.

93 Andrew M. Fairbairn, *The Place of Christ in Modern Theology* (New York: Scribner's Sons, 1911), pp.90-91.

94 Fairbairn, *The Place of Christ in Modern Theology*, p.91.

95   Harnack, *History of Dogma*, vol.4, p.162.

96   Kelly, *Early Christian Doctrines*, p.297.

97   Kelly, *Early Christian Doctrines*, p.302.

98   Paul Tillich, *A History of Christian Thought*, (New York, Touchstone Books, 1972), p.82.

99   Tillich, *A History of Christian Thought*, p. 82

100   McGiffert, *A History of Christian Thought*, vol.1, p.279.

101   Kelly, *Early Christian Doctrines*, p.306.

102   See Tillich, *A History of Christian Thought*, p.82; see for details Francis A. Sullivan, *The Christology of Theodore of Mopsuestia* (Rome: University Gregorian, 1956), pp.219 ff.

103   McGiffert, *A History of Christian Thought*, vol.1, p.280.

104   Kelly, *Early Christian Doctrines*, p.311.

105   Henry Chadwick, *The Early Church* (New York: Dorset Press, 1967), p.198.

106   Quoted from Harry A. Wolfson, *The Philosophy of the Church Fathers*, 3rd edn. (Cambridge, MA: Harvard University Press, 1970), vol.1, p.452.

107   Wolfson, *The Philosophy of the Church Fathers*, p.455.

108   Kelly, *Early Christian Doctrines*, p.312.

109   Quoted from Wolfson, *The Philosophy of the Church Fathers*, vol.1, p.456.

110   Kelly, *Early Christian Doctrines*, p.314.

111   Kelly, *Early Christian Doctrines*, p.315.

112   Wolfson, *The Philosophy of the Church Fathers*, vol.1, p.457.

113   Hardy, Richardson eds., *Christology of the Later Fathers*, p.353.

114   Hardy, Richardson eds., Ibid, p.352.

115   Hardy, Richardson eds., Ibid, p.351.

116   G. R. Driver, L. Hodgson, eds. and trans., *The Bazar of Heraclides Nestorius* (Oxford; New York: Clarendon Press, 1925), p.370.

117   Young, *From Nicaea to Chalcedon*, p.229.

118   Chadwick, *The Early Church*, p.202.

119   Kelly, *Early Christian Doctrines*, pp.339-40.

120   Grillmeier, *Christ in Christian Tradition*, p.543.

121   Kelly, *Early Christian Doctrines*, p.340.

122   William A. Wigram, *The Separation of the Monophysites* (London: The Faith Press, 1923), p.13.

123   Wigram, Ibid., p.16.

124   Robert V. Sellers, *The Council of Chalcedon: A Historical and Doctrinal Survey* (London: SPCK, 1961), p.255.

125   Sellers, Ibid, p.266.

126   Sellers, Ibid. p.301.

127   Grillmeier, *Christ in Christian Tradition*, p.553.

128   Tillich, *A History of Christian Thought*, p.90.

129   Emile Brunner, *The Christian Doctrine of God*, trans. by Olive Wyon, (OR, Wipf and Stock Publishers, 2014), vol.2, pp.324-25.

130   John Hick, *The Metaphor of God Incarnate* (London: S.C.M. Press, 1993, p.5.

131   Brunner, *The Christian Doctrine of God*, vol.2, p.349.

132   Bright, *The Age of Fathers*, vol.2, p.550.

133   John S. Whale, *Christian Doctrine* (Cambridge: Cambridge University Press, 1961), p.110.

134   McGiffert, *A History of Christian Thought*, vol.1, p.289.

135   Quoted from McGiffert, *A History of Christian Thought*, vol.1, p.173.

136   See Richard Cross, Two Models of The Trinity? Blackwell Publishers, *The Heythrop Journal*, v. 43, issue 3, 2002

137   See Dale Tuggy, "What is Modalism", http://trinities.org/blog/what-is-modalism/

138   C. Stephen Layman, *Tritheism and the Trinity*, Faith and Philosophy, vol. 5, No. 3, July 1988, p. 291

139   Dale Tuggy, "The Trinitarian Dilemma" in *The Trinity: East/West Dialogue* edited by Melville Y. Stewart, (Dordrecht, Springer, 2003), p. 23

140   William Alston, "Swinburne and Christian theology," *International Journal for Philosophy of Religion*, 41, 1997, p. 54

141   St. Augustine, *On the Trinity*, edited by Gareth B. Matthews, translated by Stephen McKenna, Cambridge, (Cambridge University Press, 2002), Books 8-15, p. xii

142   Keith E. Yandell, "The Most Brutal and Inexcusable Error in Counting? Trinity and Consistency", Religious Studies, Vol. 30, No. 2, Cambridge, Cambridge University Press, (Jun., 1994), pp. 201-217

143   Millard Erickson, *God in Three Persons: A Contemporary Interpretation of Trinity*, (Ada, MI, Baker Publication Group, 1995), p. 130

144   John Hick ed., *The Myth of God Incarnate*, (Philadelphia: The Westminster Press, 1977), p.178.

145   R. J. Hoffmann and G. A. Larue, *Jesus in History and Myth*, (Buffalo,

Prometheus, 1984, p.200.

146   Hick, *The Myth of God Incarnate*, p.179.

147   Hick, *The Myth of God Incarnate*, p.330.

148   See David F. Wells, *The Search for Salvation*, (Downers Grove, Ill.: InterVarsity, 1978); Donald Bloesch, *Christian Life and Salvation*, (Grand Rapids: Eerdmans, 1967); Anthony A. Hoekema, *Saved by Grace*, (Grand Rapids: Eerdmans, 1989)

149   See Bruce Demarest, *The Cross and Salvation: The Doctrine of Salvation*, (Wheaton, IL, Crossway Books, 2006), p. 26; D.M. Lloyd-Jones, *God's Ultimate Purpose: An Exposition of Eph* 1:1-23, (Grand Rapids: Baker, 1978)

150   See John K. Ryan, tr. *Book Eight: The Grace of Faith in The Confessions of St. Augustine.* (New York: Image Books, 1960); W.T. Whitley, ed., *The Doctrine of Grace*, (New York: Macmillan, 1931); Clark H. Pinnock, ed., *Grace Unlimited*, (Minneapolis: Bethany Fellowship, 1975)

151   See H. E. W. Turner, *The Patristic Doctrine of the Redemption: A Study of the Development of Doctrine During the First Five Centuries*, (Eugene, OR: Wipf & Stock Publishers, 2004); A. J. Wallace, R. D. Rusk, *Moral Transformation: The Original Christian Paradigm of Salvation* (New Zealand: Bridgehead, 2011)

152   See details in Demarest, *The Cross and Salvation*, p. 37ff

153   See Gerald Bonner. *St. Augustine of Hippo: Life and Controversies.* (Philadelphia: The Westminster Press, 1963); John S. Burleigh. *Faith and the Creed. In Augustine: Earlier Writings.* (Philadelphia: The Westminster Press, 1953)

154   See *The Cambridge Companion to Augustine*, eds. Eleonore Stump, Norman Kretzmann. (New York: Cambridge University Press, 2001); Stephen J. Duffy. *The Dynamics of Grace: Perspectives in Theological Anthropology.* (Collegeville, Minnesota: The Liturgical Press, 1993)

155   St. Augustine, *Admonition and Grace*, (http://www.newadvent.org/fathers/1513.htm); Karl Barth, *God, Grace and the Gospel*, trans. James S. McNab, (Edinburgh and London: Oliver and Boyd, 1959); Karl Barth, *The Knowledge of God and the Service of God*, trans. J.L.M. Haire and Ian Henderson, (New York: Charles Scribner's Sons, 1939)

156   St. Augustine, *Admonition and Grace*, (http://www.newadvent.org/fathers/1513.htm

157   See Timothy F. Lull, ed., *Martin Luther's Basic Theological Writings* (Minneapolis: Fortress, 1989), p. 224 ff.

158   Frank Leslie Cross, Elizabeth A., *Livingstone, eds. (2005). "Original sin".* The Oxford dictionary of the Christian Church (3rd rev. ed.). (Oxford: Oxford University Press, 2005)

159   Thomas Jefferson's Dec. 8, *1822 letter to James Smith, Memoir,* correspondence, and miscellanies: from the papers of Thomas Jefferson, Carr

& Co., Charlottesville, 1829, vol. IV, p.360

160   David C. Lingberg and Ronald L. Numbers eds., *God and Nature: Historical Essays on the Encounter between Christianity and Science*, (Berkeley, University of California Press, 1986), p. 169

161   See William Edward Hartpole Lecky, *History of the Rise and Influence of the Spirit of Rationalism in Europe*, (London, D. Appleton and Company, 1919), v. 1, p. 119

162   See details in Terence L. Nichols, *The Sacred Cosmos: Christian Faith and the Challenge of Naturalism.* (Eugene, WIPF & STOCK, 2003), p. 43

163   S. F. Mason, *"Science and Religion in Seventeenth Century England" in The Intellectual Revolution of the Seventeenth Century* edited by Charles Webster, (New York, Routledge, 1974), p. 207

164   See details in Mason, *"Science and Religion in Seventeenth Century England"*, p. 206ff

165   Michael Martin, *The Case Against Christianity*, (Philadelphia, Temple University Press, 1991), P. 198

166   Martin, *The Case*, p. 200

167   Martin, *The Case*, p. 201

168   See E. P. Sanders, *Paul, the Law, and the Jewish People,* (Philadelphia: Fortress, 1983), p. 123-35; H. Räisänen, *Paul and the Law,* (Philadelphia: Fortress, 1983), p. 106-7

169   Thomas Schreiner, *Did Paul Believe in Justification by Works? Another Look at Romans 2*, Bulletin for Biblical Research 3 (1993) 131-158, P. 138

170   Martin, *The Case*, p. 203

171   Robert Eisenman, *James the Brother of Jesus*, (New York, Penguin Books, 1998), p. 40

172   Calvin J. Roetzel, *"Paul in the Second Century" in the Cambridge Companion to Paul*, edited by James Dunn, (Cambridge, Cambridge University Press, 2004), p. 227

173   Gunther Bornkamm, *Paul, Paulus*, D. M. G. Stalker, trans., (New York: Harper & Row, 1969), p. 229-30.

174   Robert Eisenman, *James the Brother of Jesus*, p. 267

175   Robert Eisenman, *James the Brother of Jesus*, p. 267-268

176   Robert Eisenman, *James the Brother of Jesus*, p. 268

177   Robert Eisenman, *James the Brother of Jesus*, p. 268

178   Jerald H. Rendall, *The Epistle of St. James and Judaic Christianity*, Cambridge, (Cambridge University Press, 1927), p. 83

179   Rendall, *The Epistle of St. James*, p. 78

180   Rendall, *The Epistle of St. James*, p. 76

181   Rendall, *The Epistle of St. James*, p. 78

182   R. J. Hoffman (trans.), *Porphyry's Against the Christians*, (New York, Prometheus Books, 1994), p. 44

183   R. J. Hoffman (trans.), *Celsus: On the True Doctrine*, (New York, Oxford University Press, 1987), p. 14

184   Francis Gerald Downing, *Cynics, Paul and the Pauline Churches: Cynics and Christian Origins II*, (New York, Routledge, 1998), p. 86

185   David E. Garland, *I Corinthians*, (Grand Rapids, Michigan, Backer Academic, 2003), P. 153

186   Garland, *I Corinthians*, p. 153

187   Garland, *I Corinthians*, p. 153

188   Downing, *Cynics and Paul*, p. 86

189   Garland, *I Corinthians*, p. 160

190   Gordon D. Fee, *The First Epistle to the Corinthians*, (Grand Rapids, William B. Eerdmans Publishing Company, 1987), p. 203

191   Garland, *I Corinthians*, p. 219

192   Fee, *The First Epistle to the Corinthians*, p. 250-251

193   Fee, *The First Epistle*, p. 251

194   Hoffman, *Celsus*, p. 13

195   Hoffman, *Celsus*, p. 14

196   Hoffman, *Celsus*, p. 15

197   R. A. B. Mynors ed., Oxford Classical Texts, (Oxford, Oxford University Press, 1963), *Epistles* 10..96; Hoffman, Celsus, p. 16

198   Gerald H. Rendall trans., *Minucius Felix*, (London, Harvard University Press,1977), p. 337

199   G. W. Clark ed., *The Octavius of Marcus Minucius Felix*, Ancient Christian Writers 39, (New York, Paulist Press, 1974), p. 9

200   Hoffman, *Celsus*, p. 17

201   Hoffman, *Celsus*, p. 18

202   E. Roberts and J. Donaldson eds., *Ante-Nicene Fathers*, (New York, Cosimo Classics, 2007), v. 1, p. 165;

203   Hoffman, *Celsus*, p. 18

204   T. R. Glover trans., *Tertullian*, Apology De Spectaculis, (London, Harvard University Press, 1977), p. 9

205   Tertullian, *Apology*, p. 10

206   Tertullian, *Apology*, p. 11

207   Tertullian, *Apology*, p. 17

208   Tertullian, *Apology*, p. 19

209   Tertullian, *Apology*, p. 21

210   Tertullian, *Apology*, p. 183

211   Hoffman, *Celsus*, p. 19

212   Hoffman, *Celsus*, p. 19

213   Hoffman, *Celsus*, p. 19-20

214   Tertullian, *Apology*, p. 195-197

215   Tertullian, *Apology*, p. 227

216   Thomson Gale, Orgy: Orgy in Medieval and Modern Europe, Encyclopedia
       of Religion, 2005 http://www.encyclopedia.com/environment/encyclopedias-
       almanacs-transcripts-and-maps/orgy-orgy-medieval-and-modern-europe,
       retrieved on February 14, 2017

217   Christopher Hill, *The World Turned Up Side Down: Radical Ideas During the
       English Revolution*, (London, Penguin Books, 1975), p. 215

218   Hill, *The World Turned Up Side Down*, p. 207

219   John Bunyan, *Saved by Grace*, ReadHowYouWant.com, Limited, 2008, p. 1

220   Hill, *The World Turned Up Side Down*, p. 205

221   Hill, *The World Turned Up Side Down*, p. 215

222   Hill, *The World Turned Up Side Down*, p. 216

223   Hill, *The World Turned Up Side Down*, p. 216

224   J. F. McGregor and Barry Reay eds., *Radical Religion in the English Revolution*,
       Oxford: (Oxford University Press, 1984), p. 129

225   Clement Hawes, *Mania and Literary Style, The Rhetoric of Enthusiasm From
       Ranters to Christopher Smart*, (Cambridge, Cambridge University Press,
       1996), p. 34

226   Hill, *The World Turned Up Side Down*, p. 208

227   Hoffman, *Celsus*, p. 61

228   Hoffman, *Celsus*, p. 61-62

229   Hoffman, *Celsus*, p. 62

230   Hoffman, *Celsus*, p. 62-63

231   Hoffman, *Celsus*, p. 63

232   Hoffman, *Celsus*, p. 63-64

233   Hoffman, *Porphyry*, p. 40

234   Hoffman, *Celsus*, p. 64

235   Hoffman, *Porphyry*, p. 32

236   Hoffman, *Porphyry*, p. 33

237   Hoffman, *Celsus*, p. 64

238   Hoffman, *Celsus*, p. 65

239   Hoffman, *Celsus*, p. 65

240   Hoffman, *Celsus*, p. 65-66

241   Hoffman, *Celsus*, p. 67-68

242   Hoffman, *Celsus*, p. 68

243   Hoffman, *Porphyry*, p. 34

244   Hoffman, *Porphyry*, p. 36

245   Hoffman, *Celsus*, p. 68-69

246   Hoffman, *Celsus*, p. 71

247   Hoffman, *Celsus*, p. 70

248   Hoffman, *Celsus*, p. 75

249   Hoffman, *Celsus*, p. 75

250   Hoffman, *Celsus*, p. 72

251   D. R. Edwards and C. T. McCollough (eds), *The Archaeology of Difference: Gender, Ethnicity, Class and the "Other" in Antiquity: Studies in Honour of Eric M. Meyers*, (Boston: American Schools of Oriental Research, 2007), p. 363

252   Henry Chadwick, *Origen Contra Celsum*, (Cambridge, Cambridge University Press, 2003), p. 158

253   Chadwick, *Origen*, p. 165

254   Chadwick, *Origen*, p. 165-66

255   Hoffman, *Porphyry*, p. 78

256   Chadwick, *Origen*, p. 168

257   Chadwick, *Origen*, p. 192-93

258   Hoffman, *Porphyry*, p. 37

259   See Hoffman, *Celsus*, p. 80

260   Hoffman, *Celsus*, p. 82

261   Chadwick, *Origen*, p. 391

262   Hoffman, *Celsus*, p. 71

263   Hoffman, *Celsus*, p. 80

264   Hoffman, *Celsus*, p. 81

265   Hoffman, *Celsus*, p. 124

266   See Elaine Pagels, *The Origin of Satan*, (New York, Vintage Books, 1995), p. 141-142

267   Hoffman, *Celsus*, p. 105

268   Hoffman, *Celsus*, p. 104

269   Hoffman, *Celsus*, p. 116

270   Hoffman, *Porphyry*, p. 85

271   Hoffman, *Porphyry*, p. 86-87

272   Pagels, *Origin of Satan*, p. 143

273   Grillmeier, *Christ in Christian Tradition*, John Bowden, trans., (Atlanta: John Knox Press, 1975), vol.1, p.106.

274   Chadwick, *Origen*, p. 510

275   Heather M. Campbell, *The Ascent of the West from Prehistory through the Renaissance*, (New York, Britannica Educational Publishing, 2011), p. 103-104

276   J. G. A. Pocock, *Barbarism and Religion*, (Cambridge, Cambridge University Press, 2003), v. 3, p. 112

277   Susan Wood, *The Proprietary Church in the Medieval West*, (Oxford, Oxford University Press, 2006), P. 9

278   Campbell, *Ascent*, P. 78

279   Thomas F. X. Noble and Julia M. H. Smith (Eds.), *The Cambridge History of Christianity*, Early Medieval Christianities, C. 600-c. 1100, (Cambridge, Cambridge University Press, 2008), v. 3, p. 8

280   *Cambridge History of Christianity*, v. 3, p. 8

281   *Cambridge History of Christianity*, v. 3, p. 8

282   See Ernst Bammel and C. F. D. Moule eds., *Jesus and the Politics of His Day*, (Cambridge, Cambridge University Press, 1984), p. 1-10

283   See Elaine Pagels, *The Origin of Satan*, p. 114

284   Jacques Ellul, *Anarchy and Christianity* translated by Geoffrey W. Bromiley, (Grand Rapids, MI, William B. Eerdmans, 1991), p. 71

285   John Howard Yolder, *The Politics of Jesus*, (Cambridge, William B. Eerdmans, 1994), p. 144-145

286   Ellul, *Anarchy*, p. 56

287   Ellul, *Anarchy*, p. 58

288   Ellul, *Anarchy*, p. 58

289   Ellul, *Anarchy*, p. 59

290 See F. F. Bruce, *"Render to Caesar"* in Bammel and C. F. D. Moule eds., Jesus and the Politics of His Day, p. 249ff

291 Elaine Pagels, *Revelations, Vision, Prophecy and Politics in the Book of Revelation*, (New York, Vikings, 2012), chapter 1

292 Ellul, *Anarchy*, p. 72

293 Ellul, *Anarchy*, p. 72

294 Ellul, *Anarchy*, p. 74

295 Pagels, *Revelations, Vision, Prophecy and Politics in the Book of Revelation*, p. 35

296 See D. M. Lloyd-Jones, *Romans, An Exposition of Chapter 13*, (Edinburgh, The Banner of Truth Trust, 1967), p. 1-5

297 See a detailed study of these approaches in Seyoon Kim, *Christ and Caesar*, (Grand Rapids, MI, William B. Eerdmans, 2008), p. 34ff

298 Bernard Lategan, *Romans 13:1-7: A Review Of Post-1989 Readings*, Scriptura 110 (2012:2), pp. 259-272, http://scriptura.journals.ac.za/; p. 264-265

299 See N. T. Wright, *Paul: In Fresh Perspective,* (Minneapolis: Fortress, 2005), 63; Peter Oakes, *"Re-mapping the Universe: Paul and the Emperor in 1 Thessalonians and Philippians,"* *JSNT27* (2005): 312; Stuhlmacher, *Paul's Letter to the Romans: A Commentary,* trans. S. J. Hafemann, (Louisville, Ky., Westminster John Knox, 1994), 198-208; J. D. G. Dunn, *Romans 9-16,* WBC 38B, (Dallas: Word, 1988), 768-69; J. A. Fitzmyer, *Romans,* AB 33, (New York: Doubleday, 1993), 662-63; Richard Horsley ed., *Paul and Politics,* (Harrisburg, PA, Trinity International Press, 2000)

300 Kim, *Christ and Caesar*, p. 66

301 Kim, *Christ and Caesar*, p. 66-67

302 Kim, *Christ and Caesar*, p. 68

303 See Lategan, *Romans* 13:1-7, p. 83ff

304 Lategan, *Romans* 13:1-7, p. 269

305 John D. Crossan, *The Historical Jesus: The Life of a Mediterranean Jewish Peasant*, (San Francisco: Harper Collins, 1991), p.132.

306 See John Howard Yoder, *The Politics of Jesus*, p. 142

307 Bammel and C. F. D. Moule eds., *Jesus and the Politics of His Day*, p. 374

308 Cornelius M. Stam, *Commentary on the Epistle of Roman*, (Steven Point, WI, Berean Literature Foundation, 1984), p. 267-268

309 Bammel and C. F. D. Moule eds., *Jesus and the Politics of His Day*, p. 374

310 Cornelius M. Stam, *Commentary on the Epistle of Roman*, p. 268

311 Charles Hodge, *Commentary on the Epistle to the Romans*, (Albany, Books For The Ages, 1997), p. 630

312   Hodge, *Commentary on the Epistle to the Romans*, p. 630-631

313   Hodge, *Commentary on the Epistle to the Romans*, p. 631

314   Hodge, *Commentary on the Epistle to the Romans*, p. 630-631

315   Stam, *Commentary on the Epistle of Roman*, p. 269

316   Hodge, *Commentary on the Epistle to the Romans*, p. 628

317   Stam, *Commentary on the Epistle of Roman*, p. 269

318   Stam, *Commentary on the Epistle of Roman*, p. 269-270

319   Hodge, *Commentary on the Epistle to the Romans*, p. 631-632

320   Douglas J. Moo, *The Epistle to the Romans*, (Grand Rapids, MI, William B. Eerdmans, 1996), p. 790

321   Moo, *The Epistle to Romans*, p. 791

322   Hodge, *Commentary on the Epistle to the Romans*, p. 629

323   Hodge, *Commentary on the Epistle to the Romans*, p. 629

324   Hodge, *Commentary on the Epistle to the Romans*, p. 629-630

325   Moo, *The Epistle to Romans*, p. 791

326   Bammel and C. F. D. Moule eds., *Jesus and the Politics of His Day*, p. 263

327   Hodge, *Commentary on the Epistle to the Romans*, p. 631

328   Hodge, *Commentary on the Epistle to the Romans*, p. 632

329   Hodge, *Commentary on the Epistle to the Romans*, p. 632

330   Moo, *The Epistle to Romans*, p. 799

331   Moo, *The Epistle to Romans*, p. 802

332   Moo, *The Epistle to Romans*, p. 803

333   Hodge, *Commentary on the Epistle to the Romans*, p. 633

334   Moo, *The Epistle to Romans*, p. 804

335   Moo, *The Epistle to Romans*, p. 806

336   Marcus J. Borg and John D. Crossan, *The First Paul*, (New York, Harper Collins, 2009) p. 120

337   Marcus J. Borg and John D. Crossan, *The First Paul*, p. 117

338   Bammel and C. F. D. Moule eds., *Jesus and the Politics of His Day*, p. 381

339   http://biblehub.com/commentaries/1_peter/2-13.htm

340   Reinhard Feldmeier, *The First Letter of Peter, A Commentary on the Greek Text*, (Waco, Texas, Baylor University Press, 2008), p. 150

341   Feldmeier, *The First Letter of Peter*, p. 151

342   Feldmeier, *The First Letter of Peter*, p. 159

343   Feldmeier, *The First Letter of Peter*, p. 162

344   Kim, *Christ and Caesar*, p. 60

345   Kim, Christ and Caesar, p. 60; A. von Harnack, *The Expansion of Christianity in the First Three Centuries,* trans, and ed. J. Moffatt, 2 vols., Theological Translation Library 19-20 (New York: Putnam's Sons, 1904-5), 1:372-74.

346   The translation is taken from M. W. Holmes, *The Apostolic Fathers: Greek Texts and English Translations,* updated ed. (Grand Rapids: Baker Books, 1999), 97-98.

347   Tertullian, *Apology*, p. 151

348   Tertullian, *Apology*, p. 157

349   Kim, *Christ and Caesar*, 62-63

350   David Gwynn, *Christianity in the Later Roman Empire*, (New York, Bloomsbury, 2015), p. 33

351   Gwynn, *Christianity*, p. 34

352   R. A. Markus, *Saeculum History and Society in the Theology of St. Augustine*, Cambridge, (Cambridge University Press, 2007), p. 77

353   Markus, *Saeculum*, p. 78

354   Markus, *Saeculum*, p. 78

355   See John Cowburn SJ, Free Will, *Predestination and Determinism*, Milwaukee, Marquette University Press, 2008

356   Elaine Pagels, Adam, *Eve and the Serpent*, (New York, First Vintage Books, 1989), p. 138

357   Herbert A. Deane, *The Political and Social Ideas of St. Augustine*, (New York, Columbia University Press, 1963), p. 116

358   Elaine Pagels, Adam, *Eve and the Serpent*, p. 100

359   Henry Chadwick trans., *Augustine, Confessions*, (New York, Oxford University Press, 1991), 2.2, p. 24

360   Augustine, *Confessions*, p. 141

361   Augustine, *Confessions*, p. 150

362   Pagels, *Adam, Eve*, p. 102

363   Pagels, *Adam, Eve*, p. 108

364   Pagels, *Adam, Eve*, p. 112

365   Michael Gaddis, *There Is No Crime for Those Who Have Christ*, (Berkeley, University of California Press, 2005), p. 129

366   Pagels, *Adam, Eve*, p. 113

367   Pagels, *Adam, Eve*, p. 113

368   Markus, *Saeculum*, p. 81

369   Markus, *Saeculum*, p. 83

370   See Peter Brown, *Augustine of Hippo: A Biography*, (Berkeley, University of California Press, 2000), p. 285ff

371   Henry Chadwick, *Augustine: A Very Short Introduction*, (Oxford, Oxford University Press, 2001), p. 103

372   Markus, *Saeculum*, p. 84

373   Markus, *Saeculum*, p. 86

374   Markus, *Saeculum*, p. 89

375   Chadwick, *Augustine*, p. 107

376   Markus, *Saeculum*, p. 95

377   Perez Zagorin, *How the Idea of Religious Toleration Came to the West*, (New Jersey, Princeton University, 2003), p. 19

378   Ian Hunter, John Christian Laursen, and Cary J. Nederman eds., Heresy in Transition, (Burlington, VT, Ashgate Publishing Company, 2005), p. 1; for a useful overview, see John B. Henderson, *The Construction of Orthodoxy and Heresy: Neo-Confucian, Islamic, Jewish, and Early Christian Patterns* (Albany, SUNY Press, 1998)

379   Carlos Galvao Sabrinho, *Doctrine and Power*, (Berkeley, University of California Press, 2013), p. 16

380   Sabrinho, *Doctrine and Power*, p. 15

381   Sabrinho, *Doctrine and Power*, p. 15

382   Sabrinho, *Doctrine and Power*, p. 16

383   Sabrinho, *Doctrine and Power*, p. 17-18

384   http://st-takla.org/books/en/ecf/201/2010501.html

385   Edward Gibbon, *History of the Decline and Fall of the Roman Empire*, (London, J. O. Robinson, nd.), p. 307

386   David M. Gwynn, *Christianity in the Later Roman Empire: A Source Book*, p. 50

387   Stephen Williams and Gerard Friell, *Theodosius, The Empire at Bay*, (London, Routledge, 1994), p. 30

388   Williams and Gerard Friell, *Theodosius*, p. 33

389   Richard Lim, *"Christian Triumph and Controversy"* in G. W. Bowersock, Peter Brown, Oleg Grabar eds., Interpreting Late Antiquity: Essays on the Postclassical World, (London, *The Belknap Press of Harvard University Press, 2001)*, p. 200-201

390   Williams and Gerard Friell, *Theodosius*, p. 34

391   Williams and Gerard Friell, *Theodosius*, p. 31

392   Clyde Pharr trans., *The Theodosian Code*, (London, Oxford University Press, 1952), p. 440

393   Clyde Pharr trans., *The Theodosian Code,* P. 77

394   Ian Hunter, John Christian Laursen, and Cary J. Nederman eds., *Heresy in Transition*, p.1

395   Williams and Gerard Friell, *Theodosius*, 38

396   Lim, *Interpreting Late Antiquity*, p. 208

397   Zagorin, *How the Idea*, P. 23

398   Lim, *Interpreting Late Antiquity*, p. 206

399   Zagorin, *How the Idea*, p. 25

400   Lim, *Interpreting Late Antiquity*, p. 208

401   Zagorin, *How the Idea*, p. 27

402   Gaddis, *There Is No Crime*, p. 133

403   Zagorin, *How the Idea*, p. 29

404   Philip Schaff, *Augustin: The Writings Against the Manichaeans and Against the Donatists*, (New York: The Christian Literature Publishing Co., 1890), p. 472

405   Schaff, *Augustine*, p. 817

406   Schaff, *Augustine*, p. 817

407   Schaff, *Augustine*, p. 817

408   Gaddis, *There Is No Crime*, p. 134

409   Schaff, *Augustine*, p. 817-818

410   Schaff, *Augustine*, p. 818

411   Schaff, *Augustine*, p. 826

412   Schaff, *Augustine*, p. 809-810

413   Zagorin, *How the Idea*, p. 30

414   Zagorin, *How the Idea*, p. 30

415   Lim, *Interpreting Late Antiquity*, p. 209

416   Zagorin, *How the Idea*, p. 31

417   Zagorin, *How the Idea*, p. 32

418   Zagorin, *How the Idea*, p. 32

419   Peter Brown, "St. Augustine's Attitude to Religious Coercion." *The Journal of Roman Studies*, vol. 54, 1964, pp. 107–116., www.jstor.org/stable/298656, p. 107

420   Brown, *St. Augustine's Attitude to Religious*, p. 107

421   Brown, *Augustine's Attitude*, p. 107

422   Brown, *Augustine's Attitude*, 109-110

423   Brown, *Augustine's Attitude*, p. 110

424   Brown, *Augustine's Attitude*, p. 115-116

425   Brown, *Augustine's Attitude*, p. 115

426   William Tabbernee, *Fake Prophecy and Polluted Sacraments*, (Boston, Brill, 2007), p. 335

427   Gaddis, *There Is No Crime*, p. 142

428   See Gaddis, *There Is No Crime*, p. 145-147

429   Gaddis, *There Is No Crime*, p. 147

430   Gaddis, *There Is No Crime*, p. 150

431   Gaddis, *There Is No Crime*, p. 151

432   Gaddis, *There Is No Crime*, p. 155

433   Gaddis, *There Is No Crime*, p. 155-158

434   Gaddis, *There Is No Crime*, p. 160

435   Gaddis, *There Is No Crime*, p. 160

436   Gaddis, *There Is No Crime*, p. 181

437   Gaddis, *There Is No Crime*, p. 191

438   Gaddis, *There Is No Crime*, p. 193

439   Gaddis, *There Is No Crime*, p. 193

440   Gaddis, *There Is No Crime*, p. 194

441   Gaddis, *There Is No Crime*, p. 208

442   Gaddis, *There Is No Crime*, p. 210

443   Gaddis, *There Is No Crime*, p. 213ff

444   Gaddis, *There Is No Crime*, p. 225

445   Gaddis, *There Is No Crime*, p. 227

446   Gaddis, *There Is No Crime*, p. 250

447   Mar Marcos, *The Debate on Religious Coercion in Ancient Christianity*, Chaos e Kosmos XIV, 2013, p. 13; St. Chrysostom's Picture of His Age, (London, SPCK, 1876), p. 104

448   See S. P. Scott, *The Civil Law*, volume XII, Cincinnati, 1932, p. 65

449   J. A. S. Evans, *The Age of Justinian*, (London, Routledge, 1996), p. 246

450   Tabbernee, *Fake Prophecy*, p. 325

451 Evans, *Age of Justinian*, p. 240

452 Evans, *Age of Justinian*, p. 245

453 See Susan Ashbrook Harvey, *Asceticism and Society in Crisis: John of Ephesus and the Lives of the Eastern Saints, (London,* University of California Press, 1990)

454 Evans, *Age of Justinian*, p. 249

455 https://en.wikisource.org/wiki/History_of_the_Wars

456 Evans, The *Age of Justinian*, p. 111

457 Tabbernee, *Fake Prophecy*, p. 325-326

458 Evans, *Age of Justinian*, p. 252

459 Tabbernee, *Fake Prophecy*, p. 326

460 Tabbernee, *Fake Prophecy*, p. 326

461 Tabbernee, *Fake Prophecy*, p. 327

462 Tabbernee, *Fake Prophecy*, p. 327

463 Evans, *Age of Justinian*, p. 251

464 Evans, *Age of Justinian*, p. 251

465 Harvey, *Asceticism and Society in Crisis*, p. 25-26

466 Tabbernee, *Fake Prophecy*, p. 336

467 Tabbernee, *Fake Prophecy*, p. 336

468 See Aubrey Russel Vine, *The Nestorian Churches*, (London, Independent Press, 1937)

469 Tabbernee, *Fake Prophecy*, p. 337

470 Tabbernee, *Fake Prophecy*, p. 328

471 Evans, *Age of Justinian*, p. 249

472 Tertullian *"The Prescription against Heretics",* in Alexander Roberts and James Donaldson, eds., The Anti-Nicene Fathers (Buffalo: Christian Literature Publ. Co., 1885), vol. 3, p. 246.

473 Pagels, *Origin of Satan*, p. 164

474 Charles H. Haskins, *The Renaissance of the Twelfth Century*, (London, Harvard University Press, 1955), p. 95

475 Haskins, *Renaissance*, p. 95-96

476 Haskins, *Renaissance*, p. 96

477 Haskins, *Renaissance*, p. 96

478 Haskins, *Renaissance*, p. 97

479   Hellen Ellerbe, *The Dark Side of Christian History,* (Windermere, Florida, Morning Star and Lark, 2009), p. 29

480   Ellerbe, *Dark Side*, p. 30

481   Ellerbe, *Dark Side*, p. 41

482   See P. R. L. Brown, *The World of Late Antiquity: From Marcus Aurelius to Muhammad,* (London, Thames and Hudson, 1971)

483   Bryn Ward Perkins, *The Fall of Rome and the End of Civilisation,* (Oxford, Oxford University Press, 2006), p. 183

484   Perkins, *The Fall of Rome*, p. 87

485   Perkins, *The Fall of Rome*, p. 104

486   http://www.novaroma.org/nr/Christianity

487   http://www.novaroma.org/nr/Christianity

488   Perkins, *The Fall of Rome*, p. 41

489   Quoted from Perkins, *The Fall of Rome*, p. 2

490   Perkins, *The Fall of Rome* and p. 2

491   Perkins, *The Fall of Rome*, p. 29

492   Perkins, *The Fall of Rome*, p. 29

493   Perkins, *The Fall of Rome*, p. 30

494   Perkins, *The Fall of Rome*, p. 58

495   Ellerbe, *Dark Side*, p. 42

496   Ellerbe, *Dark Side*, p. 43-44

497   Ellerbe, *Dark Side*, p. 44

498   Ellerbe, *Dark Side*, p. 46

499   Ellerbe, *Dark Side*, p. 53

500   Williams and Gerard Friell, *Theodosius*, p. 32

501   Tillich, *A History of Christian Thought*, (New York, Touchstone Books, 1972), p.85.

502   Armstrong, *History of God*, (New York, Ballantine Books, 1994), p.131.

503   John William Draper, *History of the Conflict Between Religion and Science*, (New York, D. Appleton and Company, 1875), p. xiii; also see Alfred G. McKinney, *Mohammed, The Myths*, (New York, i Universe Inc, 2007), p. 28

504   See Thomas Dixon, Geoffrey Canter, and Stephen Pumfrey (eds.), *Science and Religion: New Historical Perspectives*, (Cambridge, Cambridge University Press, 2010), p. 113

505   W. E. H. Lecky, *History of the Rise and Influence of the Spirit of Rationalism in*

Europe, (London, D. Appleton and Company, 1919), v. 1, p. 98

506   See Draper, *History of the Conflict,* chapter III, p. 68-101

507   Martin Pugh, *Britain and Islam*, (New Haven, Yale University Press, 2019), p. 4

508   See Fred M. Donner, *Muhammad and the Believers: At the Origins of Islam*, (London, Harvard University Press, 2010), p. 2ff

509   Toshihiko Izutsu, *God and Man in the Quran: Semantics of the Quranic Weltanschauung*, (Tokyo, Keio University, 1964), p. 112

510   See detail in Barnard Lewis, *The Arabs in History*, (Oxford, Oxford University Press, 2002), p. 27-30

511   Izutsu, *God and Man*, p. 112

512   See Donner, *Muhammad and the Believers*, p. 212

513   See details in Chase F. Robinson ed., *The New Cambridge History of Islam*, Cambridge, (Cambridge University Press, 2011), v. 1, p. 81ff

514   Izutsu, *God and Man*, p. 112

515   Muhammad Ibn Isḥāq, *The Life of Muhammad : A Translation of Ishaq's Sirat Rasul Allah*, trans., Alfred Guillaume (London ; New York: Oxford University Press, 1955), 14-16. Abd al-Malik Ibn Hishām, *Al-Sīrat Al-Nabawiyah* (Egypt: Dar Al-Hadith, 2006), 38ff

516   R. H. Charles, *The Chronicle of John, Bishop of Nikiu: Translated from Zotenberg's Ethiopic Text* (Merchantville, NJ: Evolution Publishers, 2007; Christian Roman Empire Series, 4), 69–70.

517   See G. W. Bowersock, *The Throne of Adulis: Red Sea Wars on the Eve of Islam*, (Oxford, Oxford University Press, 2013), chapter 5; Corrie Jonn Block, Philoponian Monophysitism in South Arabia at the Advent of Islam with Implications for the English Translation of 'Thala'tha' in Quran 4. 171 and 5.73, *Journal of Islamic Studies* (2011) pp. 1 of 26, p. 4-5

518   Robert G. Holyland, *Arabia and the Arabs, From the Bronze Age to the Coming of Islam*, (New York, Routledge, 2001), p. 147

519   See Bowersock, *The Throne of Adulis*, chapter 6

520   For origins of Judaism in Yemen see Robert G. Holyland, *Arabia and the Arabs*, p. 146ff

521   See Amir Harrak, *The Chronicle of Zuqnin*, Parts III and IV, A.D. 488–775: Translated from Syriac with Notes and Introduction (Toronto: Pontifical Institute of Mediaeval Studies, 1999; Mediaeval Sources in Translation, 36), 78–86. Also see Irfan Shahıˆd, *The Martyrs of Najraˆn: New Documents* (Brussels: Socie´te´ des Bollandistes, 1971; Subsidia Hagiographica, 49), 46.

522   See Irfan Shahıˆd, *'Byzantium in South Arabia',* Dumbarton Oaks Papers, 33 (1979): 23–94, at 29.

523   See Lewis, *The Arabs in History*, p. 28

524 Richard C. Martin ed., *Encyclopedia of Islam and the Muslim World*, entry "Arabia-Pre-Islam," (New York, Macmillan Reference, 2004),v. 1, p. 55

525 See Holyland, *Arabia and Arabs*, p. 150

526 Fred M. Donner, *"The Background to Islam"* in Michael Maas ed., The Cambridge Companion to the Age of Justinian, (Cambridge, Cambridge University Press, 2006), p. 516

527 Lewis, *The Arabs in History*, p. 27

528 Izutsu, *God and Man*, p. 112

529 Izutsu, *God and Man*, p. 114

530 See for trade Richard L. Smith, *Premodern Trade in World History*, (New York, Routledge, 2009)

531 Donner, *Muhammad and Believers*, p. 23-24

532 Geoffrey Parrinder ed., *World Religions: From Ancient History to the Present*, (New York, Facts on File, Publications, 1983), p. 466

533 Patricia Crone, *"The Rise of Islam in the World"* in Cambridge Illustrated History of the Islamic World, (Cambridge, Cambridge University Press, 1996), p. 11

534 Antony Black, *The History of Islamic Political Thought: From the Prophet to the Present*, (Edinburgh, University Press, 2011), p. 9

535 See for details Zulfiqar Ali Shah, *Anthropomorphic Depictions of God: Concept of God in the Judaic, Christian and Islamic Traditions, Representing the Un-representable*, (London: International Institute of Islamic Thought, 2012), p.55 ff

536 Adolphe Lods, *Israel, From its Beginnings to the Middle of the Eighth Century* (London: Routledge & Kegan Paul, 1948), p.257.

537 Lods, *Israel*, p.257.

538 See Joseph P. Shultz, *Judaism and the Gentile Faiths,* Comparative Studies in Religion, (London, Associated University Presses, 1981), p. 150ff

539 See details in Matt Stefon ed., *Judaism: History, Belief, And Practice*, (New York, Britannica Educational Publishing, 2012), p. 13ff

540 See details in Mary Boyce, *Zoroastrianism, their Religious Beliefs and Practices*, (London, Routledge and Kegan Paul, 1976), p. 16-20

541 See Zulfiqar Ali Shah *"The Islamic Approach to God"* in Zafar Ishaq Ansari and Isma'il Ibrahim Nawwab eds., The Different Aspects of Islamic Culture, The Foundations of Islam, (Paris, UNESCO Publications, 2016), p. 55-109

542 Ehsan Yarshater ed., *The Cambridge History of Iran*, (Cambridge, Cambridge University Press, 2000), v. 3 (1), p. xl

543 See David Nicolle, *Sassanian Armies: the Iranian Empire Early 3rd to Mid-7th Centuries AD.* (Stockport, UK: Montvert, 1996)

544   Draper, *History of the Conflict Between Religion and Science*, p. xiii; also see Alfred G. McKinney, Mohammed, The Myths, p. 28

545   See Thomas Dixon, Geoffrey Canter, and Stephen Pumfrey (eds.), *Science and Religion: New Historical Perspectives*, p. 113

546   See Draper, *History of the Conflict*, chapter III, p. 68-101

547   Draper, *History of the Conflict*, p. 84

548   See Surah al-Kahf, verse 4 "And to warn those who say, "God has begotten a son." (18:4)

549   Draper, *History of the Conflict*, xiii

550   Draper, *History of the Conflict*, xiv

551   Izutsu, *God and Man*, p. 136

552   Franz Rosenthal, *Man Versus Society in Early Islam*, edited by Dimitri Gutas, (Leiden, Brill, 2015), p. 565

553   Lawrence Rosen, *The Justice of Islam*, (Oxford, Oxford University Press, 2000), p. 70

554   G. Parrinder, *Jesus in the Quran*, (Oxford, Oneworld, 1996), p. 153; also see Jane McAuliffe, *Quranic Christians: An Analysis of Classic and Modern Exegesis*, (Cambridge University Press, Cambridge, 2007), p. 95ff

555   See Parrinder, *Jesus in the Quran*, p. 160-161

556   Parrinder, *Jesus in the Quran*, p. 161

557   Parrinder, *Jesus in the Quran*, p. 162

558   Parrinder, *Jesus in the Quran*, p. 162

559   Parrinder, *Jesus in the Quran*, p. 163

560   Parrinder, *Jesus in the Quran*, p. 163

561   See Richard Bell, *The Origin of Islam in its Christian Environment: The Gunning Lectures*, (Edinburgh, University Press, 1925, London: Cass, repr. 1968, 6–7.

562   See details in Shah, *Anthropomorphic Depictions of God*, p. 266 ff

563   For instance see Thomas H. McCall, *Which Trinity? Whose Monotheism? Philosophical and Systematic Theologians on the Metaphysics of Trinitarian Theology*, (Grand Rapids, Wm. B. Eerdmans, 2010)

564   See Parrinder, *Jesus in the Quran*, chapter 2, p. 16ff

565   Translation taken from Muhammad Asad, *The Message of Quran*, (Bristol, The Book Foundation, 2005)

566   See details in Parrinder, *Jesus in Quran*, p. 124ff

567   Jurgen Moltmann, *The Trinity and the Kingdom: The Doctrine of God*, (Minneapolis, Fortress Press, 1993), p. 88

568   Jurgen Moltmann, *Trinity*, p. 132

569   Parrinder, *Jesus in Quran*, p. 127

570   See Neal Robinson, *Christ in Islam and Christianity*, (Albany, State University of New York Press, 1991), p. 32; Oddbjorn Leirvik ed., *Images of Jesus Christ in Islam*, (New York, Bloomsbury Publishing PLC, 2010), p. 23ff

571   See Toshihiko Izutsu, *Ethico-Religious Concepts in the Qur'án*, (Montreal, McGill-Queen's University Press, 2002)

572   See Juniper B. Carol ed., *Mariology*, (Milwaukee, Bruce Publishing Company, 1954), v. 1, p. 7ff

573   John N. D. Kelly, *Early Christian Doctrines*, p.311

574   Edward R. Hardy, ed., *Christology of the Later Fathers* (Westminster John Knox Press, 1954), p.353.

575   George Sale, *The Koran*, IX Edition of 1923 (J.B. Lippincott Company, London), p.25.

576   Edward Gibbon, *The History of the Decline and Fall of the Roman Empire* (Penguin Books, 1994), p.177.

577   See Parrinder, *Jesus in the Quran*, p. 134-35

578   See Mark Miravalle S. T. D. ed., *Mariology, A Guide for Priests, Deacons, Seminarians and Consecrated Persons*, (Goleta, CA, Seat of Wisdom Books, 2007), p. 167ff; Stephen Benko, *The Virgin Godess, Studies in the Pagan and Christian Roots of Mariology*, (Leiden, Brill, 2004), p. 196ff. "Three conclusions can be made from this view of Mary's unique associadon with Jesus: First, she has a share in the work of redemption which Christ accomplished. This means that Mary is Co-redemptnx with Jesus, who is the Redeemer. Secondly, Mary is a Mediatrix between mankind and Jesus, and thirdly, she is the Dispensatrix of all graces. These are not offical articles of faith but theses, which are very often used by Mariologists when they try to define Mary's role in the economy of salvation. " Benko, p. 222

579   "O People of the Book! Commit no excesses in your religion: nor say of Allah aught but the truth. Christ Jesus the son of Mary was (no more than) a messenger from Allah, and His Word, which He bestowed on Mary, and a spirit proceeding from Him: so believe in Allah and His Messengers. Say not "Three": desist: It will be better for you: For Allah is One God: Glory be to Him: (Far Exalted is He) above having a son. To Him belong all things in the heavens and on earth. And enough is Allah as a Disposer of affairs" [Quran 4:171].

"They surely disbelieve who say: Lo! Allah is the Messiah, son of Mary. The Messiah (himself) said: O Children of Israel, worship Allah, my Lord and your Lord. Lo! Who so ascribeth partners unto Allah, for him Allah hath forbidden paradise. His abode is the Fire. For evil-doers there will be no helpers. They surely disbelieve who say: Lo! Allah is the third of three; when there is no God save the One God. If they desist not from so saying a painful doom will fall on those of them who disbelieve. Will they not rather turn unto Allah and seek forgiveness of Him? For Allah is Forgiving, Merciful. The Messiah, son of Mary, was no other than a messenger, messengers (the like of whom) had passed away before him. And his mother was a saintly woman. And they both used to eat (earthly) food. See how We make the revelations clear for them, and see how they are turned away!"(5:72-75)

The Quran came as a rectifier of the trinitarian excesses against God. Hence, Allah revealed the Book (al-Quran) to His servant (Muhammad) "that He may warn those who say, "Allah hath begotten a son": no knowledge have they of such a thing, nor had their fathers. It is a grievous thing that issues from their mouths as a saying. What they say is nothing but falsehood" (18:4-5). The Prophet was asked to employ different arguments to bring the point across: "Say: "Praise be to Allah, Who begets no son, and has no partner in (His) dominion: nor (needs) He any to protect Him from humiliation: yea, magnify Him for His greatness and glory!" (17:111). "Say: "If the Most Gracious had a son, I would be the first to worship." Glory to the Lord of the heavens and the earth, the lord of the Throne He transcends the things they attribute to Him" (43:81-2). To the Quran, the most serious sin one can commit is the claim that God has begotten a son.

They say: "The Most Gracious has betaken a son!" Indeed ye have put forth a thing most monstrous! At it the skies are about to burst, the earth to split asunder, and the mountains to fall down in utter ruin, that they attributed a son to The Most Gracious. For it is not consonant with majesty of The Most Gracious that He should beget a son. Not one of the beings in the heavens and the earth but must come to The Most Gracious as a servant. (19:88-93).

580   Parrinder, *Jesus in Quran*, p. 135

581   See G. T. Stokes, "Sabellianism," ed. William Smith and Henry Wace, *A Dictionary of Christian Biography,* Literature, Sects and Doctrines (London: John Murray, 1877–1887), 567.

582   See Tyron Inbody, *The Faith of the Christian Church*, (Cambridge, William B. Eerdmans, 2005), p. 363

583   J. P. Moreland and W. Lane Craig, *"The Trinity"* in Michael Rea, *Oxford Readings in Philosophical Theology*, (Oxford, Oxford University Press, 2009), v. 1, p. 25

584   Jaroslav Pelikan, *The Christian Tradition: A History of the Development of Doctrine* (Chicago; London: University of Chicago Press, 1971), vol.1, p.179

585   Paul Tillich, *A History of Christian Thought*, Carl E. Braaten, ed. (New York: Simon & Schuster, 1968), p.65.

586   See John Hick, *"Islam and Christian Monotheism"* in Dan Cohn-Sherbok (eds.), *Islam in a World of Diverse Faiths*, (London, Palgrave Macmillan UK, 1997), p. 8; also Richard Cross, *"Two Models of the Trinity?"* in Michael Rea ed., Oxford Readings in Philosophical Theology, v. 1, p. 107ff

587   See details in *Augustine, The Trinity*. Translated by Stephen McKenna in *The Fathers of the Church: A New Translation*, vol. 45. (Washington, DC: The

Catholic University of America Press, 1963)

588   See Patricia Fox, *God as Communion*, (Collegeville, Minnesota: The Liturgical Press, 2001)

589   See Richard Cross, *"Two Models of the Trinity?"*, p. 107

590   Richard Cross, *"Two Models of the Trinity?"*, p. 108

591   Moreland and Craig, *"The Trinity"*, p. 30

592   Moreland and Craig, *"The Trinity"*, p. 34

593   Karl Rahner, *The Trinity*, translated by Joseph Donceel, (London, Burns and Oates, 1986), p. 19

594   See Dale Tuggy, *Divine deception, identity, and Social Trinitarianism*, Religious Studies / Volume 40 / Issue 03 / September 2004, pp 269 – 287; C. Stephen Layman 'Tritheism and Trinity', Faith and Philosophy, 5 (1988), 291–298, esp. 293–295; Cornelius Plantinga 'The threeness/oneness problem of the Trinity', *Calvin Theological Journal*, 23 (1988), 37–53, esp. 50–53; idem 'Social Trinity and tritheism', in Ronald J. Feenstra and Cornelius Plantinga (eds) *Trinity, Incarnation and Atonement : Philosophical and Theological Essays* (Notre Dame IN: University of Notre Dame Press, 1989), 21–47, esp. 27–37; Richard Swinburne *The Christian God* (New York, Oxford University Press, 1994), 180–189.

595   Edward R. Hardy ed., *Christology of the Later Fathers*, (Louisville, Westminster John Knox Press, 2006), p. 266

596   Richard Swinburne, *Was Jesus God?* (Oxford, Oxford University Press, 2008), p. 32

597   Justin Martyr in *The Early Christian Fathers*, translated by Henry Bettenson, (Oxford, Oxford University Press, 1969), p.59; see also G. R. Evans ed., *The First Christian Theologians*, (Oxford, Blackwell, 2004), p. 115ff

598   Brian Leftow, "Anti Social Trinitarianism," in *The Trinity*, ed. Stephen T. Davis, Daniel Kendall and Gerald O'Collins, (Oxford: Oxford University Press, 1999), p. 232.

599   Moreland and Craig, *"The Trinity"*, p. 36

600   Hick, *"Islam and Christian Monotheism"*, p. 8

601   See David Thomas, *"Trinity: in Encyclopedia of the Quran*, ed. Jane Dammen McAuliffe (Leiden: Brill, 2001-2006), v. 5,p. 371-72

602   Rahner, *The Trinity*, p. 42-43

603   Rahner, *The Trinity*, p. 17

604   See *Christians at the Heart of Islamic Rule*, ed. By David Thomas, (Leiden-Boston Brill, 2003), p. 23ff

605   Richard Cross, *"Two Models of the Trinity?"*, p. 114

606   Rahner, *The Trinity*, p. 43

607   Moreland and Craig, *"The Trinity"*, p. 37

608   Brian Leftow, *"Anti Social Trinitarianism,"* p. 221

609   Karl Rahner, *Theological Investigations*, translated by Kohl Margaret, London, Darton, (Longman & Todd, 1981), v. 17, p. 105

610   Block, *Philoponian Monophysitism*, p. 25

611   Block, *Philoponian Monophysitism*, p. 26

612   Block, *Philoponian Monophysitism*, p. 21

613   Block, *Philoponian Monophysitism*, p. 22

614   Block, *Philoponian Monophysitism*, p. 23

615   Block, *Philoponian Monophysitism*, p. 24

616   See Robert Morey, *The Islamic Invasion: Confronting the World's Fastest Growing Religion*, (Eugene, Oregon, Harvest House Publishers, 1992), pp. 152-153; P. Schaff, *History of the Christian Church*, (Grand Rapids, MI, Christian Classics Ethereal Library, 2002), Volume IV, Chapter III, *"Mohammedanism in its Relation to Christianity"*, p.110ff; Bell's *Introduction to the Quran*, revised by Montgomery Watt, (Edinburgh, Edinburgh University Press, 1977), Chapter 9, *"The Doctrines of the Quran"*.

617   See details in David Thomas, *"Trinity"* in J. D. McAuliffe ed., The Encyclopedia of the Quran, v. 5, p. 369

618   Parrinder, *Jesus in Quran*, p. 133

619   Parrinder, *Jesus in Quran*, p. 137

620   OddbjÃ Leirviked., *Images of Jesus Christ in Islam*, p. 24

621   David Thomas, *Trinity*, in Encyclopedia of Quran, p. 369

622   David Thomas, *Trinity*, in Encyclopedia of Quran, p. 369

623   Lewis Ayers, *Nicaea and Its Legacy, An Approach to Fourth Century Trinitarian Theology*, (Oxford, Oxford University Press, 2004), p. 344ff

624   Ayers, *Nicaea and Its Legacy* p. 186

625   Ayers, *Nicaea and Its Legacy* p. 344; see for modern interpretations of divine mystery Nicholas Lash, *Easter in Ordinary: Reflections on Human Experience and the Knowledge of God* (Notre Dame: Univ. of Notre Dame, 1990), 231-42

626   Kenneth Cragg, *The Call of the Minaret*, (Maryknoll, NY: Orbis Books, 1985), p. 263-64

627   Rahner, *Trinity*, p. 99ff

628   See Kenneth Cragg, *Jesus and the Muslim: An Exploration* (London: Allen & Unwin, 1985; reprint Oxford: Oneworld, 1999)

629   See Paul of Antioch's *Letter to a Muslim Friend*, as quoted in Thomas F. Michel, *A Muslim Theologian's Response to Christianity: Ibn Taymiyya's Al-*

Jawab al-Sahih (Delmar, NY: Caravan Books, 1984); H. Griffith, Theodore Abu⁻ Qurrah: *The Intellectual Profile of an Arab Christian Writer of the First Abbasid Century,* (Tel Aviv: Tel Aviv University, 1992); Mark N. Swanson, The Trinity in Muslim-Christian Conversation, *Dialog: A Journal of Theology.* Volume 44, Number 3. Fall 2005

630   Thomas ed., *Christians at the Heart of Islamic Rule*, p. 238

631   Thomas ed., *Christians at the Heart of Islamic Rule*, p. 238

632   Thomas, *Christians at the Heart of Islamic Rule*, p. 239

633   See Richard Dawkins, *The God Delusion*, (New York, Bantam, 2006), p.33ff

634   See Paul D. Molnar, *Divine Freedom and the Doctrine of the Immanent Trinity: In Dialogue with Karl Barth and Contemporary Theology* (London: T & T Clark, 2002)

635   David Thomas, *Christian Doctrines in Islamic Theology,* (Leiden, Brill, 2008), p. 15ff

636   See Michel, *A Muslim Theologian's Response to Christianity*

637   Thomas, *Christian Doctrines in Islamic Theology*, p. 32

638   See David Thomas and Barbara Roggema eds., *Christian Muslim Relations: A Biographical History*, (Leiden, Brill, 2009), v. 1; Emmanouela Grypeou, Mark N. Swanson and David R. Thomas, *The Encounter of Eastern Christianity with Early Islam*, (Leiden, Brill, 2006); David Thomas ed., *Syrian Christian Under Islam, The First Thousand Years*, Leiden, Brill, 2001; David Thomas, *The Bible in Arab Christianity*, (Leiden, Brill, 2007).

639   Neal Robinson, *Christ in Islam and Christianity*, p. 12

640   Robinson, *Christ in Islam and Christianity*, p. 13

641   Robinson, *Christ in Islam and Christianity*, p. 13-14

642   Leirvik, *Images of Jesus Christ in Islam*, p. 31

643   See D. J. Sahas, *John of Damascus on Islam, The Heresy of the Ishmaelites,* (Leiden, Brill, 1972); Sidney H. Griffith, *The Church in the Shadow of the Mosque: Christians and Muslims in the World of Islam,* (Princeton, Princeton University Press, 2007)

644   See Andrew Louth, *St. John Damascene*, (Oxford, Oxford University Press, 2002). "Christ is the word and spirit of God, then to deny that Christ is God is to deny the divinity of the word and spirit of God, as a result of which John calls the Muslims in turn 'mutilators' [of God] (the question of the created or uncreated status of God's word and spirit is discussed at greater length in the Dispute)." Louth, p. 79

645   See Robinson, *Christ in Islam and Christianity*, p. 10-11; See Daniel A. Madigan, "Mutual Theological Hospitality: Doing Theology in the Presence of the "Other" in Waleed El Ansari and David K. Linnan eds., *Muslim and Christian Understanding: Theory and Application of "A Common Word"*, (New York,

Palgrave Macmillan, 2010), p. 63-64

646   Madigan, *"Mutual Theological Hospitality: Doing Theology in the Presence of the "Other"*, p. 63; also see Samir Khalil Samir, *"The Quranic Non-Crucifixion"*, in Gabriel Said Reynolds ed., *The Quran in Its Historical Context*, (New York, Routledge, 2007), p. 156

647   See Harry A. Wolfson, *The Philosophy of the Kalam*, (Cambridge, Massachusetts, Harvard University Press, 1976), p. 307-309

648   See David Thomas, "The Doctrine of the Trinity in the Early Abbasid Era" *in Islam Interpretations of Christianity* edited by Lloyd Ridgeon, (New York, St. Martin Press, 2001), 83ff

649   Robinson, *Christ in Islam and Christianity*, p. 14

650   Leirvik, *Images of Jesus Christ in Islam*, p. 24

651   See Richard L. Longenecker, *The Christology of Early Christianity,* (Naperville, IL, Alec R. Allenson Inc. 1970), p. 106; Michael S. Horton, *Lord and Servant: A Covenant Christology,* (London, Westminster John Knox Press, 2005)

652   Leirvik, *Images of Jesus Christ in Islam*, p. 28

653   Leirvik, *Images of Jesus Christ in Islam*, p. 29

654   David Thomas, *Trinity*, in Encyclopedia of Quran , p. 370

655   David Thomas, *Trinity*, in Encyclopedia of Quran , p. 369

656   See David Thomas, *Anti-Christian Polemic in Early Islam,* Abu Isa al-Warra'q Against the Trinity, (Cambridge, Oriental Publications, 2002); also see S. K. Samir and J. S. Nielsen eds., *Christian-Arabic Apologetics During the Abbasid Period*, (Leiden, Brill, 1994)

657   See Abu Bakr Muhammad Ibn al-Tayyib, al-Baqilani, *Tawhid al-wa'il wa Talkhi's al-Dala'il*, (Beirut, Mu'assasat al-Kutub al-Thaqa'fiyyah, 1987); Qadi 'ABDAL-JABBAR, Abu al-Hasan, *al-Mughni fi Abwab al-Tawhid wa al-'Adl* (Volume: 5), Mahmud Muhammed al-Khudayri (ed.), (Cairo: al-Dar al-Misriyya, 1958); *Sharh al-'Usul al-Khamsa,* 'Abd al-Karim Uthman (ed.), (Cairo: Maktaba Wahba, 1965); *Critique of Christian Origins: Tathbit Dala'il al-Nubuwwa,* G. Said Reynolds- S. Khalil Samir (ed., trans.), (Provo: Brigham Young University Press, 2010); David Thomas "Early Muslim Responses to Christianity" in *Christians at the Heart of Islamic Rule*, p. 231-254; Ivor M. Beaumont, *Christology in Dialogue with Muslims: A Critical Analysis of Christian Presentations of Christ for Muslims from the Ninth and Twentieth Centuries*, (Oxford, Regnum Studies in Mission, 2005); Taqī al-Dīn Ibn Taymīyah, *Al-Jawāb al-Ṣaḥīḥli-man Baddala Dīn al-Masīḥ,* ed. 'Alī Ibn Ḥasan Ibn Nāṣir et al. (Riyadh, Dar al-A'asimah,1999); David Thomas, *A Muslim Theologian's Response to Christianity: Ibn Taymiyya's Al-Jawab Al-Sahih* (Studies in Islamic Philosophy and Science), (New York, Caravan Books, 1985); Ibn Taymiyyah, *Answering Those Who Altered the Religion of Jesus Christ,* abridged by Ash-Shahhat Ahmad al-Tahhan, Bryn Translation Services, Umm al-Qura Publishing; Abu Muhammad Ali Ibn Ahmad Ibn Hazm, *Al-Fasl fi al-Milal wa*

al-Ahwa' wa al-Nihal, (Jeddah: Sharikat Maktabat 'Uka'z, 1982); David Thomas, *Christians at the Heart of Islamic Rule*, p. 236-254

658　Muhammad Asad, *The Message of the Quran*, p. 156

659　Godron D. Newby, "Arabia, Pre-Islam" in the *Encyclopedia of Islam and the Muslim World*, (New York, Macmillan, 2003), v.1, p. 55

660　Asad, *The Message*, p. 487

661　Asad, *The Message*, p. 522-523

662　See details in Lecky, *History of the Rise and Influence of the Spirit of Rationalism in Europe*, v. 1, p. 92ff

663　G. Parrinder, *Jesus in the Quran*, p. 171

664　Parrinder, *Jesus in Quran*, p. 170-71

665　See Muhammad 'Ata' ur Rahim and Ahmad Thompson, *Jesus, Prophet of Islam*, (London, Ta-Ha Publishers, n. d.), chapter 9, p. 249ff

666　See Karl Barth, *The Doctrine of the Word of God* (Edinburgh: T & T Clark, 1956); Rudolf K. Bultmann, "New Testament and Mythology," Kerygma and Myth, Hans W. Bartsch, ed., R. H. Fuller, trans., 2nd edn. (London: Oxford University Press, 1964); John Hick ed., *The Myth of God Incarnate*, (London, SCM Press, 1977)

667　Richard C. Martin, *Islam, A Cultural Perspective*, (New Jersey: Prentice-Hall, 1982), p. 92

668　See Amitabh Pal, *Islam Means Peace*, (Oxford, Praeger, 2011)

669　I am indebted to Isma'il Faruqi's discussion of the topic.

670　Charles Le Gai Eaton, *Islam and the Destiny of Man* (Albany: State University of New York Press, 1985), p.52.

671　Sayyid Abul A'la Mawdudi, *Four Basic Quranic Terms*, Abu Asad, trans., 2nd edn. (Lahore: Islamic Publications Ltd., 1982), p.10.

672　See Calvert Watkins, ed., *The American Heritage Dictionary of Indo-European Roots*, 2nd ed., (New York, Houghton Mifflin Co., 2000).

673　See https://en.wikipedia.org/wiki/Allah, accessed on April 24, 2017

674　The translation is from Abdullah Y. Ali, *The Holy Quran* (Medina: King Fahd Holy Quran Printing Complex, 1989).

675　Mawdudi, *Towards Understanding the Quran*, translated by Zafar Ishaq Ansari, (Markfield, Islamic Foundation, 1995), vol.1, p.196; see more details about the verse Mahmoud M. Ayoub, *The Quran and its Interpreters* (Albany: SUNY, 1984), vol.1, pp.245 ff.

676　Ismail R. al-Faruqi, *Al-Tawhid: Its Implications for Thought and Life*, 2nd edn., (Virginia: International Institute of Islamic Thought, 1992), pp.9-10.

677　The terms "Allāh al-Waḥīd" and "Ilāh Waḥīd" have been used in the Quran

21 times.

678 See S. Maḥmūd al-Alusī, *Rūḥ al-Maānī* (Multan: Maktabah Imdādiyyah, n.d.), vol.15, p.314.

679 Abū Bakr Aḥmad ibn al-Ḥusayn ibn ʿAlī al-Bayhaqī, *Kitāb al-Asmāʾ wa al-Ṣifāt* (Beirut: Dār Iḥyāʾ al-Turāth al-ʿArabī, n.d.), p.32.

680 Al-Ragib al-Isfahānī, *Muʾjam Mufradāt Alfāç al-Quran* (Beirut: Dār al-Kitāb al-ʿArabī, 1972), p.294.

681 Asad, *The Message of the Quran*, p.1124.

682 Asad, Ibid.

683 The word ahl al-tawḥīd has ocurred in the hadith of Jābir ibn ʿAbd Allah. See Imam Tirmazī, *Saḥīḥ Sunan al-Tirmazī*, M. N. al-Albani, ed., 1ˢᵗ edn. (Gulf States: Maktabah al-Tarbiyyah al-ʿArabī, 1988), vol.2, p.323; and Imam Tirmazī, *Sunan al-Timazī*, Ahmad Shakir, ed. (Beirut: Dār Iḥyāʾ al-Turāth al-ʿArabī, n.d.), hadith no.2737. When the Prophet sent Muʿādh ibn Jabal as governor of Yemen in 9 AH, he told him, "You will be going to Christians and Jews (ahl al-Kitāb), so the first thing you should invite them to is the assertion of the oneness of Allah (Yuwaḥḥidu Allāh)." See al-Bukhārī, *Ṣaḥīḥ*, vol.22, p.363, hadith no.6824.

684 Very often this division is attributed to Ibn Taymiyyah and his school of thought and many scholars do not take it as a standard. But we see it in its embryonic stage in a number of earlier works. It is not that elaborate as is the case with later theological treatises but its seed is very much visible. See for instance Abū Muḥammad ʿAbd Allah ibn Abū Zayd al-Qayrawānī (died 386 AH), *Kitāb al-Jāmiʾ fī al-Sunan wa al-Adab wa al-Maghāzī wa al-Tārīkh*, M. Abu al-Ajfan, Uthman Battikh, eds. (Beirut: Muʾassasah al-Risālah, 1983), pp.107-10; and also see Ibn Khuzaymah, *Kitāb al-Tawḥīd* (Cairo: Maktabah al-Kulliyyāt al-Azhariyyah, n.d.), Here we are adopting it to help us elaborate the point at discussion and not as the standard Islamic expression of the concept of tawḥīd.

685 Al-Faruqi, *al-Tawhid*, p.21.

686 Al-Faruqi, Ibid., pp.22-23; here he refers to Paul Tillich's, *Systematic Theology* (Chicago: Chicago University Press, 1957), vol.2, p.40.

687 Al-Faruqi, *al-Tawhid*, p.23.

688 I am indebted to Al-Faruqi in discussing various contours of al-Tawhid.

689 K. Cragg, *The House of Islam*, (Grand Rapid, Dickenson Publishing, 1975), p.7.

690 Cragg, *The House of Islam*, p.7.

691 George Ferguson, *Signs & Symbols in Christian Art*, (Oxford, Oxford University Press, 1996); Steven Bigham, *Image of God the Father in Orthodox Theology and Iconography*, Torrance, (CA, Oakwood Publications,1995); Titus Burckhardt, *The Foundations of Christian Art*, (Bloomington, Indiana, World Wisdom, 2006)

692   Mohammed Hamdouni Alami, *Art and Architecture in the Islamic Tradition*, (New York, I. B. Tauris, 2011); Annette Hagedorn and Avinoam Shalem, *Facts and Artefacts: Art in the Islamic World*, (Leiden, Brill, 2007)

693   Al-Faruqi, *al-Tawhid*, pp.24-25; also see his artical *"Islam and Art,"* Studia Islamica, fasciculi XXXVII (1973), pp.81-109; and his *"Misconceptions of the Nature of the Work of Art in Islam,"* Islam and the Modern Age (May, 1970), vol.1, no.1; and his *"On the Nature of Art in Islam,"* Islam and the Modern Age (August, 1976), vol.1, no.2,; and his *"Divine Transcendence and Its Expression,"* World Faiths (Spring, 1979), vol.17; Thomas W. Arnold, *Painting in Islam* (Oxford: Clarendon Press, 1928); Richard Ettinghausen, *The Characted of Islamic Art in the Arab Heritage*, N. A. Faris, ed. (Princeton: Princeton University Press, 1944).

694   Al-Faruqi, *al-Tawhid*, p.14; I am heavily indebted to al-Faruqi in this aspect of al-Tawhid's discussion. See for details ibid., pp.9-16.

695   Izutsu, *God and Man* in the Koran, p.76.

696   Al-Faruqi, *al-Tawhid*, p.33

697   Al-Faruqi, *al-Tawhid*, p.33.

698   See John E. Kelsay's doctoral thesis titled *"Religion and Morality in Islam"* (Chalottesville: University of Virginia, 1985); F. Carney, "Some Aspects of Islamic Ethics," *Journal of Religion* (1983), vol.63, part.2, pp.159-74; Richard M. Frank, "Moral Obligation in Classical Muslim Theology," *Journal of Religious Ethics* (1983), vol.11, no.2, pp.204-23; for a general study Paul Helm, ed., *Divine Commands and Moral Requirements* (Oxford: Oxford University Press, 1981); Marshall G. S. Hodgson, *The Venture of Islam* (Chicago: Chicago University Press, 1974), vols.1-2; Janine M. Idziak, ed., *Divine Command Theory* (New York: Mellen Press, 1979); Wilferd Madelung, *"Early Sunni Doctrine Concerning Faith,"* Studia Islamica (1970), vol.32, pp.233-54; Fazlur Rahman, "Some Key Ethical Concepts of the Quran," *Journal of Religious Ethics* (1983), vol.11, no.2, pp.170-85; and A. Kevin Reinhart, "Islamic Law as Islamic Ethics," *Journal of Religious Ethics* (1983), vol.11, no.2, pp.186-203; Majid Khadduri, *The Islamic Conception of Justice* (Baltimore: The John Hopkin University Press, 1984).

699   See for details Fazlur Rahman, *Major Theme of the Quran*, (Minneapolis, Bibliotheca Islamica, 1994), chs.1-3.

700   See for details Abū Isḥāq Ibrāhīm ibn Mūsā al-Shāṭibī, *al-Muwāfaqāt fī Usūl al-Sharīʿah*, 3rd edn. (Cairo: al-Maktabah al-Tijāriyyah al-Kubrā, 1975), vol.3, p.118; Mahmud Shaltut, *al-Islām ʿAqīdah wa Sharīʿah* (Cairo: Dār al-Qalam, 1966), p.29; M. Qutb, Madhāhib Fikriyyah Muʿāâarah, 1st edn. (Beirut: Dār al-Sharq, 1983), p.13.

701   See Herald Coward, *Sin and Salvation in the World Religions: A Short Introduction*, (Oxford, Oneworld, 2003)

702   See Imam Feisal Abdul Rauf, *What is Right With Islam*, (New York, HarperCollins, 2004), p. 45ff

703   See Toshihiko Izutsu, *Ethico-Religious Concepts in the Qur'ān*, Fazlur Rahman, *Major Themes of the Quran*

704   See Mohammad Omar Farooq, *Towards Our Reformation: From Legalism to Value-Oriented Islamic Law and Jurisprudence*, (London, International Institute of Islamic Thought, 2011), p. 36ff; for a different perspective see Jacques Ellul, *Islam and Judeo-Christianity: A Critique of Their Commonality*, Translated by D. Bruce MacKay, (Eugene, OR, Cascade Books, 2015), p. 69ff

705   Black, *History of Islamic Political Thought*, p. 13

706   Kate Zebiri, "Argumentation" in Andrew Rippin ed., *The Blackwell Companion to the Quran*, (Oxford, Blackwell Publishing Ltd, 2006), p. 267

707   Zebiri, *"Argumentation"*, p. 266

708   Zebiri, *"Argumentation"*, p. 268

709   Zebiri, *"Argumentation"*, p. 268

710   Rosalind Ward Gwynne, *Logic, Rhetoric and Legal Reasoning in the Quran: God's Arguments*, (New York, Routledge, 2004), p. i

711   Gwynne, *Logic, Rhetoric and Legal Reasoning in the Quran*, p. ix

712   John Walbridge, *God and Logic in Islam: The Caliphate of Reason*, (Cambridge University Press, Cambridge, 2011), p. 16

713   Walbridge, *God and Logic in Islam*, p. 19

714   Walbridge, *God and Logic in Islam*, p. 20-21

715   Walbridge, *God and Logic in Islam*, p. 21

716   John Spurr, "Rational Religion" in Restoration England, *Journal of the History of Ideas,* Vol. 49, No. 4 (Oct. - Dec., 1988), pp. 563-585; p. 564

717   See Spurr, *"Rational Religion" in Restoration England*

718   Spurr, *"Rational Religion" in Restoration England*, p. 563

719   Walbridge, *God and Logic in Islam*, p. 22

720   Walbridge, *God and Logic in Islam*, p. 23

721   Walbridge, *God and Logic in Islam*, p. 23

722   Walbridge, *God and Logic in Islam*, p. 23

723   Walbridge, *God and Logic in Islam*, p. 24

724   Walbridge, *God and Logic in Islam*, p. 16

725   R. J. *Sternberg, Cognitive Psychology. (Belmont, CA: Wadsworth., 2009), p. 578*; David Zarefsky, *Argumentation: The Study of Effective Reasoning*, (Chantilly, VA, The Teaching Company, 2002), part 1, p. 7ff

726   See Zarefsky, *Argumentation: The Study of Effective Reasoning*, Part 1, p. 5ff

727   See *Henrique Jales Ribeiro, Systematic approaches to argument by analogy,*

(New York: Springer Verlag, *2014), pp. 23–40;* Zarefsky, Argumentation: The Study of Effective Reasoning, Part 1, p.13ff

728   See W. B. Hallaq, *The Origins and Evolution of Islamic Law,* (Cambridge, Cambridge University Press, 2005), p. 114ff

729   For details of Quranic type of reasoning see http://www.quran-miracle.info/ Quran-Reasoning.htm

730   Zebiri, *"Argumentation",* p. 272

731   Zebiri, *"Argumentation",* p. 270

732   Zebiri, *"Argumentation",* p. 272

733   Gwynne, *Logic, Rhetoric and Legal Reasoning in the Quran,* p. 192

734   Gwynne, *Logic, Rhetoric and Legal Reasoning in the Quran,* p. 206

735   Gwynne, *Logic, Rhetoric and Legal Reasoning in the Quran,* p. 204

736   Gwynne, *Logic, Rhetoric and Legal Reasoning in the Quran,* p. 206

737   Gwynne, *Logic, Rhetoric and Legal Reasoning in the Quran,* p. 206

738   Gwynne, *Logic, Rhetoric and Legal Reasoning in the Quran,* p. x

739   Shabbir Akhtar, *Islam As Political Religion,* (New York, Routledge, 2011), p. 189

740   Izutsu, *God and Man,* p. 144

741   Akhtar, *Islam As Political Religion,* p. 188

742   Akhtar, *Islam As Political Religion,* p. 196

743   A. J. Arberry, *Revelation and Reason in Islam,* (New York, Routledge, 2008), p. 14

744   Arberry, *Revelation and Reason in Islam,* p. 15

745   Binyamin Abrahamov, *"Theology"* in Rippin ed., *Blackwell Companion to the Quran,* p. 427ff ; also B. Abrahamov, *Islamic Theology, Traditionalism and Rationalism,* (Edinburgh, Edinburgh University Press, 1998)

746   See Hamid Naseem, *Muslim Philosophy. Science and Mysticism,* (New Delhi, Sarup & Sons, 2001); also his *The Attitude of Islam Towards Science and Philosophy,* (New Delhi, Sarup & Sons, 2003)

747   D. A. Madigan, *The Quran's Self-image.* (Princeton, Princeton University Press, 2001), p.149-150; also see Rippin ed., *Blackwell Companion to Quran,* p. 285ff

748   See Hashim Kamali, "Shari'a, Goals and Objectives of", in Muhammad in *History, Thought, and Culture: An Encyclopedia of the Prophet of God,* edited by Coeli Fitzpatrick and Adam Hani Walker, (Santa Barbara, ABC-CLIO, 2014), Vol. II, pp. 552–557.

749   Imam Feisal Abdul Rauf, *Defining Islamic Statehood, Measuring and Indexing Contemporary Muslim States,* (London, Palgrave Macmillan, 2015), p. 67ff

750   Amina Wadud, "Freedom and Responsibility: An Islamic Perspective" in *Freedom and Responsibility, Christian and Muslim Explorations* edited by

Simone Sinn and Martin L. Sinaga, (Minneapolis, Luther University Press, 2010), p. 27

751 See Abdullah Saeed, *Freedom of Religion,* Apostasy and Islam, (New York, Routledge, 2004)

752 Donner, *Muhammad and the Believers*, p. 69

753 Donner, *Muhammad and the Believers*, p. 69-70

754 See M. H. Khalil (ed.), *Between Heaven and Hell: Islam, Salvation, and the Fate of Others,* Oxford, (Oxford University Press, 2013)

755 Muhammad Asad, *The Message of the Qura'n,* (Gibraltar, Dar Al-Andlus, 1980), p. 31, note 50.

756 Donner, *Muhammad and the Believers*, p. 70

757 Muhammad b. Jarir al Tabari, *Jami' al Bayan 'an Ta'wi'l Ay al Quran,* translated in English by J. Cooper, (Oxford, Oxford University Press, 1989), P. 364

758 Fazlur Rahman, *Major Theme of the Quran*, p.166

759 See Rashid Rida, *Tafseer al-Quran al Hakeem,* (Cairo, Dar al-Manar, 1367 A.H.), pp-70-74

760 Muhammad Asad, *Ibid*, p. 95, note:85

761 Donner, *Muhammad and the Believers*, p. 70

762 B. Lewis, *The Jews of Islam,* (Oxford, Princeton University Press, 1987), p. 13

763 Jacques Waardenburg ed., *Muslim Perceptions of Other Religions*, (Oxford, Oxford University Press, 1999), p. 6

764 Jane McAuliffe, *Quranic Christians*, p. 93

765 Kate Zebiri, *Muslims and Christians Face to Face,* (Oxford, Oneworld, 2003), p. 16

766 See Charles Anthony Cimball, *Striving Together in the Way of God: Muslim Participation in Christian-Muslim Dialogue,* UMI Dissertation Services, 1996, p. 31ff; also Kate Zebiri, *Muslims and Christians Face to Face,* p. 15ff

767 McAuliffe, *Quranic Christians*, p. 287

768 McAuliffe, *Quranic Christians*, p. 287

769 McAuliffe, *Quranic Christians*, p. 290

770 McAuliffe, *"Christians in the Quran and Tafsi'r"*, p. 115

771 McAuliffe, "Christians in the Quran and Tafsi'r" in *Muslim Perceptions of Other Religions edited by Jacques Waardenburg*, p. 105

772 Waardenburg, *Muslim Perceptions of Other Religions*, p. 9

773 Waardenburg, *Muslim Perceptions of Other Religions*, p. 9

774 Asma Afsaruddin, "In Defense of All Houses of Worship? Jihad in the

Context of Interfaith Relations" in Sohail H. Hashmi ed., *Just Wars, Holy Wars and Jihads: Christian, Jewish and Muslim Encounters and Exchanges*, (Oxford, Oxford University Press, 2012), p. 47

775   Afsaruddin, *"In Defense of All Houses of Worship?"*, p. 50

776   Afsaruddin, *"In Defense of All Houses of Worship?"*, p. 65

777   Leslie Holden (ed.), *Jesus in History, Thought and Culture: An Encyclopedia*, (Oxford, ABC CLIO, 2003)

778   Jane D. McAuliffe, *Quranic Christians*, p. 204

779   Antony Black, *The West and Islam, Religion and Political Thought in World History*, (Oxford, Oxford University Press, 2008), p. 13; also see Crone, *God's Rule*, p. 8-9

780   Black, *History of Islamic Political Thought*, p. 11

781   Black, *History of Islamic Political Thought*, p. 11

782   Michael Cook, *Forbidding Wrong In Islam: An Introduction*, (Cambridge, Cambridge University Press, 2003); also his *Commanding Right and Forbidding Wrong in Islamic Thought*, (Cambridge, Cambridge University Press, 2004)

783   Michael Cook, *Muhammad*, (Oxford, Oxford University Press, 1996), p. 44

784   N. J. Coulson, *A History of Islamic Law*, (Edinburgh, Edinburgh, University Press, 1964, p. 9

785   Black, *History of Islamic Political Thought*, p. 11

786   Black, *History of Islamic Political Thought*, p. 11

787   Black, *History of Islamic Political Thought*, p. 12

788   See Wael B. Hallaq, *A History of Islamic Legal Theories*, (Cambridge, Cambridge University Press, 1997), p. 125ff

789   Hallaq, *A History of Islamic Legal Theories*, p. 125

790   See Hallaq, *A History of Islamic Legal Theories*, p. 127 ff

791   See Abdul Hamid A. Abu Sulayman, *The Quranic World View, A Springboard for Cultural Reform*, (London, International Institute of Islamic Thought, 2011), p. 63ff

792   See Birgit Krawietz, "Justic as a Pervasive Principle in Islamic Law" in *Islam and the Rule of Law* edited by Birgit Krawietz and Helmut Reifeld, (Berlin, Konrad-Adenauer-Stiftung, 2008), p. 35-48; Mahmoud Ayuob, "The Islamic Concept of Justic" in *Islamic Identity and the Struggle for Justice* edited by Nimat Hafez Barazangi, (Miami, University of Florida Press, 1996), p. 19-26

793   Lawrence Rosen, *The Justice of Islam*, (Oxford, Oxford University Press, 2002), p. x

794   Rosen, *The Justice of Islam*, p. 96

795   Rosen, *The Justice of Islam*, p. 96-97; see also K. Cragg, Counsels in
       Contemporary Islam, (Edinburgh, Edinburgh University Press, 1965), p. 186ff

796   For an introduction to Islamic law see Wael B. Hallaq, *An Introduction to
       Islamic Law*, (Cambridge, Cambridge University Press, 2009)

797   Black, *History of Islamic Political Thought*, p. 12

798   See Imam Feisal Abdul Rauf, *What is Right With Islam,* p. 45ff

799   See Toshihiko Izutsu, *Ethico-Religious Concepts in the Qur'án*

800   See Mohammad Omar Farooq, *Towards Our Reformation: From Legalism to
       Value-Oriented Islamic Law and Jurisprudence*, London, p. 36ff; for a different
       perspective see Jacques Ellul, *Islam and Judeo-Christianity: A Critique of Their
       Commonality*, p. 69ff

801   See Bryn S. Turner ed., *Islam: Critical Concepts in Sociology,* (New York,
       Routledge, 2004), p. 169ff

802   Sayed Khatab and Gary D. Bouma, *Democracy in Islam*, (New York,
       Routledge, 2007), p. 12

803   See Sayed Khatab and Gary D. Bouma, *Democracy in Islam,* p. 12-13; also
       John N. Figgis, *The Divine Right of Kings,* (Cambridge, Cambridge University
       Press, 1914)

804   Black, *The West and Islam, Religion and Political Thought in World History*, p. 16

805   Jacques-Benigne Bossuet, *Politics drawn from the Very Words of Holy Scripture,*
       translated and edited by Patrick Riley, (Cambridge, Cambridge University
       Press, 1990), p. 81

806   See details in *Bossuet, Politics,* p. 58ff

807   Bossuet, *Politics*, p. 87

808   Bossuet, *Politics*, p. 89

809   Bossuet, *Politics*, p. 96

810   Bossuet, *Politics*, p. 58

811   Sayed Khatab and Gary D. Bouma, *Democracy in Islam*, p. 12

812   Rose W. Lane, *The Discovery of Freedom, Man's Struggle Against Authority,*
       (New York, The John Day Company, 1943), p. 83

813   Lane, *The Discovery of Freedom,* p. 85-86

814   Black, *The West and Islam*, p. 13

815   Black, *History of Islamic Political Thought*, p. 14

816   Crone, *God's Rule*, p. 7

817   See C. G. Weeramantry, *Islamic Jurisprudence, An International Perspective,*
       (London, Macmillan Press, 1988), p. 113-125; David Pearl, *A Textbook on
       Muslim Personal Law,* (London: Croom Helm,1979), pp. 41–57, 77–84,

100–120; Sayed Khatab and Gary D. Bouma, *Democracy in Islam*, p. 24-25

818   See Muhammad Shafiq, *The Role And Place Of Shura In The Islamic Polity*, Islamabad, Islamic Studies, Vol. 23, No. 4 (Winter 1984), pp. 419-441

819   Ilyas Ahmad, The Social Contract and the Foundations of the Islamic State, *The Indian Journal of Political Science,* Vol. 4, No. 2 (October—December, 1942), pp. 132-169

820   Feisal Abdul Rauf, *Defining Islamic Statehood*, p. 63ff

821   See details in Azizah Y. al-Hibri, Islam and American Constitutional Law: Borrowing Possibilities or a History of Borrowing, University of Pennsylvania *Journal of Constitutional Law* 1.3 (1999): 492-527.

822   Sayed Khatab and Gary D. Bouma, *Democracy in Islam*, p. 18-19

823   Sayed Khatab and Gary D. Bouma, *Democracy in Islam*, p. 19

824   Sayed Khatab and Gary D. Bouma, *Democracy in Islam*, p. 19-20

825   Sayed Khatab and Gary D. Bouma, *Democracy in Islam*, p. 20

826   Sayed Khatab and Gary D. Bouma, *Democracy in Islam*, p. 20

827   J. Wellhausen, *The Arab Kingdom and Its Fall*, translated by Margaret Graham Wier, Calcutta, (Calcutta University Press, 1927), p. 8-9

828   See M. H. Kamali, *Caliphate and Political Jurisprudence in Islam: Historical and Contemporary Perspectives.* Muslim World, 106, 2016, p. 384–403. doi:10.1111/muwo.12145; For Shi'ite concept of "Deputyship of Imam" see Abdulaziz A. Sachedina, *The Just Ruler* (al-Sultan al-'Adil) in Shi'ite Islam, (Oxford, Oxford University Press, 1998), p. 29ff

829   See Hugh Kennedy, *Caliphate, The History of an Idea*, (New York, Basic Books, 2016), p. chapter 1

830   See details in Sayed Khatab and Gary D. Bouma, *Democracy in Islam*, p. 7-23

831   See Laura Etheredge (ed.), *Islamic History*, (New York, Britannica Publishing Services, 2010, p. 63-64

832   See Julius Wellhausen, *Die religiös-politischen Oppositionsparteien im alten Islam*, Berlin, 1901, esp. pp. 61-71; tr. R. C. Ostle and S. M. Walzer as *The Religious-Political Factions in Early Islam*, (Amsterdam, 1975), pp. 105-20; Wilferd Madelung, *The Succession to Muhammad: A Study of the Early Caliphate.* (Cambridge, Cambridge University Press, 1997)

833   Karen Armstrong, *Islam: A Short History*, (New York, Modern Library, 2002), p. 43; see also Crone, *God's Rule*, p. 24-25

834   See Lewis, *The Arabs in History*, p. 68

835   See Andrew Rippin, *Muslims, Their Religious Beliefs and Practices*, (New York, Routledge, 2005), p. 64

836   Armstrong, *Islam*, p. 44

837   Crone, *God's Rule*, p. 36

838   See Lewis, *The Arabs in History*, p. 66

839   Lewis, *The Arabs in History*, p. 66-67

840   Armstrong, *Islam*, p. 42

841   Lewis, *The Arabs in History*, p. 67

842   See Lewis, *The Arabs in History*, p. 69

843   See Lewis, *The Arabs in History*, p. 75

844   See Khaled Abou El Fadl, Islam and the Challenge of Democratic
       Commitment, Berkeley Electronic Press, *Fordham International Law Journal,*
       v. 27, Issue 1, 2003, Article 2

845   See Imam Feisal Abdul Rauf, *Defining Islamic Statehood*, p. 30ff

846   See Wael B. Hallaq, *The Origins and Evolution of Islamic Law,* Majid Fakhry,
       Islamic Philosophy, *Theology and Mysticism: A Short Introduction,* (Oxford,
       Oneworld, 2000)

847   Muhammad Hamidullah, *The First Written Constitution in the World: An
       Important Document of the Time of the Holy Prophet,* (Lahore, Ashraf Press,
       1975); Michael Lecker, *The Constitution of Medina: Muḥammad's First Legal
       Document.* (Princeton, NJ: Darwin, 2004); Sayed Khatab and Gary D. Bouma,
       Democracy in Islam, p. 32

848   Hamidullah, *The First Written Constitution in the World*, p. 2

849   Sayed Khatab and Gary D. Bouma, *Democracy in Islam*, p. 32

850   Sayed Khatab and Gary D. Bouma, *Democracy in Islam*, p. 33

851   Hamidullah, *The First Written Constitution in the World*, p.13

852   Sayed Khatab and Gary D. Bouma, *Democracy in Islam*, p. 33

853   Lewis, *The Arabs in History*, p. 40

854   Sayed Khatab and Gary D. Bouma, *Democracy in Islam*, p. 31. See the Quran
       'Not all of them are alike. There are among the People of the Book some
       upright men, who all night long recite the revelations of God and prostrate
       themselves in adoration; who believe in God and the Last Day; who enjoin
       justice and forbid wrong and vie with each other in good works. These are
       the righteous: whatever good they do, shall not be denied them. God knows
       the righteous' (Quran 3:113–114). 'And there are among the People of the
       Book those who truly believe in God; and in the revelation to you; and in the
       revelation to them. They humble themselves before God; and do not sell His
       revelations for a miserable gain. These shall be rewarded by their Lord. Swift
       is God's reckoning' (Quran 3:199).

855   John L. Esposito, *What Everyone Needs to Know About Islam*, (Oxford, Oxford
       University Press, 2002), p. 70

856   Esposito, *What Everyone Needs to Know About Islam*, p. 70-71

857   Lewis, *The Jews of Islam,* p. 20

858   Tamara Sonn, *Islam: A Brief History,* (Oxford, Wiley-Blackwell, 2010), p. 1

859   John L. Esposito, *What Everyone Needs to Know About Islam,* p. 71

860   Lewis, *The Jews of Islam,* p. 8

861   W. M. Watt, *Muhammad at Medina,* (Oxford, Clarendon Press, 1956), p. 241

862   Wellhausen, *Arab Kingdom,* p. 14

863   Maxime Rodinson, *Muhammad,* translated by Anne Carter, (New York, Penguin Books, 1985), p. 152

864   Michael Cook, *Muhammad,* p. 75

865   Sonn, *Islam,* p. 34-35

866   Watt, *Muhammad at Medina,* p. 244

867   Cook, *Muhammad,* p. 20

868   See the text in Watt, *Muhammad at Medina,* p. 221ff

869   Sayed Khatab and Gary D. Bouma, *Democracy in Islam,* p. 32

870   Carl W. Ernst, *Following Muhammad, Rethinking Islam in the Contemporary World,* (Chapel Hill, University of North Carolina Press, 2003), p. 89

871   Ernst, *Following Muhammad,* p. 43

872   Sayed Khatab and Gary D. Bouma, *Democracy in Islam,* p. 33

873   Uri Rubin, The "Constitution of Medina", Some Notes, Studia Islamica, No. 62 (1985), pp. 5-23, p. 12, http://www.jstor.org/stable/1595521, Accessed: 04-04-2017 22:23 UTC, JSTOR

874   Uri Rubin, *The "Constitution of Medina",* p. 13; also see M. Lecker, *The Constitution of Medina,* p. 89-91

875   Uri Rubin, *The "Constitution of Medina",* p. 13

876   Uri Rubin, *The "Constitution of Medina",* p. 10

877   Uri Rubin, *The "Constitution of Medina",* p. 16

878   Sayed Khatab and Gary D. Bouma, *Democracy in Islam,* p. 34

879   Rodinson, *Mohammed,* p. 154

880   Watt, *Muhammad at Medina,* p. 228

881   See Watt, *Muhammad at Medina,* p. 223

882   Sonn, *Islam,* p. 28

883   Hamidullah, *The First Written Constitution in the World,* p.25

Bibliography

Arberry, A. J., *Revelation and Reason in Islam*, (New York: Routledge, 2008)

Abdul Rauf, F., *Defining Islamic Statehood, Measuring and Indexing Contemporary Muslim States*, (London: Palgrave Macmillan, 2015)

Abdul Rauf, F., *What is Right with Islam*, (New York: HarperCollins, 2004)

Abrahamov, B., *Islamic Theology, Traditionalism and Rationalism*. (Edinburgh: Edinburgh University Press, 1998)

Abu Sulayman, A. A., *The Quranic World View, A Springboard for Cultural Reform*, (London: International Institute of Islamic Thought, 2011)

Akhtar, S., *Islam As Political Religion*, (New York: Routledge, 2011)

Al-Tabari, Muhammad b. Jarir, *Jami' al Bayan 'an Ta'wi'l Ay al Quran*, translated in English by J. Cooper, (Oxford: Oxford University Press, 1989)

Al-Alusī, S. Maḥmūd, *Rūḥ al-Maʿānī* (Multan: Maktabah Imdādiyyah, n.d.)

Alami, M. H., *Art and Architecture in the Islamic Tradition*, (New York: I. B. Tauris, 2011)

Al-Baqilani, Abu Bakr Muhammad Ibn al-Tayyib, *Tawhid al-wa'il wa Talkhiṣ al-Dala'il*, (Beirut: Mu'assasat al-Kutub al-Thaqa'fiyyah, 1987)

Al-Bayhaqī, Abū Bakr Aḥmad ibn al-Ḥusayn ibn ʿAlī, Kitāb *al-Asmāʾ wa al-Ṣifāt* (Beirut: Dār Iḥyāʾ al-Turāth al-ʿArabī, n.d.)

Al-Faruqi, I. R., *Al-Tawhid: Its Implications for Thought and Life*, 2nd edn., (Virginia: International Institute of Islamic Thought, 1992)

Ali, A. Y., *The Holy Quran* (Medina: King Fahd Holy Quran Printing Complex, 1989)

Al-Isfahānī, al-Ragib, *Muʿjam Mufradāt Alfāẓ al-Qurʾān* (Beirut: Dār al-Kitāb al-ʿArabī, 1972)

Al-Shāṭibī, Abū Isḥāq Ibrāhīm ibn Mūsā, *al-Muwāfaqāt fī Uṣūl al-Sharīʿah*, 3rd edn. (Cairo: al-Maktabah al-Tijāriyyah al-Kubrā, 1975)

Altizer, Thomas J. J. ed., *Toward a New Christianity*, (New York: Harcourt, Brace & World Inc., 1967)

Angus, S., *The Mystery Religions*, (New York: Dover Publications, 1975)

Ansari, Z. I. and Nawwab, I. I. eds., *The Different Aspects of Islamic Culture, The Foundations of Islam*, (Paris: UNESCO Publications, 2016)

Armstrong, K., *History of God*, (New York: Ballantine Books, 1994)

Armstrong, K., *Islam: A Short History*, (New York: Modern Library, 2002)

Asad, M., *The Message of the Quran*, (Bristol: The Book Foundation, 2003)

Ata' ur Rahim, M. and Thompson, A., *Jesus, Prophet of Islam*, (London: Ta-Ha Publishers, n. d.)

Ayers, L., *Nicaea and Its Legacy*, An Approach to Fourth Century Trinitarian Theology, (Oxford: Oxford University Press, 2004)

Bammel, E. and Moule, C. F. D. eds., *Jesus and the Politics of His Day*, (Cambridge: Cambridge University Press, 1984)

Barazangi, N. H., *Islamic Identity and the Struggle for Justice*, (Miami: University of Florida Press, 1996)

Barth, K., *God, Grace and the Gospel*, trans. James S. McNab, (Edinburgh and London: Oliver and Boyd, 1959)

Barth, K., *The Doctrine of the Word of God* (Edinburgh: T & T Clark, 1956)

Barth, K., *The Knowledge of God and the Service of God*, trans. J. L. M. Haire and Ian Henderson, (New York: Charles Scribner's Sons, 1939)

Bell, R., *The Origin of Islam in its Christian Environment: The Gunning Lectures*, (Edinburgh University, 1925, London: Cass, repr. 1968)

Benko, S., *The Virgin Godess, Studies in the Pagan and Christian Roots of Mariology*, (Leiden: Brill, 2004)

Bettenson, H. trans., *The Early Christian Fathers*, (Oxford: Oxford University Press, 1969)

Bigg, Charles, *The Christian Platonists of Alexandria*, (Oxford, Oxford University Press, 1913)

Bigham, S., *Image of God the Father in Orthodox Theology and Iconography*, (Torrance, CA: Oakwood Publications,1995)

Black, A., *The History of Islamic Political Thought: From the Prophet to the Present*, (Edinburgh: Edinburgh University Press, 2011)

Black, A., *The West and Islam, Religion and Political Thought in World History*, (Oxford: Oxford University Press, 2008)

Bloesch, D., *Christian Life and Salvation*, (Grand Rapids: Eerdmans, 1967)

Bonner, G., *St. Augustine of Hippo: Life and Controversies*, (Philadelphia: The Westminster Press, 1963)

Borg, M. J. and Crossan, J. D., *The First Paul*, (New York: Harper Collins, 2009)

Bornkamm, G., *Paul, Paulus, D. M. G. Stalker*, trans. (New York: Harper & Row, 1969)

Bossuet, J. B., *Politics Drawn from the Very Words of Holy Scripture*, translated and edited by Patrick Riley, (Cambridge: Cambridge University Press, 1990)

Bowersock, G. W., Brown, P. and Grabar, O., *Interpreting Late Antiquity: Essays on the Postclassical World*, (London: The Belknap Press of Harvard University Press, 2001)

Bowersock, G. W., *The Throne of Adulis: Red Sea Wars on The Eve of Islam*, (Oxford:

Oxford University Press, 2013)

Boyce, M., Zoroastrianism, *Their Religious Beliefs and Practices*, (London: Routledge and Kegan Paul, 1976)

Bright, W., *The Age of Fathers* (New York: AMS Press, 1970)

Brown, P. R. L., *The World of Late Antiquity: From Marcus Aurelius to Muhammad*, (London: Thames and Hudson, 1971)

Brown, P., *Augustine of Hippo: A Biography*, (Berkeley: University of California Press, 2000)

Brunner, E., *The Christian Doctrine of God*, trans. by Olive Wyon, (OR, Wipf and Stock Publishers, 2014)

Bultmann, R. K., "*New Testament and Mythology*," Kerygma and Myth, Hans W. Bartsch, ed., R. H. Fuller, trans., 2nd edn. (London: Oxford University Press, 1964)

Burckhardt, T., *The Foundations of Christian Art*, (Bloomington, Indiana: World Wisdom, 2006)

Burleigh, J. S., Faith and the Creed. *In Augustine: Earlier Writings*. (Philadelphia: The Westminster Press, 1953)

Burridge, Richard A., *What Are the Gospels? A Comparison with Graeco-Roman Biography* (New York: Cambridge University Press, 1992)

Campbell, H. M., *The Ascent of the West from Prehistory through the Renaissance*, (New York: Britannica Educational Publishing, 2011)

Carol J. B. ed., *Mariology*, (Milwaukee: Bruce Publishing Company, 1954)

Chadwick, H., *Augustine: A Very Short Introduction*, (Oxford: Oxford University Press, 2001)

Chadwick, H., *Early Christian Thought and the Classical Tradition* (New York: Dorset Press, 1967)

Chadwick, H., *Origen Contra Celsum*, (Cambridge: Cambridge University Press, 2003)

Chadwick, H., *The Early Church* (New York: Dorset Press, 1967)

Chadwick, H., trans., Augustine, *Confessions*, (New York: Oxford University Press, 1991)

Charles, R. H., *The Chronicle of John*, Bishop of Nikiu: Translated from Zotenberg's Ethiopic Text (Merchantville, NJ: Evolution Publishers, 2007)

Cimball, C. A., *Striving Together in the Way of God: Muslim Participation in Christian-Muslim Dialogue*, (UMI Dissertation Services, 1996)

Clark, G. W., ed., *The Octavius of Marcus Minucius Felix*, Ancient Christian Writers 39, (New York: Paulist Press, 1974)

Clarke, C. P. S., *Short History of The Christian Church* (London: Longman, 1966)

Cook, M., *Forbidding Wrong in Islam: An Introduction*, (Cambridge: Cambridge University Press, 2003); Commanding Right and Forbidding Wrong in Islamic Thought, (Cambridge: Cambridge University Press, 2004); Muhammad, (Oxford: Oxford University Press, 1996)

Coulson, N. J., *A History of Islamic Law*, (Edinburgh: Edinburgh University Press, 1964)

Coward, H., *Sin and Salvation in the World Religions: A Short Introduction*, (Oxford: Oneworld, 2003)

Cowburn SJ., J., *Free Will, Predestination and Determinism*, (Milwaukee: Marquette University Press, 2008)

Cragg, K., *Counsels in Contemporary Islam*, (Edinburgh: Edinburgh University Press, 1965)

Cragg, K., *Jesus and the Muslim: An Exploration* (London: Allen & Unwin, 1985; re-print Oxford: Oneworld,1999)

Cragg, K., *The Call of the Minaret*, (Maryknoll, NY: Orbis Books, 1985)

Cragg, K., *The House of Islam*, (Grand Rapid: Dickenson Publishing, 1975)

Crone, P., *God's Rule, Government and Islam*, (New York: Columbia University Press, 2004)

Cross, F. L. and Livingstone, E. A., eds., *The Oxford dictionary of the Christian Church*, (Oxford: Oxford University Press, 2005)

Crossan, J. D., *The Historical Jesus: The Life of a Mediterranean Jewish Peasant*, (San Francisco: Harper Collins, 1991)

Crossan, J. D., *The Historical Jesus: The Life of a Mediterranean Jewish Peasant* (San Francisco: Harper Collins, 1991)

Dampier, C. W., *A History of Science and its Relation to Philosophy and Religion*, (Cambridge: Cambridge University Press, 1966)

Davis, S. T., Kendall, D. and O'Collins, G. eds., *The Trinity*, (Oxford: Oxford University Press, 1999)

Deane, H. A., *The Political and Social Ideas of St. Augustine*, (New York: Columbia University Press, 1963)

Demarest, B., *The Cross and Salvation: The Doctrine of Salvation*, (Wheaton, IL: Crossway Books, 2006)

Dixon, T., Canter, G. and Pumfrey, S. eds., *Science and Religion: New Historical Perspectives*, (Cambridge: Cambridge University Press, 2010)

Donner, F. M., *Muhammad and the Believers: At the Origins of Islam*, (London: Harvard University Press, 2010)

Downing, F. G., *Cynics, Paul and the Pauline Churches: Cynics and Christian Origins II*, (New York: Routledge, 1998)

Driver, G. R., Hodgson, L., eds. and trans., *The Bazar of Heraclides Nestorius* (Oxford; New York: Clarendon Press, 1925)

Duffy, S. J., *The Dynamics of Grace: Perspectives in Theological Anthropology*, (Collegeville, Minnesota: The Liturgical Press, 1993)

Dunn, J. D. G., *Romans 9-16*, (Dallas: Word, 1988)

Dunn, J., *Cambridge Companion to Paul*, (Cambridge: Cambridge University Press, 2004)

Eaton, C. G., *Islam and the Destiny of Man* (Albany: State University of New York Press, 1985)

Edwards, D. R. and McCollough, C. T., (eds), *The Archaeology of Difference: Gender, Ethnicity, Class and the "Other" in Antiquity: Studies in Honor of Eric M. Meyers* (Boston: American Schools of Oriental Research, 2007)

Eisenman, R., *James the Brother of Jesus*, (New York, Penguin Books, 1998)

El Ansari, W. and Linnan, D. K. eds., *Muslim and Christian Understanding: Theory and Application of "A Common Word"*, (New York: Palgrave Macmillan, 2010)

Ellerbe, H., *The Dark Side of Christian History*, (Windermere, Florida: Morning Star and Lark, 2009)

Ellul, E., *Anarchy and Christianity* trans. by Geoffrey W. Bromiley, (Grand Rapids, MI: William B. Eerdmans, 1991)

Ellul, J., *Islam and Judeo-Christianity: A Critique of Their Commonality*, Translated by D. Bruce MacKay, (Eugene, OR: Cascade Books, 2015)

Erickson, M., *God in Three Persons: A Contemporary Interpretation of Trinity*, (Ada, MI: Baker Publication Group, 1995)

Ernst, C. W., *Following Muhammad, Rethinking Islam in the Contemporary World*, (Chapel Hill: University of North Carolina Press, 2003)

Esposito, J. L., *What Everyone Needs to Know About Islam*, (Oxford: Oxford University Press, 2002)

Etheredge, L. (ed.), *Islamic History*, (New York: Britannica Publishing Services, 2010)

Ettinghausen, R., *The Characters of Islamic Art in the Arab Heritage*, N. A. Faris, ed. (Princeton: Princeton University Press, 1944)

Evans, G. R., ed., *The First Christian Theologians*, (Oxford: Blackwell, 2004)

Evans, J. A. S., *The Age of Justinian*, (London: Routledge, 1996)

Fairbairn, A. M., *The Place of Christ in Modern Theology* (New York: Scribner's Sons, 1911)

Fakhry, M., *Islamic Philosophy, Theology and Mysticism: A Short Introduction*, (Oxford: Oneworld, 2000)

Fee, G. D., *The First Epistle to the Corinthians*, (Grand Rapids: William B. Eerdmans Publishing Company, 1987)

Feldmeier, R., *The First Letter of Peter, A Commentary on the Greek Text*, (Waco, Texas: Baylor University Press, 2008)

Ferguson, G., *Signs & Symbols in Christian Art*, (Oxford: Oxford University Press, 1996)

Figgis, J. N., *The Divine Right of Kings*, (Cambridge: Cambridge University Press, 1914)

Fitzmyer, J. A., *Romans*, (New York: Doubleday, 1993)

Fitzpatrick, C. and Walker, A. H., *Muhammad in History, Thought, and Culture: An Encyclopedia of the Prophet of God*, (Santa Barbara: ABC-CLIO, 2014)

Fox, P., *God as Communion*, (Collegeville, Minnesota: The Liturgical Press, 2001)

Fox, R. L., *Pagans and Christians* (New York: Alfred & Knopf Inc., 1987)

Gaddis, M., *There Is No Crime for Those Who Have Christ*, (Berkeley: University of California Press, 2005)

Garland, D. E., *I Corinthians*, (Grand Rapids, Michigan: Backer Academic, 2003)

Gibbon, E., *The History of the Decline and Fall of the Roman Empire* (London: Penguin Books, 1994)

Glover, T. R., trans., *Tertullian, Apology De Spectaculis*, (London: Harvard University Press, 1977)

Gore, Charles, *The Incarnation of the Son of God* (New York: Scribner's Sons, 1960)

Grant, Robert M., *The Formation of The New Testament*, (New York, Harper and Row, 1965)

Griffith, H., *Theodore Abu⁻ Qurrah: The Intellectual Profile of an Arab Christian Writer of the First Abbasid Century*, (Tel Aviv: Tel Aviv University, 1992)

Griffith, S. H., *The Church in the Shadow of the Mosque: Christians and Muslims in the World of Islam*, (Princeton: Princeton University Press, 2007)

Grillmeier, A., *Christ in Christian Tradition, John Bowden, trans.* (Atlanta: John Knox Press, 1975)

Grypeou, E., Swanson, M. N. and Thomas, D. eds., *The Encounter of Eastern Christianity with Early Islam*, (Leiden: Brill, 2006)

Guthrie, Jr., Shirley C., *Christian Doctrine* (Richmond: CLC Press, 1968)

Gwatkin, H. M., *Studies of Arianism* (New York: AMS Press, 1978)

Gwynn, D. M., *Christianity in the Later Roman Empire: A Source Book*, (London: Bloomsbury, 2015)

Gwynne, R. W., Logic, *Rhetoric and Legal Reasoning in the Quran: God's Arguments*, (New York: Routledge, 2004)

Hagedorn, A. and Shalem, A., *Facts and Artefacts: Art in the Islamic World*, (Leiden: Brill, 2007)

Hallaq, W. B., *A History of Islamic Legal Theories*, (Cambridge: Cambridge University Press, 1997)

Hallaq, W. B., *An Introduction to Islamic Law*, (Cambridge: Cambridge University Press, 2009)

Hallaq, W. B., *The Origins and Evolution of Islamic Law*, (Cambridge: Cambridge University Press, 2005)

Hamidullah, M., *The First Written Constitution in the World: An Important Document of the Time of the Holy Prophet*, (Lahore: Ashraf Press, 1975)

Hardy, E. R., ed., *Christology of the Later Fathers*, (Louisville: Westminster John Knox Press, 2006)

Harnack, A., *History of Dogma*, (OR, Wipf and Stock Publishers, 1997)

Harnack, A., *The Expansion of Christianity in the First Three Centuries, trans, and ed. J. Moffatt*, (New York: Putnam's Sons, 1904-5)

Harrak, A., *The Chronicle of Zuqnin*, Parts III and IV, A.D. 488–775: Translated from Syriac with Notes and Introduction (Toronto: Pontifical Institute of Mediaeval Studies, 1999)

Harvey, S. A., *Asceticism and Society in Crisis: John of Ephesus and the Lives of the Eastern Saints*, (London: University of California Press, 1990)

Hashmi, S. H., ed., *Just Wars, Holy Wars and Jihads: Christian, Jewish and Muslim Encounters and Exchanges*, (Oxford: Oxford University Press, 2012)

Haskins, C. H., *The Renaissance of the Twelfth Century*, (London: Harvard University Press, 1955)

Hawes, C., *Mania and Literary Style, The Rhetoric of Enthusiasm from Ranters to Christopher Smart*, (Cambridge: Cambridge University Press, 1996)

Helm, P. ed., *Divine Commands and Moral Requirements* (Oxford: Oxford University Press, 1981)

Hick, J. ed., *The Myth of God Incarnate*, (London: SCM Press, 1977)

Hick, J., *The Metaphor of God Incarnate* (London: S.C.M. Press, 1993)

Hill, C., *The World Turned Up Side Down: Radical Ideas During the English Revolution*, (London: Penguin Books, 1975)

Hodge, H., *Commentary on the Epistle to the Romans*, (Albany: Books for The Ages, 1997)

Hodgson, M. G. S., *The Venture of Islam* (Chicago: Chicago University Press, 1974)

Hoekema, A. A., *Saved by Grace*, (Grand Rapids: Eerdmans, 1989)

Hoffman, R. J., trans., *Celsus: On the True Doctrine*, (New York: Oxford University Press, 1987)

Hoffman, R. J., trans., *Porphyry's Against the Christians*, (New York, Prometheus Books, 1994)

Holden, L. (ed.), *Jesus in History, Thought and Culture: An Encyclopedia*, (Oxford: ABC CLIO, 2003)

Holmes, M. W., *The Apostolic Fathers: Greek Texts and English Translations*, updated ed. (Grand Rapids: Baker Books, 1999)

Holyland, R. G., *Arabia and the Arabs, From the Bronze Age to the Coming of Islam*, (New York: Routledge, 2001)

Hopkins, R. P., *How Greek Philosophy Corrupted the Christian Concept of God*, (Springville, Utah, Horizon Publishers, 2009)

Horsley, R. ed., *Paul and Politics*, (Harrisburg, PA: Trinity International Press, 2000)

Horton, M. S., *Lord and Servant: A Covenant Christology*, (London: Westminster John Knox Press, 2005)

Hunter, I., *Laursen, J. C., and Nederman, C. J.*, eds., Heresy in Transition, (Burlington,

VT: Ashgate Publishing Company, 2005)

Ibn Hazm, Abu Muhammad Ali Ibn Ahmad, *Al-Fasl fi al-Milal wa al-Ahwa' wa al-Ni-hal*, (Jeddah: Sharikat Maktabat 'Uka'z, 1982)

Ibn Hishām, A., *Al-Sīrat Al-Nabawiyah* (Egypt: Dar Al-Hadith, 2006)

Ibn Isḥāq, M., *The Life of Muhammad: A Translation of Ishaq's Sirat Rasul Allah*, trans., Alfred Guillaume (London; New York: Oxford University Press, 1955)

Ibn Taymīyah, Taqī al-Dīn, *Al-Jawāb al-Ṣaḥīḥli-man Baddala Dīn al-Masīḥ*, ed. 'Alī Ibn Ḥasan Ibn Nāṣir et al. (Riyadh: Dar al-A'asimah,1999)

Idziak, J. M. ed., *Divine Command Theory* (New York: Mellen Press, 1979)

Inbody, T., *The Faith of the Christian Church*, (Cambridge: William B. Eerdmans, 2005)

Beaumont, I. M., *Christology in Dialogue with Muslims: A Critical Analysis of Christian Presentations of Christ for Muslims from the Ninth and Twentieth Centuries*, (Oxford: Regnum Studies in Mission, 2005)

Izutsu, T., *Ethico-Religious Concepts in the Qur'án* (Montreal: McGill-Queen's University Press, 2002)

Izutsu, T., *God and Man in the Quran: Semantics of the Quranic Weltanschauung*, (Tokyo: Keio University, 1964)

Jeremias, J., *New Testament Theology*, John Bowden, trans. (New York: Charles Scribner's Sons, 1971)

Henderson, J. B., *The Construction of Orthodoxy and Heresy: Neo-Confucian*, Islamic, Jewish, and Early Christian Patterns (Albany: SUNY Press, 1998)

Kelly, John N. D., *Early Christian Doctrines* (New York: Harper and Brothers, 1958)

Kelsay, J. E., *"Religion and Morality in Islam"*, (Charlottesville: University of Virginia, 1985)

Kennedy, H., Caliphate, *The History of an Idea*, (New York: Basic Books, 2016)

Khadduri, M., *The Islamic Conception of Justice* (Baltimore: The John Hopkin University Press, 1984)

Khalil, M. H. (ed.), *Between Heaven and Hell: Islam, Salvation, and the Fate of Others*, (Oxford: Oxford University Press, 2013)

Khatab, S. and Bouma, G. D., *Democracy in Islam*, (New York: Routledge, 2007)

Krawietz, B. and Reifeld, H. ed., *Islam and the Rule of Law*, (Berlin: Konrad-Adenauer-Stiftung, 2008)

Lane, R. W., *The Discovery of Freedom, Man's Struggle Against Authority*, (New York: The John Day Company, 1943)

Lash, N., *Easter in Ordinary: Reflections on Human Experience and the Knowledge of God* (Notre Dame: University of Notre Dame, 1990)

Lecker, M., *The Constitution of Medina: Muḥammad's First Legal Document*, (Princeton, NJ: Darwin, 2004)

Leirviked, O., *Images of Jesus Christ in Islam*, (New York: Bloomsbury Publishing

PLC, 2010)

Lewis, B., *The Arabs in History*, (Oxford: Oxford University Press, 2002)

Lewis, B., *The Jews of Islam*, (Oxford: Princeton University Press, 1987)

Lewis, C. S., *The Incarnation of the Word of God*, Being the Treatise of St. Athanasius, Geoffrey Bles, trans. (London: The Centenary Press, 1944)

Lloyd-Jones, D. M., *God's Ultimate Purpose: An Exposition of Eph* 1:1-23, (Grand Rapids: Baker, 1978)

Lloyd-Jones, D. M., *Romans, An Exposition of Chapter 13,* (Edinburgh: The Banner of Truth Trust, 1967)

Lods, A., *Israel, From its Beginnings to the Middle of the Eighth Century* (London: Routledge & Kegan Paul, 1948)

Longenecker, R. L., *The Christology of Early Christianity*, (Naperville, IL: Alec R. Allenson Inc. 1970)

Louth, A., *St. John Damascene*, (Oxford: Oxford University Press, 2002)

Lull, T. F., ed., *Martin Luther's Basic Theological Writings* (Minneapolis: Fortress, 1989)

Maas, M., *The Cambridge Companion to the Age of Justinian*, (Cambridge: Cambridge University Press, 2006)

Madelung, W., *The Succession to Muhammad: A Study of the Early Caliphate*, (Cambridge: Cambridge University Press, 1997)

Madigan, D. A., *The Quran's Self-image.* (Princeton: Princeton University Press, 2001)

Markus, R. A., *Saeculum History and Society in the Theology of St. Augustine*, (Cambridge: Cambridge University Press, 2007)

Martin, M., *The Case Against Christianity*, (Philadelphia: Temple University Press, 1991)

Martin, R. C., ed., *Encyclopedia of Islam and the Muslim World*, (New York: Macmillan Reference, 2004)

Martin, R. C., *Islam, A Cultural Perspective* (New Jersey: Prentice-Hall, 1982)

Stefon, M., ed., *Judaism: History, Belief, And Practice*, (New York: Britannica Educational Publishing, 2012)

Matthews, G. B., ed., *St. Augustine, On the Trinity*, translated by Stephen McKenna, (Cambridge: Cambridge University Press, 2002)

Mawdudi, Sayyid Abul A'la, *Four Basic Quranic Terms*, Abu Asad, trans., (Lahore: Islamic Publications Ltd., 1982)

McAuliffe, J. D. ed, *Encyclopedia of Quran ed.*, (Leiden: Brill, 2006)

McAuliffe, J. D., *Quranic Christians: An Analysis of Classic and Modern Exegesis*, (Cambridge: Cambridge University Press, 2007)

McCall, T. H., *Which Trinity? Whose Monotheism? Philosophical and Systematic Theologians on the Metaphysics of Trinitarian Theology*, (Grand Rapids, MI: Wm. B. Eerdmans, 2010)

McGiffert, A. C., *A History of Christian Thought* (New York: Charles Scribner's Sons, 1960)

McGregor, J. F., and Reay, B. eds., *Radical Religion in the English Revolution*, (Oxford: Oxford University Press, 1984)

Meijering, E. P., *God Being History: Studies in Patristic Philosophy* (Amsterdam: North-Holland Publishing Company, 1975)

Meloney, G. S. J., *The Cosmic Christ, From Paul to Teilhard* (New York: Sheed & Ward, 1968)

Michel, T. F., *A Muslim Theologian's Response to Christianity: Ibn Taymiyya's Al-Jawab al-Sahih* (Delmar, NY: Caravan Books, 1984)

Miravalle, M. ed., Mariology, *A Guide for Priests, Deacons, Seminarians and Consecrated Persons*, (Goleta, CA: Seat of Wisdom Books, 2007)

Molnar, P. D., *Divine Freedom and the Doctrine of the Immanent Trinity: In Dialogue with Karl Barth and Contemporary Theology* (London: T & T Clark, 2002)

Moltmann, J., *The Crucified God* (New York: Harper & Row, 1974)

Moo, D. J., *The Epistle to the Romans*, (Grand Rapids, MI: William B. Eerdmans, 1996)

Morey, R., *The Islamic Invasion: Confronting the World's Fastest Growing Religion*, (Eugene, Oregon: Harvest House Publishers, 1992)

Mynors, R. A. B., ed., *Oxford Classical Texts*, (Oxford: Oxford University Press, 1963)

Naseem, H., *Muslim Philosophy. Science and Mysticism,* (New Delhi: Sarup & Sons, 2001); *The Attitude of Islam Towards Science and Philosophy*, (New Delhi, Sarup & Sons, 2003)

Netton, I. R., *Text and Trauma: An East-West Primer* (Richmond: Curzon Press, 1996)

Nicolle, D., *Sassanian Armies: the Iranian Empire Early 3rd to Mid-7th Centuries AD.* (Stockport, UK: Montvert, 1996)

Noble, T. F. X. and Smith, J. M. H. eds, *The Cambridge History of Christianity*, Early Medieval Christianities, C. 600-c. 1100, (Cambridge: Cambridge University Press, 2008)

Norris, Jr., R. A., ed. and trans., *The Christological Controversy* (Philadelphia: Fortress Press, 1980)

Odahl, C. M., *Constantine and the Christian Empire*, (New York, Routledge, 2010)

Omar Farooq, M., *Towards Our Reformation: From Legalism to Value-Oriented Islamic Law and Jurisprudence*, (London: International Institute of Islamic Thought, 2011)

Pagels, E., *Revelations, Vision, Prophecy and Politics in the Book of Revelation*, (New York: Vikings, 2012)

Pagels, E., *The Origin of Satan*, (New York: Vintage Books, 1995)

Pagels, P., *Adam, Eve and the Serpent*, (New York: First Vintage Books, 1989)

Pal, A., *Islam Means Peace*, (Oxford: Praeger, 2011)

Parrinder, G. ed., *World Religions: From Ancient History to the Present*, (New York:

Facts on File Publications, 1983)

Parrinder, G., *Jesus in the Quran*, (Oxford: Oneworld, 1996)

Pearl, D., *A Textbook on Muslim Personal Law*, (London: Croom Helm,1979)

Pelikan, J., *The Christian Tradition: A History of the Development of Doctrine* (Chicago; London: University of Chicago Press, 1971)

Perkins, B. W., *The Fall of Rome and the End of Civilization*, (Oxford: Oxford University Press, 2006)

Pharr, C., trans., *The Theodosian Code*, (London: Oxford University Press, 1952)

Pinnock, C. H., ed., *Grace Unlimited*, (Minneapolis: Bethany Fellowship, 1975)

Pocock, J. G. A., *Barbarism and Religion*, (Cambridge: Cambridge University Press, 2003)

Qadi, 'Abdal Jabbar, *Abu al-Hasan, al-Mughni fi Abwab al-Tawhid wa al-'Adl* (Volume: 5), Mahmud Muhammed al-Khudayri (ed.), (Cairo: al-Dar al-Misriyya, 1958); Sharh al-'Usul al-Khamsa, 'Abd al-Karim Uthman (ed.), (Cairo: Maktaba Wahba, 1965)

Qutb, M., *Madhāhib Fikriyyah Mu`āåarah*, 1st edn. (Beirut: Dār al-Sharq, 1983)

Rahman, F., *Major Theme of the Quran*, (Minneapolis: Bibliotheca Islamica, 1994)

Rahner, K., *The Trinity, translated by Joseph Donceel*, (London: Burns and Oates, 1986)

Rahner, K., *Theological Investigations*, translated by Kohl Margaret, (London: Darton, Longman & Todd, 1981)

Räisänen, H., *Paul and the Law* (Philadelphia: Fortress, 1983)

Rea, M. C., *Oxford Readings in Philosophical Theology*, (Oxford: Oxford University Press, 2009)

Rendall, G. H., trans., *MINUCIUS FELIX*, (London: Harvard University Press,1977)

Rendall, G. H., *The Epistle of St. James and Judaic Christianity*, (Cambridge: Cambridge University Press, 1927)

Reynolds, G. S and Samir, S. K. (ed., trans.), Critique of Christian Origins: Tathbit Dala'il al-Nubuwwa, (Provo: Brigham Young University Press, 2010)

Reynolds, G. S, ed., *The Quran in Its Historical Context*, (New York: Routledge, 2007)

Ribeiro, H. J., *Systematic Approaches to Argument by Analogy*, (New York: Springer Verlag, 2014)

Richard Dawkins, R., *The God Delusion*, (New York: Bantam, 2006)

Rida, R., *Tafseer al-Quran al Hakeem*, (Cairo: Dar al-Manar, 1367 A.H.)

Ridgeon, L., *Islam Interpretations of Christianity*, (New York: St. Martin Press, 2001)

Rippin, A. ed., *The Blackwell Companion to the Quran*, (Oxford: Blackwell Publishing Ltd, 2006)

Rippin, A., Muslims, *Their Religious Beliefs and Practices*, (New York: Routledge, 2005)

Roberts, A. and Donaldson, J. eds., *The Anti-Nicene Fathers* (Buffalo: Christian Literature Publ. Co., 1885)

Roberts, E., and Donaldson, J., eds., *Ante-Nicene Fathers*, (New York: Cosimo Classics, 2007)

Robertson, A., *A Select Library of Nicene and Post-Nicene Fathers of the Christian Church* (Grand Rapids: W. B. Eerdmans, 1957)

Robinson, C. F. ed., *The New Cambridge History of Islam*, (Cambridge: Cambridge University Press, 2011)

Robinson, F. ed., *Cambridge Illustrated History of the Islamic World*, (Cambridge: Cambridge University Press, 1996)

Robinson, N., *Christ in Islam and Christianity*, (Albany: State University of New York Press, 1991)

Rodinson, M., *Muhammad*, translated by Anne Carter, (New York: Penguin Books, 1985)

Rosen, L., *The Justice of Islam*, (Oxford: Oxford University Press, 2002)

Rosenthal, F., *Man Versus Society in Early Islam*, edited by Dimitri Gutas, (Leiden, Brill, 2015)

Ryan, J. K., trans. *Book Eight: The Grace of Faith in The Confessions of St. Augustine*, (New York: Image Books, 1960)

Sabrinho, C. G., *Doctrine and Power*, (Berkeley: University of California Press, 2013)

Sachedina, A. A., *The Just Ruler* (al-Sultan al-'Adil) in Shi'ite Islam, (Oxford: Oxford University Press, 1998)

Saeed, A., *Freedom of Religion, Apostasy and Islam*, (New York: Routledge, 2004)

Sahas, D. J., *John of Damascus on Islam, The Heresy of the Ishmaelites*, (Leiden: Brill, 1972)

Sale, G., *The Koran*, (London: J.B. Lippincott Company, 1850)

Samir, S. K. and Nielsen, J. S. eds., *Christian-Arabic Apologetics During the Abbasid Period*, (Leiden: Brill, 1994)

Sanders, E. P., *Paul, the Law, and the Jewish People* (Philadelphia: Fortress, 1983)

Sayers, D. L., *The Emperor Constantine*, (New York: Harper & Brothers, 1951)

Schaff, P., *Augustin: The Writings Against the Manichaeans and Against the Donatists*, (New York: The Christian Literature Publishing Co., 1890)

Schaff, P., *History of the Christian Church*, (Grand Rapids, MI: Christian Classics Ethereal Library, 2002)

Sellers, R. V., *The Council of Chalcedon: A Historical and Doctrinal Survey* (London: SPCK, 1961)

Kim, S., *Christ and Caesar*, (Grand Rapids, MI: William B. Eerdmans, 2008)

Shah, Z. A., *Anthropomorphic Depictions of God: Concept of God in the Judaic, Christian and Islamic Traditions, Representing the Un-representable*, (London: International Institute of Islamic Thought, 2012)

Shahı^d, I., *The Martyrs of Najra^ n: New Documents* (Brussels: Socie´te´ des Bollan-distes, 1971)

Shaltut, M., *al-Islām `Aqīdah wa Sharī`ah* (Cairo: Dār al-Qalam, 1966)

Shultz, J. P., *Judaism and the Gentile Faiths, Comparative Studies in Religion*, (London: Associated University Presses, 1981)

Sinn, S. and Sinaga, M. L., *Freedom and Responsibility, Christian and Muslim Explorations*, (Minneapolis: Luther University Press, 2010)

Smith, R. L., *Premodern Trade in World History*, (New York: Routledge, 2009)

Smith, W. and Wace, H., *A Dictionary of Christian Biography, Literature, Sects and Doctrines* (London: John Murray, 1877–1887)

Sonn, T., *Islam: A Brief History*, (Oxford: Wiley-Blackwell, 2010)

St. Augustine, *The Trinity*. Translated by Stephen McKenna in The Fathers of the Church: A New Translation, vol. 45. (Washington, DC: The Catholic University of America Press, 1963)

Stam, C. M., *Commentary on the Epistle of Roman*, (Steven Point, WI: Berean Literature Foundation, 1984)

Sternberg, R. J., *Cognitive Psychology*. (Belmont, CA: Wadsworth., 2009)

Stewart, M. Y., ed., *The Trinity: East/West Dialogue*, (Dordrecht: Springer, 2003)

Stuhlmacher, P., *Paul's Letter to the Romans: A Commentary*, trans. S. J. Hafemann (Louisville, Ky.: Westminster John Knox, 1994)

Stump, E. and Kretzmann, N., eds., *The Cambridge Companion to Augustine*, (New York: Cambridge University Press, 2001)

Sullivan, F. A., *The Christology of Theodore of Mopsuestia* (Rome: University Gregorian, 1956)

Swinburne, R., *Was Jesus God?* (Oxford: Oxford University Press, 2008)

Sykes, S. W., and Clayton, J. P., eds., *Christ, Faith and History: Cambridge Studies in Christology*, (Cambridge: Cambridge University Press, 1972)

Tabbernee, W., *Fake Prophecy and Polluted Sacraments*, (Boston: Brill, 2007)

Thomas D. ed., *Syrian Christian Under Islam, The First Thousand Years*, (Brill: Leiden, 2001)

Arnold, T. W., *Painting in Islam* (Oxford: Clarendon Press, 1928)

Thomas, D. and Roggema, B. eds., *Christian Muslim Relations: A Biographical History*, (Leiden: Brill, 2009)

Thomas, D. ed., *Christians at the Heart of Islamic Rule*, (Leiden-Boston: Brill, 2003)

Thomas, D., *A Muslim Theologian's Response to Christianity: Ibn Taymiyya's Al-Jawab Al-Sahih* (Studies in Islamic Philosophy and Science), (New York: Caravan Books, 1985)

Thomas, D., *Anti-Christian Polemic in Early Islam, Abu Isa al-Warra'q Against the Trin-*

ity, (Cambridge: Oriental Publications, 2002)

Thomas, D., *Christian Doctrines in Islamic Theology*, (Leiden: Brill, 2008)

Thomas, D., *The Bible in Arab Christianity*, (Leiden: Brill, 2007)

Tillich, P., *A History of Christian Thought*, (New York: Touchstone Books, 1972)

Tillich, P., *Systematic Theology* (Chicago: Chicago University Press, 1957)

Tirmazī, Imam, *Saḥīḥ Sunan al-Tirmazī*, M. N. al-Albani, ed., 1st edn. (Gulf States: Maktabah al-Tarbiyyah al-`Arabī, 1988)

Turner, B. S. ed., *Islam: Critical Concepts in Sociology*, (New York: Routledge, 2004)

Turner, H. E. W., *The Patristic Doctrine of the Redemption: A Study of the Development of Doctrine During the First Five Centuries*, (Eugene, OR: Wipf & Stock Publishers, 2004)

Urban, L., *A Short History of Christian Thought* (New York: Oxford University Press, 1995)

Vine, A. R., *The Nestorian Churches*, (London: Independent Press, 1937)

Whitley, W. T., ed., *The Doctrine of Grace*, (New York: Macmillan, 1931)

Waardenburg, J. ed., *Muslim Perceptions of Other Religions*, (Oxford: Oxford University Press, 1999)

Walbridge, J., *God and Logic in Islam: The Caliphate of Reason*, (Cambridge: Cambridge University Press, 2011)

Wallace, A. J., Rusk, R. D., *Moral Transformation: The Original Christian Paradigm of Salvation* (New Zealand: Bridgehead, 2011)

Watkins, C. ed., *The American Heritage Dictionary of Indo-European Roots*, 2nd ed., (New York: Houghton Mifflin Co., 2000)

Watt, W. M., *Muhammad at Medina*, (Oxford: Clarendon Press, 1956)

Weeramantry, C. G., *Islamic Jurisprudence, An International Perspective*, (London: Macmillan Press, 1988)

Wellhausen, J., *Die religiös-politischen Oppositionsparteien im alten Islam*, trans. R. C. Ostle and S. M. Walzer as The Religious-Political Factions in Early Islam, (Amsterdam, North Holland,1975)

Wellhausen, J., *The Arab Kingdom and Its Fall*, translated by Margaret Graham Wier, (Calcutta: Calcutta University Press, 1927)

Wells, D. F., *The Search for Salvation*, (Downers Grove, IL.: InterVarsity, 1978)

Whale, J. S., *Christian Doctrine* (Cambridge: Cambridge University Press, 1961)

Wigram, W. A., *The Separation of the Monophysites* (London: The Faith Press, 1923)

Williams, S. and Friell, G., *Theodosius, The Empire at Bay*, (London: Routledge, 1994)

Wolfson, H. A., *The Philosophy of the Church Fathers*, (Cambridge, MA: Harvard University Press, 1970)

Wolfson, H. A., *The Philosophy of the Kalam*, (Cambridge, Massachusetts: Harvard University Press,1976)

Wood, S., *The Proprietary Church in the Medieval West*, (Oxford: Oxford University Press, 2006)

Wright, N. T., *Paul: In Fresh Perspective* (Minneapolis: Fortress, 2005)

Yarshater, E. ed., *The Cambridge History of Iran*, (Cambridge: Cambridge University Press, 2000)

Yolder, J. H., *The Politics of Jesus*, (Cambridge: William B. Eerdmans, 1994)

Young, F. M., *From Nicaea to Chalcedon* (London: S.C.M. Press, 1983)

Zagorin, P., *How the Idea of Religious Toleration Came to the West*, (New Jersey: Princeton University, 2003)

Zarefsky, D., *Argumentation: The Study of Effective Reasoning*, (Chantilly: VA, The Teaching Company, 2002)

Zebiri, K., *Muslims and Christians Face to Face*, (Oxford: Oneworld, 2003)

Index

'Abba'sid rule 286
Abduh, Muhammad 270
Abelard 170
Abraham 26, 182-5, 261, 267-8, 281
family of 266-9, 272-4, 280, 295
Abrahamic connection 266-74
Abrahamov, Binyamin 263
abrogation 270, 282
absolute submission to worldly authorities 115-28, 139
absolutism 117, 135, 139, 171, 180, 281-2
Abu Ha'ritha 208
abuse of authority 118
Adam 21, 66-9, 93, 105, 131-6, 194, 265, 275
Adoptionism 34-5, 47, 60, 63, 191-5, 198, 200, 210
Aelurus, Timothy 56
Afsaruddin, Asma 273-4
A'ad 229
Ahktar, Shabbir 255
al-Akbar, al-A'sha 181
Allah 198-9, 203, 213, 218-19, 223-30, 235-8, 241, 265-8, 271-3
allegory 106
Alston, William 62
al-Alusi 229
Ambrose, St. 145, 158
analogical reasoning 253
Ananias 149
anarchy 118
anti-imperialism 114-15, 128
Antinomianism 75-95, 276-8, 282
Antirationalism 95-111
Apollinaris 41-2

Apologists 26-7, 42, 89, 91, 141, 209-14
Apostolic Creed 145
Aquinas, St. Thomas 34, 73, 168
Arabic language 207-8, 279
Arabism 286-7
Arberry, A.J. 262-3
Arcadius 164
argumentation 247-8, 254, 276
Aristides 24
Aristotle and Aristotelianism 73, 167, 248-9, 254, 263
Arius and Arianism 36-40, 46, 63, 143-6, 206
Armstrong, Karen 178, 286
art, Islamic 238
Asad, Muhammad 217-18, 230-1, 269, 271
asceticism 143
Ataric 136
Athanasius, St. 15, 38-48, 144, 197
Athenagoras 24, 26, 39
atonement 67, 82, 100, 166, 202
Augustine, St. 34, 60-3, 69, 130-9, 147-58, 172, 175
Augustinian doctrine 68-9, 202-3, 207, 232
authoritarianism 171
Ayat 255
Ayman, Umm 189

Bahi'ra 189
Bammel, E. 117, 124
Barth, Carl 34, 61, 72, 221
Battle of Ditches 296
al-Bayhaq ī 229
beasts, political powers seen as 112-13

believers and *non-believers*, separation of 269

Bell, Richard 190, 208

Benedict, St. 17

biblical passages 166, 233, 267; *see also* Hebrew Bible

Biel, Gabriel 68

Bigg, Charles 23, 28, 30

bin Ali, Hussain 286

bin Nawfel, Waraqah 182, 189

bishops, role of 111, 133-4, 163, 171, 277

Black, Anrony 184, 246-7, 282

Blake, William 13

blasphemy 218, 266

Block, C.J. 207-8, 212

bloodshed 117

Borg, M. 123

Bornkamm, Paul G. 77

Bouma, Gary D. 284, 289

Brandon, S.G.F. 18

Brethren of Free Spirit 92-3

Bright, William 38, 59

Brown, Peter 110, 154-6

Brunner, E. 58-9

Bruno, St. 17

Bunyan, John 94

Burridge, Richard 14

Byzantium and the Byzantine Empire 109-10, 166, 171, 175-6, 180-3, 288, 296

Caelestius 68

Cain 87

Caliphate system 285

Calvin, John 93

Campbell, Heather 109

canonisation process 15-16, 21

capital punishment 117, 153, 157, 164

Cappadocian Fathers 48, 60-2, 201, 203, 209

carnal concupiscence 131-2

Cassian, John 68

caste system 276

Catholic communion 146-53, 160-2, 166

Celsius 17, 22, 95-109, 126, 141

Chadwick, Henry 50, 54, 138

Chalcedonian Christianity 182, 202, 205, 208, 210; *see also* Council of Chalcedon

Chilton, Bruce 18

Christendom 171, 177, 282, 288, 292

medieval 139

Christian tradition 137, 170, 177, 217

Christianity

Arab knowledge of 181, 190, 217

central doctrine of 11-12, 20, 72-3, 95, 100, 102, 121-2

criticisms of 88, 96-7, 103, 106-8, 263

declared as Roman state religion 11-12, 109, 292

Gospel-type and *Church-type* 250

hostility to worldly authorities 113-14

importance of Jesus to 13-14

Islamic reformation of 179-80, 186-90, 223, 232-3, 296

paganisation of 125-6

political climax of 110

primitive 95

role in the fall of the Roman Empire 173-5

Roman 76, 119, 166

social consequences of the spread of 103

stagnation in Medieval period 13

Christocentrism 77

Christology 18-23, 33, 39, 45, 48-54, 57-63, 67, 180, 213-14

Chrysostom, John 132-4, 158-9

Church, Christian

establishment of 146

formulation of doctrine 16-17, 171-2, 177

provision of spiritual guidance 133

relations with the state 109-11, 126-8, 134, 138-9, 143, 147, 172

wealth and power acquired by 110, 176-7

Cicero 170

Circumcelliones 149

civic society 294

civil authority 119-20

civil rights 265

civil unrest 118

clan ties 277

Clarke, C.P.S. 15

Clarkson, Lawrence 94

class divisions 170-1

Claudius, Emperor 125

Clement of Alexandria 23, 29-30

Clement of Rome 127, 132

Cleomenes 31

clericalism 285

'coding' 115

coercion in matters of religion 263-4, 295

Collyridianism 213
Congar, Yves 154
Constantine, Emperor 12, 16, 38, 40, 43-4, 109, 134-5, 142-4
    as the ideal Christian ruler 129
Constantius II, Emperor 144
constants, universal 279
constitutional monarchy 288
consultation 282-4
controversies, theological 143-5, 163
conversion to Christianity 161
Cook, Michael 277-8, 292
Corinth 82-8, 93-4, 140
corporealism 52
cosmic order 130
Coulson, N.J. 278
Council of Carthage (398) 169
Council of Chalcedon (451) 52-60, 63, 226
Council of Ephesus (431) 52-3, 68
Council of Nicaea (325) 38-47, 142, 146, 226
Council of Trent (1547) 68-9
Councils of Constantinople (381, 533 and 680) 50-1, 56, 144, 197, 226
Cragg, Kenneth 208, 210, 214, 237-8
creeds, Islamic and Christian 226
Crisp, Tobias 93
Crone, Patricia 183, 282, 286
Crossan, John D. 17-18, 123
crucifixion 115, 161, 192, 201, 218, 232
Crusades 274
cult saviours 100
Cupitt, D. 17
custom 279
Cyril of Alexandria 51-5, 197

Dampier, W.C. 12
dangerous messages 102, 107
Daniel 117-18
Dark Ages 12, 166, 172, 177
death penalty *see* capital punishment
democracy 283-5
Deucalion 106
Deuteronomy, Book of 121
dignity, human 264-5
Diocletian 144
Diodous of Tarsus 49
Dioscorus of Alexandria 54
disciplinary procedures 133

divine attributes 186-7, 192-6, 212; *see also* God, attributes of
divine right monarchy 111, 117, 127, 129, 134, 139, 186, 278-88
Docetism 23, 30, 43, 47, 63
dogmas 95-6, 104, 106, 167, 171, 217-21
Donatus and Donatists 136-8, 147-56, 169
Donner, Fred 267-71
Downing, Francis 84
Draper, William 179, 186-7
Dunn, J.D.G. 114
Duns Scotus, John 68, 168
Dyothelitism 56

Eaton, Charles 224
Ebionitism 80
edicts 111, 142
egalitarianism 284-5
Eisenman, Robert 79-80
Ellicott, C.J. 124
Ellul, Jacques 112
Enlightenment thought 13, 250, 252, 257-60
Epicurean philosophers 167
Epiphanius 11, 31, 89, 159, 200
Erickson, Millard 64
Ernst, Carl W. 293
Esposito, John L. 280, 291
eternal life 65, 77
eternity, concept of 216
Ethiopia 181-2
Eucharist, the 249
Eusebius of Caesarea 43, 128-30, 134
Eutyches 53-4
Evagrius Scholasticus 164
Evans, J. 160, 162
Eve 69, 194, 265, 275
excommunication 144
exegesis 269-74
exousiology 111, 116, 138

Fairbairn, Andrew 46-7
faith 12, 59, 68, 78-83, 103-4, 108, 167, 255, 263-4
    definition of 81
    justification by 77-8, 86, 92, 95, 114
    see also salvation by faith
Falk, Harvey 18
the fall 66

Farsi, Salman 189
al-Faruqi 228, 233-4, 240-1
Fee, Gordon 85-6
Feldmeier, Reinhard 125
Fitzmyer, J.A. 114
five freedoms 265
Flavian 54
flogging 157
foreknowledge and foretold happenings
    97-8
Fox, R.L. 44
free will 132
freedom of choice 135
freedom of religion 147, 266, 274, 281,
    288-96
Fronto, Marcus Cornelius 88

Gaddis, Michael 133, 148
Galatia 84
Gale, Thomas 92
Galerius 144
Garland, David 83, 85
Geneva Convention 69
geopolitics 147
Gerasa (Jordan) 111
al-Ghazali 254, 276
Ghassanids 181, 207
Gibbon, Edward 142, 173, 198
Gibraltar 282
Gnostic sect 23, 158
God
    attributes of 232-7, 264
    Christian concept of 108
    comprehension of 221
    oneness of 177, 225-8, 231-2, 235, 271
    Quranic concept of 223-4, 237
    transcendence and unity of 221-2
    use of the word 225
God the Father and God the Holy Spirit
    13, 194, 210; see also Holy Spirit
God-ordained government 116-24
God-talk 239
Godhead 61
good deeds 68, 75-6, 80, 92, 246, 268, 270,
    273, 276
Goranson, Stephan 103
Gore, Charles 14
Gospel writers 75
delivering contradictory and secondhand

reports 98, 101
Gospels 14-18, 21-2
grace 66-9, 92-5
of God 245-6
Grant, R.M. 14
Gratian 170
Greco-Roman civilization 11-12, 30, 74,
    139, 176, 220, 275
Greek language 226
Greek philosophy 35, 251, 254, 256, 260,
    262
Gregory the Great 169
Gregory Nazianzen 48
Gregory of Nyssa 145, 203
Griffith, Sidney 209
Grillmeier, Alois 55-6, 108
Grotius, Hugo 281
Guibert de Nogent 170
Guthrie, S.C. Jr 13
Gwynn, David M. 129, 143
Gwynne, Rosalind Ward 248, 254

hadith 276
Hagar 151-2
Hamidullah, M. 289, 296
Harnack, Adolph 32, 43-8, 126
Harrington, Daniel J. 17-18
Harvey, V.A. 64
Haskins, Charles 169-70
Hawes, Clement 94
Hebrew Bible 15, 182, 185, 222, 226
hedonism 83, 92-5, 141
Heracleides 141
hereditary form of government 285
heresy 108, 139-57, 160-5, 172
definition of 160
Herod, King 101, 112
Hick, John 64, 204, 221
hierarchical levels of authority 119
Hijaz 285
Hill, Christopher 93
Hippolytus 26, 30-1
Hobbes, Thomas 281
Hodge, Charles 118, 121-3
Hodgson, L. 279
Hoffman, R.J. 87, 91
Holocaust, the 114
Holy Spirit 210, 215-16
Holyland, Robert G. 181

homoousios 39, 45
Honourius, Emperor 153, 165
Honourius of Autun 170
human rights 265-6, 280
hypostasis 52

Ibn Abbas 270
Ibn Hazm 217
Ibn Ishaq 181, 189
Ibn Kathir 274
Ibn Taymiyyah 217
Ibn Zubair 286
Ignatius Loyola 17
al-Ihklās 229-30
ilāha 224-5
imperialism 285
Incarnation doctrine 47, 63-4, 67, 78, 95,
    105, 177-8, 187, 198-9, 208-13, 217-20,
    224, 275
incest 83, 88-90
inductive reasoning 253
Inquisitions 153, 165
Iraq 285
Irenaeus 29-30, 140-1
Irving, T.B. 229
Isaac 26, 266
Ishmael 266
Islam 184, 187-8, 206, 211-12, 220, 263,
    268-70, 275-96
and divine right monarchy 280-8
fundamental doctrine of 269, 282
inclusive and *missionary* nature of 263
meaning of the word 222
as a purified and simplified form supersed-
    ing Christianity 179-80
and religious freedom 288-96
lslamic civilization and culture 238
Islamic creed 224-31
Islamic identity 278
Islamic states 283
Israelites 184-5
Izutsu, Toshihiko 182, 241, 255

Jabbar, Qadi Abdul 217
Jacob 26, 184-5
Jafnid family 180-1
Jahweh 185
James, brother of Jesus 78-82
Jaspers, Karl 255

Jefferson, Thomas 70
Jeremias, J. 14
Jerome, St. 169
Jesus Christ 47-58, 63, 225, 242
    among the Jews 15
    belief in 76
    centrality to Christian religion 13-14
    divinity of 22-4, 32-8, 46-9, 57, 63,
        96-102, 105-8, 141, 180, 186-7, 190,
        196-202, 210, 217, 233
    encounters with power structures
        112-14
    as a historical personage 11
    humanity of 38, 49, 52, 57, 67, 102, 108,
        192, 209, 213
    identity of 17-19
    Islamic attitude to 275
    person of 13, 47-53, 81
    as prophet, angel, Messiah and Lord 21
    relevance to humanity 187
    two natures of 47-55, 58, 63, 95, 99,
        167, 181-2, 199-201
    Jesus connection 274-5
Jewish Christians 79, 121
Jewish communities and Judaism 160-2,
    181-5, 232, 234, 269, 290-6
Jihad 273-4
Josephus 139
John of Damascus 213
John of Ephesus 161, 165
John of Nikiu 181
John's Gospel 16-20, 37, 67, 70, 72, 76-8,
    113-14, 118, 213-15
Jones, A.H.M. 174
Judaism see Jewish communities
Judas Iscariot 96, 149
Julian, Emperor 144
Julius of Rome 46
Justin Martyr 17, 24-30, 140
Justinian I, Emperor 51, 110, 160-5, 171,
    176

Kelly, John N.D. 15, 26, 31, 43-4, 49, 51, 55
al-Khawarij 288
Khatab, Sayed 284, 289
Khora's rebellion 87
Khusro 1 Anushirwan, King 182
Kim, Seyoon 114-15, 126
al-Kindī, Abū Yūsuf 204

kingdom of heaven on Earth 129
kingship, hereditary 285
Koran, the see [the] Quran

Lane, Rose W. 281
Lategan, Bernard 115
Latin language 169
law
    enforcement of 119
    eternal character of 137-8
Lecky, W.E.H. 179
Leftow, Brian 204, 206
Leirvik, Oddbjorn 215-16
Leo, Pope 54-5
Lewis, Barnard 182, 271, 286, 290-1
Lewis, C.S. 40
libertinism 87, 89
Lightfoot, R.H. 18
Lim, Richard 146, 152
literature 14, 96-7, 116, 128, 176-7
Locke, John 251, 289
Lod, A. 185
Logos, the 19, 21, 25-30, 35-9, 42, 49-50,
    144, 212-15
    Greek concept of 99, 249, 252
loving God and loving one's neighbour
    68, 70
loving one's enemies 128
loyalty 126-7, 292
Lucian of Antioch 39
Luke's Gospel 16-17, 150, 217
Luther, Martin 68-9, 93, 187

McAuliffe, Jane D. 271-5
McGiffert, Arthur C. 28, 34, 42, 50, 59
McGregor, J.F. 94
Madigan, Daniel 213-14, 263
magistrates acting by divine appointment
    118-23
Mahometanism 179
Manicheans 152, 154, 163
Marcellus 45
Marcian 54-5
Mariolatry 196-8
Mark's Gospel 14, 61
Markus, R.A. 129
Martin, Richard C. 221
martyrdom 149, 151, 158, 291
Mary Magdalene 101

Mary the Virgin 35, 43, 49-55, 63, 107, 162,
    181-2, 186, 192, 196-7, 209-10, 275
    worship of 197-8
Mason, S.F. 73
massacres 156
Matthew's Gospel 75-6
Mawdudi, Sayyid Abul A'la 227-8
Maximinus 144
Mecca 182-3
Medina 289-96
metaphysics 61
Middle Platonism 19, 27
miracles 101
Modalism 32, 34, 42, 60-3, 191, 199-202
    definition of 60-1
Moltmann, J. 193
Monarchism 30-6, 45, 63
    Modalist or *Dynamic* 34-6, 200-2
monarchy 287; see also kingship
Monophysites 48-9, 56, 63, 162, 165, 197,
    201-2, 207-8
Monotheism 15-16, 21, 24-7, 30, 35, 40,
    50, 56, 107, 165-6, 180, 191, 200, 206,
    217, 221-4, 268
    functional 203, 205
    Islamic understanding of 241-2
Montanists 164-5
Moo, Douglas J. 123
morality and moral standards 75-6, 82-4,
    88, 277-80
Moreland, J.P. 202-3
Morey, Robert 208
Moses 21, 185, 222, 225, 237, 242, 280
Mu'awaiya, Caliph 285-6
Muhammad the Prophet 177, 184-90,
    208-9, 217-18, 225-8, 242-3, 251, 254,
    277, 281-2, 285-6, 289-92, 295
Muqatil ibn Sulayman 274
Muslim communities 274-5, 285-9
    rapprochement with Christians 275
mystery cults 78, 88, 95

al-Nabighah 181
Najarani Monophysites 207
natural disasters 164, 171
Nebuchadnezzar 117-18
Negus, King 190
Neoplatonism 73, 220
Nero 120, 125

Nestorius and Nestorianism 50-6, 63, 162-5, 197
Netton, I.R. 13-14
New Testament 14-20, 50, 67, 77, 111, 114, 116, 124-8, 140, 143, 196, 215, 282
Newby, Gordon D. 217
Nicene Creed 38, 44, 48, 54-5, 145, 207
Nicene theology 46-7, 146
Nimrud, King 261
Noah 117, 242
Noetus and Noetianism 31, 34, 63, 199
Nomianism 276-80
Norris, Richard A. 24-5, 36-7
Northern Reformation of Christianity 179, 186

Oaks, Peter 114
obedience to God, church and state 119-23, 137, 146
Occam, William 68
Old Testament 15, 77, 98, 121, 155, 194
ophthalmology 133
Origen 19-20, 27-30, 39, 42, 96, 132, 141
  Celsum 108
original sin 69-70, 105, 131-4, 167-8, 187-8, 192, 201, 275
orthodoxy
  Christian 63, 141-6, 149-50, 171, 199-202, 205-10, 216, 220
  Islamic 276
Othman, Caliph 285
Overbury, Sir Thomas 93

pacifism 125
paganisation 125-6
paganism 83-4, 108, 134, 139-41, 146-7, 155, 161-2, 165-7, 175, 205-6, 254, 271
Pagels, Elaine 113, 132
Papacy, the 281, 291
Parmenian, Bishop 148
Parrinder, Geoffrey 194, 198, 208, 220
Patripassianism 63, 199
Paul , St. 14, 36-7, 61, 67, 70, 76-88, 92-5, 114-30, 136-40, 149-50, 154, 167-8, 198, 214-15, 282
Paul of Antioch 210
Paul of Samosata 35, 49, 200
Pelagius 68
Pelikan, Jaroslav 38

'People of the Book' 267-74, 280, 288, 291-3
Perkins, Bryan 172, 175-6
persecution, religious 16, 115, 128, 139, 141-3, 147, 149, 151-3, 156-60, 164, 264, 291, 296
  just and unjust 152
Persermenian, Narses 161
Persian state 186
Peter, St. 96, 124-6, 145
Phibionites 89
Philo of Alexandria 19-20
Philoxenus 56
Phocas the Patrician 161
Pilate, Pontius 101, 115, 118
pilgrimage 278
plague, bubonic 164, 176
Plantingian Arianism 206
Plato and Platonism 19-20, 27, 33, 45, 167, 170
Pliny the Younger 88
pluralism, religious 272, 293, 296
poetical expressions 222
polemicists 212-13
policing 119
polytheism 32, 106, 192, 204-6, 260, 267
Porphyry of Tyre 82, 98, 101, 104-7
power-sharing 287
Praxeas 31
predestination 117, 123, 130, 156
priests 281
Proclamations of Peter 78-9
Procopius 160-1
promiscuity 84, 89-90, 93, 95
prophecies 98-9
prostitution 84-6
psychological needs of writers 213
Psychology Trinity model 60
Ptolemy 23
public opinion 133
Pugh, Martin 179-80
punishment 76-7, 117, 119, 122, 140-2, 145, 149-50

al-Qāsim, Zaydi Imām 204
questioning, limits to 169
the Quran 14, 70, 179-82, 188-98, 201-9, 234-48, 254, 262-9, 272-3, 280-4, 290-5

admonitions against Trinitarianism in 219
Christian interpretation of 212
styles used in 262
terminology used in 238-9
al-Qurtubi, al-Razi 274
Qurysh tribe 182
Quss, Bishop 189

Rahman, Fazlur 270
Rahner, Karl 34, 61, 71, 203-6, 210
Raisanen, H. 77, 215
Ranters 93-4
reason and rationality 252-9
    inductive or analogical 253
    qualitative or quantitative 257
'reasonable' laws 118
redemption 41
Reformation, Protestant 180
Relativism 251-2
'reluctant readers' 114
Rendall, Gerald 81
'rendering unto Caesar' 112-15, 121-3, 292
Resurrection 78, 100-1
Revelation, Book of 112-13
Rida, Rashid 270
Rightly-Guided Caliphs 285, 287
Robertson, William 174
Robinson, Neal 212
Rodinson, M. 292, 295
Roetzel, Calvin 78
Roman Empire 11, 109-10, 113-15, 120-1,
    126, 128, 136, 140, 156, 165-6, 171-2,
    281, 288, 292
    fall of 172-7
Rome, city of
    expulsion from 125
    sack of 136, 138, 172, 175
Rosen, Lawrence 188, 279
Rubin, Uri 294
rule of the many 179
Russia 163

Sabellius and Sabellianism 31-2, 42-5, 63,
    200
Sabinus of Heraclea 46
Sabrinho, Carlos Galvao 141
Sale, George 197
salvation 48-52, 57, 64-8, 75-83, 86, 94,

106, 108, 145, 157, 166, 178, 201, 219,
    243-7, 268-9, 273, 280
    Christian and Islamic schemes of 244-6
    by faith 87-8
salvationism 87-8
al-ṣamad 229-30
Samaritans 160
Sanders, E.P. 18, 77
Satan 107
Sayers, Dorothy 36
Schaff, Philip 14, 149
Schedl, German C. 213
schism 140, 148
Schleiermacher, Friedrich 34, 61
Scholasticism 249-52
Schweizer, Eduard 125
Scientific Era 251
sectarianism 186-7, 193
secularisation 287
Secundus of Ptolemais 45-6
Semitic Christianity 11-12, 220
Separationism 63
Sermon on the Mount 128, 282
'Servant of God', use of the term 214-15
Severus of Antioch 111
sexual perversions 83-95
shahādah 224-8
Shahi^d, Irfan 207
Shari'ah 265, 276-80, 283-4, 287
Shenoute, Abbot 157
silk and the Silk Road 183
Simon Magus 79
sinners and saints in earthly states 130-1
Smaragdus 169
Smith, Morton 18
Social Trinitarians 205-7
sociopathy, allegations of 108
'Son of God', use of term 41-2, 193-4, 208
Sonn, Tamara 291-2, 296
soteriology 77-83, 86, 95, 162, 280
Southern Reformation of Christianity
    178-80, 186-7
sovereignty 280-1, 295
    of God 283
sozo 64-5
speculative theology 23
Stam, C.M. 117
standards of living 172, 176
state activities, participation in 138

Stoics 167, 249
Stuhlmacher, P. 114
submission, reasons for 124–5; see also
    absolute submission
Sunnah 227
Sura Maryam 192
Sūrah al-Kāfirūn 228
al-Suyuti, Imam 254
Swinburne, Richard 203–4
Sylvester, St. 109–10
Synesius 129
Synod of Carthage (418) 68
Synoptic Gospels 18, 21–2, 67–8, 76, 78,
    112

al-Tabari 270, 274
Tabbernee, William 156, 160, 164
Tatian 17, 24, 26
Al-Tawhid 264
categories of 231–8
concept of 223, 239–41
taxation 117, 120, 123
Ten Commandments 242
Tertullian, Emperor 27–8, 32–3, 89–91,
    127–8, 140, 167–9, 200
Themistius 129
Theodore of Mopsuestia 21, 49–51
Theodosius II, Emperor 52, 54, 109, 145–7,
    158
Theodotus 34
Theognosta 181
Theophanes 286
Theophilus 24
theos 19–20
Thomas, St. 21
Thomas, David 211, 216–17
Thomas of Marmarka 45–6
Thomas the Quaestor 161
'Throne Verse' 227
Tillich, Paul 35–8, 57, 177–8, 200, 233
Tisdall, W. St. Clair 197–8
toleration, religious 280, 293
the Tora 125, 268
torture 157
trade in luxury goods 183
transcendence 50, 108, 223, 234–40, 243
    Islamic version of 178
translation problems 19, 21
transmigration of souls 167

tribal structure 293
tribalism 275, 287
Trinitarian theology 12–13, 16, 33, 46,
    59–64, 69–74, 106, 108, 141, 162,
    186–92, 196–8, 201–7, 210–17, 220, 223,
    230, 264, 273, 275
    Augustinian or *Cappadocian* 68–9,
        202–3, 207, 232
    immanent or *economic* 210, 212
    Islamic rejection of 188, 220
    and the Quran 190–2
    social or *anti-social* 60–2, 202–4
Trinity Monotheism 205–6
tri-theism 62, 71–2, 106, 200–8, 275
triune God 13, 186, 195, 206, 219, 262, 275
trust in human capacities and goodness
    137
al-Tufi, Najm al-Din 254
Tuggy, Dale 62, 203
tyrannical kings 282

cUlama 254, 287
Umayyad rule 286–7
umma 266–7, 278, 292, 295
uniformity of worship and of belief 160
unipersonality 58
Unitarian doctrine 15–16, 74, 142, 180 ,
    191, 223
Unity, *Ontological* or *of Actions* 210
Urban, Linwood 32–3
cUthman b. al-Huwayrith 189
Utilitarian reasoning 251

Vermes, Geza 18
violence associated with sainthood 158
Visigoths 172
vocabulary, religious 238–9
the Vulgate 169

Waardenburg, Jacques 271, 273
Wadud, Amina 265
al-Warraq, Abu Isa 211, 217
war, waging of 293–4
Watt, W.M. 291–2
Wellhausen, J. 284, 291, 294
Whale, J.S. 59
Wigram, W.A. 55
Wiles, Maurice 58
World War II 114

worldview, supernatural 74
worship 103, 107, 160, 218-19
of idols 119
Wright, N.T. 114

Yahweh 222
Yandell, Keith E. 63
Yarshater, E. 186
Yemen 181-2
Yoder, John Howard 112
Young, Frances 39-41, 53

Zaehner, R.C. 208
Zagorin, Perez 140, 146, 152-3
Zaid b. Ha'ritha 189
zealots 158
Zebiri, Kate 247-8, 272
Zenobia, Queen 35
Zephyrinus 33
Zoroastrianism 185-6, 280